THE GENIUS OF SHAKESPEARE

'Ambitious, exceptionally well informed and immensely engaging book . . . Bate has, to an exceptional degree, the virtue of readability. He writes with unflagging energy, intelligence, wit and enthusiasm'
STANLEY WELLS, *Daily Telegraph*

'The great strength of Jonathan Bate's new book is the willingness to take seriously the questions which the general reader always asks and which the average academic, it sometimes seems, would rather die than answer. What was Shakespeare like? Did he write his own works? Why is he supposed to be such a great genius? *The Genius of Shakespeare* aims, and deserves, to be a popular book'
LOIS POTTER, *Times Literary Supplement*

'An insight on every other page . . . Anyone who has ever wondered why Shakespeare's head appears on cheque guarantee cards as a mark of authenticity will find this volume of interest. It is not just for scholars'
ROBERT NYE, *Scotsman*

'Excellent. Amusing and stylishly written. Non-dogmatic. Wide-ranging and at times touching on the profound. Well worth reading'
FELIX PRYOR, *Spectator*

'There are many fresh insights as Bate charts the continual reinvention of Shakespeare by succeeding ages, and by different cultures and nationalities, to suit their own passing ends'
ANTHONY HOLDEN, *Sunday Times*

JONATHAN BATE was born in 1958. He is King Alfred Professor of English Literature at the University of Liverpool, and was previously a Fellow of Trinity Hall, Cambridge. Professor Bate has lectured on Shakespeare throughout the world and has held visiting posts at Harvard, Yale, the University of California and the Folger Shakespeare Library in Washington DC. His many acclaimed books include *Shakespeare and Ovid* (1993) and the new Arden edition of *Titus Andronicus* (1995). His first novel, *The Cure for Love*, is also published by Picador.

THE GENIUS OF
SHAKESPEARE

JONATHAN BATE

PICADOR

First published 1997 by Picador

This edition published 1998 by Picador
an imprint of Macmillan Publishers Ltd
25 Eccleston Place, London SW1W 9NF
Basingstoke and Oxford

Associated companies throughout the world

ISBN 0 330 37101 0

579864

A CIP catalogue record for this book is available from
the British Library.

Typeset by SetSystems Ltd, Saffron Walden, Essex
Printed and bound in Great Britain by
Mackays of Chatham plc, Chatham, Kent

To P. J. B.,
without whose love and inspiration
it could not have been written.

PREFACE

Ask for the name of a writer of universally acknowledged genius and the answer is sure to be Shakespeare. The two words 'William Shakespeare' have become synonymous with the two words 'great literature'. His birthday is celebrated annually in Germany; there is a Globe Theatre in Tokyo; a library devoted to him stands on Capitol Hill in Washington, DC, a stone's throw from the legislature – where every other author has to make do with a niche in the vast Library of Congress, the Bard of Avon has his special place across the road, the Folger Shakespeare Library.

In British life, he seems to be everywhere. He is quoted and adapted daily in newspaper headlines and advertising copy. He is the only compulsory author in the National Curriculum and in Advanced Level English Literature in schools. He has a national, massively subsidized theatre company named after him and committed to the regular revival of all his works. Driving down the M6 motorway, you pass signs indicating the new county you are entering: Cheshire, Staffordshire, Warwickshire. But the sign does not say 'Warwickshire' – it says 'Warwickshire: Shakespeare's County'. Handing over a cheque guarantee card, one presents as a mark of its authenticity a hologram of Shakespeare's head.

Where did Shakespeare come from? From what raw materials was his work created? By what process did his genius come to be acknowledged and celebrated? Why has a sixteenth-century English dramatist of humble origins become the best-known and most admired author in the history of the world? And, anyway, what exactly *is* so special about his works?

Over the last hundred years, scores of books on Shakespeare have been written for those whom the editors of the first collected edition of the plays (the 'First Folio') described as 'the great Variety of Readers'. Nearly all such books are either biographies or accounts of the works in which each of the plays and poems is examined in what is presumed to be chronological order. The organizing principle of the biography is the writer's life; that of the literary-critical survey is his career. It is my argument that neither Shakespeare's life nor his career can account for his genius. I propose that the genius of Shakespeare is not co-extensive with the life of William Shakespeare. A knowledge of the 'pre-life' and the 'after-life' of his art is essential to an understanding of his power. Thus the first half of the book explores the *origins* of Shakespeare, while the second half tells of his *effects*.

'The words of a dead man', wrote W. H. Auden in a poem about how poetry works its magic, 'Are modified in the guts of the living'. This book is a kind of biography of Shakespeare, but one which takes Auden's thought seriously: what I mean by Shakespeare is not just a life which lasted from 1564 to 1616, but a body of words and stage-images which live because they were originally Shakespeare's modifications of the words and stage-images of his predecessors and because they have subsequently been modified again and again in the guts of successive generations of the living.

The astonishing variety of the plays has helped to keep the name of Shakespeare alive in different ages and cultures whilst the names of his fellow-dramatists are now dead to all but experts and aficionados. The fortunes of individual plays rise and fall through time, in an endless unfolding of the potential, the latent power, within the Shakespearean oeuvre as a whole. In my final chapter, for instance, I suggest that a true critical appreciation of *Measure for Measure* only became possible in the relativistic twentieth century. Other ages will bring other plays to special prominence – if, for example, the science of cryonics takes off in the twenty-first century there will be productions and readings of *The Winter's Tale* and *Pericles* as allegorical anticipations of the art of bodily deep-freeze and reanimation. My closing pages ask, with the assistance of the philosopher Ludwig Wittgenstein, what it is about the world of Shakespearean drama that has made it continue to live in so many different eras and cultures. The answer to that question will be the closest we can get to a definition of the genius of Shakespeare.

CONTENTS

List of Illustrations

1. *William Shakespeare*, engraving by Martin Droeshout in the First Folio of Shakespeare. Woodcut. (Folger Shakespeare Library, Washington, DC.)

2. *Henry Wriothesley, third Earl of Southampton*. Engraving. (Folger Shakespeare Library, Washington, DC.)

3. *John Florio*. Drawing from engraving. (Huntington Library.)

4. *Samuel Daniel*. Engraving. (Folger Shakespeare Library, Washington, DC.)

5. Max Beerbohm, *William Shakespeare, his method of work*. Lithograph.

6. William Blake, illustration to Thomas Gray's *The Progress of Poesy*. Watercolour and black ink. (Yale Centre for British Art, Paul Mellon Collection.)

7. After William Hogarth, *David Garrick as Richard III*. Engraving.

8. Laurence Olivier as Hamlet. Still from the film *Hamlet* (1948) by courtesy of Rank Film Distributors Ltd.

9. Laurence Olivier and Eileen Herlie as Hamlet and Gertrude. Still from the film, *Hamlet* (1948) by courtesy of Rank Film Distributors Ltd.

10. Jean Simmons as Ophelia in Olivier's *Hamlet*. Still from the film *Hamlet* (1948) by courtesy of Rank Film Distributors Ltd.

11. J. E. Millais, *Ophelia*. Oil on canvas. (Tate Gallery.)

12. J. H. Fuseli, *Garrick and Mrs Pritchard as Macbeth and Lady Macbeth after the murder of Duncan*. Watercolour. (Kunsthaus, Zurich.)

13. J. H. Fuseli, *Garrick and Mrs Pritchard in Macbeth*. Oil on canvas. (Tate Gallery.)

PART ONE

WHO IS SHAKESPEARE? WHAT IS HE?

And almost thence my nature is subdued
To what it works in, like the dyer's hand.
(Sonnet 111)

1

A LIFE OF ANECDOTE

All that is known with any degree of certainty . . .

The first formal biography of William Shakespeare appeared nearly a hundred years after his death. It was written by the dramatist Nicholas Rowe and prefixed to the *Works of Mr William Shakespear*. Published in 1709, this was also the first modern edition of the plays in the sense that it had a named editor who 'corrected' the text. But by the end of the eighteenth century scholars were questioning the veracity of some of the most celebrated stories narrated by Rowe, for instance the tale of how Shakespeare was forced to leave Stratford for London because he had been caught stealing deer from the park of the local squire. In 1780 the scholar George Steevens wrote:

> As all that is known with any degree of certainty concerning Shakespeare, is − *that he was born at Stratford upon Avon, − married and had children there, − went to London, where he commenced actor, and wrote poems and plays, − returned to Stratford, made his will, died, and was buried,* − I must confess my readiness to combat every unfounded supposition respecting the particular occurrences of his life.

For Steevens, the criterion for 'certainty' was written contemporary proof. The evidence to which he gave credence was that which could be found in the official record. Thus the documents which he trusted most were Shakespeare's will (signed on 25 March 1616, proved 22 June 1616) and certain parish records from Stratford–upon–Avon: the christening of William Shakespeare, son of John Shakespeare, on 26 April 1564; the marriage of William Shakespeare and Anne Hathaway on 28 November 1582; the christening six months later of Susanna, daughter to William Shakespeare (26 May 1583); the christening of the twins Hamnet and Judith, son and daughter to William Shakespeare,

on 2 February 1585; and the burial of William Shakespeare in Holy
Trinity Church on 25 April 1616.

Two centuries on from Steevens, we know that the official record is
much more comprehensive than this. There are over fifty documents
relating to Shakespeare, his family, and his acting company in the
London Public Record Office alone. For instance, on 15 March 1595
the Treasurer of the Queen's Chamber made payments to William
Kempe, William Shakespeare, and Richard Burbage for performing
plays at court; on 16 May 1599 an inquisition in Chancery allowed
Shakespeare and his fellows to occupy the Globe playhouse; and in
May 1603 warrants were issued under the royal seal authorizing
Shakespeare and his company to call themselves the King's Men. Other
PRO documents relate to Shakespeare's defaulting on his taxes, serving
as witness in a marital dispute involving the household where he lodged
in London, and purchasing property near the Blackfriars theatre where
the King's Men played in the last years of his career. Other Stratford
documents show him accumulating property in his home town and
becoming involved in petty legal disputes.

We know a great deal more about Shakespeare's life than we do
about the lives of most of his fellow-dramatists and fellow-actors. But it
is in the nature of official documents that they pertain either to the
bare facts of birth, marriage, and death, or to legal and financial matters
– wills, conveyances of property, debts, and taxes. We learn from them
that Shakespeare invested his income shrewdly and was mildly litigious.
We do not learn very much from them about his character as it affects
what we are interested in: his plays.

And we can all too easily read too much into them. It used, for
example, to be suggested that because the first draft of Shakespeare's
will made no mention of his wife and the final version only did so in
order to give her his second-best bed, then he must have been
unhappily married or not a very good husband. But legal historians
have shown that, though it was unusual not to include a specific
provision for a wife, this does not amount to a disinheritance, since
under common law Anne Shakespeare would have been entitled to a
third of her husband's estate and to residence in his house for the
remainder of her life. The second-best bed is certainly a curious detail,
but whether it was a sign of contempt or affection or neither, we
cannot tell. It is pure speculation to infer that Shakespeare intended to

cut his wife off 'not indeed without a shilling, but with an old bed', as Edmond Malone supposed in 1780. It is equally pure speculation to infer that the best bed would have been reserved for visitors, the second one therefore 'rich in tender marital associations', as Samuel Schoenbaum supposed in 1975.

Far more interesting is a different body of early evidence which reveals a surprising amount about how Shakespeare was viewed by his contemporaries. 'Genius' in Shakespeare's own time did not mean what *The American Heritage Dictionary of the English Language* says that it means now: 'exceptional and transcendent creative power'. The emergence of that meaning is examined in chapter six. Rather, the word's primary meaning was 'characteristic disposition, bent, or inclination; natural character or constitution'. The word suggested the particular combination of astral influences represented in a person's horoscope. Most of the records we have concerning Shakespeare as an actor-dramatist are anecdotal, but the *representative anecdote*, like the horoscope, is precisely a form of which the purpose is to distil someone's characteristic disposition, their 'genius'. The point of the anecdote is not its factual but its representative truth.

John Keats said that 'A Man's life of any worth is a continual allegory – and very few eyes can see the Mystery of his life – a life like the scriptures, figurative . . . Shakspeare led a life of Allegory: his works are the comments on it'. From the end of this chapter onwards, we will be hearing a lot about the 'Mystery' of Shakespeare's life and we will be encountering many allegorical or figurative readings of him. The key point to grasp at the outset is that the mystery and the allegories were only born after Shakespeare's death. The mystery had to be invented in order to account for the genius. I offer my initial Anecdotal Life as an antidote to the later Allegorical Lives, for what is striking about the record left by his contemporaries is not the mystery but the *mobility* of William Shakespeare.

The boy William

Shakespeare's anecdotal life begins at thirty – or to be precise, twenty-eight. His early years, like those of Jesus Christ, are shrouded in mystery and consequently dressed up with myth. The relevant records of the

Stratford-upon-Avon grammar school do not survive, so we do not know for sure when the boy William was enrolled there and when he left. We do know from the parish records that at the age of eighteen he married an already pregnant older woman, Anne Hathaway, and that the couple had three children, including a pair of twins. The boy, Hamnet, died in 1596 at the age of eleven. But there are no records of Shakespeare's professional activities in the decade after his marriage. There is no reason why there should have been any: only when he began to make his name as a dramatist did others begin to pay attention to him. Some time in the late 1580s he became a player in London; sooner or later, he tried his hand as a writer of plays. Of his early career, this is all we know for sure.

In the absence of external evidence, biographers have sought to unearth anecdotes of the author's youth from details in his plays. This is a very dubious procedure. An Elizabethan play was a collaborative work that belonged to the theatrical company which performed it every bit as much as to the dramatist who wrote it. For this reason, plays were rarely the medium for self-portraiture on the part of the writer. But for the same reason, they were quite likely to include in-jokes for the enjoyment of the company.

There is a good example in *Hamlet*. When the players arrive at Elsinore, Polonius boasts that he was a bit of an actor himself in his university days. He starred as Julius Caesar: 'I was killed i'th'Capitol. Brutus killed me.' Never one to miss the opportunity for a clutch of puns, Hamlet replies, 'It was a brute part of him to kill so capital a calf there.' A couple of scenes later, Hamlet will – brutally – kill Polonius. In the original performance, there may well have been an added twist to this neat parallelism. Shakespeare wrote *Julius Caesar* for his acting company, the Lord Chamberlain's Men, about a year before *Hamlet*; the two plays were almost certainly in the repertoire together. Richard Burbage, the company's leading actor, would have played both Brutus and Hamlet. If another actor in the company who specialized in the roles of older men played both Julius Caesar and Polonius, then we have a company joke: poor old so-and-so always ends up being stabbed to death by Burbage before the play is half done.

Burbage seems to have made his name playing the role of Shakespeare's Richard III. The coincidence with his own Christian name became another company joke, as will be seen from a bawdy tale to be told later in this chapter. It may be inferred that if we are to find any Shakespearean self-portraits in the plays, the chances are that they will take the form of company jokes, perhaps involving correspondences of name.

Shakespeare invented two characters called William. One of them was the simple-minded country fellow in *As You Like It* who loses Audrey the goatherd to the witty court Fool, Touchstone. 'Art thou wise?' Touchstone asks William. 'Ay, sir, I have a pretty wit', he replies. Pretty indeed: these seven words are the longest sentence that the witless William manages to string together.

We are explicitly told that countryman William was born in the Forest of Arden. His creator, William Shakespeare, son of Mary Arden, was born in Warwickshire, where there was a Forest of Arden. William of Arden is surely William of Stratford's wittily self-deprecatory portrait of himself as tongue-tied country bumpkin.

Tradition has it that Shakespeare excelled more as a writer than an actor. He may well have given most of his energies in rehearsal to 'directing' the company, showing them how to translate his words into stage actions; his own acting roles were therefore likely to have been confined to brief cameos. He is supposed to have played old Adam, Orlando's loyal servant, in the opening scenes of *As You Like It*. The company joke would be complete if he also doubled in the role of young William towards the end of the play. William plays William in order to make fun of his own rural origins.

This, then, is a first image of Shakespeare: a country boy, provincial and therefore assumed to be boorish. He rose to prominence in the 1590s as *the dramatist without a university education*. Soon after his death, he was mythologized as a pure genius, a child of nature *warbling his native wood-notes wild*. Rural origins came to be regarded as synonymous with lack of culture. But William Shakespeare's ignorance is part of the myth; it is very far from being the historical fact. The self-representation as tongue-tied William of Arden is deliciously ironic because Shakespeare's true wit and verbal facility are amply on display in the character of Touchstone. See this, and the question then becomes: how could the country boy have learnt the sophisticated language of the court jester who is no fool? And at this point we see one of the reasons for the emergence of the Shakespeare Authorship Controversy. People who do not believe that Shakespeare wrote the plays say that William of Stratford really did resemble boneheaded William of Arden. They say that courtly characters – dukes and princesses and sophisticated jesters – could only have been created by a courtier. A courtier such as, for instance, the Earl of Oxford.

The authorship controversy will be discussed in detail in chapter three. The point to grasp here is that it is based on a false premiss, namely the assumption that someone who was not a courtier and did not go to university could not have written learned plays with court settings. This assumption can only be made by someone who knows little of Shakespeare's contemporaries. The most successful of all Elizabethan tragedies was a learned play with a court setting: entitled *The Spanish Tragedy*, it was written by Thomas Kyd, who was not a courtier and did not go to university. Kyd did not need a higher education or inside knowledge of courtly matters in order to be able to write *The Spanish Tragedy*. It was enough that he went to a good grammar school, which equipped him with the necessary arts of reading and writing.

In act four scene one of *The Merry Wives of Windsor*, a boy called William is given a Latin grammar lesson by Sir Hugh Evans, a Welsh schoolmaster. Was this scene written by an earl such as Oxford who never set foot inside a grammar school in his life? Or by a man called William who as a boy was entitled, by virtue of his father's status as an alderman of the town, to attend the grammar school at Stratford-upon-Avon, where there was a Welsh schoolmaster, one Thomas Jenkins? The lesson of Sir Hugh Evans in *Merry Wives* is based on the Latin grammar book that was the standard school text of the period. It is all the evidence we need that young William Shakespeare attended the King's Free Grammar School of Stratford-upon-Avon.

What would he have been taught there? The Stratford syllabus does not survive, but those of comparable institutions do. Here, for example, are the curricular instructions for the grammar school at Witton in Cheshire. We may assume that Stratford would have offered a very similar education, not least because John Brownsword, the master there in the period immediately before Shakespeare reached grammar school age, was formerly a pupil, then a teacher, at Witton:

> I will [that the boys be] taught always the good literature both Latin and Greek, and good authors such as have the very Roman eloquence

joined with wisdom, especially Christian authors that wrote their wisdom with clean and chaste Latin, either in verse or in prose; for mine intent is by founding of this School specially to increase knowledge and worship of God and our Lord Jesus Christ, and good Christian life and manners in the children. And for that intent I will the children learn the *Catechisma*, and then the *Accidence and Grammar* set out by King Henry the Eighth, or some other if any can be better for the purpose, to induce children more speedily to Latin speech; and then *Institutum Christiani Hominis* that learned Erasmus made, and then *Copia* of the same Erasmus, *Colloquia Erasmi*, *Ovidius: Metamorphoseos*, Terence, Mantuan, Tully, Horace, Sallust, Virgil and such other as shall be thought most convenient to the purpose unto true Latin speech.

Shakespeare's education would, then, have begun with the fundamentals of Christian doctrine, as laid out in the catechism of the Anglican Church. From there, it would have proceeded to a thorough grounding in Latin grammar. Having been drilled in his grammar, the young William would then have been led line by line through a range of set texts — first, a variety of anthologies and selections, then some original works by the major authors of classical Rome.

The instructions for Witton School indicate that an Elizabethan grammar school education would have placed a particular emphasis upon the 'pure' neo-Latin of the great humanist educator of the early sixteenth century, Desiderius Erasmus. His *Institutum Christiani Hominis* combined the wisdom of the classics with the faith of the Christian; his *De Copia* taught the art of linguistic copiousness, of rhetorical embellishment and variation; his *Colloquies* were dialogues which trained boys in the speaking of Latin. The young William's initial step towards the drama would have been taken when his class performed their Erasmian dialogues: a colloquy is a miniature play, in which appropriate words are found for particular situations and character-types.

Shakespeare's first attempts in the art of literary *composition* would have come a little further up the grammar school. He would have been set the exercise of writing letters in Latin in the style of different characters from classical myth and history. The art of fitting the emotion to the moment would have begun here. Thereafter, he would have been made to write compositions on particular themes, perhaps beginning from an edited version of Erasmus' great collection of proverbial wisdom, the *Adagia*. Many of the 'wise saws' for which Shakespeare's plays have become so renowned – the quotable generalizations about human life – can be traced back to the *Adagia* or comparable textbooks.

If Shakespeare reached the top of the school, he would have found himself composing formal orations and declamations. He would still have been writing in Latin, but he would have learned an art of rhetorical disposition – of lucidly structured argument – which would serve him well when he came to put speeches in the mouths of his dramatic creations. Meanwhile, he would have read a range of Latin literary works, most notably that great storehouse of classical mythology, Ovid's *Metamorphoses*. Scholarly studies have shown that the classical learning in Shakespeare's plays corresponds very closely to that provided by the grammar school syllabus.

Grammar school techniques of composition, and in particular the emphasis on rhetorical elaboration or copiousness, stayed with Shakespeare throughout his career. He learnt in school to read a 'source' and embellish it, expand upon it; sometimes he would have to turn prose into verse. This is exactly how he worked as a playwright. He would take a history book – the English chronicles of Holinshed, the classical lives of Plutarch – and turn passages of it into a history play. He would take a prose romance or a novella and turn it into a comedy or a tragedy: a pastoral called *Rosalynd* by Thomas Lodge becomes *As You Like It*; an Italian tale about a Moor and his scheming ensign is dramatized as *Othello*. Or he would simply borrow the plot of an old play from the existing repertoire – *The True Chronicle History of King Leir* or *The Famous Victories of Henry the Fifth* – and make it his own by greatly complicating it.

Here is an example of his compositional method in action. A passage in Sir Thomas North's translation of Plutarch's *Life of Marcus Antonius* describes the moment when Antony first sees Cleopatra, splendidly arrayed on her barge on the River Cydnus:

> the poop whereof was of gold, the sails of purple, and the oars of silver, which kept stroke in rowing after the sound of the music of flutes, hautboys, citherns, viols, and such other instruments as they played upon in the barge. And now for the person of her self: she was laid under a pavilion of cloth of gold of tissue, apparelled and

attired like the goddess Venus, commonly drawn in picture; and hard by her, on either hand of her, pretty fair boys apparelled as painters do set forth god Cupid, with little fans in their hands, with the which they fanned wind upon her. Her ladies and gentlewomen also, the fairest of them were apparelled like the nymphs Nereids (which are the mermaids of the waters) and like the Graces, some steering the helm, others tending the tackle and ropes of the barge, out of the which there came a wonderful passing sweet savour of perfumes, that perfumed the wharf's side, pestered with innumerable multitudes of people. Some of them followed the barge all along the river's side; others also ran out of the city to see her coming in. So that in the end, there ran such multitudes of people one after another to see her, that Antonius was left post alone in the market-place, in his imperial seat to give audience.

Shakespeare wrote for a bare stage and an appreciative ear. Where the director of a modern musical would tell his designer to build that barge, Shakespeare let his audience fashion the scene in their imagination by turning North's prose into richly evocative verse:

> The barge she sat in, like a burnished throne
> Burned on the water. The poop was beaten gold;
> Purple the sails, and so perfumèd that
> The winds were love-sick with them. The oars were silver,
> Which to the tune of flutes kept stroke, and made
> The water which they beat to follow faster,
> As amorous of their strokes. For her own person,
> It beggared all description. She did lie
> In her pavilion – cloth of gold, of tissue –
> O'er-picturing that Venus where we see
> The fancy outwork nature. On each side her
> Stood pretty dimpled boys, like smiling Cupids,
> With divers-coloured fans whose wind did seem
> To glow the delicate cheeks which they did cool,
> And what they undid did. . . .
> Her gentlewomen, like the Nereides,
> So many mermaids, tended her i'th' eyes,
> And made their bends adornings. At the helm
> A seeming mermaid steers. The silken tackle
> Swell with the touches of those flower-soft hands

> That yarely frame the office. From the barge
> A strange invisible perfume hits the sense
> Of the adjacent wharfs. The city cast
> Her people out upon her, and Antony,
> Enthroned i'th' market-place, did sit alone,
> Whistling to th'air, which but for vacancy
> Had gone to gaze on Cleopatra too,
> And made a gap in nature.
>
> (*Antony and Cleopatra*, 2.2.198–225)

Our modern conception of genius makes creativity synonymous with originality. In matters artistic, there is no more severe accusation than that of plagiarism. Students are therefore surprised when you show them these two passages. They are scandalized that Shakespeare did not make up his own story. The barge and all its accoutrements, the apparel of Cleopatra herself, her gorgeous attendants, the common people running out of the city to gaze upon the exotic queen, imperial Antony left alone on his throne in the market place: each successive detail is lifted straight from the source.

But to the Elizabethans, this procedure would have been admirable, not reprehensible. For them, there was no higher mark of artistic excellence than what they called the *lively turning* of familiar material. This was the art of copiousness which they were taught in school: take a piece of received wisdom (a proverb, a phrase, a historical incident, a story out of ancient myth), *turn* it on the anvil of your inventiveness, and you will give it new life.

The genius is in the embellishment. Shakespeare takes the golden poop and the purple sails from North's Plutarch, but adds 'and so perfumèd that / The winds were love-sick with them'. Where the historian has offered mere description, the dramatist adds reaction. He imagines the wind being affected by Cleopatra's aura. Then the water follows suit: the strokes of the oars and their musical accompaniment are in Plutarch, but in Shakespeare the water falls in love even as it is beaten. That pain and love have something to do with each other is a thought he developed later in the play, when Cleopatra compares the stroke of death to a lover's pinch 'which hurts and is desired'.

In Plutarch, Cleopatra is like a picture of Venus, the goddess of love; in Shakespeare, she out-pictures the best imaginable picture of Venus.

The poet proves his art by transforming the historian's plain simile into an astonishingly complex effect: a work of art usually imitates nature, whereas the very best work of art seems to 'outwork' nature, whereas Cleopatra surpasses even that. So does her allure come from nature or from art? Through the poet's imagination, Cleopatra can contrive her goddesslike appearance so that the very elements of nature – first the winds and the waves, then the rope of the tackle, then the stone of the wharf, and finally the air itself – fall in love with her. After this, is it surprising that Antony does so too? Soon he will vacate that throne on which he has been left in the empty market place, looking rather ridiculous. The image of vacation becomes symbolic of the whole process of the play, whereby politics and power are left behind, such is the lure of Cleopatra's erotic aura.

To read Enobarbus' description in accompaniment with its source is simultaneously to see why Shakespeare was a genius in our modern sense and why he did not need more than an Elizabethan grammar school education in order to write his plays. The raw material was there in a readily accessible source. The method of *lively turning* such material was learnt in school. The uniqueness of Shakespeare is the quickness of mind and fertility of imagination that, Cleopatra-like, make effects of art seem like effusions of nature.

The upstart crow

The two characters called William stand as symbols for the essentials of Shakespeare's youth. William of Arden embodies his origins in rural Warwickshire; William of Windsor enacts his exposure to a grammar school education. Country and not city, grammar school and not university: the image precisely fits the earliest surviving allusions to William Shakespeare as dramatist.

The occupation of dramatist in late-Elizabethan England was neither dignified nor secure. In the late 1580s, that other grammar school boy, Thomas Kyd, wrote his hugely successful *Spanish Tragedy*. In 1594, Kyd died in poverty. In the same period, Christopher Marlowe achieved fame with his *Tamburlaine the Great*, *Dr Faustus*, and *The Jew of Malta*. In 1593, Marlowe was killed in a brawl over a tavern bill in Deptford. If Shakespeare had known that Marlowe was exactly the same age as himself, he could not but have been chastened by the thought that Marlowe had achieved so much before he himself had hardly begun; nor could he but have been haunted by imaginings of what Marlowe might have gone on to achieve had he not been struck down. That chastening and that haunting are my subject in chapter four.

Marlowe was one of a group of Cambridge-educated dramatists who have become known as the 'university wits'. But neither their education nor the success of their plays brought them status or prosperity. Among the leading wits were George Peele, who was frequently in debt and died in poverty in 1596; Thomas Nashe, who eked out a living as a pamphleteer and died in poverty in 1601; and Robert Greene, whose death was as notorious as Marlowe's.

Greene's demise was described in a letter dated 5 September 1592 and published that same year. The author was Gabriel Harvey, another Cambridge man, but no friend to the playmakers. Harvey tells of how he went to London 'to enquire after the famous Author: who was reported to lie dangerously sick in a shoemaker's house near Dow-gate: not of the plague, or the pox, as a gentleman said, but of a surfeit of pickled herring and rhenish wine.' He hears that Greene has died a couple of days earlier. Hostess Isam, the shoemaker's wife, tells him, with tears in her eyes, of how on his deathbed Greene called for a 'penny-pot of Malmsey' and then scribbled 'a letter to his abandoned wife, in the behalf of his gentle host: not so short as persuadable in the beginning, and pitiful in the ending.' For all his animosity towards Greene, Harvey is impelled to pity at the decline whereby the last words of a gifted wit, noted for his fine quips and quaint disputes, are these:

> Doll, I charge thee by the love of our youth, and by my soul's rest, that thou wilt see this man paid: for if he and his wife had not succoured me, I had died in the streets. Robert Greene.

Within two weeks of the date of Harvey's letter, the printer and writer Henry Chettle lodged in the Stationers' Register his right to publish 'a book entitled GREENE'S Groatsworth of Wit bought with a million of Repentance'. Apparently reconstructed by Chettle from manuscripts left by Greene at his death, the *Groatsworth of Wit* narrates the picaresque adventures of a younger son called Roberto, whose life-story closely resembles Greene's. Roberto complains about the treatment of writers at the hands of the London players: the actors pay the playwrights a pittance, whilst becoming rich and famous themselves. For this reason, Greene urges his fellow Cambridge men, Marlowe, Nashe, and Peele, to renounce the stage.

Recently, he protests, the players have added insult to injury. It is not merely that they have taken advantage of the university playwrights; now, one of the actors has trespassed on their territory by setting himself up as a writer:

> Yes, trust them not: for there is an upstart Crow, beautified with our feathers, that with his *Tiger's heart wrapped in a Player's hide,* supposes he is as well able to bombast out a blank verse as the best of you; and, being an absolute *Johannes fac totum,* is in his own conceit the only Shake-scene in a country.

There can be no doubt that this refers to Shakespeare. A pun on his name is combined with a parody of one of his lines. In *The True Tragedy of Richard Duke of York,* the historical drama which the 1623 First Folio of Shakespeare's collected plays calls *Henry VI Part Three,* the Duke of York is taunted by his enemies as they place a paper crown on his head. He hits back at the 'she-wolf of France', Queen Margaret, with the words 'O tiger's heart wrapped in a *woman's* hide!' By parodying the line, Greene is complaining that Shakespeare has started writing plays in the elevated blank-verse style which was the trademark of the university wits.

Johannes fac totum means Jack-of-all-trades. Applied to Shakespeare, it means first actor, then dramatist. A Jack, furthermore, was no gentleman. Greene goes on to refer to the players as 'rude grooms'. This is a scornful allusion to the acting companies' status as 'servants' or 'grooms of the chamber' to their royal or aristocratic patrons. The narrative of *Greene's Groatsworth of Wit* is a downward spiral from respectability (Master of Arts in the University of Cambridge) to poverty to death; Shakespeare is introduced antagonistically because his path seems to be going in the opposite direction, from country clown to rude groom to successful writer.

The image of the crow and the accusation 'beautified with our feathers' suggest that Shakespeare may even have been filching with his pen. The phrasing is based on that of Thomas Nashe in the preface he contributed to one of Greene's earlier works, *Menaphon.* Nashe had gibed at writers who 'in disguised array vaunt Ovid's and Plutarch's plumes as their own' and at those who trick up the acting companies 'with their feathers'. The image of borrowed plumes is itself a borrowed plume, in that it is taken from a fable in Aesop concerning a crow with borrowed feathers, which the Roman poet Horace applied to literary thieves. For Greene, then, Shakespeare's is a double offence: as an actor, he gains credit for mouthing fine lines which really belong to the university wits, and as an upstart writer he is now imitating their style, even borrowing their phrases, in his own plays.

'Upstart' is a word which entered the English language with the social mobility of the mid-sixteenth century. It means 'one who has newly or suddenly risen in position or importance; a newcomer in respect of rank or consequence; a parvenu'. The word precisely denotes Greene's perception of Shakespeare: a man of low origins who has suddenly come on the scene and is being touted as an important new voice in the theatre.

We do not know whether 'in his own conceit' means that it really was Shakespeare's own joke that he was the only 'Shake-scene in a country', but it certainly was the case that apt punning on his name became commonplace once his reputation was established. Greene's principal emphasis is the new boy's 'rudeness', his lack of an advanced education. It is one of the ironies of the Shakespeare story that the first surviving reference to him concerns the very lack of a university degree which three hundred years later led people to start supposing that the plays must have been written by someone more educated.

How did Shakespeare react to Greene's insults? Like so much pertaining to his life, the answer can only be a matter of inference.

In the autumn of 1592, when the *Groatsworth* was published, the London theatres were closed. This was an occupational hazard which Shakespeare faced throughout his career: fear of public disorder and the risk of plague infection spreading through closely packed audiences meant that there were frequent bans on performance. Save for two brief seasons in midwinter (when the cold weather diminished the risk of plague), the theatres remained closed from June 1592 until June 1594. This must have been frustrating for Shakespeare, since, thanks to the *Henry VI* plays, his new career as a writer was just taking off.

According to Nashe, writing in the summer of 1592, the play featuring the brave Lord Talbot's battles against the French in the time of Joan of Arc was a triumphant success, drawing some ten thousand spectators. The play in question was printed as Shakespeare's in the First Folio, where it is called *Henry VI Part One*. It may, however, have been a work of collaboration between Shakespeare and one or more of the university wits, perhaps even Greene himself. A partnership which ended in tears, with Shakespeare ending up gaining all the credit for the hit play, is as good an explanation as any for Greene's bitterness.

With the future of the London theatres uncertain, Shakespeare had two choices: to continue as an actor and follow his company on a provincial tour, or to try to make his way through his writing. Touring was hard work with little reward; the financial returns from the provinces were too poor for it be worth writing new plays for performance there. Shakespeare made the other choice. Greene's death in poverty at exactly this moment would have been a stark reminder that this was a high-risk decision. Publishers paid writers as poorly as the actors did. One could not sustain a living as a full-time writer. The only means of advancement was to gain aristocratic or court patronage: flatter a lord or lady with an elegant and complimentary dedication and they might give you at least a guinea or two for it. Continue to ingratiate yourself with them and if you were very lucky they might then employ you in some secretarial or other post in their household. This seems to have been Shakespeare's plan of action.

Suddenly to find himself publicly tarred with the feathers of the upstart crow must have been a setback. What incentive would there be for a lord to employ a *Johannes fac totum* when there were university-educated wits aplenty on the market? It looks as if Shakespeare arranged for measures to be taken to defuse Greene's bombshell. Within three months, Henry Chettle, who had been responsible for the publication of the *Groatsworth*, was prevailed upon to offer an apology in the preliminary epistle to his collection of stories, *Kind-Heart's Dream*. He disclaimed the insult to Shakespeare, but admitted to editing Greene's papers and said that he was 'as sorry as if the original fault had been my fault'. He then added a commendation of Shakespeare:

> my self have seen his demeanour no less civil than he excellent in the quality he professes. Besides, divers of worship have reported his uprightness of dealing, which argues his honesty, and his facetious grace in writing, that approves his art.

Chettle's language inverts that of the *Groatsworth*. Social derogation is replaced by cordial respect: civility of demeanour and uprightness of dealing are the marks of the gentleman. 'Honest' means 'of good birth'; the word is intended to repair the damage done by 'upstart'. Chettle defends Shakespeare's poetic language as well as his social status; the bombastic player is transformed into a polished writer, characterized by 'art' and 'facetious grace'. 'Facetious' suggests elegance and urbanity. This is the image needed if one is to gain aristocratic patronage: Chettle's characterization marks Shakespeare's first step on the literary and social road of upward mobility.

His image intact, Shakespeare then targeted his potential patron. In April 1593 his *Venus and Adonis*, an erotic narrative poem of supreme wit and polish, was entered on the Stationers' Register in which the right to publish was assigned. The publisher was Richard Field, a fellow old-boy of the Stratford-upon-Avon grammar school. The title-page of *Venus and Adonis* came adorned with a Latin epigraph which began '*Vilia miretur vulgus*' – 'let the vulgar mass admire trash'. The quotation is an implicit renunciation of the 'low' art of playwrighting. 'I know my Latin – despite not having a university degree,' Shakespeare is also saying, 'and I am capable of drinking from the Castalian spring of classical inspiration, writing in the style of Ovid (from whom the epigraph is quoted); I have aspirations to be considered the English equivalent of that most urbane of classical poets.'

Venus and Adonis carries a dedication 'To the Right Honourable Henry Wriothesley, Earl of Southampton, and Baron of Titchfield'. Southampton was a young aristocrat who was about to come of age. It was therefore assumed that he was also about to come into considerable power of patronage. 'Your Honour's in all duty, William Shakespeare', the flattering dedicatory letter is signed. Shakespeare had made his debut in print.

We do not know exactly what form Southampton's patronage took, but it does seem that he gave Shakespeare some support in the course of 1593, since a year after the publication of *Venus and Adonis* Shakespeare considered it worthwhile to dedicate a second elegant poem to him, *The Rape of Lucrece*. The tone of the second dedication is more confident and suggests some form of acquaintance: 'The love I dedicate to your Lordship is without end', it begins. By the standards of Elizabethan dedications, this is full but not excessive. We cannot infer from it 'love' in any personal sense. Nevertheless, there is strong evidence to suggest that in 1593 Shakespeare had a degree of intimacy with Southampton's household, and that he was building up his poetic portfolio by writing sonnets as well as narrative poems for the delectation of the young Earl. This episode will be my subject in chapter two.

If, as seems highly likely, the sonnets do belong to this period, then the opening of number 112 looks striking:

> Your love and pity doth th'impression fill
> Which vulgar scandal stamped upon my brow;
> For what care I who calls me well or ill,
> So you o'er-green my bad, my good allow?

The previous two poems in Shakespeare's sonnet sequence have hinted at the social stigma attached to the trade of acting: 'Thence comes it that my name receives a brand' (111); 'Alas, 'tis true, I have gone here and there / And made myself a motley to the view' (110) – 'motley' is a technical term for the dress of the stage Fool. What is the 'brand' of sonnet 111, the 'vulgar scandal' of 112? If the rejection of the 'vulgus' proclaimed on the title-page of *Venus and Adonis* was Shakespeare's way of trying to put the *Groatsworth* scandal behind him, we have our answer. It may be, then, that the verb in line four is a private joke. It is a nonce-word, a Shakespearean coinage never used again. In the original text it is spelt 'ore-greene'. Could it mean 'cover over Greene's insult'? The sonnet would then be saying: 'I do not care that Greene calls me ill and Chettle calls me well, all I care is that you, my fair young patron, should care for me.'

If I were reading Shakespeare's life as one of allegory and finding comments on it in his works, in the manner suggested by Keats, I would say that Will's social mobility and his ability to remake himself are dramatized in the figure of Prince Hal, whilst his recognition that to have a great wit does not necessarily lead to financial reward is dramatized in the character of Sir John Falstaff – who dies in Hostess Quickly's tavern, calling out for sack and remembering a woman called Doll in an uncanny replication of Greene's death in Hostess Isam's house, calling out for malmsey and writing to a wife called Doll. But Shakespeare's life of contemporary anecdote tells us nothing of whether the relationship with Southampton ended in reward or in neglect.

There is only a posthumous tradition that the Earl provided financial support (to the tune of a thousand pounds), so it can only be fancy that Southampton's funds provided Shakespeare with the money which enabled him to become a leading shareholder in the company of the Lord Chamberlain's Men, formed when the London theatres reopened in the summer of 1594.

From that point on, Shakespeare was house dramatist to the Chamberlain's (later King's) Men, regularly writing two or three plays a year, devoting himself fully to the theatre. Where the university wits' relationship with the acting companies had been one-sided, Shakespeare saw that the dramatist's best hope was to have a stake in the company himself. In that sense, he invented the *profession* of dramatist. Within a few years, others were following the trail he had blazed: Thomas Heywood carved out an analogous position for himself as house dramatist with the Lord Admiral's Men, the other leading company of the later 1590s, and Ben Jonson became the second commercially successful dramatist without a university background.

Instead of leading to a career as a secretary in an aristocratic household, the two narrative poems worked wonders for Shakespeare's public image. *Venus and Adonis* was his most successful work, being reprinted in 1594, 1595, 1596, twice in 1599, and three times in 1602. The number of reprintings suggests that it sold over ten thousand copies in a decade, which would make it the best-selling poem of the Elizabethan age. It was certainly quoted and imitated more frequently than any other poem. Because of it, Shakespeare was known above all as a witty, sophisticated writer, as 'rich conceited', 'sweet', and 'honey-flowing'.

Most excellent in both kinds for the stage

By 1598 his dramatic works were being widely praised too. That year Francis Meres, an Oxford man resident in London and with his finger on the pulse of the literary scene, published a comparison between living English writers and dead classical ones. Meres gave the impression of being in the know among the literati by mentioning that Shakespeare was circulating 'sugared' sonnets 'among his private friends'. But he was in fact a representative witness rather than a privileged one. His opinions were nearly all Elizabethan commonplaces; precisely because they are unoriginal, they are evidence of the general view of Shakespeare. Meres regarded Shakespeare as the wittiest, most mellifluous poet of the age: this was the common currency of literary opinion. He considered *Venus and Adonis* and *Lucrece* to have made Shakespeare a reincarnation of Ovid: this is proof of those poems' success in the work of self-promotion.

Meres described Shakespeare as 'the most excellent' English dramatist for both comedy and tragedy. He listed the plays on which his judgement was based: in comedy, *The Two Gentlemen of Verona*, *The Comedy of Errors*, *Love's Labour's Lost*, the now lost *Love's Labour's Won*, *A Midsummer Night's Dream* and *The Merchant of Venice*; in tragedy, *Richard II*, *Richard III*, *Henry IV*, *King John*, *Titus Andronicus* and *Romeo and Juliet*. Six years on from Greene's scornful dismissal, and before the writing of the plays most admired in later ages, the upstart crow had made it to the top.

By the end of the 1590s Shakespeare was admired for both his verbal facility and his variety of modes and moods. He was seen to move with ease between lyric and dramatic forms, and between tragedy and comedy. No other poet, either English or classical, was praised by Meres in so many different categories of writing.

Around 1600, Gabriel Harvey gave further witness to Shakespeare's variety, remarking that the 'younger sort' took much delight in the playful *Venus and Adonis*, while 'the wiser sort' preferred the tragic matter of *Lucrece* and *Hamlet*. Then in 1604 one Anthony Skoloker praised Shakespeare for combining light and heavy matter, comedy and tragedy, in a single play: '*Friendly Shakespeare's Tragedies*, where the *Comedian* rides when the *Tragedian* stands on tip-toe . . . pleas[ing] all, like Prince *Hamlet*.' As the image of Shakespeare the man was associated with social mobility, so the image of Shakespeare the dramatist was characterized by stylistic range and generic flexibility.

In the sixteenth century, the selling point of a play was generally its title, not the name of the dramatist. No writer's name is included on the title-pages of Shakespeare's earliest printed plays, *Titus Andronicus* (1594), *The First Part of the Contention betwixt the Two Famous Houses of York and Lancaster* (1594) and *The True Tragedy of Richard Duke of York* (1595). But by 1598–9 Shakespeare's name had sufficient recognition value for publishers to think it worth a place on their title-pages. The first printed editions of plays to bear Shakespeare's name were the Quartos (slim volumes, analogous to the modern paperback) of *Love's Labour's Lost* and *Richard II* which appeared in 1598, and *Henry IV Part One* and *Richard III* which appeared the following year.

That there was a widespread vogue for Shakespeare by this time is also demonstrable from a fascinating series of allusions in a pair of plays called *The Return from Parnassus*, produced by Cambridge University students between 1599 and 1601.

A character in the first of these plays is a foolish gentleman called Gullio, who wishes to impress both his mistress and the aristocracy. He thinks that the way to do this is to quote copiously from *Venus and Adonis*, *Lucrece* and *Romeo and Juliet*. He mouths Shakespeare's lines, pretending that they are his own. 'We shall have nothing but pure Shakespeare, and shreds of poetry that he hath gathered at the theatres', complains Ingenioso, a representation of the Cambridge-educated Thomas Nashe, as Gullio launches into a 'monstrous theft' from *Romeo*, then lifts a stanza from *Venus*:

> Thrice fairer than my self, thus I began,
> The gods' fair riches, sweet above compare,
> Stain to all nymphs, more lovely than a man,
> More white and red than doves and roses are:
> > Nature that made thee, with herself at strife,
> > Saith that the world hath ending with thy life.

The primary anecdotal value of the *Parnassus* plays is that they show us which Shakespearean styles were regarded in the dramatist's own time as his most characteristic and popular. Surprisingly from the point of view of what has been most valued down the ages, one answer proves to be the elegant verbal play, the polished symmetry and rhetorical elaboration, of stanzas such as this. In a later scene, however, lines that are more familiar to us are shown to have been already memorable in their own time. A character is auditioned for a Shakespearean tragic lead, and the passage he is given is the astonishingly arresting start of *Richard III*:

> Now is the winter of our discontent
> Made glorious summer by this son of York.

The scene featuring Gullio the Shakespeare-worshipper continues with Ingenioso composing imitations of Chaucer, Spenser, and Shakespeare, then asking for a choice to be made between them. The foolish Gullio's choice of Shakespeare above the venerable Chaucer and Spenser carries the clear implication that from the play's 'university' point of view the vogue for Shakespeare has grown severely out of proportion. The *Parnassus* plays were a continuation of the battle between university and non-university writers.

This becomes even clearer in a later scene, when the leading actors of the Chamberlain's Men, the tragedian Richard Burbage and the clown Will Kempe, are impersonated. Burbage and Kempe stand up for their fellow Shakespeare and condemn the university wits for larding their plays with an excess of mythological imagery: 'they smell too much of that writer *Ovid* and that writer *Metamorphoses*'. Kempe's ignorance of the fact that *Metamorphoses* is a work by Ovid, not the name of another writer, is a typical 'university' put-down of the vulgar players. Ironically though, Shakespeare – as Meres recognized – had a better claim than any university dramatist to the mantle of Ovid. His immensely popular *Titus Andronicus* was the most notable Ovidian drama of the age.

Titus is characterized by a bold combination of high tragedy and black comedy, of pathos and grotesquerie, of love-language and bloody spectacle. It deliberately flouts the classical decorum which would prevent these differing tones from keeping company. Its indecorum seems to be the object of satire in another scene in *The Return from Parnassus*, when a character called Judicio, having equivocally praised the non-university Ben Jonson as 'the wittiest fellow of a Bricklayer in England', produces what is intended to be a critically judicious summary of the art of William Shakespeare:

> Who loves not *Adon's* love, or *Lucrece'* rape?
> His sweeter verse contains heart-robbing lines,
> Could but a graver subject him content,
> Without love's foolish lazy languishment.

As so often, Shakespeare's capacity to touch the heart is singled out for praise, together with the sweetness of his poetic language. The phrase 'graver subject' alludes to 'some graver labour', Shakespeare's own description in the dedication to *Venus and Adonis* of the yet-to-be-written *Rape of Lucrece*. But the final line of Judicio's characterization sounds like a parody of *Titus*, the other Shakespearean work on the classical theme of rape. In that play, the villainous Aaron compares love to 'lingering languishment' (2.1.111); he recommends rape as a better course of action. With 'love's foolish lazy languishment', the *Parnassus*-author parodies both Shakespeare's rococo alliteration and his indecorous contamination of the heroic form of tragedy with the lyric matter of erotic desire.

Ovid would have us believe that one of the functions of love poetry is to persuade people to jump into bed with you. We have one tantalizing piece of evidence that Shakespeare's quickness of wit – manifested nowhere more richly than in the lovers' wit-combats of Biron and Rosaline in *Love's Labour's Lost*, Beatrice and Benedick in *Much Ado about Nothing*, Rosalind and Orlando in *As You Like It* – served him well in this regard. The story comes to us from two different sources, one of them a diary entry made on 13 March 1602 by a law student and playgoer called John Manningham. Since the existence of this diary was not known until the nineteenth century, the version of the story which circulated in the theatrical tradition in earlier centuries provides independent corroboration of the incident's underlying truth.

The story first reached print in Thomas Wilkes' *General View of the Stage*, published in 1759:

> One evening when *Richard III* was to be performed, Shakespeare observed a young woman delivering a message to Burbage in so cautious a manner as excited his curiosity to listen to. It imported, that her master was gone out of town that morning, and her mistress would be glad of his company after Play; and to know what signal he would appoint for admittance. Burbage replied, 'Three taps at the door, and "It is I, Richard the Third."' She immediately withdrew, and Shakespeare followed till he observed her to go into a house in the city; and enquiring in the neighbourhood, he was informed that a young lady lived there, the favourite of an old rich merchant. Near the appointed time of meeting, Shakespeare thought proper to anticipate Mr Burbage, and was introduced by the concerted signal. The lady was very much surprised at Shakespeare's presuming to act Mr Burbage's part; but as he (who had wrote *Romeo and Juliet*), we may be certain, did not want wit or eloquence to apologize for the

intrusion, she was soon pacified, and they were mutually happy till Burbage came to the door, and repeated the same signal; but Shakespeare popping his head out of the window, bid him be gone; for that William the Conqueror had reigned before Richard III.

There may be a little embroidery here (the cuckolding of a rich old merchant is a classic folk-tale motif), but the version of the story in Manningham's diary is identical in substance, save that in his account the citizen herself attends the play and is so impressed by Burbage's performance that before leaving the theatre she finds him backstage and makes the assignation. Manningham is also crisper on the substance of the matter: Shakespeare was 'at his game' with the woman when Burbage knocked on the door.

There is no more vivid anecdote of the life of Shakespeare's theatre. Richard Burbage puts in such a charismatic performance as Richard III that the female theatregoer responds by offering him her body, every bit in the manner of a modern pop star's groupie. Shakespeare, with his usual eye for the main chance, pops in between the erection and Burbage's hopes, then pops out of the window with a stunningly witty punchline. Burbage has no cause to complain about Shakespeare presuming to act his part, because Shakespeare has himself written the part of Richard. Shakespeare's art may not have advanced him among the aristocracy, but it has got him into a citizen's bed.

As far as Shakespeare's more serious social aspirations were concerned, they received a boost in 1596 when, acting on behalf of his father, he obtained a coat of arms and a motto to attach to the family name. By 1596, then, his plays and poems had earned enough for him to buy a piece of gentility; by the following year they had earned enough for him to buy New Place, the second-largest house in Stratford-upon-Avon. There may be some affectionate mockery of Shakespeare's social climbing in a scene in Ben Jonson's *Every Man in his Humour* (1599) in which a country character called Sogliardo comes up to London and buys a patent for a coat of arms, which costs him thirty pounds but enables him to sign himself gentleman. The motto for the Shakespeare arms seems to have been 'non sanz droict', 'Not without right'. Sogliardo's motto is '*Not without mustard*'. Mustard was proverbially sharp – John Marston snarled out 'sharp mustard rhyme / To purge the snottery of our slimy time' – so the allusion could be translated as *it is not without a certain piquancy that Shakespeare claims a 'right' to gentlemanly status*. Mustard was also the cheapest of condiments: where a true gentleman would have spiced his food more exotically and expensively, mustard is a betrayal of Shake-scene's base origins.

Art or nature?

Affectionate mockery was the tone of most of Ben Jonson's allusions to Shakespeare during his lifetime. In the prologue to his revised version of *Every Man in his Humour*, he gently derided the lack of realism in the history plays. On Shakespeare's stage, the Wars of the Roses are fought with 'three rusty swords' and 'some few foot-and-a-half words', while the Chorus in *Henry V* 'wafts you o'er the seas' by pure authorial fiat. Then in the induction to *Bartholomew Fair*, Jonson teased the audience for their preference for old plays like *Titus Andronicus* and Kyd's *Spanish Tragedy* over newer works – implicitly his own. He also 'apologized' for not including in his play such popular Shakespearean vulgarities as 'a *Servant-monster*' (Caliban) and '*Jigs* and *Dances*' (the musical interludes in the sheep-shearing feast of *The Winter's Tale*). The features picked out for mockery both here and in Jonson's later pronouncements – for example that *Pericles* was a 'mouldy tale' and *The Winter's Tale* was absurd because it has a shipwreck on the coast of Bohemia, a country located one hundred miles from the sea – are breaches of that classical decorum which on the one hand demands verisimilitude in drama and on the other prescribes the separation of tragedy from comedy, high style from low.

In one of his conversations with the Scottish poet William Drummond, Jonson famously said 'that Shakespeare wanted Art'. Jonson's own method of compensating for his lack of a university education was the introduction into English Renaissance theatre of a new degree of classical regularity, an imitation of the admired examples of Roman comedy and tragedy. This is the 'art' which he claimed Shakespeare lacked.

Jonson set himself up as the English Horace. One of the arguments of Horace's *Art of Poetry* had been that the true poet combines nature with art, inspiration with perspiration. In the words of Jonson's own translation of the *Ars Poetica*: 'A good and wise man will cry open shame / On artless verse.' The true artist will go over his work again and again, and 'blot out' his 'careless' lines 'with his turned pen'.

Shakespeare's extraordinary linguistic facility had given him a reputation for composing at great speed. When his fellow-actors John Heminges and Henry Condell published his collected plays in the First Folio of 1623, they included a prefatory address 'To the Great Variety of Readers' in which they said that 'His mind and hand went together, and what he thought he uttered with that easiness that we have scarce received from him a blot in his papers'. According to Jonson's Horatian poetics, this absence of 'blots' was a deficiency, not a strength. It meant that the poet had not returned to his text and turned over his 'careless' passages. Jonson dissented from Heminges and Condell's praise in a passage 'concerning our Shakespeare' in his literary notebook:

> I remember the Players have often mentioned it as an honour to Shakespeare that in his writing, whatsoever he penned, he never blotted out a line. My answer hath been 'Would he had blotted a thousand!', which they thought a malevolent speech. I had not told posterity this, but for their ignorance, who choose that circumstance to commend their friend by, wherein he most faulted. And to justify mine own candour (for I loved the man, and do honour his memory – on this side Idolatry – as much as any), he was indeed honest, and of an open and free nature, had an excellence Fancy, brave notions and gentle expressions, wherein he flowed with that facility that sometimes it was necessary he should be stopped . . . His wit was in his own power; would the rule of it had been so too.

Jonson's praise of Shakespeare's character is unstinting: 'he was indeed honest' roundly confirms Chettle's reply to Greene's abuse, while 'an open and free nature' suggests exactly that openness to all impressions and possibilities, that willingness to experiment and unwillingness to close the mind which John Keats later described as 'negative capability'. The reason for the element of criticism in Jonson's memorandum is his view that Heminges and Condell did Shakespeare no favours by praising him for never having a second thought.

This was a matter of great concern to the classically inclined Jonson. He dwelt upon it in his poem, 'To the Memory of my Beloved, the Author Master William Shakespeare, and what he hath left us', which was printed prominently in the First Folio, immediately after Heminges and Condell's address to the reader.

Jonson opens his poem by writing that he will not offer ignorant praise or blind affection; he will seek to explain as well as to commend. The explanation begins with an enumeration of Shakespeare's predecessors, the writers who shaped the theatre he inherited: Thomas Kyd, author of the vastly influential *Spanish Tragedy*, John Lyly, the age's first great writer of comedies, and Christopher Marlowe, who forged the 'mighty line' which is late Elizabethan verse-drama's greatest glory. Shakespeare outdid them all. Jonson then goes on to make a higher claim: that the works of Shakespeare even outdid those of the ancients. He was greater than Aeschylus, Sophocles, and Euripides in tragedy, than Aristophanes, Terence, and Plautus in comedy. His achievement is regarded as nothing less than the making of British literature as something superior to the classics.

Such a claim might sound 'insolent' and 'haughty', but Jonson neatly forestalls this potential criticism by applying those very adjectives to the drama of Greece and Rome which Shakespeare is said to overgo. 'Triumph, my Britain, thou hast one to show / To whom all scenes of Europe homage owe', proclaims one of the poem's several prophetic invocations. In later centuries, the writers of every country of Europe would indeed pay homage to Shakespeare, just as Shakespeare did indeed 'shine forth', as Jonson exhorts him to, as a star to light later poets and artists along the way of creativity.

One of the poem's chief conceits is that Shakespeare has succeeded in outdoing the ancients without having a great knowledge of them. That is to say, he has surpassed his predecessors in spite of his 'small Latin and less Greek'. Jonson's purpose in mentioning Shakespeare's lack of advanced accomplishment in the ancient languages was not to condemn his friend for ignorance or to say that he had no education. This, however, is what later readers have often assumed was his point, with all sorts of unfortunate consequences which I discuss in later chapters. The point is rather that Shakespeare's genius has reanimated the spirits of the fathers of tragedy without any attempt at a conscious imitation of them. What has enabled him to do this is his direct truth to nature: 'Nature herself was proud of his designs, / And joyed to wear the dressing of his lines.'

But then, keeping in mind his Horatian sense of the need for both inspiration and perspiration, Jonson writes,

> Yet must I not give Nature all; thy Art,
>   My gentle Shakespeare, must enjoy a part.
> For though the poet's matter nature be,
>   His art doth give the fashion; and that he
> Who casts to write a living line must sweat –
>   Such as thine are – and strike the second heat
> Upon the muses' anvil, turn the same,
>   And himself with it that he thinks to frame;
> Or for the laurel he may gain a scorn,
>   For a good poet's made as well as born.
> And such wert thou.

Here Shakespeare is praised for doing exactly what Heminges and Condell said that he did not do: having second thoughts, blotting and improving his lines. Jonson goes on to write of his fellow-dramatist's 'well-turned and true-filed lines': turning and filing constitute Horace's praise of the poet as *craftsman* rather than as natural genius. Turning is the art of chiselling raw blocks of Plutarch's prose into the finely honed verse of *Antony and Cleopatra*.

But Jonson failed in his attempt to create an image of Shakespeare as both poet of nature and scrupulous craftsman who knew the need to work and rework his material. The image from the opening pages of the First Folio which endured was that of Heminges and Condell: Shakespeare writing so smoothly and so perfectly that he scarce blotted a line. This image paved the way for the later apotheosis of Shakespeare as pure genius untrammelled by art.

In 1640, a new edition of Shakespeare's *Poems* was published with a dedicatory epistle by Leonard Digges. It was a point-for-point reply to Jonson's poem in the First Folio. It opens with the words 'Poets are born, not made.' This is a deliberate rebuff to Jonson's 'a good poet's made as well as born'. In Digges' poem, Shakespeare's works are characterized by 'Art without art unparalleled as yet'. A series of claims are then made about Shakespeare's achievement. Whilst Jonson's image of Shakespeare revising and polishing his work – striking the second heat upon the Muses' anvil – has been forgotten, Digges' praises became critical commonplaces:

Next, nature only helped him, for look through
This whole book, thou shalt find he doth not borrow
One phrase from Greeks, nor Latins imitate,
Nor once from vulgar languages translate,
Nor plagiary-like from others glean,
Nor begs he from each witty friend a scene
To piece his acts with. All that he doth write
Is pure his own: plot, language exquisite.

In 1623, Jonson's Shakespeare had held nature and art in Horatian balance; in 1640, Digges' Shakespeare is all nature, all instinct. Misunderstanding Jonson's phrase about Shakespeare's 'small Latin and less Greek' as an insult, Digges fashions an image of the playwright's autonomy. His Shakespeare never plagiarizes and never collaborates.

Digges' claims are false: Shakespeare is full of borrowed phrases and almost all his plots are gleaned from others. The story about Shakespeare's encounter with the citizen's wife was not the only allusion to the dramatist in John Manningham's diary of 1602: that February, he noted that he had seen *Twelfth Night* and that it was 'much like the *Comedy of Errors*, or *Menechmi* in Plautus, but most like and near to that in Italian called *Inganni*'. For Manningham, it was noteworthy, not deplorable, that a Shakespearean comedy should resemble an ancient Roman play or a modern Italian one. Far from being 'pure his own', Shakespeare's plays relied on inherited material. Some of them imitated the 'Latins': *The Comedy of Errors* is a version of Plautus' *Menaechmi*. Others translated elements from the 'vulgar languages': *Twelfth Night* is only one of several comedies to rework Italian sources.

Digges' poem goes on to single out a number of Shakespeare's characters for special praise. The biggest crowd-pullers in the early seventeenth-century theatre are said to be 'Honest Iago' and 'the jealous Moor', 'Falstaff, Hal, Poins, the rest', Beatrice and Benedick, and 'Malvolio that cross-gartered gull'. Shakespeare's characters have always had a unique life in the memories of playgoers, but even they are not 'pure his own': most of them are fleshed out from what he found in his sources.

Ironically for Jonson's attempt to extol Shakespeare's art, the very existence of Ben's own works added to the sense that Will was a 'natural'. Digges' poem asserted that audiences greatly preferred Shakespeare's nimble lines to Jonson's 'tedious though well-laboured *Catiline*'. Jonson's plays do frequently seem *laboured*, Shakespeare's *easy*. It is somehow appropriate that the Jonson Folio was entitled *Works*, whereas the Shakespeare Folio went into print under the easier and more mobile title of *Comedies, Histories and Tragedies*.

A number of anecdotes which circulated in the first half of the seventeenth century turn on the contrast between Jonson's ponderous learning and Shakespeare's quick wit. In Thomas Fuller's *Worthies of England*, for instance, Jonson is compared to a great Spanish galleon, 'solid but slow in his performances'; Shakespeare, meanwhile, is a nimble English warship, 'lesser in bulk, but lighter in sailing, [which] could turn with all tides, tack about and take advantage of all winds, by the quickness of his wit and invention.' The earliest, and most likely to be authentic, of these anecdotes is the following, recorded in several different sources:

> Shakespeare was Godfather to one of Ben Jonson's children, and after the christening being in a deep study, Jonson came to cheer him up and asked him why he was so melancholy. 'No, faith, Ben,' says he, 'Not I – but I have been considering a great while what should be the fittest gift for me to bestow upon my God-child, and I have resolved at last.' 'I prithee, what?' says [Jonson]. 'Ifaith, Ben, I'll e'en give him a dozen good Latin Spoons, and thou shalt translate them.'

Here Shakespeare is imagined to play upon his own small Latin. But one of the points of the joke is that an inscription on a christening spoon would be easy Latin indeed, and it would not take Jonson's great learning to translate it. Shakespeare is sufficiently confident in the Latin he has from his grammar school education to be able to make a joke about Jonson having a great deal more from his. The other point of the story is that it illustrates Shakespeare's quick wit and verbal inventiveness. The punchline turns on a pun: christening spoons were frequently made of a metal alloy called 'latten'.

Regardless of its factual origin, this story has the authentically *representative* truth of anecdote. It shows us a Shakespeare who thinks quickly and likes to tease. But above all it shows us a Shakespeare who loves to act a role: when Ben comes to him after the christening, Will is in the *pose* of melancholy. We know very little of Shakespeare's early life as an actor on the London stage, but what we know for sure was that he retained all his life the ability to act. It is because he was an actor that he could, in Fuller's words, 'turn with all tides, tack about and take advantage of all winds'.

Jonson realized this, as may be seen from a brilliant moment of invention in the poem on his 'beloved' colleague's art. Shakespeare, writes Jonson, did not only 'turn' his poetry on the anvil, he turned *himself with it*. In each line 'he seems to shake a lance': in the heat of composition he fashions a spear. That spear is himself: Shake-spear. What we mean by 'Shakespeare' is not the life but the work. As a dramatist, he never speaks in his own voice, he makes and remakes, turns and returns, himself. He does not tell us about his life; for this we have to rely on the anecdotes of others. The only road from the works themselves to the life is Keats's path of allegorical interpretation.

A life of allegory

In his ingenious image of the framing of Shake-speare upon the Muses' anvil, Jonson, who knew Shakespeare so well, foreshadows what Jorge Luis Borges unravels in the greatest of all brief allegories of Shakespeare's life.

To begin with, says Borges, 'There was no one in him'. His words were copious, but behind his face 'there was only a bit of coldness, a dream dreamt by no one'. How, then, to fill that brain, that domed forehead which looks out at us from the Droeshout engraving on the title-page of the First Folio (Fig. 1)? Was reading the answer? With his little bit of Latin, Shakespeare began to find out. It was not enough. Was living to the moment the answer? He 'let himself be initiated by Anne Hathaway one long June afternoon' – a woman eight years his senior, she was six months pregnant when they married. It was not enough.

He goes to London and becomes an actor. He gains a singular satisfaction from impersonating other beings. But still this is not enough, so he takes to imagining other beings. He writes plays himself:

And so, while his flesh fulfilled its destiny as flesh in the taverns and brothels of London, the soul that inhabited him was Caesar, who disregards the augur's admonition, and Juliet, who abhors the lark, and Macbeth, who converses on the plains with the witches who are also Fates. No one has ever been so many men as this man, who like the Egyptian Proteus could exhaust all the guises of reality.

Did he ever leave any hints in these plays as to his true identity? Borges thinks that he only did so at those moments when he recognized that identity is itself play – when Richard III says that he plays the part of many and Iago proclaims 'I am not what I am'. His most famous passages – Hamlet's soliloquies, Jaques' oration on the seven ages, Prospero's 'Our revels now are ended' – suggest that 'existing, dreaming and acting' are all three one and the same thing.

For twenty years he persisted in that controlled hallucination, but one morning he was suddenly gripped by the tedium and the terror of being so many kings who die by the sword and so many suffering lovers who converge, diverge and melodiously expire.

He sells his share in his theatre and returns to his native town. He takes up another role, that of 'a retired impresario who has made his fortune'. He has to do something: he concerns himself with 'loans, lawsuits and petty usury'. But

History adds that before or after dying he found himself in the presence of God and told Him: 'I who have been so many men in vain want to be one and myself.' The voice of the Lord answered from a whirlwind: 'Neither am I anyone; I have dreamt the world as you dreamt your work, my Shakespeare, and among the forms in my dream are you, who like myself are many and no one.'

'Are you', not 'is you': the form of Shakespeare is plural. Borges called his allegory 'Everything and Nothing'.

2

SHAKESPEARE'S AUTOBIOGRAPHICAL POEMS?

Brief lives

The first biographies of Shakespeare were anecdotal. In his *Brief Lives*, John Aubrey recorded that the dramatist's father was a butcher and that the boy William used to help him in the family shop, killing calves in a 'high style' to an accompanying dramatic speech. Aubrey also reported that between leaving school and becoming a player in London, William was himself a country schoolmaster. And he said that he had been told that during Shakespeare's working life in London the dramatist returned to his native Stratford once a year, stopping off in Oxford at a tavern owned by a Mr and Mrs Davenant, the latter being a witty and beautiful woman who just might have borne him an illegitimate son who grew up to be Sir William Davenant, Poet Laureate.

Like the anecdotes from Shakespeare's own lifetime, each of these three items of gossip has symbolic meaning. The first attests to his humble and rural origins. It sows the seed for the excesses of later Bardolatry: the butcher's son from provincial Stratford has the same kind of background as the carpenter's son from provincial Nazareth. 'After God,' said the Romantic novelist Alexandre Dumas, author of *The Three Musketeers* and *The Count of Monte-Cristo*, 'Shakespeare created most'. The second anecdote contributes to the long debate about whether Shakespeare's genius was a matter of nature or art. The schoolmastering story had fairly good authority, in that it came from the actor William Beeston, whose father was the actor Christopher Beeston, a member of Shakespeare's company. Aubrey introduced it specifically in order to modify Ben Jonson's 'small Latin and less Greek'. The third piece of gossip serves the dual purpose of suggesting that Shakespeare was a bit of a lad and making him the 'father' of later creative endeavour. Davenant, especially after a few drinks, seems positively to have encouraged the story about his origins: he thought it was worth impugning his mother's good name for the sake of establishing his own poetic pedigree. The royal imprimatur of Davenant's Laureateship is symbolically passed back to Shakespeare, who thus begins his long career as England's National Poet.

After Aubrey came Nicholas Rowe. Though more substantial than anything that had gone before, and formally billed as 'Some Account of the Life of Mr William Shakespear', his biography, prefaced to his 1709 edition of the *Works*, was still anecdotal rather than documentary. Rowe begins by saying that his prime interest is the kind of 'little Personal Story' which brings colour to the life of a great man. This 'Life' gave currency to such memorable anecdotes as the deer-stealing incident – Shakespeare the lad once more – and the casting of William himself as the ghost of Hamlet's father. The latter lays the ground for later readings of Hamlet as the dramatist's most favoured son among all his characters – a reading reinforced by the discovery that Shakespeare really did name his son Hamnet, which appears to be a variant of Hamlet.

The eighteenth century is full of narratives, both historical and fictional, of men who rose from low to high in English society. Rowe's Shakespeare is just such a man. He begins by offending against the Game Laws, which in Rowe's time remained one of the primary means of protecting the property rights of country gentlemen; he is drummed out of town by Sir Thomas Lucy, the local landowner, and, like Dick Whittington or Henry Fielding's Tom Jones, is forced to go to London to seek his fortune. He ends up hobnobbing with the rich and famous:

> He had the Honour to meet with many great and uncommon Marks of Favour and Friendship from the Earl of *Southampton* . . . There is one instance so singular in the Magnificence of this Patron of *Shakespear's*, that if I had not been assur'd that the Story was handed down by Sir *William D'Avenant*, who was probably very well acquainted with his Affairs, I should not have ventured to have inserted, that my Lord *Southampton*, at one time, gave him a thousand Pounds, to enable him to go through with a Purchase which he heard he had a mind to.

He even attracts the attention of the Queen herself:

Queen *Elizabeth* had several of his Plays Acted before her, and
without doubt gave him many gracious Marks of her Favour . . . She
was so well pleas'd with that admirable Character of *Falstaff*, in the
two Parts of *Henry the Fourth*, that she commanded him to continue
it for one Play more, and to shew him in Love. This is said to be the
Occasion of his writing *The Merry Wives of Windsor*.

This tradition of a royal command was first recorded by John Dennis in
the preface to his adaptation of *The Merry Wives of Windsor*, published
in 1702. He added for good measure that the Queen was so keen to
see Sir John in love that she gave Will just ten days to write the play –
and he duly obliged.

The anecdote retains its point whether or not the commission came
from the Queen: Shakespeare is imagined to have the gift of dashing
off a new play in less than a fortnight, while Falstaff is made into a
larger-than-life character who bursts the bounds of the play in which
he originally appeared. He generates not only a second part of *Henry
IV*, but also *The Merry Wives*. We cannot have enough of Falstaff, so
what better than a play which shows him in love? One of the first
things we want to know about our heroes is who they fell in love with.

Shakespeare unlocks his heart?

What, then, about the love life of Shakespeare himself? Rowe and his
successors among the eighteenth-century Shakespeareans did not take
much interest in the question, though they repeatedly returned to the
anecdote about Davenant being the dramatist's natural son. It certainly
did not occur to them to seek in the plays for hidden clues to
Shakespeare's amorous inclinations. They did not regard literature as
encoded autobiography. This was an idea which only emerged towards
the end of the century and which was at the centre of the great cultural
shift that we call the Romantic movement.

The point is crucial and a failure to grasp it has done more than
anything else to create misconceptions and myths about Shakespeare.
In a book on Sir Philip Sidney, John Buxton provides the best summary
I know of the cardinal difference between late sixteenth- and early
nineteenth-century poetry:

The Elizabethans wrote for Penelope Devereux, or Lucy Harington, or Magdalen Herbert, for a gentleman or noble person, for the court, for the benchers of the Middle Temple. Their audience was not vaguely perceived through a mist of universal benevolence: they could kiss its hand, or hear the tones of its voice. From this arises the paradox that the Romantics, writing for the patronage of the unknown man in the bookshop, are much more personal than the Elizabethans, writing, as often as not, for someone with whom they had dined a few days ago. For the Romantic, with everyone to write for, and therefore with no one to write for, wrote for and about himself in a way 'unprecedented in literary history', as Wordsworth remarked; whereas the Elizabethan tried to produce a poem to suit a particular occasion and a known taste.

'Scorn not the sonnet,' wrote Wordsworth in his sonnet on the sonnet: 'with this key / Shakspeare unlocked his heart'. 'Did Shakespeare?' answered Robert Browning, who knew the habits and conventions of the Renaissance, the arts of *persona* and role-play, rather better. 'If so, the less Shakespeare he!'

When Romantics get their hands on Shakespeare's sonnets, the trouble begins. In 1796 August Wilhelm von Schlegel, a central figure in the German Romantic movement, remarked that the sonnets appeared to have been inspired by real love and therefore gave unique access to the poet's life. In his lectures on drama delivered in Vienna in 1808, he amplified the point:

It betrays more than ordinary deficiency of critical acumen in Shakspeare's commentators that none of them, as far as we know, have ever thought of availing themselves of his sonnets for tracing the circumstances of his life. These sonnets paint most unequivocally the actual situation and sentiments of the poet; they make us acquainted with the passions of the man; they even contain remarkable confessions of his youthful errors.

In 1838 another German Romantic, Heinrich Heine, confidently proclaimed that the sonnets were authentic records of the circumstances of Shakespeare's life and in particular his misery. Before our eyes Shakespeare becomes a Romantic, making poetry – as Heine himself did – out of his personal misery.

It is to Schlegel and Romanticism, then, that we owe the idea that the sonnets are *Shakespeare's Autobiographical Poems* – a book of this title by Charles Armitage Brown was also published in 1838. Brown had been a close friend of John Keats, whose sonnets most certainly are autobiographical poems. But that Keats inspired Brown and Shakespeare inspired Keats does not mean that Shakespeare's sonnets were like Keats's. Shakespeare was not a Romantic poet like Wordsworth who just sat down and wrote a sonnet when he felt one coming on, or like Keats for whom the sonnet was above all a way of expressing his own intense feelings.

There is some reason to suppose that the order in which the one hundred and fifty-four sonnets appeared in their first Quarto edition of 1609 was carefully thought out. Often a particular sonnet is a contin-uation of, or a reply to, the one before. Occasionally there seems to be deliberate play between a sonnet's subject matter and its place in the sequence. For instance, the first sonnet on the power of time is number 12 and its first line concerns a 'clock' – which counts in twelves. The climactic sonnet on the same theme, which begins 'Like as the waves make towards the pebbled shores, / So do our minutes hasten to their end', is 60 – the number of minutes that are ended by an hour.

But even if we discount the significance of individual placements, the sonnets as a whole unquestionably fall into three discrete groups. The first one hundred and twenty-six appear to be addressed to a youthful 'you'/ 'thou' who is 'right fair', who seems always to be one and the same person, and who, whenever his sex is identified, is male; the next twenty-six are concerned with a woman, who is 'coloured ill'; the final two sonnets – a pair of vignettes of Cupid – are addressed to neither of them. The break after sonnet 126 might even be marked in the text: uniquely in the collection, that poem has twelve lines instead of fourteen, and it ends with a pair of lines consisting of blanks inside parentheses. Whether the origins of these marks are the author's or the publisher's, they highlight the fact that sonnet 126 is a kind of 'envoy' and they effect a pause before the change of subject represented by 127.

If we read the sonnets in the sequence in which they were printed, the outline of a story is fairly clear. It is not so sequential a narrative as that of Sir Philip Sidney's *Astrophil and Stella*, the most celebrated previous collection of Elizabethan sonnets. By no means every poem fits the pattern – thus for example, numbers 78 to 86 are a discrete group about 'rival poets', yet 81 is an exception. But the grouping of like themes is such that one has a sense of a beginning, a middle, and an end. Charles Armitage Brown's division of the sequence into six phases was the first attempt to summarize it as a narrative, and it remains representative:

1. To his friend, persuading him to marry (1–26)
2. To his friend, who had robbed the poet of his mistress, forgiving him (27–55)
3. To his friend, complaining of his coldness, and warning him of life's decay (56–77)
4. To his friend, complaining that he prefers another poet's praises, and reproving him for faults that may injure his character (78–101)
5. To his friend, excusing himself for having been some time silent, and disclaiming the charge of inconstancy (102–126)
6. To his mistress, on her infidelity (127–152)

Like most readings of the sonnets, this one involves a degree of projection on Brown's part. Subsequent commentators regard the first seventeen sonnets, not the first twenty-six, as the 'marriage-group' – and, strictly, their subject is reproduction rather than marriage. Sonnets 40 to 42 seem to imply that the poet's friend has slept with the poet's mistress, but it is fantasy to make this the matter of all the poems from 27 to 55. Again, phrases like 'reproving' and 'injure his character' owe more to a Victorian notion of gentlemanly conduct than to an Elizabethan patron–client relationship. But it remains true that the sequence begins with seventeen sonnets urging the youth to reproduce his beauty, is focused on time and mortality in the sixties, becomes exceptionally embittered in the nineties, and turns to the 'dark lady' at 127. It is hardly surprising that in a biographical age like the nineteenth century, people started extrapolating Shakespeare's love life from this narrative.

One factor which may have prevented biographical readings of the sonnets from emerging rather earlier was the embarrassing fact that the first one hundred and twenty-six of them were apparently addressed to a young man, not, as was customary in the form, to the poet's lady-love. In 1640 the opportunistic publisher John Benson got round this problem by producing an edition which cheerfully changed some of the pronouns from 'he' to 'she' and 'him' to 'her', but this ceased to be a possible course of action once the eighteenth-century code of editorial responsibility had been carved out. The non-dramatic works were generally excluded from eighteenth-century editions of Shakespeare, such as Dr Johnson's of 1765. When Edmond Malone included them in his 1780 *Supplement* to the revision of the Johnson edition which had appeared two years earlier, George Steevens added notes in which he said that the sonnet form was characterized by 'the highest strain of affectation, pedantry, circumlocution, and nonsense'. Steevens went so far as to say that 'the strongest act of Parliament that could be framed would fail to compel readers into their service'; of sonnet 20, 'A woman's face with nature's own hand painted / Hast thou, the master-mistress of my passion', he wrote 'It is impossible to read this fulsome panegyrick, addressed to a male object, without an equal mixture of disgust and indignation'. This distaste is manifestly moral as well as aesthetic. In the Victorian era, Henry Hallam, father of Alfred Tennyson's dear friend Arthur, was so disturbed by the implied sexual orientation of the sonnets that he wished they had never been written. It was left for a long succession of later commentators to salvage the situation by declaring that the poet's love for the Fair Youth was a matter of pure friendship rather than homosexual desire.

The fortunes of biographical reading

Two great questions have dominated discussion of the sonnets: to whom are they addressed, and are they indeed autobiographical? Who was the beautiful young man whom the poet is urging to marry in the first seventeen sonnets? Since he is the presumed addressee of the next one hundred and nine, did Shakespeare himself fall in love with him? And was he synonymous with the mysterious 'Mr W. H.' described in the publisher's prefatory statement to the 1609 edition as 'the only begetter of these ensuing sonnets'?

The difficulty of answering these questions with any degree of assurance may be seen from the handling of them by Sir Sidney Lee, one of the begetters of the *Dictionary of National Biography* and the author of what was hailed on its publication in 1898 as the fullest and most responsible biography of Shakespeare yet written.

In the early 1890s, Lee contributed entries to the *Dictionary of National Biography* (*DNB*) in which he stated categorically that the dedication to the 1609 Quarto 'is addressed to [the Earl of] Pembroke, disguised under the initials of his family name – William Herbert' and, furthermore, that Shakespeare's young friend 'was doubtless Pembroke himself, and "the dark lady" in all probability was Pembroke's mistress, Mary Fitton. Nothing in the sonnets directly contradicts the identification of W. H. . . . with William Herbert, and many minute internal details confirm it.' But by 1897 the serially issued biographical dictionary had reached the letter S and thus included Lee's article on Shakespeare (some 40,000 words, the longest entry in the entire *DNB*). Here it was announced that 'There is no evidence that [Pembroke] was in his youth acquainted with the poet, or at any time closely associated with him'. The identification of the fair youth of the sonnets with Pembroke rested 'on wholly erroneous premisses'. As for Mary Fitton, she had proved distinctly unfitting to be the dark lady: in her *Gossip from a Muniment Room*, also of 1897, Lady Newdigate-Newdegate reproduced two portraits which showed that her complexion was fair not dark, her hair brown not black, and her eyes grey not black.

In his *DNB* article on Shakespeare, and the biography into which he expanded it the following year, Lee shifted his allegiance to the other leading candidate for fair youth: the sonnets clearly affirm that the youth is Shakespeare's patron and Shakespeare's only known patron was Henry Wriothesley, third Earl of Southampton (Fig. 2). By the time Lee reached the letter W in 1900, he was as convinced of this theory as he had been a decade earlier of the other one: his *DNB* entry on Wriothesley states that 'Southampton doubtless inspired Shakespeare with genuine personal affection'.

In later editions of the earlier entry, the argument that the fair youth was 'doubtless' Pembroke was quietly dropped. As H. E. Rollins put it with the dry humour which characterizes his admirable Variorum edition of the *Sonnets*, 'Of course Lee had a perfect right to move abruptly from one side to another (his doing so speaks well for his open-mindedness); though, in view of the flat contradictions between the 1889 (Fitton) and 1891 (Herbert) volumes and the 1897 (Shakespeare) and 1900 (Wriothesley) volumes of the *DNB*, it might have been fairer to students, and more sporting, if he had mentioned his change of creed'.

The identity of the fair youth matters much more to those who believe that the poems grew from personal experience than to those who believe that they are poetic fictions, influenced more by sonnet-eering convention than by life. So where did Lee stand on this other great question? When his *DNB* article on Shakespeare was published in London in 1897, readers were given the following categorical statement:

> Attempts have been made to represent [the sonnets] as purely literary exercises, mainly on the ground that a personal interpretation seriously reflects on Shakespeare's moral character. But only the two concluding sonnets (153 and 154) can be regarded by the unbiased reader as the artificial product of a poet's fancy. . . . In the rest of the 'Sonnets' Shakespeare avows, in phraseology that is often cryptic, the experiences of his own heart. Their uncontrolled ardour suggests that they came from a youthful pen – from a man not more than thirty.

But as soon as these words were in print, Lee ordered them to be cut from the dictionary's type-plates. Readers of the New York edition, published a few months later, were informed that the sonnets were 'to a large extent undertaken as literary exercises' – Shakespeare's 'ever-present dramatic instinct may be held to account for most of the illusion of personal confession which they call up in many minds'.

Lee went on to devote a substantial section of his 1898 *Life* to the 'anti-biographical' theory. A chapter entitled 'The Borrowed Conceits of the Sonnets' asserted that most of the poems are 'little more than professional trials of skill' and that to seek a biographical original for the dark lady would be as ridiculous as to suppose that Cleopatra was based upon some dusky woman of Shakespeare's acquaintance and not upon the historical Cleopatra. Two chapters later, Lee turns to 'The Supposed Story of Intrigue in the Sonnets'. Readers might themselves suppose from this chapter title that Lee will argue that the youth's affair with the dark lady is another quasi-dramatic fiction. But at this point the biographer cannot stop himself slipping back to his former position: 'The definite element of intrigue that is developed here is not found anywhere else in the range of Elizabethan sonnet-literature. The character of the innovation and its treatment seem only capable of explanation by regarding the topic as a reflection of Shakespeare's personal experience.' There is something about the sonnets which irresistibly pulls Lee's instincts back to the biographical reading that his reason has rejected.

But the most extraordinary volte-face remains the one whereby Lee passed instantly from the ultra-Romantic position which was first articulated by Schlegel to the ultra-anti-Romantic position which has become dominant among modern scholars. Anti-Romanticism reached its culmination in Stephen Booth's 1977 edition of the *Sonnets*, where it was polemically stated that 'William Shakespeare was almost certainly homosexual, bisexual, or heterosexual. The sonnets provide no evidence on the matter.' Resistance to the biographical approach has even led one critic to argue that since Shakespeare was playing with traditional sonnet-matter, and since in number 130 (and indeed in *Love's Labour's Lost*) he explicitly parodies the conventions of praise so dear to sonneteers, the whole sequence should be read as nothing more than a parody of sonneteering conceived for the delight of his witty friends.

The sonnets have an extraordinary capacity to elicit categorical statements from their interpreters. It is announced that the youth *is* Southampton, the youth *is* Pembroke, the youth *is* nobody, the dark lady *is* Mary Fitton, she *is* Aemilia Lanyer, she *is* nobody, the sonnets *are* based on experience, they are *not* based on experience, the love was *not* homosexual, the love *was* homosexual, the love was a dramatic fiction which had *nothing* to do with Shakespeare's sexuality. Somehow the poems convince each reader that what he or she sees in them is what is really there. But somehow they then sneak up behind you and convince you of something completely different.

They can do this partly because of what they leave out. Sidney's *Astrophil and Stella* consists of one hundred and eight sonnets, each crystallizing a lover's mood, and nine songs in which the 'plot' is carried forward – Astrophil confesses his love to Stella, she rejects him, and so on. Shakespeare left out the songs; all the 'events' take place off stage. Since the poems imply a plot without actually spelling it out, there is room for readers to step in with their version of affairs. As the plays leave interpretive space for the audience – we have to decide whether to side with Hal or Falstaff, we are not *told* how to react – so the sonnets drop hints to draw the reader into their implied narrative, but have a cunning reticence which allows our fantasies to run riot.

This, then, *is* the genius of the sonnets: their power to generate readings. In the nineteenth century, most of those readings were biographical. In the late twentieth-century academy, most of them are linguistic. The Stephen Booth edition came equipped with a four-hundred-page commentary which discovered multiple wordplays in almost every line of every sonnet. This kind of reading had its origin in an essay on sonnet 94 by William Empson which begins as follows:

> It is agreed that *They that have power to hurt and will do none* is a piece of grave irony, but there the matter is generally left; you can work through all the notes in the Variorum [edition] without finding out whether flower, lily, 'owner,' and person addressed are alike or opposed. One would like to say that the poem has all possible such meanings, digested into some order, and then try to show how this is done, but the mere number of possible interpretations is amusingly too great. Taking the simplest view (that any two may be alike in some one property) any one of the four either is or is not and either should or should not be like each of the others; this yields 4096 possible movements of thought, with other possibilities. The niggler is routed here.

But Empson was a brilliant biographical critic as well as a brilliant linguistic one; his essay is as shrewd on the poem's implied relationship with its author's patron as it is on the dazzling wordplay. For Empson it was proper to speculate about biographical origins, but the problems of the sonnets were by no means 'solved' by biography.

This seems to me the best position to hold. A story about where the sonnets came from is necessary for an understanding of their nature, but not sufficient for an appreciation of their complexity.

The professed aim of Booth's edition, stated in its preface, was to give the modern reader as much as the editor could 'resurrect of a Renaissance reader's experience of the 1609 Quarto'. This was a rather curious ambition in view of the fact that the 1609 Quarto seems to have attracted the attention of hardly any Renaissance readers. Unlike Shakespeare's two best-selling narrative poems, *Venus and Adonis* and *The Rape of Lucrece*, which went through edition after edition and were praised by dozens of his contemporaries, the 1609 *Sonnets* were never reprinted and hardly ever referred to. Conceivably the book was actively suppressed; more probably, it quietly languished and soon died. That some, at least, of the sonnets circulated in manuscript in the 1590s shows that their intended Renaissance readers were Shakespeare's 'private friends', who would by definition have known something of the circumstances of composition. They, surely, are a more interesting audience to recover than the equally small and even more hypothetical readership of the 1609 volume. Shakespeare's sonnets were at least initially written for a specific purpose and a specific reader or coterie of readers, and we will understand them better if we try to find out who those readers were.

To establish as best we can the circumstances of composition and initial consumption is not to fall in with the Romantic biographical fallacy. Consider the comparable case of Sir Philip Sidney's *Astrophil and Stella*. 'Astrophil' is not synonymous with Sir Philip, nor 'Stella' with Penelope Devereux, but there is no doubt that Penelope Devereux was the ideal implied reader of the sequence. We do not know, and it does not matter much, whether Philip was really in love with Penelope, but we do know, and it matters a great deal, that in the thirty-seventh sonnet of the sequence Sidney puns on the name of Lord Rich, to whom Penelope was unhappily married and whom the poet clearly regarded as unworthy of her. In other sonnets in the sequence the poet-narrator 'Astrophil' manifestly alludes to Sir Philip's status at court, his coat of arms, and his father. There is a character in Sidney's *Arcadia* called Philisides, a name which plays wittily on Philip and Sidney; by the same account, 'Astrophil' means more than 'lover of Stella' (from Greek, 'astro-', star, and 'phil-', love) – the name also contains Phil Sidney himself. These facts do not prove the poems to be fully autobiographical, but they do show that Elizabethan sonneteering makes uses of personal material as well as rhetorical convention. Astro-Phil is at some level Sir Philip; so too, 'Will' in sonnets 135, 136, and 143 is at some level William.

Penelope Devereux is and is not 'Stella', but she was the first implied reader of *Astrophil*; the Countess of Pembroke almost certainly is not 'Delia', but she was the first implied reader of Samuel Daniel's sonnet sequence, *Delia*. So too, Shakespeare's potential patron is and is not the 'fair youth', but he was the first implied reader of the sonnets. Furthermore, the gap between the patron as reader and as subject is smaller than in other cases, for – unusually – Shakespeare does not give a mythical name to his subject of praise, along the lines of Stella, Delia, or Ganymede (the name of the lovely lad in Richard Barnfield's overtly homosexual sequence, *The Affectionate Shepherd*).

We may reasonably assume that to begin with there was only one fair youth. It is a further reasonable inference that he was a patron or potential patron: sonnets 26 and 57–8 include words and phrases like 'Lord', 'vassalage', 'written ambassage', 'duty', 'waiting', 'your servant' and 'being at your beck', while the 'rivals poets' sequence only makes sense in the context of a jostle for patronage. For this reason, the only two serious candidates for 'fair youth' are those between whom Lee wavered: William Herbert, third Earl of Pembroke, a noted patron of poets (and one of the dedicatees of the posthumous Folio of Shakespeare's works) who on two occasions in the late 1590s vigorously resisted attempts to marry him off; and Henry Wriothesley, third Earl of Southampton, a noted patron of poets (and the dedicatee of Shakespeare's unquestionably authorized publications, *Venus and Adonis* and *The Rape of Lucrece*), who in the early 1590s vigorously resisted an attempt to marry him off. Either of them is thus a possible candidate as recipient of the first group of sonnets, on the subject of begetting an heir.

The language of this first group – and indeed of many more of the sonnets – is very close to the language both of the two narrative poems which Shakespeare dedicated to Southampton in 1593–4 and of the plays of that vintage, notably *Love's Labour's Lost*. Furthermore, references such as that in sonnet 16 to 'my pupil pen' suggest early work. A starting-date of around 1592–4 favours Southampton, since Pembroke would only have been twelve or thirteen years old at the time. It is also striking that sonnet 26, which makes such extensive use of the language of patronage, reads like a versification of the prose dedication to Southampton which Shakespeare prefixed to *Lucrece* in 1594. The case for Pembroke is much weaker for the simple reason that we have no evidence that Shakespeare – as opposed to his fellow-actors after his death – sought William Herbert's patronage. Many, if not all, of the sonnets were written in the 1590s, yet no Pembrokite has established any link between Shakespeare and Pembroke in the 1590s.

The lovely boy

It is not inconceivable that Shakespeare began writing sonnets to Southampton in the early 1590s, then, when it became clear that the young Earl was not going to be an especially munificent patron, the poet changed course and started addressing sonnets to Pembroke in the late 1590s and early 1600s. Since very few of the sonnets had been published by this time, individual poems could even have been recycled for a new 'ideal reader'. The 1609 Quarto would then have had the effect of collapsing two glamorous aristocrats into one composite lovely boy. The dedicatory address might then be read as a sleight-of-hand: an assurance to Pembroke (W[illiam] H[erbert]) that he was the *only* inspirer of the sonnets, whereas in fact he was one of two male inspirers.

In the absence of new evidence, hypotheses such as this cannot be refuted, but in deciding on the identity of the *original* recipient of the first of the sonnets, we should apply the metaphorical razor of the medieval philosopher William of Occam. Occam's estimable principle was that for purposes of explanation things not known to exist should not, unless it is absolutely necessary, be postulated as existing. *All candidatures for the fair youth with the exception of Southampton's depend on things not known to exist; it is not necessary to postulate any of these things as existing, since the origin of the sonnets can be explained with things we do know to exist.*

Among these things are the following.

The vogue for writing sonnets of praise in an attempt to gain literary patronage belongs to the early 1590s. Of all surviving Elizabethan sonnet-cycles, the closest to Shakespeare's in language and structure is Samuel Daniel's *Delia*, published in 1592. The London theatres were closed, for fear of spreading plague, for much of the period 1592–4. In 1593–4 Shakespeare sought the patronage of the Earl of Southampton by dedicating his two narrative poems to him. Through his mother, Mary Arden, Shakespeare was a distant relative of Southampton. In the period 1591–4 Southampton was notably recalcitrant about marriage. The obvious inference of all this is that Shakespeare began writing sonnets to Southampton in the period 1592–4, probably beginning with a group somehow concerning marriage.

Internal evidence needs to be treated with great caution, but the following could also be numbered among Occam's 'things known to exist'. The sonnets seem to refer to the fair youth's mother as being alive, his father dead: this fits Southampton's case in the early 1590s (and not Pembroke's in the late 1590s). In the nineteenth century, Henry Wriothesley's descendants said that their name was pronounced 'Rosely'; Southampton's most authoritative biographer claims that in the sixteenth century the family name was pronounced 'Rye-ose-ley'. Either way, the word 'Rose' may be audible in the name. Furthermore, Southampton's home at Titchfield was emblazoned with a heraldic representation of roses. Sonnet 1 begins 'From fairest creatures we desire increase, / That thereby beauty's *Rose* might never die'; this *Rose* is one of the few words italicized in the original text, which suggests that it was stressed deliberately. 'Rose' is frequently played on in the sonnets to the youth, for example in sonnet 95, where 'the fragrant rose' is juxtaposed to 'thy budding name'. Additionally, the Southampton family motto was 'one for all, all for one'. Though wordplay on 'one' and 'all' was common in Elizabethan times, it seems almost obsessive in Shakespeare's *Sonnets* – for instance, in sonnet 8 'all in one' occurs in the context of family, and in 53 'all', 'one', and 'none' come into conjunction in the context of a comparison of the fair youth to Adonis, the mythical fair youth of Shakespeare's first poem dedicated to Southampton.

Again, italicization and wordplay give mysterious significance to the word '*Hews*' in sonnet 20, perhaps suggesting a twist on the four initial letters of Henry Wriothesley, Earl of Southampton. 'HEWS' is and is not 'H.W.E.S.', just as in Maria's riddling letter in *Twelfth Night* 'M.O.A.I.' is and is not Malvolio. Insofar as the fair youth is made of language, is a fictional creation, he is not Southampton; but insofar as he has a human original, that original is Southampton and not Pembroke or anyone else.

The first book to be dedicated to Southampton was a Latin poem called *Narcissus*, written in 1591 by John Clapham, a secretary to Lord Burghley. Southampton was Burghley's ward and at this time Burghley wanted him to marry his own granddaughter, Elizabeth de Vere. Southampton refused – with the result that when he came of age he had to pay a substantial fine to Burghley, which crippled him financially. Since Narcissus comes to a watery end as the result of his resistance to womankind, it is likely that Clapham's poem was commissioned by Burghley to put pressure on Southampton in the marriage stakes. Given the similarity of the Narcissus theme to the *Venus and Adonis* one, and the tissue of allusions to Narcissus in the first seventeen sonnets, the so-called 'marriage' group, it seems highly plausible that Shakespeare was aware of what was going on in the Southampton household – though exactly how the sonnets relate to the marriage question is a complicated matter which we will have to pursue further.

It would have been assumed that Southampton would gain control of a considerable fortune once he came of age in 1595 (though because of Burghley's fine this did not in fact prove to be the case), so in 1593–4 we find a number of poets, including Thomas Nashe and Barnabe Barnes, positioning themselves as potential recipients of his patronage by dedicating works to him. This situation provides a reasonable explanation for Shakespeare's sonnets on the theme of rivalry for patronage, though there is no hard evidence to enable us to name the particular poet or poets whom he singles out as his own rivals.

Once all these facts are collected, the case for Southampton as the original patron/youth looks irrefutable. To regard the sonnets as parody, exercise, or pure play is to forget the economic urge which drove Shakespeare to write. He wrote plays to win audiences for his theatre company; when the theatres were closed, he wrote *Venus and Adonis* and *The Rape of Lucrece* to gain the patronage of Southampton. In the 1590s, sonnets were part of a poet's repertoire in the quest for patronage and this is what must initially have drawn Shakespeare to the form. The vast sum of a thousand pounds is hard to credit, but if there is any truth in Rowe's story of Southampton giving Shakespeare financial support, then it looks as if the sonnets might have done the trick.

Bearing this in mind, we must do away with the notion that the first seventeen sonnets were written with the intention of literally urging Southampton to get married. It may have been all very well for John Clapham, under Burghley's protection, to remind the young Earl of the dangers of narcissism, but it is wholly implausible that Shakespeare would have begun his quest for patronage by urging his patron to do the very thing he didn't want to do, namely get married quickly. *Venus and Adonis*, the second book to be dedicated to Southampton, is an essentially comic treatment of the theme of male resistance to woman. It may be regarded as a playful riposte to Clapham that would have been more likely to please Southampton. I suspect that the first few sonnets were conceived in similar terms, perhaps even as a joke at Burghley's expense.

Shakespeare is saying something like the following: 'Burghley wants you to marry, but you're far too smart to be influenced by Clapham's wooden, moralizing Latin poem warning you of the fate of Narcissus; it would be easy to write a more persuasive set of poems on the marriage theme; after all, it's a highly traditional theme (Erasmus wrote a dialogue on it); look, here are all the traditional arguments (that propagation is natural, that it's a way of cheating age and time), but – and here's a twist on convention – the best argument of all is not the traditional one about the need to pass on your *virtue*, but rather it's the need to pass on your *beauty*. We'll begin with Clapham's Narcissus image (sonnet 1: "But thou, contracted to thine own bright eyes"; sonnet 3: "Look in thy glass"), but instead of condemning narcissism, and moralizing about the transience of beauty, we'll positively revel in it.'

Once he started down this line, he quickly saw the next trick: to locate the propagation and immortalization of his subject's beauty not in an heir, but *in the sonnets themselves*. Thus the couplet of 12 reads 'And nothing 'gainst Time's scythe can make defence / Save breed to brave him when he takes thee hence', whereas that of 15 reads 'And all in war with Time for love of you, / As he takes from you I engraft you new'; 17 proposes a double immortality, in a child and in 'my rhyme', but then 18 and 19 make the strongest claims yet for the poet's 'eternal lines' and their power to defeat Time. The initial theme of getting an heir has served its purpose – crudely, that of grabbing the reader's (and especially Southampton's) attention – and we do not hear of it again. Shakespeare has written himself into the most ancient role of the poet: as someone who sings for his supper, immortalizes his master or mistress in return for their patronage.

But now Shakespeare is hooked on writing sonnets arising from this theme. His restless wit and sharp intelligence lead him to press hard upon every word, every idea. Daniel had written his *Delia* to gain the patronage of a great lady, the Countess of Pembroke; his purpose was well served by the two senses of the word 'mistress' – as the idealized fair lady *in* the poems was his mistress in the sense of lover, so the real fine lady *intended to read* the poems was his mistress in the sense of employer. Shakespeare needs a different trick, since he has a male patron and the word 'master' does not contain the same double meaning. He therefore invents in sonnet 20 the double epithet 'Master Mistress'. He playfully, and perhaps tactfully, adds that he does not really want to do with his master what poets traditionally want to do with their mistresses, namely 'use' their beauty in the act of physical lovemaking: thus the 'one thing' with which nature has '*prickt*' the Master out is left for 'women's pleasure'; it is said to be 'to my purpose nothing'.

One cannot, however, go on writing on a subject without thinking oneself deeply into it. If the sonnets are to work on a profounder level than that of the playfulness which characterizes the tone of the first seventeen of them, the poet has to imagine himself really falling in love with the narcissistic youth. In sonnet 53, the youth becomes Adonis, but generally Shakespeare eschews the use of classical names which had characterized the work of his predecessors. He nevertheless retained a controlling classical myth beneath the surface. If the youth is Narcissus, he himself has to be Echo. One meaning of Echo, the girl whose unrequited love for Narcissus causes her to waste away and become a disembodied voice, is that love is by its nature dependent on an Other. Narcissism is a perverted form of love exactly because it denies the Other. To speak words of love and hear them echoed by one's partner is love's lovely requital. But at the same time, an echo does not exist: it is merely a repetition of one's own words. Echo and Narcissus belong in the same story because erotic love itself is a projection of one's own desires and ideals, not an answering to the other. Shakespeare knows that when you look in your lover's eyes, it is a reflection of yourself that you see. Where he had begun sonnet 3 by telling the youth to look in his mirror, he begins sonnet 22 by looking in his own glass. Is love a reception within of the 'thou', the beloved other perceived by the 'eye', or is it a projection outward of the 'I', the voracious self?

Exactly for the reason that the sonnets are about this problem, it is a mistake to make a choice between biographical and anti-biographical readings of them. To make such a choice implies that a love poem must be either fact or fancy. Shakespeare either *really loved* the fair youth or *only imagined* his love. But one of the things that Elizabethan sonnets, Shakespeare's above all others, are very good at showing is that it is simple-minded to envisage such a distinction. Love does not work like that: being in love is very exactly something that happens *in the imagination*. In *A Midsummer Night's Dream*, Theseus says that lunatics, lovers, and poets are of imagination 'all compact' – their mental states lead to kinds of transformed vision whereby they see the world differently from how one sees it when in a 'rational' state of mind.

The task of love poets is to find ways of describing this changed vision; their problem is that so many people have tried doing this before that they very quickly start repeating all the clichés of their poetic predecessors.

They start, for instance, to enumerate the beauties of their beloved from top to toe, in a convention known as the blazon. Shakespeare parodies this convention in sonnet 130, 'My mistress' eyes are nothing like the sun', ending by saying that he loves his mistress more truly than those who embellish their mistresses with 'false compare'. Does this mean that he has written a 'sincere' love poem? No, because the anti-blazon was a convention almost as old as the blazon. Does it mean, then, that he has merely written an exercise? Only insofar as all writing is an exercise of the wits, the arts of expressions, as much as it is a record of feeling or experience.

Because they are highly self-conscious about the fact that any kind of recording of feeling or experience is a rhetorical art, Shakespeare's sonnets are peculiarly amenable to the extreme anti-realist practice of deconstruction, which endlessly generates interpretations, always deferring reversion to 'real experience'. But this does not mean that their sole purpose is pure linguistic play or, in the reductive version of this position, that they are 'mere literary exercises' or parodies with no origin in feeling or experience. The tone of those of them that are parodies, notably 'My mistress' eyes are nothing like the sun', is very different from the tone of the rest – I would say that 'My mistress' eyes' was deliberately placed at 130 to lighten the tone after the agonized energies of 129, 'Th'expense of spirit in a waste of shame / Is lust in action'.

Yet in making this distinction, I am projecting, as do all readers of these mesmerizing, puzzling poems. To my ear, the bitterness of tone in certain of the sonnets is incompatible with the idea that they are mere exercises. But it could equally well be argued that Shakespeare knew how to mimic bitterness in his plays – think of Hamlet's soliloquies – and that he may therefore be feigning it in his sonnets. The only solution to this problem is to allow the sonnets to rest in a middle space between experience and imagination. We must not reduce them to their origin, probable as it is that Shakespeare began to write them around the time he was seeking Southampton's patronage by dedicating his two narrative poems to him.

The sonnets are best thought of as *imaginings of potential situations which might have grown* from the initial Southampton situation. We will never know exactly which of them are rhetorical transmutations of actual occurrences and which are rhetorical enactments of potential situations that Shakespeare imagined. *And it is of their essence that they deny us this knowledge*: they do so precisely in order to show us that we cannot know whether love is 'real' or 'imagined'. We do not need to know what happened in the bed, because what the sonnets are interested in is how love happens in the head.

Does love come from the 'I' or the 'eye', is it a 'truth' or is it a 'lie'? The sonnets meditate and pun obsessively on this, until they end (save for their light mythological coda concerning Cupid's bath) with an extraordinary couplet which holds together all four terms, 'I', 'eye', 'truth', and 'lie':

> For I have sworn thee fair – more perjured eye
> To swear against the truth so foul a lie.

The 'thee' addressed here is the 'dark lady', not the 'fair youth'. The introduction of her into the sequence is the inevitable consequence of sonnet 20's invention of the Master-Mistress and its splitting apart of spiritual and sexual love. If the fair youth is to be the idealized object of unrequited desire, physicality and requital must be siphoned off and directed elsewhere: hence the lady's darkness. Sonnet 144 marks the formal division of the two kinds of love:

> Two loves I have, of comfort and despair,
> Which like two spirits do suggest me still.
> The better angel is a man right fair,
> The worser spirit a woman coloured ill.

But the dramatist in Shakespeare recognizes that human beings are not made of such sharp distinctions. His plays are built upon the dissolution of differences, the unravellings whereby we see some soul of good in things evil and vice-versa, whereby we cannot reject the worser spirit of Falstaff just because we admire Hal's transformation into a better angel. Fairness in Shakespeare is always contaminated with foulness, and vice-versa. The sonnets' way of dramatizing this paradoxical alliance is to imagine a liaison between the man right fair and the woman coloured ill. Their relationship is the subject of sonnets 35 (perhaps), 40, 41, 42, 134, and the vicious closing couplet of 144 in which the woman is imagined to 'fire' the man out with venereal disease.

The dark lady

There is no reason to suppose that the sonnets cease to be anchored to Southampton when the dark lady is introduced. The patron remains the first implied reader. Our reconstruction of origins therefore requires us to imagine a situation in which Southampton would have enjoyed reading about himself betraying Shakespeare by going to bed with his mistress. If we are to maintain our principle that the sonnets are imaginings of potential situations which might have grown from the initial Southampton situation, we would do well to locate the dark lady in the same household.

Biographical sleuths have usually looked for Shakespeare's supposed mistress in the wrong place, namely the London acting world. The leading candidates are a notorious dark-skinned Clerkenwell prostitute known as Lucy Negro and a poetess of Italian extraction, Aemilia Bassano (later Lanyer), who was the mistress of Lord Hunsdon, the patron of Shakespeare's acting company. Yet there is nothing to connect either of these women to Southampton in the 1590s, let alone to his household.

When A. L. Rowse made the case for Aemilia Bassano, for whom there is not a scrap of direct evidence, he announced in a wonderfully circular statement that his answers to the problems of the sonnets 'cannot be impugned, for they are the answer', while adding that anyone who disagreed with him was talking 'complete rubbish'. Without anything approximating to this assurance, I would like to propose that our understanding of the sonnets will be assisted if we *suppose* – not if we confidently assert – that they are tied to some rather sordid intrigue in the Southampton household around 1593–4.

The imagined relationship between the poet and the youth grows from routine flattery to intense love to bitter disillusionment and a sense of betrayal. The articulated relationship between the poet and the dark lady veers between mutual sexual use, regarded sometimes casually and sometimes guiltily, and bitterness stemming from the intervention of the fair youth. The element of guilt, and the sexual disgust that explodes in the single extraordinary sentence of sonnet 129's anatomy of desire, may be caused by the fact that the union involves a breach by both parties of what sonnet 152 calls the 'bed-vow', which in Elizabethan English strongly implies marriage vows.

The 'profile' of the dark lady, as a criminal investigator would put it, therefore sounds as if it should be a married woman in or close to the household of Southampton, whom both Shakespeare and Southampton slept with. The 'William the Conqueror' incident discussed in the previous chapter suggests that a married woman's quick wit and willingness would have been sufficient incentive for Shakespeare to sleep with her, but we perhaps need to find some further incentive for Southampton to do so at precisely the time when he was resisting marriage, especially since there was a rumour in the 1590s that he preferred the sexual company of men to that of women.

It seems to me that an Elizabethan earl of possibly homosexual orientation would be more likely to sleep with a married woman of lower social status because he wanted to score off her husband than because he desired her in herself. Suppose that the young Earl's guardian, who wishes to marry him off against his will, places an agent in his household in order to report back on the progress of the marriage suit and related affairs. Suppose that the agent is married. To sleep with his wife would be the most delicious revenge for the man's presumption in reporting intimate matters back to Burghley.

In the period from 1592–4 there was such an agent in Southampton's household. Placed there by Burghley, he acted as the Earl's language tutor. His name was John Florio (Fig. 3). His presence in the household seems to have been of considerable importance for the development of Shakespeare's career – it accounts for much of the dramatist's broad, though very patchy, acquaintance with Italian literature and his slight knowledge of the Italian language. It seems to have been immediately after the period of Southampton's patronage during the closure of the theatres that Shakespeare began to make extensive and ambitious use of Italian settings and plots in his plays. Florio was the obvious person to introduce him to his sources for these. In the same period, phrases from Florio's Italian language manual, *First Fruits*, start appearing in Shakespeare's works; it is even possible that the Italian's affected language is parodied in the character of Don Armado and his pedantry in the character of Holofernes in *Love's Labour's Lost*, Shakespeare's sonnet-ridden play of circa 1595. That play's title and subject matter, its merry demolition of stale courtly love-language, are strongly suggested by a passage in *First Fruits*: 'We need not speak so much of love, all books are full of love, with so many authors, that it were labour lost to speak of Love.'

Unromantic as the thought may be, there is no reason why we should not imagine Shakespeare sleeping with Florio's wife as well as pilfering his library and mocking his phrases. Florio himself (born about 1553) was declining into the vale of years and, to judge from his prodigious literary productivity, devoting himself entirely to his work. At the time in question, he was labouring not of love, but at the massive task of single-handedly compiling the first English–Italian dictionary. A spirited and neglected wife, like the young lady of the city in the William the Conqueror story, could easily enjoy a turn in the bed with the witty poet. And she would find it hard to resist the advances of the Earl, knowing that her husband's income and hence her children's well-being depended on his retaining his post.

My dark lady, then, is John Florio's wife, who happens to have been the sister of Samuel Daniel, the sonneteer. It is a pleasing fancy that the dark lady sonnets might be addressed to the sister of a poet who wrote to a more conventionally fair mistress. One could even complicate the plot by proposing Daniel (Fig. 4) as the 'rival poet' – there is no direct evidence that he sought Southampton's patronage, but the presence of his sister in the household suggests that he might have seen an opening (which might have been closed pretty quickly as a result of the sexual intrigue involving Shakespeare and Southampton which I am supposing).

Florio wrote that in order to be 'accounted most fair' a woman should have 'Black eyes, black brows, black hairs', though we have no way of knowing whether Mrs Florio lived up to this dark ideal. But to concern ourselves overmuch with literal physical attributes is to miss the point. In Elizabethan love literature, fairness and darkness have a great deal more to do with social status than with actual hair and eye colour. Fairness was regarded as synonymous with aristocratic and courtly elevation, darkness with low origins. A dark woman means a country wench. One thing we do know about Miss Daniel is that she was a low-born Somerset lass.

If genes are to be trusted, we may also surmise that she was witty and talented. Her brother Samuel became one of the most admired poets of the age, whilst another brother, John, became a highly regarded musician and composer. According to Thomas Fuller's *Worthies of England*, the Daniels' father was himself a music master. Miss Daniel's musical ability is a sure bet. In sonnet 128, the dark lady proves herself to be accomplished at the keyboard. The poet envies 'those jacks that nimble leap / To kiss the tender inward of thy hand'. Might the jacks be not only the keys but also the husband, John – which is Jack – Florio? Give husband Jack thy fingers, lover Will thy lips to kiss, the sonnet would then end.

The Florios had four children. A daughter called Aurelia was probably the eldest; another daughter, Joan, was born in 1585, then Edward in 1588 and Elizabeth in 1589. The simile in sonnet 143 whereby 'Will' compares himself to his mistress's 'neglected child' would gain added poignancy if Mrs Florio really were neglecting young Edward and Elizabeth as she lay in bed with Will.

As for Florio himself, he was not a poet but he was in the 'pay and patronage' of Southampton. He states as much in the dedication to *A World of Words*, his Italian dictionary. Shakespeare introduces the theme of rival writers in sonnet 78 with the phrase 'every *Alien* pen'. 'Alien', one of the handful of italicized words in the 1609 Quarto, had a very specific meaning in Elizabethan English: it referred to a foreigner. The Italian Florio was the only writer of Shakespeare's acquaintance who was an 'alien'. Could he have been the initial rival who inspired Shakespeare to imagine a series of greater rivals in the sequence through to 86? (In chapter four, I will suggest the identity of the greatest of them.) And might Shakespeare be tacitly alluding to Florio's other presumed function when in the couplet of sonnet 125 he introduces the figure of a 'suborned informer'?

We do not know Mrs Florio's first name. Our ignorance is tantalizing but fitting. She has hitherto survived in literary history only as 'Daniel's sister' and 'Florio's wife'. To this we may add 'and perhaps Shakespeare's mistress'. She has been made immortal only in terms of her relationships with others: as sister/wife/mistress to a succession of male writers and as mother to the Florio children whose names do survive. The dark lady is always the *addressee*: the fact that we do not know her first name is a token of how we never hear her voice, her side of the story.

We will never know whether Shakespeare and/or Southampton really slept with Florio's wife and the sonnets knowingly allude to actual events, or whether the sonnets are knowing imaginings of possible intrigue. To reiterate, their reticence on this matter is essential to their purpose: we *must* be denied knowledge of the original bed deeds, because the sonnets are interested not so much in who lies with whom as in the paradoxes of eyeing and lying.

My story is and is not a fantasy. To adapt what Oscar Wilde once said of Will Hughes, his candidate for the 'fair youth': you *must* believe in Mrs Florio – I almost do myself. I began to work on the sonnets with a determination to adhere to an agnostic position on the question of their autobiographical elements. But, like Sidney Lee, I have been unable to hold fast to my unbelief. The sonnets have wrought their magic upon me and forced from me yet one more reading to add to all those which they have generated since the Romantic period. Their genius is still at work.

Master W. H.

Shakespeare did not publish his sonnets with a dedication to South-ampton, as he published *Venus and Adonis* and *Lucrece* with such dedications, and as Samuel Daniel published *Delia* with a dedication to the Countess of Pembroke. The reason for this may be mundane: perhaps by the time he got around to contemplating publication, Southampton had been hit with Burghley's fine and Shakespeare realized there wouldn't be much money left for patronage. Perhaps Southampton had already come up with the goods – that gift which, according to Rowe, Davenant knew about. Perhaps the reopening of the theatres in 1594 and the formation of the Chamberlain's Men meant that all Shakespeare's energies went into his playwrighting. Or it may be that the implied narrative of the sonnets was a little too private for publication to be appropriate.

The fact that Shakespeare didn't rush his sonnets into print shows that their purpose wasn't really the immortalizing of his love's name in 'eternal lines' of black ink. Neither the youth nor the lady is overtly named. The only name that is written and thus immortalized is that of Will himself.

Consider sonnet 55:

> Not marble nor the gilded monuments
> Of princes shall outlive this powerful rhyme,
> But you shall shine more bright in these contents
> Than unswept stone besmeared with sluttish time.
> When wasteful war shall statues overturn,
> And broils root out the work of masonry,
> Nor Mars his sword nor war's quick fire shall burn
> The living record of your memory.
> 'Gainst death and all oblivious enmity
> Shall you pace forth; your praise shall still find room
> Even in the eyes of all posterity
> That wear this world out to the ending doom.
>   So, till the judgement that yourself arise,
>   You live in this, and dwell in lovers' eyes.

In a way it is extraordinary that Shakespeare wrote this poem but did not get it printed. Did he really believe that a single sheet of paper with a poem inked on it would outlive marble and gilded monuments? Multiple printed copies would have stood a much better chance. And if the poem is intended to make his love live in the eyes of posterity, why is the 'you' not named? Writing poetry of praise but forgetting to name the person praised is an oxymoronic activity if ever there was one.

But then we stop to think: it is not Shakespeare's 'love' in the sense of his beloved that is at stake here; it is Shakespeare's 'love' in the sense of his capacity to write of love. Who is it that 'dwells in lovers' eyes' when this poem is read? If we read it to our lover, we might imagine that it is him or her. But if we look our lover in the eyes as we recite it, the person we see dwelling in those eyes is ourself. The only person who is immortalized in the sense of speaking beyond the grave, being reanimated, is William Shakespeare.

Once the poems are *published*, then, it is Shakespeare, not the fair youth, who is immortalized. This brings us to what has been the greatest stumbling block in the way of sensible biographical discussion of the sonnets. I mean of course the inscription which the publisher Thomas Thorpe inserted at the beginning of the 1609 text:

TO . THE . ONLIE . BEGETTER . OF . THESE . INSVING . SONNETS . Mᴿ .
W.H . ALL . HAPPINESSE . AND . THAT . ETERNITIE . PROMISED . BY . OVR .
EVER–LIVING . POET . WISHETH . THE . WELL–WISHING . ADVENTVRER .
IN.SETTING.FORTH. T.T.

All biographical approaches to the sonnets have assumed that 'the only begetter' must mean either the procurer of the manuscript or the inspirer of the poems.

Of the candidates advanced by those who have supposed it refers to whoever passed the manuscript to Thorpe, the least implausible was brought forward in *The Athenaeum* in April 1867. Southampton's father died in his youth, but in 1598 his mother married Sir William Hervey or Harvey; she died in late 1607 and Hervey remarried the following year. Could he have been the one to pass the sonnets to Thorpe – perhaps while he was clearing out the Southampton effects before his remarriage – and earn the dedication in return? Though he was a 'Sir', knights were sometimes referred to in the period as plain 'Master'. Perhaps Thorpe even knew about Hervey's new young wife and the prospect that Sir William might be eternized through the birth of a son. This is a charming little story. The scholar Mario Praz confessed to 'a partiality for the picture of the widowed husband roaming about the empty house and finding, among dusty family papers, "Shakespeare's Sonnets": it is so delightfully Victorian.' But, alas, there is a severe problem with the case for Hervey or any other procurer: there is not the slightest piece of evidence that in the language of the period the word 'begetter' could refer to a person who 'acquired' something.

The biographers who have had most fun are those who have assumed that 'begetter' means 'inspirer' and that 'Mr W. H.' is therefore the fair youth himself. The candidates are legion, the fantasies a delight – none more so than Oscar Wilde's in his *Portrait of Mr W. H.*, in which we meet a gorgeous boy actor called Willie Hughes. But, though half-seduced by his own theory, Wilde was quite aware that his lovely Willie was a *jeu d'esprit*, invented to help make the case for a homoerotic Shakespeare. Less easily countenanced is the tendency even of reputable critics who remain sceptical of the 'biographical fallacy' to slip into the way of calling the addressee of the sonnets 'Mr W. H.'

W[illiam] H[erbert], the Earl of Pembroke, has the right initials to have been Master W. H., while H[enry] W[riothesley], the Earl of Southampton, has the right initials though in the wrong order. But would Thorpe have identified an earl of the realm as a mere 'Master'? And would he have written such a cursory dedication if its recipient were an earl? Dedicating books to noblemen in the period was a serious business which required a great many ornate sentences, not a few enigmatic words. In certain respects, Thorpe's inscription is not a dedication at all: it makes no appeal for patronage. Nor is there any reason to suppose that Thorpe would have known the identity of the fair youth in the first place. And don't the sonnets have two inspirers, the youth and the dark lady, not an 'only' one?

In Renaissance book dedications, 'begetter' only infrequently meant 'inspirer'. It usually meant 'author'. A poet begets his poems upon his Muse. According to the customary usage, the writer is the father or begetter, while the patron is the sponsor or godfather – this is what Shakespeare calls Southampton in his dedication to *Venus and Adonis*.

Let us assume the customary usage, leave out the mysterious initials, and modernize the wording and word order of Thorpe's statement. It will then read as follows: 'Thomas Thorpe, the well-wishing publisher of the following sonnets, takes the opportunity upon publishing them to wish their only author all happiness and that eternity promised by our ever-living poet.' Had Thorpe not included the initials W. H., would not everyone have assumed that he was addressing Shakespeare? His inscription is not printed like a dedication to a third party; it reads as an acknowledgement to the author himself. If the publication of the sonnets was authorized by Shakespeare, the publisher's statement would have been a word of thanks; if unauthorized, it could have been a kind of apology.

Amidst all the speculation about W. H., two facts about Thorpe's book are often overlooked. First, that it was not the first book to call itself Shakespeare's sonnets. As we saw in the previous chapter, Shakespeare came fully into vogue in 1598–9. In 1599 William Jaggard cashed in on the fashion by publishing *The Passionate Pilgrime. by W. Shakespeare*. Elizabethan booksellers advertised their wares by pasting title-pages to posts outside their shops in St Paul's Yard. On the basis of the displayed title, readers purchasing Jaggard's book from W. Leake at the sign of the Greyhound would have gained the impression that they were obtaining a collection of love sonnets by the author of the hugely popular *Venus and Adonis*. It would have looked like a very good buy indeed. Having paid their pence, they would have discovered that Jaggard's tiny volume consisted of twenty sonnets and lyrics. The first was 'When my love swears that she is made of truth', which (with slight alterations) became sonnet 138 in the collection published by Thorpe a decade later; the second was 'Two loves I have, of comfort and despair', number 144 in Thorpe. Two of the next three were sonnets lifted from the text of *Love's Labour's Lost*. But apart from one further lyric from *Love's Labour's Lost*, the rest of the collection contains no more authenticated Shakespeare.

The Passionate Pilgrime. by W. Shakespeare in fact had several begetters, including Christopher Marlowe and two lesser poets, Richard Barnfield and Bartholomew Griffin. Jaggard's deception in trying to pass it off as all Shakespeare's makes it highly plausible that Thorpe would have wanted his prospective buyers to know that here was an authentic collection which really did consist entirely of Shakespeare – hence the prefatory claim that W. S. was the *only* begetter.

The second important fact is that Thorpe, as was usual in the period, did not print the book himself. He farmed the work out to the printing shop of George Eld. Some of its misprints suggest that it was poorly proof-read. One of the elaborate Elizabethan secretary-hand forms of capital 'S' closely resembles another secretary form of capital 'H'. Could it have been that in the holograph copy for the prefatory statement Thorpe or an assistant wrote 'Mr W. S.', but that the initials were misread in Eld's shop as W. H.? Might the mysterious Mr W. H., over whom so much ink has been spilt for so long, be no more than an inky slip, the creation of a misprint?

It might be objected that the proof-reader was unlikely to have overlooked an error on the capitalized opening page of the book, but it is surprising how often errors are not picked up on title-pages and in preliminary matter. A careless proof-reader might only start paying serious attention on reaching the main body of the text. Title and dedication-page errors are common in the books of the period. For instance, a play by Thomas Goffe called *The Raging Turke* has its title printed in huge letters – except that in one of the two states of the title-page it appears as THE RANING TURKE.

A further objection to the proposition that W. H. is really W. S.

would be that it seems odd for Thorpe to refer to Shakespeare twice, first by initials, then as 'our ever-living poet'. But Thorpe's language is highly wrought: 'wisheth the well-wishing' might be said to be equally redundant. It is quite possible that Thorpe was making an elegant conceit: he wishes earthly happiness and heavenly eternity for the mortal person Master William Shakespeare, just as the immortal poet of the sonnets eternizes the fair youth. If Thorpe had read the sonnets carefully, he would have noticed that they do *not* follow the classical convention of claiming immortality for the poet – they claim immortality for the poet's beloved. Where Horace or Ovid would have written 'So long as men can breathe or eyes can see, / So long lives this, and this gives life to me', Shakespeare writes in sonnet 18, 'So long as men can breathe or eyes can see, / So long lives this, and this gives life to *thee*' (my italics). It is thus left for Thorpe to wish life to Shakespeare.

An alternative explanation is that 'our ever-living poet' does not in fact refer to Shakespeare. 'Ever-living' was an epithet applied to dead poets, not living ones. The point was that they were dead, but they lived eternally through their work. 'Our ever-living poet' might therefore refer to a great dead English poet who had written on the great theme of poetic immortality. Certain poets were so well known that they did not have to be named. In *The Merchant of Venice*, Shakespeare writes, 'Therefore the poet / Did feign that Orpheus drew trees, stones, and floods' (5.1.79–80) – the poet is not named because it is assumed that everyone will know it is Ovid (though some scholars have argued that it is Horace). By the same account, Thorpe's 'our ever-living poet' could refer to Sir Philip Sidney or Edmund Spenser, by 1609 both routinely associated with the idea of poetic immortality. Spenser famously wrote in his *Ruins of Time* that the Muses gave eternity to poets; he ended his translation of Joachim du Bellay's sonnet sequence, *Ruins of Rome*, with an envoy addressed to du Bellay himself, saying that the great dead French poet was 'worthy of immortality' and would 'all eternity survive'. As Spenser promises immortality to du Bellay, so Thorpe imagines Spenser, now immortal, welcoming Shakespeare to the same eternal company.

Of all the candidates for the identity of Master W. H., the misprint seems to me the strongest. But whoever it was that Thorpe really meant, there could be no more appropriate origin for the subsequent history of Shakespeare's *Sonnets*. The metamorphosis of W. S. into W. H. is symbolical of the achievement of the sonnets: they were begotten in Shakespeare's own brain, but they invent 'character' and 'situation' so powerfully that they make us believe in their subject. They perform their work of immortalization so effectively that they have made thousands of readers project that immortalization into the dedication by inventing 'Master W. H.' It is a lovely suppose that Thorpe knew what he was doing: saluting the genius and predicting the immortality of Master William Shakespeare. But I salute George Eld's hypothetical incompetent compositor as an unconscious genius who by substituting W. H. for W. S. allowed Shakespeare to perform in his sonnets the very disappearing act which is always available to a dramatist who loses himself in his characters but which should by rights be impossible for a lyric poet who writes in the first person.

3

THE AUTHORSHIP
CONTROVERSY

The mystery

There is a mystery about the identity of William Shakespeare. The mystery is this: why should anyone doubt that he was William Shakespeare, the actor from Stratford-upon-Avon?

It is the first question which the professional Shakespearean is always asked in casual conversation outside the walls of the academy – who wrote the plays? When told of the hard core of evidence that the man from Stratford did so, people are surprised. Sometimes it is suspected that the academics are covering up a scandal: it is said that *we do not know who wrote the plays attributed to Shakespeare.* Every now and then – it has been happening for over a hundred years – an amateur literary sleuth comes forward and, amidst a flurry of publicity, claims to have *solved the mystery.* The professors are likened to the plodding Inspector Lestrade; the truth can only be revealed by some unacknowledged Sherlock Holmes.

As I sit writing in my flat in Toxteth, a neighbour in the same apartment building is labouring at the project to which he has devoted the last forty years: his book which will prove conclusively that the works of Shakespeare were written by the Anglo-Italian translator and dictionary maker John Florio. A few miles away in South Liverpool a retired solicitor of my acquaintance is decoding cryptic allusions in the *Henry VI* plays which, he is convinced, will show that the works of Shakespeare were written by Gilbert Talbot, seventh Earl of Shrewsbury. At work in the University of Liverpool I give my lectures in the Rendall Building, named after Canon Gerald H. Rendall, the university's first Gladstone Professor of Greek, who became converted at the age of eighty to the theory that the plays were written by Edward de

Vere, seventeenth Earl of Oxford. He remained alive long enough to write four books on the subject, the last of them published in 1939. That same year, A. W. Titherley, formerly Dean of Science in the same university, published the first of his four books arguing the case for William Stanley, sixth Earl of Derby. Four 'Anti-Stratfordians' in one northern English city, arguing for four different candidates. The story will be the same in every city in which Shakespeare is known – which must be almost every city in the world.

Most academic Shakespeareans are as dismissive of the large and colourful army of Anti-Stratfordians as Lestrade is of Holmes. But I have taken an interest in the authorship question ever since, at the age of fourteen, I fell under the influence of a brilliant but eccentric Greek master. He tried to persuade me that the plays were written by the Earl of Oxford. He was so convinced of this himself that he changed his name by deed poll to Edward, in honour of Edward de Vere, the author of 'Shake-speare'. He triumphantly drew my attention to phrases in the sonnets. 'That every word doth almost sel my name' (Sonnet 76): 'every', he said, almost sells or tells or spells 'e-vere', which was proof positive.

Admittedly, I began to become sceptical when I discovered that the original proponent of de Vere's claim was an Edwardian schoolmaster who rejoiced in the name of J. Thomas Looney. It was also more than a little unfortunate that de Vere died in 1604. *Macbeth* could not have been composed before the Gunpowder Plot of 1605; *The Winter's Tale* was licensed by Sir George Buc, who only began licensing plays for performance in 1610; *The Tempest* was impelled by a voyage which took place in 1609; and *Henry VIII* was described by at least two witnesses as a 'new play' in 1613. How de Vere managed to write these plays from beyond the grave is a profound mystery indeed. But I persevered in my interest until I had examined all the evidence, and I remain fascinated by the mystery of the persistence of the Anti-Stratfordian position. It has something of the power of a myth, and myths are fictions from which there are always truths to be learned.

Henry VIII was one of Shakespeare's three collaborations with John Fletcher, who subsequently took over as house dramatist of the King's Men. Fletcher had intimate links with Shakespeare's fellow-actors, but no connection with Oxford's circle. If there is one thing we can say for certain about Shakespeare's plays it is that they were written by a man of the theatre. An early play like *Titus Andronicus* was composed under the influence of the hit plays of the late 1580s, notably Thomas Kyd's *The Spanish Tragedy* and Christopher Marlowe's *The Jew of Malta*; a middle play like *Hamlet* was intricately bound up with the rivalry between the adult and children's acting companies around 1600; the late plays were responsive to Fletcher's innovations in the writing of tragicomic romance and the King's Men's purchase of the lease on the indoor playhouse at Blackfriars. Countless technicalities of staging in every one of the plays reveal that only a professional theatrical insider could have written them.

Amateur aristocrats such as the Earl of Oxford did write plays, but these were static and rarefied things in comparison with the mobile mingle-mangle of the public drama, with its mix of kings and clowns that so offended purists like Sir Philip Sidney. The difference between popular stage drama and aristocratic 'closet' drama may be instantly apprehended by anyone who takes the trouble to read, say, Shakespeare's *Antony and Cleopatra* in conjunction with the neoclassical version of *Antony* that was Englished by Sir Philip's sister, the Countess of Pembroke. For reasons that will be discussed later in this chapter, a motley collection of writers has been seduced by the Baconian and Looney hypotheses. But a much more striking fact is that no major actor has ever been attracted to Anti-Stratfordianism. That is because actors know from the inside that the plays must have been written by an actor.

Insofar as Looney and later Oxfordians address the problem of chronology at all, they have to argue that the later plays were written before 1604, kept in manuscript, and subsequently revised by the players with topical allusions to post-1604 events added in. But this argument is fatally flawed in the cases of *Macbeth* and *The Tempest*: the former does not merely allude to the Gunpowder Plot, it is a Gunpowder play through and through, while the latter could only have been written after the publication of Florio's translation of Montaigne in 1603 and the tempest that drove Sir George Somers' ship to Bermuda in 1609.

Nor can Oxfordians provide any explanation for the manifest stylistic differences between Shakespeare's Elizabethan and his Jacobean plays, or the technical changes attendant upon the King's Men's move to the Blackfriars theatre four years after their candidate's death. Unlike the

Globe, the Blackfriars was an indoor playhouse; it therefore depended on artificial lighting; candles would not burn unattended for the full length of a play, so act-divisions were introduced, during which they could be trimmed or replaced (the audience, meanwhile, was entertained with music). The plays written after Shakespeare's company began using the Blackfriars in 1608, *Cymbeline* and *The Winter's Tale* for instance, have what most of the earlier plays do not have: a carefully planned five-act structure. No Oxfordian has addressed this difficulty for their faith. Presumably they would say that Oxford wrote a batch of five-act plays just in case the King's Men one day happened to acquire an indoor playhouse and that he gave instructions on his deathbed for these plays to be kept in a closet until such a day arrived. That there is no record of Oxford ever having had any contact with any of the King's Men has not deterred Oxfordians in the past and will not deter them in the future.

The evidence

Since the theory that William Shakespeare of Stratford did not write the works of Shakespeare still retains a strong hold on the popular imagination and is bolstered by a steady trickle of television programmes and magazine articles, it is worth making a simple statement of the evidence that William Shakespeare of Stratford did write the works of Shakespeare. The Anti-Stratfordian position begins from incredulity at the idea of a provincial grammar-school boy being the greatest artistic genius the world has ever seen. Some reasons for that incredulity will be discussed later, as will the history of the idea of a great artistic genius. For now, I want to remain with bare facts.

Only a few of the Anti-Stratfordians deny that the William Shakespeare who was born and died in Stratford-upon-Avon spent much of his life as an actor in London. John Shakespeare of Stratford, William's father, was granted a coat of arms in 1596; that same coat of arms appears on the monument to William Shakespeare which was erected in the Stratford parish church some time between his death in 1616 and the publication of the First Folio of the collected plays in 1623. In 1602 a member of the College of Heralds complained about his colleagues having granted arms to a number of supposedly unworthy persons, among them 'Shakespear the Player'. Shakespeare of Stratford must therefore have been Shakespeare the Player. Furthermore, in his will the Stratford man left money to buy mourning rings to 'my fellows, John Heminges, Richard Burbage and Henry Condell'. This establishes beyond doubt that he was the same William Shakespeare who was a sharer with those actors in the company of the Lord Chamberlain's (later King's) Men.

The more widespread Anti-Stratfordian argument is that the actor was merely a front man and that the true author of the plays was someone else who for some reason could not reveal himself (or herself) as the true author. This is usually imagined to be an aristocrat unwilling to stigmatize his name by attaching it to something so undignified as a play. There is, however, not a single example of any aristocrat of the sixteenth or seventeenth centuries having expressed regret publicly or privately at not being able to write plays. As I have said, many of them, including the Earl of Oxford, did write plays – only not for public performance. The last thing an aristocrat would have wanted was his work being exposed to the garlic-breathed multitude. There is but one record of an aristocrat penning comedies for the common players, and it sounds more like malicious gossip than fact – it occurs in an informer's letter. The aristocrat in question was not Oxford, but William Stanley, the Earl of Derby. Since Stanley had the Christian name 'William', qualifying him to write the phrase 'my name is *Will*' (Sonnet 136), it is surprising that the case for him as the author of Shakespeare has never had the popularity of that for Oxford. Where Oxford's problem is that he died too soon to have written half Shakespeare's plays, Stanley's is that he lived long enough to have written all Beaumont and Fletcher's as well. He did not die until 1641.

The supposed 'fact' on which all Anti-Stratfordian arguments rest is the claim that there is no hard evidence to link the Stratford man to the *writing*, as opposed to the acting, of the plays. But this is not a fact at all: several contemporaries explicitly make the link.

Above all, there is the testimony of Ben Jonson. He knew Shakespeare intimately. He spoke about him privately and wrote about him publicly. He knew him as both an actor – Shakespeare was in the cast of at least two of Jonson's plays – and a writer. He remarked upon his fellow-dramatist's compositional practices. In his poem in praise of his 'beloved' friend, which I examined in my first chapter, he christened him 'Sweet Swan of Avon'. There is the decisive link with Stratford-upon-Avon.

Then there is Francis Beaumont. He co-wrote plays with Shakespeare's collaborator, John Fletcher. Beaumont penned some famous verses celebrating the wits who drank at the Mermaid Tavern. When in 1613 'William Shakespeare of Stratford upon Avon in the County of Warwick gentleman' bought a gatehouse in Blackfriars, one of the trustees he named in the purchase deed was William Johnson, the owner of the Mermaid. The obvious inference is that William Shakespeare of Stratford-upon-Avon, gentleman and actor, knew Johnson well because he was a regular customer at the Mermaid and thus a drinking companion of Beaumont. Now, in a manuscript verse-letter addressed to Jonson, Beaumont specifically praised Shakespeare for writing his best lines 'by the dim light of Nature', without 'Learning'. Beaumont thus knew Shakespeare the actor and spoke of him as a writer. Furthermore, his statement that Shakespeare achieved poetic greatness without the benefit of advanced learning precisely refutes the foremost claim of all the Anti-Stratfordians, namely that the plays could only have been written by someone who had benefited from a better formal education than Shakespeare's.

Then there is William Camden. He was both Jonson's schoolmaster and an officer in the College of Heralds. In 1602, he co-wrote with William Dethick a reply to the complaint of another heraldic officer that they had demeaned the profession by granting coats of arms to base-born persons such as 'Shakespear the Player'. Camden and Dethick replied that Shakespeare's father was a magistrate in Stratford-upon-Avon, a justice of the peace who had married a daughter and heir of the highly respectable Arden family, that he 'was of good substance and habelité', and therefore thoroughly merited the grant of arms. The following year Camden completed his *Remains of a greater Work concerning Britain*, in which he listed William Shakespeare, together with his fellow-dramatists Ben Jonson, George Chapman, and John Marston, among 'the most pregnant wits of these our times'. Within the space of a year, then, Camden describes Shakespeare as a leading writer and answers the complaint about granting a coat of arms to the player by delineating Shakespeare's Stratford pedigree. The writer therefore has to be the player.

Then there is John Davies of Hereford. A teacher of penmanship, he went to London, got to know the literary scene, and penned many poems himself. In his *Microcosmos* of 1603, he wrote:

> *Players*, I love ye, and your *Quality*,
> As ye are Men, that pass time not abus'd:
> And some I love for *painting, poesy*.

In the margin he helpfully identified the 'some' he had in mind: 'W. S.' and 'R. B.' There can be no doubt to whom he refers: William Shakespeare and Richard Burbage, the two leading lights of the acting company who in that same year of 1603 gained the ultimate accolade of patronage, the title of King's Men. Davies wished to defend Burbage and Shakespeare against the common accusation that acting was a vile 'abuse' of time and morals; he did so by pointing out that these two actors had additional, more noble qualities – Burbage as a painter and Shakespeare as the writer of poesy. Davies reiterated his admiration for Shakespeare and Burbage in another poem two years later. Some years after that he published an epigram addressed to Will Shakespeare, which simultaneously alluded to his acting and praised him as a great playwright, the English equivalent of the revered Roman dramatist Terence.

Then there is Sir George Buc. His work at the Revels Office, involving the licensing of plays, led him to enquire after the names of the authors of certain plays that had been published anonymously. On the title-page of his copy of the play *George a Greene, the Pinner of Wakefield*, he scribbled a note to the effect that it was written by a minister who had played the pinner's part himself. 'Teste W. Shakespea', he added: 'according to the testimony of William Shakespeare'. This is hard evidence that Shakespeare was known to be a central figure in the London theatre world, intimately acquainted with the dramatic repertoire. It is inconceivable that Buc would have sought out Shakespeare for information concerning authorship had he been the mere bit-part player of Oxfordian fantasy.

Then there is Leonard Digges. He was an Oxford don who had connections with Stratford-upon-Avon and knew the London literary scene. His stepfather, Thomas Russell, was an overseer of Shakespeare's will. In a manuscript note written during Shakespeare's lifetime Digges, like Camden, affirmed what the proponents of Bacon, de Vere, and others have continually denied – the Stratford man's authorship of the plays. Digges' note was a memorandum to himself on the flyleaf of a book. He remarked that Lope de Vega was admired in Spain as both a dramatist and a poet just as Shakespeare was admired in England for both his plays and his sonnets. Since Digges was brought up by his stepfather in a village on the outskirts of Stratford-upon-Avon in the 1590s, his note's reference to 'our Will Shakespeare' establishes a firm link between his home town and the author of the sonnets and plays. Furthermore, as a manuscript note scribbled for his own personal use, not intended for publication, this evidence cannot be dismissed as part of a 'conspiracy' to pass off Shakespeare as the author of the plays, which is what the Anti-Stratfordians assume of the prefatory material to the First Folio by Digges, Jonson, and others.

Digges' commendatory poem for the Folio refers to the dramatist's 'Stratford monument'. The inscription on that monument gives the highest imaginable praise to Shakespeare's writing, just as the inscription on the grave of his daughter, Susanna, speaks of her inheriting her father's 'wit'. As was seen in chapter one, wit, in the sense of verbal facility, was what William Shakespeare was especially known for in his own lifetime. Proponents of the Looney hypothesis, on the other hand, always regard the Stratford actor as a kind of Tony Lumpkin, an illiterate rustic clown.

Then there is Francis Meres. As we have already seen, he was close enough to Shakespeare to know that in the 1590s the dramatist circulated unpublished sonnets 'among his private friends'; he had no doubts about ascribing both the sonnets and the plays to Shakespeare. The sonnets were not intended for publication. A pseudonym to disguise the authorship of published works is one thing, but if a writer circulates a batch of his poems in manuscript among his personal friends and includes in one of those poems the phrase 'for my name is *Will*', one has to be something of a Looney to conclude that his name was in fact Edward (de Vere) or Francis (Bacon). In addition, proponents of de Vere's claim have long been embarrassed by the fact that Meres' list of contemporary dramatists includes the names of both Shakespeare and Edward, Earl of Oxford – if Oxford wrote plays under his own name, why did he also have to do so under Shakespeare's?

Several passages in the *Parnassus* plays, performed in Cambridge around 1600, discussed in my first chapter, only make sense if Shakespeare the actor and Shakespeare the dramatist were one and the same person. Again, in 1613 the Earl of Rutland paid William Shakespeare and Richard Burbage just over two pounds each for designing him an impresa (emblem and motto for a shield) to use at a celebratory tilt. Burbage was a painter as well as an actor: he obviously provided the design, which means that his fellow-actor composed the poetic inscription. It follows that Shakespeare the actor was also a writer.

Anti-Stratfordians like to say that none of William Shakespeare's letters survive. This is also false. Letters addressed by William Shakespeare to Henry Wriothesley, the Earl of Southampton, may be read at the beginning of the texts of *Venus and Adonis* and *The Rape of Lucrece* in any complete edition of his works. The letter prefixed to *Venus and Adonis* is couched in the servile language which low-born writers had no choice but to use if they aspired to the patronage of aristocrats: 'only if your Honour seem but pleased, I account my self highly praised, and vow to take advantage of all idle hours, till I have honoured you with some graver labour'. Pride of place was so important to Elizabethan society that the idea of the mighty Earl of Oxford in the forty-third year of his life writing such words to one of Burghley's whipper-snapper wards is even more fantastic than the thought of him writing plays after his own death.

The list of contemporary testimonies and evidence could be considerably extended. *No one in Shakespeare's lifetime or the first two hundred years after his death expressed the slightest doubt about his authorship.* So why did people start expressing such doubts?

That nobody raised the question for two hundred years proves that there is no intrinsic reason why there should be a Shakespeare Authorship Controversy. There must therefore be extrinsic reasons for the origin and growth of the controversy. The likeliest would seem to be a change in the idea of Shakespeare, or a change in the idea of authorship, or both. In chapter six I will show that in the course of the eighteenth century there were indeed closely related changes in these two ideas.

There was no Shakespeare Authorship question at the beginning of the eighteenth century for two reasons. First, though Shakespeare was highly regarded, he was not sufficiently highly regarded for anybody to worry themselves about his provincial origins and lack of a university degree. For much of the century, the argument was not so much 'How could such clever plays have been written by the Stratford lad?' as 'Are the plays totally lacking in learning or just somewhat lacking in learning?' It would have been much more probable for there to have been a Jonson Authorship question: 'How could such genuinely learned plays have been written by a sometime bricklayer's apprentice who didn't go to university and who may even have left school before the sixth-form?' Secondly, the myth of the solitary author, alone with his blank sheet of paper, his thoughts springing fully-formed from his own innate genius, had not yet taken hold. As the sonnet mystery discussed in the previous chapter was consequent upon a Romantic idea of poetry as autobiography, so the Authorship mystery is consequent upon a Romantic idea of authorial genius.

By the end of the eighteenth century, Shakespeare had been hailed as a genius, even a God. The moment a faith takes hold, heretics emerge. In a curious way, they are actually required in order to sustain the orthodoxy. Shakespearean heretics come in two brands.

There are those who question his genius, who say that the plays are not all they are cracked up to be. The most noble of these heretics was Count Leo Nikolayevich Tolstoy, who wrote a notable essay arguing that *King Lear* was a rotten play, far inferior to the anonymous old play of *King Leir* from which Shakespeare adapted it. That essay will be discussed in chapter five. The heresy which proposes that Shakespeare might not be such a great writer after all is, however, rare because it invites the easy riposte, 'Write something better yourself, then.' It is a position that has only been held successfully by great writers like Tolstoy, arrogant writers like George Bernard Shaw, and troubled thinkers like Ludwig Wittgenstein, whom I discuss in my final chapter.

The easier heresy is the other brand, which calls into question not the genius but the authorship. Holders of this position are the classic heretics – the other kind might better be described as professed atheists. True heretics are even more fanatical about their beliefs than the orthodox. They claim to be regarded as the true keepers of the flame. Most Stratfordians admit that Shakespeare had his off days (the Gentleman's entrance with a bloody knife in the final scene of *King Lear* heralds a truly abysmal passage of dialogue), whilst all Oxfordians admire every word of the works indiscriminately – or if there is a sequence they don't like, they simply dismiss it as an interpolation on the part of the vulgar players.

Keepers of the flame undoubtedly they are. The problem is with 'true'. And it is at this point that we must turn to the original Shakespeare Authorship Controversies of the eighteenth century. Both affairs concerned individual documents, not the whole Works, but they were essential prerequisites for the full-scale authorship debates of the following two centuries. One took place in the 1720s, the other in the 1790s; the differences between them are revelatory of the transformation of Shakespeare from admired dramatist into cult-figure.

The first authorship controversy

Between 1700 and 1740, Shakespeare took over from Beaumont and Fletcher as the most performed dramatist on the London stage. The expansion of publishing and book-buying in the same period, combined with the effects of the introduction in 1709 of England's first Copyright Act, meant that in the same period there was a proliferation of rival editions of the plays. But in many cases the plays as performed on stage were different from the texts reproduced in the editions. The Restoration habit of 'regularizing' Shakespeare's language and plots to fit with 'modern' decorums took a long time in dying – Nahum Tate's alteration of *King Lear* back to the kind of happy ending which had characterized the old *King Leir* was not finally banished from the stage until the 1830s. The prevalence of adaptation shows that in the early eighteenth century there was no sense of Shakespeare's original texts being utterly sacrosanct like Holy Writ.

In 1725, the leading poet of the day, Alexander Pope, completed his edition of Shakespeare. It carried over into textual editing the custom of 'improving upon the original' which was the mark of stage performance. The text was frequently emended to make both the language and the metre of the plays conform to eighteenth-century norms. Passages which Pope regarded as 'excessively bad', and which he therefore assumed must have been interpolations by hands other than Shakespeare's, were 'degraded to the bottom of the page'. Pope's presumption led Lewis Theobald, a lawyer turned scholar and all-round hack writer, to publish the following year his *Shakespeare Restored: or a specimen of the many errors, as well committed, as unemended, by Mr Pope in his late edition of this poet, designed not only to correct the said edition, but to*

restore the true reading of Shakespeare in all the editions ever yet publish'd.
Pope took his revenge on Theobald's pedantry by making him the hero
of *The Dunciad*, but it is to *Shakespeare Restored* that modern Shakespearean editing owes its origins. Theobald went on to produce a rival
edition of his own, textually far superior to Pope's.

In the late 1720s, then, Pope and Theobald were rivals for the
mantle of Shakespeare. Pope's poetic eminence gave him the stronger
claim, despite Theobald's superior scholarship. But in 1727 Theobald
tipped the balance in his own favour: he announced that he had got
hold of a lost Shakespearean play which he was preparing for the stage.
It was duly staged that December, running for ten nights and being
revived on a number of subsequent occasions. A correspondent in the
Weekly Journal wrote that it was received with 'unanimous Applause'
by 'considerable Audiences' and that its success marked the rightful
repossession of the stage on the part of its great author. The correspondent praised Theobald for rescuing the play from oblivion and added
that the editor's veneration for 'the Genius of that Author', as
manifested by *Shakespeare Restored*, was 'too sincere to permit him to
impose a spurious piece on the World in his Name'.

An anonymous poetic contribution to *The Gentleman's Magazine*
took a different view:

> See! T— leaves the lawyer's gainful trade,
> To wrack with poetry his tortur'd brain:
> Fir'd, or not fir'd, to write resolves with rage,
> And constant pores o'er Shakespear's sacred page;
> – Then starting cries, I something will be thought,
> I'll write – then – boldly swear 'twas Shakespear wrote.

So was it a forgery or was it not? Was the *Weekly Journal* correct in its
assumption that Theobald revered Shakespeare too much to fabricate a
play? Or was *The Gentleman's Magazine* closer to the mark? Did
Theobald revere Shakespeare so much, and so want to be more like
him than Pope was, that he wrote the play himself and passed it off as
being by the immortal Bard? The play was called *Double Falsehood*.
Which begs the question: the surviving text is manifestly not authentically Shakespearean, but exactly what kind of falsehood does it
perpetrate?

The whole affair is extremely bizarre. The previous year Theobald had scrupulously set about restoring Shakespeare's original text. So if he had a manuscript of an authentic lost play in his possession, why did he not publish it in scrupulously original form? Why, when he went on to edit the collected plays, did he neither include nor mention *Double Falsehood*? And why did he never publish a reasoned refutation of the accusation of forgery? Did he keep the manuscript close to his chest because it was a fabrication or out of a desire to keep a precious piece of Shakespeare to himself?

Though not included in Theobald's edition of Shakespeare's plays, *Double Falsehood* was published in 1728. Perhaps the most striking thing about this publication is its opening statement:

> GEORGE THE SECOND, by the Grace of God, King of *Great-Britain*, *France* and *Ireland*: Defender of the Faith, etc. To all to whom these Presents shall come, Greeting. Whereas our Trusty, and Well-beloved *Lewis Theobald*, of our City of *London*, Gent. hath, by his Petition, humbly represented to Us, That He having, at considerable Expense, Purchased the Manuscript Copy of an Original Play of WILLIAM SHAKESPEARE, called, *Double Falsehood; Or, the Distrest Lovers*; and, with great Labour and Pains, Revised, and Adapted the same to the Stage; has humbly besought Us to grant him Our Royal Privilege, and Licence, for the Sole Printing and Publishing thereof, for the Term of Fourteen Years: We, being willing to give all due Encouragement to this his Undertaking, are graciously pleased to condescend to his Request.

Theobald, then, obtained special royal permission to retain the exclusive right to publish *Double Falsehood*. Are we really to suppose that Theobald's humble representation to the King of England was a lie? That he would have asked for the royal warrant to be affixed to a forgery? It seems much more likely that Theobald wanted exclusive rights to publication for fourteen years (1) because he saw that his find was a money-spinner, and (2) to stop Pope getting his hands on it.

Theobald asserted in his preface to the published text of *Double Falsehood* that 'those great Judges' to whom he had communicated the work in manuscript had vouched for its authenticity. But he neglected to mention who those judges were, and no one at the time said that they had seen the manuscript. Nevertheless, in a letter sent to an aristocratic lady, enclosed with some free tickets to the play, Theobald invited his correspondent to come round and look at the manuscript whenever she might care to – so he must have had something to show her.

In his preface, Theobald actually claimed that he had in his possession not one but *three* manuscripts of the play. The principal one was said to be in the handwriting of John Downes, a theatre prompter from the time of the Restoration. Theobald said that it had formally belonged to Thomas Betterton, the leading Shakespearean actor of the late seventeenth century, who, according to tradition, had received it via an illegitimate daughter of Shakespeare. Nicholas Rowe's biography gave Shakespeare three daughters, whereas he had only two by Anne Hathaway, but we should not attach too much weight to the 'tradition' of which Theobald speaks. It is best viewed as a neat metaphor for the play itself: *Double Falsehood* is to be regarded as an illegitimate child which is truly the offspring of Shakespeare but which was born outside the licensed fold of the First Folio.

Of the two other purported manuscripts, one was said to be a later copy, the other to be of high quality, with 'fewer Flaws and Interruptions in the Sense' than the Downes manuscript. Did Theobald merely say that he had three manuscripts in order to lend credibility to his story? But, then again, what would he have said if someone had asked to see them? It is a very strange forger who goes to the trouble of producing three different manuscripts of the same work.

As for the play itself, it has many verbal similarities to a number of Shakespearean plays, notably *Hamlet*, which were frequently staged in Theobald's time. This suggests that it could be a good imitation. But then most of acts four and five are in a style that is highly reminiscent of the tragicomic dramatic romances which John Fletcher pioneered between 1608 and 1613. The end offers revelation upon revelation; the love-induced madness of the central character is comparable to that of the jailer's daughter in Fletcher's most affecting scenes in *The Two Noble Kinsmen*; a pair of pompous fathers, one of whose daughters is cross-dressed, are also highly Fletcherian; even some of the linguistic and metrical features resemble Fletcher's. If Theobald were fabricating a Shakespeare play, why on earth did he write the second half of it in the style of Fletcher?

This brings us to the most decisive reason for thinking that Theobald was telling the truth when he said he had an old manuscript (or manuscripts): *nobody in Theobald's time knew that Shakespeare wrote plays in collaboration with Fletcher.* Until the early nineteenth century, it was assumed that *The Two Noble Kinsmen* was by either Fletcher alone or Beaumont and Fletcher; until 1850, it was assumed that *Henry VIII* was by Shakespeare alone. Only since then has it been known that Shakespeare ended his career by writing in collaboration with the dramatist who subsequently stepped into his shoes as in-house writer for the King's Men.

Indeed, Theobald complained in his preface to *Double Falsehood* that some of his antagonists had denied that the play was Shakespeare's on the very grounds that 'the *Colouring, Diction,* and *Characters,* come nearer to the Style and Manner of FLETCHER.' Had he known that *The Two Noble Kinsmen* was first published not in the Beaumont and Fletcher Folio of 1647, but in 1634 as 'by John Fletcher and William Shakespeare', he would have made the connection and been able to argue that the marks of Fletcher's hand are, paradoxically, proof of the play's authenticity, not its fabrication.

Theobald answered the point that the play sounded more like Fletcher than Shakespeare with the weak argument that he wished 'that Every Thing which is good, or pleasing, in our Tongue, had been owing to [Shakespeare's] Pen.' It may well be true that Shakespeare has influenced all subsequent English literature, but it is going a little far to claim that he actually penned every good work in the language. In the second edition of *Double Falsehood,* Theobald accordingly changed 'in our Tongue' to 'in that other great poet'. This suggests that he was coming round to the view that Fletcher did have a hand in it.

And here one sees the probable answer to some of our perplexing questions. Theobald never wrote a reasoned defence of Shakespeare's authorship because he could not deny the marks of Fletcher; he lost enthusiasm for the play not because it was a forgery but because he found himself in the embarrassing position of having obtained a royal warrant for the exclusive reproduction of a Shakespeare play and then discovering that it appeared to be a Fletcher play.

Furthermore, Theobald did not edit *Double Falsehood* in the scholarly way in which he edited the plays in the First Folio because he attached it to the theatrical tradition rather than the textual one. His approach to Shakespeare's *reading texts* was regressive: he attempted to restore the originals. His approach to Shakespeare's *theatre scripts* was progressive: as

Tate had 'improved' *King Lear* and Davenant had updated *Macbeth* with a full chorus of singing and dancing witches, so he regularized *Double Falsehood*. He recognized that sixty years earlier Betterton or Downes would have been likely to improve their original, and that quite possibly sixty years before that Fletcher may have done the same, so he did not hesitate to do so himself. He would have regarded this as fidelity to Shakespeare's continuing theatrical life. Since his manuscript came from the theatrical tradition, there would have been no point in treating it as he treated the plays he included in his reading edition.

Double Falsehood is a dramatization, with altered names, of one of the best-known incidents in Cervantes' *Don Quixote*, the story of the love-madness of Cardenio. Theobald did not know that in 1613 the King's Men were paid for two performances at court of a play called *Cardenno* or *Cardenna*. He did not know that this was exactly the period during which Fletcher was taking over from Shakespeare as the company's house dramatist, beginning with collaborations on *Henry VIII* and *The Two Noble Kinsmen*. Nor did he know that in 1653 an entry was placed on the Stationers' Register for a play (never published) called '*The History of Cardenio* by Mr Fletcher and Shakespeare'. As *The Two Noble Kinsmen* was Shakespeare and Fletcher's dramatization of the famous love-story of Palamon and Arcite from Chaucer's *Knight's Tale*, so *Cardenio* must have been their dramatization of the famous love-story of Cardenio and Luscinda from *Don Quixote*.

Close linguistic parallels show that the ultimate source of *Double Falsehood* was the first English translation of Cervantes, published in 1612. The probability of Theobald having fabricated a Shakespeare play, unintentionally written half of it in the style of Fletcher, and used for its source the very book which Shakespeare and Fletcher used for a play of whose existence he was ignorant, is infinitesimal. The inference has to be that Theobald's play is indeed a version of *Cardenio*, which Shakespeare and Fletcher must have written while Thomas Shelton's 1612 translation was new and popular. The fact that the original *Cardenio* could not have been written before 1612 is, incidentally, another nail in the coffin of the Earl of Oxford as putative author of Shakespeare.

One of Theobald's *Double Falsehood* manuscripts was kept as a treasure in the library of Covent Garden Theatre – it was referred to in an advertisement for a revival of the play in 1770. Presumably it was destroyed when that theatre burned down in 1808. What happened to the other two manuscripts, if they ever existed, remains a mystery. The published text of Theobald's adaptation, which is probably an adaptation of an adaptation from the time of Betterton and Downes, survives. Reading it, one hears the faint cry of a Shakespeare and Fletcher original trapped below the layers of rewriting:

> What you can say is most unseasonable; what sing,
> Most absonant and harsh: nay, your perfume,
> Which I smell hither, cheers not my sense
> Like our field-violet's breath.
>
> (1.3.54–7)

The rare sixteenth-century word 'absonant' (meaning discordant) and the specificity of imagination which chooses 'field-violet' rather than plain 'violet': these do not have the feel of decorous eighteenth-century imitation, they sound the authentically late-Shakespearean note.

For our purposes, three things are interesting about the case of *Double Falsehood*. First, insofar as we can make out the original *Cardenio* beneath the surface, with its marked distinction between Shakespearean and Fletcherian scenes, it confirms Shakespeare's status as a collaborator, a man of the theatre who frequently worked together with his colleagues. Some of Shakespeare's early theatrical efforts were almost certainly towards collaborative plays – the Countess of Salisbury scenes in the history-play of *Edward III* are now regarded as his by nearly all scholars. He almost certainly wrote only the second half of *Pericles*. And his last three plays – *Henry VIII*, *Cardenio*, and *The Two Noble Kinsmen* – were shared out with Fletcher. The fact of collaboration is one of the strongest pieces of evidence that the author of Shakespeare's plays was, like the authors of all other public plays of the period, a professional writer, not an aristocrat.

Secondly, *Double Falsehood* shows that Shakespeare's status was on the rise by the 1720s. The exceptional nature of the royal warrant for exclusive publication shows that a lost Shakespeare play was regarded as something very special. And the fact that Theobald's critics regarded the play as a fabrication shows that Shakespeare had become sufficiently special for fabrication to be considered a possibility. In 1660 Fletcher was more highly regarded than Shakespeare; by 1730, intimations of Fletcher's hand caused the devaluation of *Double Falsehood*. Shakespeare is no longer merely first among equals: by this time he is regarded as having unique value.

But although the *Gentleman's Magazine* poem spoke of 'Shakespear's sacred page', the works had not yet quite become a sacred icon. This is the third notable feature of the *Double Falsehood* affair: comparatively little interest was shown in the manuscript itself. After David Garrick boosted Shakespeare to full apotheosis with his Stratford Jubilee of 1769, any object associated with the Bard would have been treated with reverence. Had a lost manuscript been recovered then, people would have queued up to touch it, even to kiss it; an accurate edition would have been published, an alteration for the stage not contemplated. The difference will be seen if we turn to the second great controversy concerning Shakespeare and authorship.

The second authorship controversy

The Romantic idea of authorship locates the essence of genius in *the scene of writing*. With Romanticism, the quintessential image of the poet becomes that of Samuel Taylor Coleridge alone in a farmhouse, transcribing his opium-induced dream of 'Kubla Khan' onto a blank piece of paper, being interrupted by the knock of a person from Porlock, thus losing for ever that part of the inspired vision which he had not yet written down. This conception of what it is to be a genius has the effect of investing talismanic power in *the author's original manuscript*. This in turn has the effect of removing Shakespeare from the playhouse – it was in the Romantic period that idealists began complaining that the plays were too great to be soiled by the stage. It also creates a problem out of his manuscripts' failure to survive. Previously, the absence of original holograph manuscripts of the plays in Shakespeare's own hand had been an inconvenience to editors in their attempts to correct the printed texts, but not cause for serious consternation. The historical origin of the authorship controversy was the attempt to fill the gap left by the absence of original manuscripts.

The rise of Bardolatry in the eighteenth century was such that by 1800 the lawyer and gentleman of letters George Hardinge could write, 'Every thing, Sir, now-a-days has to do with Shakespeare: the difficulty is, to find out what has not to do with him.' Hardinge was thinking especially of a debate which had raged in the mid-1790s, in tandem with the great controversies about the rights and wrongs of the French Revolution. It was a matter about which everybody on the literary scene had an opinion.

In the course of 1795, one Samuel Ireland of Norfolk Street introduced the London public to a variety of documents and relics purporting to be newly discovered Shakespeareana. First there was a mortgage deed with the Bard's own signature, then a promissory note from Shakespeare to his fellow-actor John Heminges. These documents seemed to confirm the image of the dramatist that had been established by Edmond Malone's 1790 edition of the *Plays and Poems of William Shakspeare*, a landmark in Shakespearean scholarship which set new standards in scholarly responsibility and textual rigour. Malone's introductory material had played down the 'folk' image of Shakespeare, transmitted via oral tradition – the undisciplined youth stealing deer from Sir Thomas Lucy's Charlecote Park – and brought forward instead a series of documents concerning his business dealings, for instance a conveyance proving that he purchased a house in Blackfriars from one Henry Walker in 1613. The National Poet thus ceased to be a man of the people, careless of authority, and was recreated as an impeccable bourgeois gentleman, busily accumulating property and respectability in London and Stratford.

Great excitement attended upon Ireland's discovery, provoking an appetite for more – and preferably for something more intimate than a miscellany of legal instruments. Ireland duly obliged: he announced that he had obtained from his mysterious anonymous source an exchange of letters between Shakespeare and the Earl of Southampton. These letters only confirmed what was already known, Shakespeare's debt to his patron, but they bestowed a patina of aristocratic glamour upon the proceedings.

What was needed next was something which answered one of the Shakespearean puzzles that were earnestly debated in the late eighteenth century. In 1757 an apparently authentic 'Spiritual Testament' by John Shakespeare had been found in the rafters of the birthplace house in Stratford. Shakespeare's father was a Roman Catholic! There was thus a potential conflict, causing some alarm, between the National Poet and the National Church. Could Will have been tainted by his father's allegiance to the old religion? Samuel Ireland was able to put English minds at rest: he produced a 'Spiritual Testament' purportedly in William Shakespeare's own hand which showed that, whatever his father's beliefs, the dramatist himself remained a devout Anglican all his life.

Next came a portrait (the very countenance of the Bard!), then Shakespeare's library catalogue (he was not an untutored genius after all!), then a pair of priceless letters to the ladies in his life (Queen Elizabeth and Anne Hathaway), and then the grail itself of which every Shakespearean dreams — the lost original manuscripts of *The Tragedye of Kynge Leare* and some scenes of *Hamblette*. Finally, beyond even the grail: the full text of what was announced as a complete lost Shakespearean play, *Vortigern, An Historical Tragedy.*

Samuel Ireland's humble abode became a shrine where literary pilgrims could pay their homage to the immortal Bard. The newspapers could not get enough of the story. There was tremendous demand for the documents to be published. And so it was that on Christmas Eve 1795 Samuel Ireland produced his present for the national heritage: *Miscellaneous Papers and Legal Instruments under the Hand and Seal of William Shakspeare, including the Tragedy of King Lear, and a Small Fragment of Hamlet, from the Original MSS. in the Possession of Samuel Ireland.* It was not, however, a free gift: elaborately typeset and beautifully bound in folio, it cost four guineas per copy by subscription.

Ireland's son, William Henry, had been curiously reluctant for the documents to go into print, where they could be closely examined. But his father insisted, and besides, preparations were soon under way for an even greater event: the world premiere of *Vortigern* at the Theatre Royal, Drury Lane, with the greatest actor of the age, John Philip Kemble, in the leading role. It was originally scheduled for the first of April 1796; Kemble — who did admit to doubts about the text's authenticity — was persuaded to postpone the premiere by a day, for fear of the enterprise seeming Foolish.

But then, with consummate timing, there appeared on 31 March a weighty book entitled *An Inquiry into the Authenticity of Certain Miscellaneous Papers and Legal Instruments, published Dec. 24, 1795 and Attributed to Shakspeare, Queen Elizabeth, and Henry, Earl of Southampton: Illustrated by Fac-Similes of the Genuine Hand-Writing of that Nobleman, and of Her Majesty; a new Fac-simile of the Hand-Writing of Shakspeare, never before Exhibited; And other Authentick Documents: In a Letter*

Addressed to the Right Hon. James, Earl of Charlemont. The author was Edmond Malone, the foremost Shakespearean scholar of the age. He conclusively demonstrated that the Ireland documents were all fakes, riddled with the most elementary errors and anachronisms. An amazing five hundred copies of his pricey four-hundred-page book were sold within forty-eight hours. Unsurprisingly, the performance of *Vortigern* on the second of April provoked uproar during act five scene two when Kemble pronounced the unfortunate lines

> And with rude laughter, and fantastic tricks,
> Thou clap'st thy rattling fingers to the sides;
> And when this solemn mockery is ended . . .

The Ireland butterfly had been broken upon the wheel of Malone's formidable scholarship. The solemn mockery was soon ended, leaving only egg on the faces of the believers.

How on earth, we now wonder, can so many of the leading literati of the day, from the Poet Laureate and James Boswell downwards, have been taken in by such farragos as 'A Letter from Shakspeare to Anna Hathcrrewaye' and 'A Deed of Gift from William Shakspeare to William Henry Ireland', in which Elizabethan spelling was represented as a matter of including as many double consonants as possible and adding lots of 'e's to the ends of words? Thus Shakespeare's memorandum to himself appended to his letter from Queen Elizabeth: 'Thys Letterre I dydde receyve fromme mye moste gracyouse Ladye Elizabethe ande I doe requeste itte maye bee kepte withe alle care possyble.' But we should not merely laugh. For all the scholarly advances of the last two hundred years, a very distinguished historian could still authenticate the Hitler Diaries. When you want something badly enough, it is easy to close your eyes.

Boswell knelt down in front of the Ireland documents and pronounced the Nunc Dimittis. Any student of medieval religion can tell you about the manufacture of relics: the forger William Henry Ireland was simply performing a service for true believers in the cult that had been formalized by David Garrick's Jubilee of 1769, when London society descended on rural Stratford in order to celebrate the genius of Shakespeare. Very soon after Malone's exposure, Ireland junior wrote a confession – itself another tidy little earner – and in it he claimed that he was only trying to please father Samuel. The latter was an arch-

Bardolater, and his son thought that it would make the old man happy to have a document in Shakespeare's hand, so he fabricated one for him. But once it was widely credited, William Henry, 'urged, partly by the world' and partly by his 'own vanity', could not stop himself producing another one – and another, and another, until he eventually got round to some *Lear* and *Hamlet* manuscripts and the complete text of *Vortigern*. One cannot help admiring his energy.

Samuel Ireland's motives for publishing the material were presumably primarily financial – hence the expensive format in which the *Miscellaneous Papers and Legal Instruments* was produced – and secondarily associated with reputation. He hoped that his family name and his home just off the Strand would for ever be associated with this greatest of all literary discoveries. His ambition anticipates the unspoken dream of all Anti-Stratfordians: that they will be the one to gain immortality as the unmasker of the 'true' identity of 'Shake-speare'. Samuel Ireland continued to believe in the authenticity of the documents even after his son had confessed that they were fabrications. So too will Anti-Stratfordians continue to believe in their theories even after scholarship has shown them to be groundless.

What did the Ireland affair do to Shakespeare? It made him into a commodity. Garrick had done exactly the same when he sold tickets for his Jubilee, as had the citizens of Stratford-upon-Avon who turned out holy relics manufactured from the suspiciously prolific wood of 'Shakespeare's Mulberry Tree'. The birth of the Shakespeare industry is paradigmatic of eighteenth-century England as a consumer society. Samuel Ireland was an archetypal entrepreneur in that he began from low origins as a weaver, but then made his money as a print-seller. He was a beneficiary of the economic expansion whereby more and more people had the leisure and the money to purchase prints and books.

Forgery was a threat in the eighteenth-century cultural market place for the same reason that the counterfeiting of coin and paper money is a threat to the economy of any such society. William Dodd has two claims to fame: his *Beauties of Shakespear*, a hugely successful anthology of purple passages that made Shakespeare available to a much wider audience than ever before (the *Reader's Digest* principle), and his unhappy end, hanged as a counterfeiter after forging the signature of his former pupil, Lord Chesterfield, on a bond for over four thousand pounds. The 1709 Copyright Act made literature into property; thereafter, forgery was the capital literary crime. The Ireland affair, then, was very much of its age – it was the last and greatest of the eighteenth-century literary forgery scandals, a replay, with increased financial stakes, of the controversies that had surrounded James Macpherson's 'discovery' of the legendary Gaelic bard Ossian, Thomas Chatterton's invention of the medieval poet Rowley, and William Lauder's forgery-based claim that Milton was a plagiarist. Malone was troubled by the Ireland forgeries and needed to suppress them because they debased the cultural coinage and potentially devalued such genuine Shakespearean documents as existed.

Subsequent authorship controversies have been premised on the proposition that since there are no play manuscripts in William Shakespeare's hand, William Shakespeare could not have written plays. The Ireland controversy was premised on a simpler, and in its way more beautiful, idea: since there are no play manuscripts in William Shakespeare's hand, we will have to invent some. The announcement of their discovery was calculated as a major media event – just as later stirrings of authorship controversies and manuscript discoveries have been so calculated. The Irelands wanted there to be original manuscripts and relics to worship, so William Henry manufactured them. Father and son incurred the wrath of the professional scholar Malone because he had laboured for years on the task of establishing the true text and biography of Shakespeare in the absence of more than a handful of original corroborating documents. He could not see the genuineness of the passion for Shakespeare that led to the forgeries; all he could see was that the Irelands were upstarts and cheats.

In his book *Forgers and Critics*, the scholar Anthony Grafton shows, principally by means of examples from the Renaissance, that there is a curious symbiosis between literary forgery and authentic scholarship – historical criticism 'has been dependent for its development on the stimulus that forgers have provided'. The Ireland affair certainly bears this argument out, in that the forgeries provoked significant scholarly research concerning Shakespeare's times from both Malone and his antagonist Alexander Chalmers, who entered the lists after the exposure of the forgeries by publishing two large books which controverted Malone's idealizing, royalist view of Elizabethan England.

The same thing happened a century later with the Baconian theory.

By the end of the 1880s, the question of whether Shakespeare's works were really written by Francis Bacon had been debated in hundreds of books, pamphlets, and newspaper and magazine articles. A need to lay the Bacon theory to rest by laying out the full details of Shakespeare's life stimulated Sidney Lee into the researches which led to his *Dictionary of National Biography* entry and subsequent 'definitive' biography. The latter has an appendix on 'The Bacon–Shakespeare Controversy' which ends with a paragraph of truly Malonean exasperation:

> The abundance of the contemporary evidence attesting Shakespeare's responsibility for the works published under his name gives the Baconian theory no rational right to a hearing; while such authentic examples of Bacon's efforts to write verse as survive prove beyond all possibility of contradiction that, great as he was as a prose writer and a philosopher, he was incapable of penning any of the poetry assigned to Shakespeare. Defective knowledge and illogical or casuistical argument alone render any other conclusion possible.

But just as Lee's biography failed to prove itself definitive, so his lofty dismissal of the Baconians failed to settle the question. As soon as Bacon had been laid to rest, up rose the Earl of Oxford, courtesy of J. Thomas Looney and his followers, and another generation of latter-day Malones had to undertake the painstaking work of refutation.

Anti-Stratfordian method

The Ireland affair provides the paradigm for all subsequent Shakespeare Authorship controversies. Its timing is all-revealing: it occurred in the 1790s because by 1790 new conceptions of Shakespeare and of Authorship had emerged which made it inevitable that it would occur. Coincidentally, its occurrence in a decade of extreme social turbulence raised the political stakes over what Hardinge called 'things to do with Shakespeare'. Nationalism and class interest thus came to play a major role in the controversy.

As for the form of the controversy, it has repeated itself in every subsequent Shakespeare Authorship debate: the battle-lines are drawn between amateur and professional, enthusiasm and scholarship, desire and documentation. Because surviving Elizabethan playhouse documents do not concern personal intrigue and high passion, the heretics have to invent colourful Romantic fantasies of their hero's life. War is waged in weighty tomes which stir tremendous passions at the time of publication, but are soon forgotten. The section of the Folger Shakespeare Library devoted to the authorship question has over three hundred dusty books on the case for Bacon, many of them over a thousand pages long.

Anti-Stratfordians, cognisant of the Irelands' demise, have not usually resorted to the fabrication of documents. Like the Irelands, they begin from the absence of original Shakespearean manuscripts and with a Romantic conception of authorship, but their strategy is a subtler one. Instead of fabricating Shakespeare, they propose that *Shakespeare fabricated his own identity*. And since 'Shake-speare' was a genius, he disguised himself so brilliantly that nobody has been able to decipher his true identity – until the Anti-Stratfordians themselves, that is.

The chief device of the late-nineteenth- and early-twentieth-century Baconians was the *cryptogram*. By selecting individual letters and words from the voluminous works of Shakespeare they discovered hidden messages from Francis Bacon saying that he was the true author. Here is an example of the method in action, taken from Ignatius Donnelly's *The Great Cryptogram: Francis Bacon's Cipher in the So-called Shakespeare Plays*. First you must deduce the formula of the cipher. It is '516−167=349−22b&h=327'. Then, using square roots, you must select a number of words from the columns of the First Folio. Thus from pages 74−6 of the *Histories* you will find:

Seas
ill
said
that
More
low
or
Shak'st
Spur
never
wrote
a
word

of
them

With a little allowance for Elizabethan pronunciation, the meaning is obvious, is it not? 'Cecil said that Marlowe or Shakespur never wrote a word of them'.

We thus have the word of no less a witness than William Cecil, Lord Burghley, chief minister to the Queen herself, that Bacon wrote the works traditionally attributed to Shakespeare – and, for good measure, those of Marlowe too. The problem with this, quite apart from the fact that writing plays filled with cryptograms is a very bizarre thing to have supposed Bacon to have spent his already extremely busy life engaging in, is that there are so many words and letters in Shakespeare that it would be possible to extract from them cryptograms naming anybody one cares to think of as the hidden author – any Elizabethan, any dead writer, you, me, Elvis Presley, or Malcolm X.

Oxfordians, cognisant of the Baconians' demise, have on the whole eschewed cryptograms. Their favoured code is the *hidden personal allusion*. Typically, the argument runs: Polonius is a satirical 'portrait' of Lord Burghley; the Earl of Oxford had personal reasons to dislike Lord Burghley; therefore the Earl of Oxford wrote *Hamlet*. But this method is in essence no different from the cryptogram, since Shakespeare's range of characters and plots, both familial and political, is so vast that it would be possible to find in the plays 'self-portraits' of, once more, anybody one cares to think of.

There is no evidence whatsoever that Elizabethan plays were vehicles for self-portraiture. The idea that they might have been is another back-projection of the Romantic notion of authorship: the Oxfordian attempt to find the life and character of their Earl hidden in the works of Shakespeare is no different in kind from the Ireland attempt to flesh out the life and character of Shakespeare by fabricating letters from him to Queen Elizabeth and Anne Hathaway.

More locally, it is absurd to suppose that any Elizabethan play might contain satiric references to particular aristocrats of the day. Polonius cannot be a satirical portrait of Lord Burghley for the simple reason that if he were, the author of the portrait would have found himself in prison before he could turn round. Dramatists ran the risk of censorship when they portrayed even relatively obscure long-dead aristocrats, like

Sir John Oldcastle: complaints from Sir John's descendants about a certain character in *Henry IV Part One* meant that Shakespeare had to change the fat knight's name from Oldcastle to Falstaff. The supposition that Polonius – who, besides, is not intended as the old dodderer for whom Oxfordians take him – could bear any resemblance to the most powerful man in the land betrays another respect in which Anti-Stratfordians resemble William Henry Ireland: their ignorance of the age in which Shakespeare lived.

But at this point one begins to see that a curious reversal has taken place over the last two hundred years. William Henry was disastrously ignorant of Elizabethan spelling and handwriting, but his father Samuel and his defender Alexander Chalmers knew something of the history of the age. Malone thought that one of the fatal flaws in 'A Letter from Shakspeare to Anna Hatherrewaye' was a certain contempt for monarchy which slipped out in the phrasing; he argued that since Shakespeare's plays showed reverence for the principle of monarchy, this proved that the letter could not have been written by Shakespeare. In his published reply to Malone, Samuel Ireland argued that of course you can find loyalist passages in Shakespeare, spoken by kings, bishops, and courtiers, but that this loyalism is only what is natural in the mouths of such characters; it belongs to them and does not necessarily represent Shakespeare's own political outlook. Since his form is dramatic, Shakespeare can put forward a plurality of political positions:

> Hence it is, that in the writings of Shakspeare, it is easy to select passages, in which the most servile, and submissive principles are inculcated. But on the other hand, it is by no means difficult to find sentiments, which breathe the spirit of a proud and dignified independence.

Chalmers added that the apparent orthodoxy of Shakespeare's plays was attributable to the censorship, not to the dramatist's natural loyalty. He drew attention to the 1589 Licensing Act which prevented the players from handling 'certain matters of *divinity* and of *state* unfit to be suffered'. You don't need a censorship if there isn't sedition in the air: 'The privy-council did not so much partake of the scenic enthusiasm of the people, as they viewed the popular concourse to scenic representations, in the light of a political disorder; which, having increased under restraint, required correction, rather than countenance.'

It was Malone who idealized the Queen and her courtiers, and he did so, Ireland and Chalmers insisted, for contemporary political reasons. Malone may have had truth on his side, but he mortgaged that truth to nostalgia for an age of chivalry which never really existed.

In the light of this, we should pause to reflect upon the identity of some of the leading candidates for the authorship of 'Shake-speare'. Among those who have been advanced are: Francis Bacon, first Baron Verulam and Viscount St Albans; Edward de Vere, seventeenth Earl of Oxford; William Stanley, sixth Earl of Derby; Roger Manners, fifth Earl of Rutland; the third Earl of Southampton; the second Earl of Essex; the first Earl of Salisbury; the seventh Earl of Shrewsbury; the Earl of Devonshire and eighth Lord Mountjoy; Sir Walter Ralegh; Sir Anthony Sherley; the bastard son of the Earl of Hertford and Lady Catherine Grey. These names seem to have something in common.

Anti-Stratfordianism promulgates not just a Romantic idea of authorship, but an aristocratic one. The traditional image of Shakespeare made much of his humble birth; the absence of privilege suited the idea of his innate genius. But the Anti-Stratfordians cannot abide the thought of Shakespeare resembling an untutored Romantic genius of low origins like John Clare. They require something more glamorous: a background similar to that of the Romantic whose life became his greatest work, Lord Byron.

Fully fledged Anti-Stratfordianism was a late-Victorian phenomenon. It was in the Victorian period that, for the first time, English culture became resolutely middle-class. The middle classes were highly sensitive to intruders from 'below' and firmly committed to the ideals of 'above'. The paradigmatic Victorian literary career was that of Alfred Tennyson, who came from middling stock and ended up as not just a Laureate but a Lord. A cult attached itself to the memory of Byron because he had the glamour of Lordship from birth. John Clare, meanwhile, was shut away in a madhouse; his work fell into neglect because he was a peasant. Anti-Stratfordianism makes William of Stratford into the peasant, shuts him away, and attributes his work to any lord it can find.

The argument that Shakespeare must have been an aristocrat because he wrote so knowingly about courts is facile. Every Elizabethan and Jacobean professional dramatist wrote about courts, yet none of them was a courtier. Courts are things you can learn about from books and gossip; besides, the dramatists saw the court from the inside when their companies were commissioned to put on special performances there. What is much harder to imagine is an aristocrat like Oxford reproducing the slang of the common tavern and the intonations of the low-born which are as characteristic of Shakespeare's plays as any polished mimickings of courtly language.

The Anti-Stratfordian aristocratic principle is a matter of prejudice, not argument. The sentiment behind it is best summed up by a statement of Christmas Humphreys of the Inner Temple, Barrister at Law, on the first page of his introduction to Miss Hilda Amphlett's *Who was Shakespeare?*, an Oxfordian work which is absolutely representative in its modes of both argument (emphasis above all on hidden personal allusions) and presentation (the Sherlock Holmes method of sniffing out clues, the introduction by a senior lawyer to confer bogus authority). Judge Christmas, as he later became, writes:

> It is offensive to scholarship, to our national dignity, and to our sense of fair play to worship the memory of a petty-minded tradesman while leaving the actual author of the Shakespeare plays and poems unhonoured and ignored. Moreover, I have found the plays of far more interest when seen as the work of a great nobleman and one very close to the fountainhead of Elizabethan England.

'Our national dignity', 'a petty-minded tradesman', 'a great nobleman': these three phrases tell the whole story. Like so many English questions, it all boils down to class.

This, then, is the curious reversal: whilst in their fantasies the Oxfordians are descendants of Ireland, in their social allegiance they are the true heirs of Malone. The latter wrote in his attack on the forgeries that our 'respect and veneration' for the author of the plays compels us 'to preserve them pure and unpolluted by any modern sophistication or foreign admixture whatsoever'. In accordance with their Byronic elision of the work and the life, Oxfordians transfer this compulsion to the identity of the author: they cannot allow him to be tainted by anything so vulgar as *trade*. They regard blue blood as the prerequisite for genius. Like Malone, they have swallowed the myth of herself which Queen Elizabeth carefully propagated. They are in thrall to the glamour of her court; they desperately want Shakespeare to be 'very close to the fountainhead'.

For this reason, we should salute the Anti-Stratfordians who have taken this desire to its logical extreme: George Elliot Sweet, who sweetly proposed in 1956 that Queen Elizabeth herself wrote the plays, and – a little surprisingly, given his own political convictions – Malcolm X, who (whilst in prison) proposed that King James wrote them.

Malone's phrase 'foreign admixture', a gibe at French Revolutionary innovation, also has its resonances in later authorship controversies. As will be shown in chapter six, the eighteenth-century elevation of Shakespeare to the rank of supreme genius had a lot to do with nationalism and Francophobia. One of the most frequently reiterated Anti-Stratfordian claims is that William Shakespeare could not have written the plays because he had never been to Italy, of which the plays supposedly reveal intimate knowledge. Let us set aside the fact that in the first scene of the *Two Gentlemen of Verona* the impression is given that it is possible to travel by sea from Verona to Milan, which makes one suspect that the plays could not have been written by anyone who had ever actually been to Italy (Milan is a seaport once again in *The Tempest*). The interesting thing about this claim is not its falsity but the conclusion which tends to be drawn from it: the plays must have been written by an English aristocrat who visited Italy. The alternative possibility, that the plays must have been written by an Italian, has never found favour: perish the thought that the works of Shakespeare might have been written by a *foreigner*. As I remarked in the previous chapter, Shakespeare's knowledge of matters Italian can be attributed to the presence of John Florio in the household of the Earl of Southampton. Because Shakespeare knew Florio and his works, the belief that Shakespeare's works were actually written by Florio is harder to refute than the case for any aristocrat's authorship – but because Florio was not an Englishman, the case for him has never made much headway. Except in Italy, of course, where one Santi Paladino published his *Un italiano autore delle opere Shakespeariane* to much acclaim in 1955.

The case for the Earl of Oxford was first made by J. Thomas Looney. The two key things to remember about Looney are who he thought he was, and when he wrote his book. He claimed descent from the Earls of Derby, who, like Piers Gaveston in Marlowe's *Edward II*, were Lords of Man – the Isle of Man, that is. Whilst this ancestry makes it surprising that Looney believed in the authorship of the Earl of Oxford rather than the Earl of Derby, it is symptomatic of the Oxfordians' concern for good pedigree. Looney was an ancient Isle of Man name, the correct pronunciation of which is 'Low-ney', and for this reason J. Thomas proudly refused to write under a pseudonym even though one of the publishers to whom he showed his manuscript offered to publish it provided there was a less risible name on the title-page. When the book appeared in 1920, it had Hamlet's 'What a wounded name' as an epigraph on its title-page immediately below the name Looney. The phrase is supposed to be applied to the name of de Vere, but its proximity to that of Looney is more than serendipitous.

As for the time of the book's writing, it is revealed in the first sentence of Looney's preface: 'The solution to the Shakespeare problem, which it is the purpose of the following pages to unfold, was worked out whilst the Great European War was in progress.' That war was being fought against Germany, which patriotic Englishmen like Looney believed to have made some provocative bids for the ownership of Shakespeare. It was time to reclaim him not just for England, but for the highest rank of Englishness.

By a sad and elegant irony, the Great European War tolled the final death knell of the English aristocracy as a power in the land. Within a few years, there was a Labour government and the earls started selling off their great houses to the National Trust. In the final decade of the twentieth century, the leading exponent of Oxfordianism is Charles Francis Topham de Vere, Earl of Burford – who just happens to be a descendant of the Earl of Oxford. He has realized that he can resuscitate the ailing family estate by touring America giving lectures on the case for his ancestor. He is a living embodiment of the heritage industry which is all that is left of Britain's Greatness.

Burford's chief American lieutenant has been Charlton Ogburn Jr., author of a thousand-page study of *The Mysterious William Shakespeare*. I still have a vivid memory of Ogburn appearing on one of the television programmes that are periodically devoted to the authorship controversy. He was filmed at his beautiful plantation house in Beaufort, South Carolina. A charming gentleman, he stressed that his was an ancient and distinguished Southern family. He was, in short, one of the Anglophiles of the old South who discerned a lamentable symmetry between the defeat of the Cavaliers by Oliver Cromwell in the English Civil War and the defeat of the plantation owners by the Yankees in the American Civil War. By 1990, however, Ogburn had made his peace with the North. In that year he dedicated the second edition of his book to a New Englander, Philip Saltonstall Weld. But these two surnames reveal that Ogburn was still obsessed with class, for they are unmistakable calling cards of the American aristocracy – the Welds are New England newspaper magnates (Hearsts without the vulgarity) and the Saltonstalls are among the most venerable of Boston's old colonial families.

The Anti-Stratfordian phenomenon is not only a question of class. It also has a psychological dimension. The most revealing of William Henry Ireland's forgeries was a document in which Shakespeare thanked one William Henry Ireland for jumping in and saving his life when he had fallen into the River Thames on his way back from the playhouse one day. Malone's discovery of Shakespeare's Blackfriars lease had revealed that an earlier tenant of the gatehouse had been a William Ireland. William Henry Ireland took the liberty of projecting his own middle name onto William Ireland and inventing the life-saving story, thus giving his father and himself an enviable ancestry: an Ireland had saved Shakespeare's life in 1604, allowing him to go on to write *King Lear* and his other later plays! Anti-Stratfordians repeat this pattern: they claim to be saving the life, the fame, of their candidate whereas they are in fact attempting to write an identity for themselves.

An excellent private asylum

If the father of all Anti-Stratfordians was William Henry Ireland the forger, the mother was Delia Bacon, whose *The Philosophy of the Plays of Shakspere Unfolded* set the bandwagon of full-blown Authorship Controversy in motion in 1857. No prizes are to be awarded to readers guessing the surname of Delia Bacon's chosen candidate for the authorship. Though she was a Baconian, Delia was irresistibly drawn to William's birthplace. She went to Stratford and attempted to open his grave, in which she hoped she would find some authentic Baconian relics. In December of the year in which her book was published she was, her family biographer writes, 'removed to an excellent private asylum for a small number of insane persons at Henley-in-Arden – in "the forest of Arden" – eight miles from Stratford.'

One of the men who enquired after her welfare there was Shake-

speare's American Romantic apostle, Ralph Waldo Emerso.
more, Delia's book carried a preface by Nathaniel Hawthorne.
not explicitly endorse her claims, but it did not explicitly deny the.
either. The author of *The Scarlet Letter* was not the only one to be
fascinated. At opposite extremes of American literary culture, Mark
Twain and Henry James became Anti-Stratfordians. James, obsessed as
he was with the supernatural, said that he was *haunted* by the thought
that the divine William was a fraud. Haunting in the context of
Shakespeare immediately makes one think of the ghost of Hamlet's
father. The Freudian explanation is obvious: Shakespeare is the haunting
father, the later writer is the haunted Hamlet. Writers, especially
American ones who want to throw off the burden of their English
literary patrimony, are drawn to the Anti-Stratfordian heresy out of
what Harold Bloom calls 'the anxiety of influence', the knowledge of
Shakespeare's unsurmountable superiority. They cannot actually kill
Shakespeare, so the next best thing is to kill his name, for it is as a name
that a literary father exercises authority. The works are thus displaced
onto a different name which carries the weight of aristocratic instead of
literary tradition. It is no coincidence that the most distinguished of all
Oxford's supporters was none other than Sigmund Freud. As Bloom
has brilliantly argued, Freud submitted to the Looney hypothesis as a
way of taking revenge on William of Stratford for being the one person
in the history of the world with a more powerful map of the human
passions than his own.

Freud knew that rejection of the father was a necessary psychological
defence mechanism to enable us to develop our own identities. The
desire to kill off William of Stratford is only a mark of the power of
William of Stratford. It follows that, paradoxical as it may seem, *in order
to have the Genius of Shakespeare, we also have to have the Authorship
Controversy*. I have found it both boring and infuriating to read the
fantasies and misrepresentations of the Anti-Stratfordians, but I comfort
myself with the knowledge that their outpourings are but the tarnished
flipside of a coin the head of which shines with the gold of Berlioz's
Roméo et Juliette, Verdi's *Otello*, Fuseli's paintings, Aimé Césaire's *Une
tempête*, and a host of other creations inspired by Shakespeare. The
Genius of Shakespeare means people getting obsessed with Shakespeare,
Shakespeare infusing himself into their very being, filling their whole
lives. With Berlioz the result was a series of musical works of

extraordinary beauty and originality, not to mention some wonderful memoirs and a (not-so-wonderful) marriage to a Shakespearean actress. With Delia Bacon, J. Thomas Looney, and their successors, the result is fat, bad, sad books. So be it: they are a price worth paying for the achievements of a Berlioz, a Verdi, a Fuseli, a Césaire.

As we have seen, the Authorship Controversy became possible – indeed inevitable – because of the apparent failure to survive of William Shakespeare's play manuscripts. Since printers did not return copy to authors or acting-companies after plays were published, hardly any Elizabethan play manuscripts survive. That is why there was an opening for William Ireland to forge his purported manuscripts of *Lear* and *Hamlet*.

A manuscript which does survive is that of the multi-authored history play, *Sir Thomas More*. One scene of it is in a handwriting which most experts agree to be Shakespeare's. Even if the palaeographic evidence is disputed, the vocabulary, the movement of ideas, and the way of representing the crowd are authentically Shakespearean.

The scene is a classic Shakespearean encounter between a spirited crowd, resembling the followers of Jack Cade in *Henry VI* or the citizens in *Coriolanus*, and the manipulative rhetoric of a politician seeking to control them, like Mark Antony in *Julius Caesar* or Buckingham addressing the mayor and citizens in *Richard III*. Shakespeare characteristically combines, on one side, an earthy prose and a healthy contempt for authority (inconceivable from the hand of the Earl of Oxford), with, on the other side, a supple verse and a weighty invocation of authority.

His marvellous ear for the idiom of the commons is apparent from the scene's first words: 'Peace, hear me! He that will not see a red herring at a Harry groat, butter at eleven pence a pound, meal at nine shillings a bushel, and beef at four nobles a stone, list to me.' His rhetoric of order is at full force in More's homily:

> For to the King God hath his office lent
> Of dread, of justice, power and command,
> Hath bid him rule, and willed you to obey;
> And to add ampler majesty to this,
> He hath not only lent the King his figure,
> His throne and sword, but given him his own name,

Calls him a god on earth. What do you then,
Rising 'gainst him that God himself installs,
But rise 'gainst God?

As in *Coriolanus*, when we hear the voices of the crowd we sympathize with their complaint even as we laugh at their chopped logic,
but when we submit to the rhetoric of the authority figure we find
the commoners contemptible. The authors of *Sir Thomas More* had
run into trouble with the censor over their first version of the
insurrection scene, so it looks as if they went to Shakespeare to ask
him for a revision exactly because they knew he had a knack for
the delicate art of writing crowd scenes that were both sufficiently
robust to please the groundlings and sufficiently orthodox to please the
censor.

Shakespeare's contribution to *Sir Thomas More* reveals a number of
things about his working life. He was a man of the theatre. He did
jobbing work, fulfilling particular commissions as well as creating plays
of his own. He contributed to plays which had different scenes written
by different dramatists. He revised other writers' work. He wrote
fluently but did occasionally 'blot a line' or have a second thought. He
did not own his play manuscripts: they were the property of whichever
acting company he was writing for; they would be shown to the
licenser of plays, marked up, changed if necessary, then given to the
company bookkeeper for copying into the prompt book, then either
sold to a printer or otherwise disposed of. Such a Shakespeare is utterly
unlike the Romantic image of authorship in which the poet works
alone in his study, is answerable only to his own inspiration, and
cherishes his manuscripts.

The case of *Sir Thomas More* establishes the collaborative nature of
Shakespeare's genius. His art was dependent not only on inherited
literary materials, but also upon his place as one of many people within
the theatrical profession. He could not have written one powerful scene
for *Sir Thomas More* if other dramatists such as Anthony Munday and
Henry Chettle had not written the rest of it. Only the perverse will
share Tolstoy's view of the relative merits of *King Lear* and the old *Leir*
play, but the fact remains that *Lear* could not have been written without
the old *Leir* play, just as *Henry IV* and *Henry V* could not have been
written without the old anonymous play of *The Famous Victories of*

Henry the Fifth, and a whole swath of the plays could not have been written without the prior achievements of Marlowe.

The Anti-Stratfordians are more right than they know in proposing that the genius of Shakespeare cannot be synonymous with the life of the country-bred actor. They are wrong only in their supposition that the mystery of the achievement of the plays will be solved by finding an alternative, romantically conceived author. In the next two chapters we will discover some of the ways in which Shakespeare's plays were written by other people: not by Bacon or Oxford, but by William Shakespeare's predecessors in the theatre, and the authors of the narrative and dramatic source material on which he depended.

4

MARLOWE'S GHOST

The death of the author

Sherlock Holmes is the most powerful and exemplary character in late-Victorian fiction. By the 1890s, population growth and urban expansion, coal fires, and heavy industrialization had caused the streets of London to be blanketed in a pea-soup fog. A mist had also settled on the order of things. Even after the earth was 'decentred' by the sixteenth-century Copernican revolution in astronomy, it was possible to retain a 'top-down' view of the universe: from God to man to the higher animals and so on. The nineteenth-century Darwinian evolution turned the model upside-down and began with the protozoa; it proposed furthermore that natural selection was an inexorable but unpredictable process governed by laws of survival, not a matter of divine providential design. The idea of man's evolution from the apes was regarded by many as an appalling affront; humankind's sense of its own privileged place was shrouded in doubt and controversy.

It is not coincidental that British detective fiction came of age with Wilkie Collins in the 1860s, the decade immediately after the publication of Charles Darwin's *Origin of Species*. The detective, Holmes above all others, was a reassuring figure because he cut through the fog. He penetrated to the quick of every mystery, deduced brilliant solutions to every problem. He was an embodiment of man's unconquerable mind; apparently immortal (surviving his descent into the Reichenbach Falls), he was proof of our superiority to Darwin's apes.

As Darwin's book cast doubt upon God's authorship of the world, so Delia Bacon's *The Philosophy of Shakespeare's Plays Unfolded*, published two years earlier, cast doubt upon Shakespeare's authorship of the works. The Baconian controversy reached its peak in the 1880s and '90s. Enough had been done to establish doubt in the public imagination; Max Beerbohm published a popular caricature of Sir Francis

Bacon slipping a scroll of works to a *lumpen*-looking William of Stratford (Fig. 5). But the theory that *it was Bacon* failed to convince because the deduction of it depended upon elaborate cryptograms. An alternative suspect was needed. Above all, a Sherlock Holmes was required to come forward and deduce the true identity of the author of the plays. And, sure enough, in 1895, when Holmes-mania was at its height, one William Gleason Zeigler published a detective story about Elizabethan England entitled *It Was Marlowe: A Story of the Secret of Three Centuries*. It was neither William of Stratford nor Francis of St Albans. It was Christopher of Canterbury.

Zeigler had the grace to present his case in the form of a novel, so his candidate for the authorship of Shakespeare's plays was not taken very seriously. But he established a paradigm whereby the Authorship Investigator sets him or herself up as a literary-historical Sherlock Holmes. Thomas Looney began his book on the case for the Earl of Oxford by drawing up a list of what he saw as the characteristics of the plays. These are the 'clues'. He then examined every possible 'suspect' and came up with the name of the perpetrator. In the Authorship story, however, the perpetrator is not the *villain*, but the unfairly maligned and neglected *hero* of the story. The detective-story structure is thus given a romance ending – which is why the hero usually turns out to be a nobleman in disguise. Since the 1890s, Anti-Stratfordian books have almost invariably been structured like detective stories, with their unfoldings of the mystery and deductions of the solution.

Zeigler saw that a good detective story must have a murder. In this respect, the Earl of Oxford, the Earl of Derby, and all the other aristocrats who have been brought forward as suspects turn out to be red herrings. If there is to be a murder, then Marlowe has to be the man. Was not his stabbing during a Deptford tavern brawl in 1593 the most infamous murder in English literary history? Sixty years on from Zeigler, Calvin Hoffman, a Broadway press agent, published the result of his twenty years' detective work concerning the identity of the dramatist: *The Murder of the Man who was 'Shakespeare'*. Written in high swashbuckling style, it is a glorious tale of all manner of colourful skulduggery.

Less than two weeks before Marlowe's death, a warrant for his arrest on charges of blasphemy and atheism had been issued by the Privy Council. Can it be a coincidence that he was murdered just before his period of bail was due to end? No, says Hoffman. What happened was this: Sir Thomas Walsingham, his noble employer and homosexual lover, arranged for three ruffians – the sinister Frizer, Poley, and Skeres – to murder someone who was *said* to be Marlowe (an abducted Spanish seaman, perhaps), while the lovely youth himself was spirited away to France and then Italy. From there, he would continue writing plays, which were passed off as Shakespeare's. The dedication of the *Sonnets* is to Mr W. H., that is to say *W*alsing-*H*am.

For Hoffman, there were two key pieces of evidence in support of the theory that Marlowe wrote Shakespeare. The first was the existence of many verbal parallels between the two dramatists' works; it was as a result of jotting these down over the years that Hoffman began to formulate his theory. Secondly, there was the fact that the first we hear by name of Shakespeare as an author is the dedication to his poem *Venus and Adonis* – a work published at a time uncannily close to the day when Marlowe was supposedly killed. It will be the contention of this chapter that Hoffman's initial instincts were correct. The verbal parallels are signs that there are close links between the works of Marlowe and those of Shakespeare. Furthermore, it is not a coincidence that Shakespeare's career took off at exactly the moment when Marlowe's came to its untimely end.

Where Hoffman went wrong was in his conception of the nature of authorship. He inherited the Romantic idea of authorship, that which makes the identity of an author synonymous with the biological life and the personality of the person who actually pens the 'Collected Works'. The key tactic of all Anti-Stratfordians is to read the sonnets as coded autobiography. In 1995 A. D. Wraight published a six-hundred-page tome, devoted to the case for Marlowe, under the title *The Story that the Sonnets Tell*. But, as we have seen, Elizabethans did not write sonnets as coded autobiography. Let us strip away the Romantic notion of authorship and then ask afresh whether Marlowe in some sense wrote the works of Shakespeare.

Robert Greene seems to have accused Shakespeare of pluming his own plays with the feathers of the university wits. It was of the essence of Shakespeare's art that he inherited – or stole – materials and transformed them. Nearly all Shakespeare's plays are rewritings of one kind or another. His works were in all sorts of respects prewritten by others, just as they have been subsequently rewritten by others. The manuscript of *Sir Thomas More* is like a palimpsest. Munday, Chettle, and their collaborators had run into trouble with the censor over the original version of the play, so they brought in Shakespeare to revise or *write over* the May Day riot scene.

Shakespeare knew the work of such dramatists as Greene, Peele, Munday, and Chettle; he borrowed certain techniques of dramatic cross-dressing and comic overhearing from John Lyly. But the influence of Marlowe stands out: *he is the only contemporary whom Shakespeare overtly alludes to rather than subliminally absorbs*. That Shakespeare felt the need to express his admiration for Marlowe may paradoxically suggest that Marlowe was the one contemporary about whom he had a certain anxiety.

In his book *The Anxiety of Influence*, Harold Bloom proposes that literary creation is a form of misinterpretation. Paradoxically, original writing occurs in the act of *re*-creation, the wresting of the great literature of the past to the purposes of the later artist. For Bloom, writers are the most powerful readers of previous writers; their creativity functions by means of what he calls 'strong misreading'. All poems are thus 'antithetical' to their precursor poems. Indeed, 'A poem is not an overcoming of anxiety, but is that anxiety'; it has force precisely because it is energized by a sense of belatedness, of the need to turn the burden of tradition into the shock of the new. Bloom regards the business of criticism as being to learn poets' own metaphors for their acts of reading.

Shakespeare is excluded from Bloom's argument about the anxiety of influence on the grounds that his 'prime precursor was Marlowe, a poet very much smaller than his inheritor'. But I am not so sure that Shakespeare knew that he was very much greater than Marlowe. I think that Bloom's method is more applicable to the relationship between Shakespeare and Marlowe than Bloom himself admits. I would like to suggest that some of Shakespeare's works are antithetical readings of Marlovian precursors; that they *are* his anxiety about Marlowe; that some of his most characteristic thinking about reading, writing, and theatricalizing occurs during his engagements with Marlowe. And it seems to me that one of Shakespeare's key metaphors for such thinking is murder.

In his comparative discourse upon classical and English poets, which I discussed in chapter one, Francis Meres sought a classical equivalent for Marlowe. He found one in a poet named Lycophron, who was shot to death by a rival. So, he says, was Marlowe killed by a rival for his lewd love. Metaphorically, not literally, Shakespeare was the rival who killed Marlowe. For a few quick bright years, Marlowe was the greatest dramatist whom the English nation had ever seen. Yet he has ever after been given second place. Literary history always reads him as the precursor to Shakespeare. In this sense, Bloom's analysis is right: the inheritor has absolutely – or, as we will see, *almost* absolutely – absorbed the precursor. But what Bloom underestimates is the magnitude of the battle which Shakespeare had to fight with Marlowe *and his ghost*. In a way that was quite different from what they imagined, Zeigler and Hoffman hit upon a truth.

Throughout his work on influence and its anxieties, Bloom has denied the importance of verbal parallels. He argues that the transmission of words and ideas from poet to poet is just something that happens, that it is a fit subject for mere source-hunters, but should not be the concern of truly strong critics, since it reveals little about the deeper dynamics of literary relations. As a general rule, I think it is true that Shakespeare's snapping-up of phrases from his reading and the plays of his contemporaries is of no great moment. Given the nature of memory-training in Elizabethan grammar schools and the fact that Shakespeare began his career as an actor whose trade was the learning of other people's lines, it is hardly surprising. But Greene's gibe in the *Groatsworth* does suggest that it is a habit which was noticed by his contemporaries: the parodic quotation from *Henry VI Part Three*, 'tiger's heart wrapped in a player's hide', seems to throw Shakespeare's habit back at him. It seems to me that when a famous phrase from a previous writer is clearly audible in a literary work, it is usually a sign of interauthorial confrontation. For this reason, I will be paying attention to Shakespeare's 'quotations' of Marlowe. I will not be attending to the many individual phrases that are simply assimilated without attention being drawn to them. Overt quotations apart, the more interesting similarities than those of phrasing are those of character-type and structure.

Shakespeare, I suggest, only became Shakespeare because of the death of Marlowe. And he remained peculiarly haunted by that death. In 1593 the chance of death gave Shakespeare the opportunity to emerge from the shadow of Marlowe's mighty line; but for many years afterwards the Canterbury grammar school boy (born 1564) continued to haunt the Stratford–upon–Avon grammar school boy (born 1564). Bloom's theory of poetic influence depends upon an Oedipal model, in which the precursor poet is the slain father. But Marlowe and Shakespeare were of the same generation. A better model for their relationship is that of *sibling rivalry*. I propose that Shakespeare was born as a dramatist by way of his strong (mis)reading of Marlowe, and that he matured as an author by grace of the (mis)fortune of his dramatic brother's death.

The rivals

Let me begin with a neat fable by the critic Marjorie Garber:

> Imagine for a moment a scene set in Arthur's bosom – that peculiarly English afterworld Shakespeare invented as the final resting place of Falstaff.
>
> Up there in Arthur's bosom, seated at a table (if it's Arthur's bosom it's probably a round table), are Shakespeare and Marlowe, busy playing what looks at first to be a game of cards. But when we get a little closer, we can see that instead of cards, they're using plays – each has a handful of quartos, octavos, and, on Shakespeare's part, some sheets of folio. Marlowe plays first, and he puts down *The Jew of Malta*. '*The Merchant of Venice*,' Shakespeare replies, laying down a quarto from his own hand. '*Dido Queen of Carthage*,' says Marlowe. '*Antony and Cleopatra*,' Shakespeare answers. Now Marlowe, considering, puts down *Edward II*, and Shakespeare counters immediately with *Richard II*. '*Dr Faustus*,' offers Marlowe, in some desperation, but with a half-smile of triumph. A pause – and then Shakespeare says softly, '*Macbeth*.' Marlowe takes a deep breath, and looks through his depleted hand. Finally he speaks. '*Tamburlaine the Great Parts One and Two*.' And Shakespeare, with an apologetic smile, lays down his cards. '*Henry IV Part One*,' he says deliberately, '*Henry IV Part Two*, and *Henry V*!'

There is the outline of a profound truth here, but the story offers a simplified version of that truth. For one thing, it implies that Marlowe and Shakespeare took turns to make their plays, as in a regular card game. In fact, Marlowe had revealed his entire hand almost before Shakespeare had started. But not quite before: in the early 1590s, I shall argue, there was something of the tit for tat which Garber imagines. Secondly, I shall suggest that some of Marlowe's moves were so strong that Shakespeare could not immediately outplay them. He required up to three moves, typically (1) imitation, (2) parody, and (3) outstripping. And thirdly, although *Henry V* was a key move in the game, it wasn't quite the final move which Garber implies. We will see that Marlowe had a right to that half-smile of triumph when he played *Dr Faustus*.

The other problem with Garber's version is that it garbles chronology for the sake of rhetorical effect. The chronology of all Marlowe's plays and all Shakespeare's early ones are greatly disputed matters. This makes any argument about the nature of the relationship between the two dramatists in the early 1590s very difficult to prove. There was a time when it was argued that the *Henry VI* plays were reworkings of Marlovian originals, and that Marlowe might even have had a hand in *The First Part of the Contention betwixt the Two Famous Houses of York and Lancaster* (published 1594) and *The True Tragedy of Richard Duke of York* (published 1595). These two plays are versions of what in the First Folio are called the second and third parts of *Henry VI*. Their texts are somewhat corrupt, which meant that there emerged in the mid-twentieth century a consensus that they were not the 'sources' of *Henry VI Parts Two and Three* but rather 'memorial reconstructions' of them, put together by actors. The exact nature of these early texts is still hotly debated, but we can be fairly certain of three things: that they are by Shakespeare, not Marlowe; that they are nevertheless strongly *influenced* by Marlowe; and that they are an original two-part play. I shall therefore refer to *The First Part of the Contention* and *The True Tragedy*, not *Henry VI Parts Two and Three*.

Again, exactly how *Richard III* relates to Marlowe will depend on whether we assign it an early or late date. For my purposes, the precise chronology of the earlier plays does not matter: whatever the local movement, there was two-way traffic between Marlowe and Shakespeare until the latter's death. Things only started changing after the Deptford stabbing. That is why Calvin Hoffman was right to see a symbolic coincidence between the fateful day of Marlowe's death (30 May 1593) and the entry on the Stationer's Register of *Venus and Adonis* on 18 April 1593. The fact that the latter date was *before* the former is the fatal flaw in Hoffman's argument that Marlowe literally – as opposed to metaphorically – *became* 'Shakespeare' after the Deptford affair.

We could say that Marlowe and Shakespeare, born in the same year, were originally a pair of dramatic twins. The relationship between their work was initially symbiotic. But then, like the twins in Shakespeare's plays, they were split apart. A year after Marlowe's death in May 1593, the theatrical repertoire was divided when the London companies reorganized themselves: the newly formed Chamberlain's Men took the Shakespeare plays to their theatre in Shoreditch and the works of Marlowe remained with – and continued to work box-office magic for – Philip Henslowe's company at the Rose on Bankside. As is the way with twins, however, the closeness of the bond meant that the ghost of the dead one haunted the living.

Thomas Kyd's *Spanish Tragedy* invented revenge drama for the English public stage. Christopher Marlowe's *Tamburlaine the Great* invented much more: heroic drama, historical drama, the high-sounding stalking giant of the stage, and the two-part play. *Tamburlaine*, it seems certain, made the name of both Marlowe as writer and Edward Alleyn as actor. According to my chronology, Shakespeare's first attempt in history and tragedy was a two-part play on the subject of the Wars of the Roses: *The First Part of the Contention betwixt the Two Famous Houses of York and Lancaster* and *The True Tragedy of Richard Duke of York*. To write a two-parter was to challenge Marlowe.

But the title of the first part implies an immediate change of direction. The Marlovian structure is based upon the hero: Tamburlaine rises in the first part and falls in the second. The Shakespearean structure is based upon historical process. The subject is not a mighty foreign warlord, but the very nation of England. In a sense, the action opens where *Tamburlaine* closes: with the question of what to do after a conquering warrior is dead and there is no single strong inheritor to take over from him. Henry V united England by fighting a war against France; what is to be done when the king is dead, the foreign war is over, the new king is a weakling, and rival factions are jostling for power? The Marlovian theme of the conquest of land is replaced by a Shakespearean interest in the government of land; instead of expanding without, the nation destroys itself from within. Scheming regents and lords replace tributary kings and loyal generals.

But Shakespeare's most striking innovation is not at the level of high politics. Dramatically, the strongest scenes in the play are those concerning Jack Cade's rebellion. Shakespeare's first history play, possibly his first play of any kind, is notable above all for its introduction into publicly staged historical drama of the common crowd.

Shakespeare, then, counters Marlowe with two moves: the shift from the exotic to the domestic, and the stylistic innovation which replaces Marlowe's univocal high-astounding terms with a dialogue between high and low, verse and prose, lords and commons. Tamburlaine's idiom is the only memorable one in his plays. Marlovian history is strikingly uninterested in the vulgar: *Edward II* begins with Gaveston's pushing aside of three poor men – rude grooms are not men for Marlowe. Marlowe taught Shakespeare the art of blank verse as the medium for noble characters and heightened emotions. Shakespeare's personal hallmark was the rapid switch between Marlovian and more vulgar idioms. Only in *Dr Faustus* and a few passages of *The Jew of Malta*, and then without his usual assurance, did Marlowe combine soaring blank verse with knockabout prose. Even Marlowe's own first printer took a dim view of his abilities in comedy: he took it upon himself to excise from the text of *Tamburlaine* all 'fond and frivolous gestures' and digressions from the play's high epic matter.

A groundling standing in the pit of the Rose theatre would have gaped at Tamburlaine because of the sheer difference between himself and the Scythian. Tamburlaine removes his shepherd's garb at the beginning of part one and acts like a lord for the rest of his life. With Jack Cade & Co., a groundling would have seen himself mirrored on the stage. He would have seen a plain man speaking of new-dressing the commonwealth of England from below. The Cade sub-plot is about a potential revolution. The historical fact of Cade's defeat and the knowledge that the play would have to pass through the hands of the censor before it could be performed ensured that Shakespeare rejected the possibility of realizing that potential on stage. His own political position cannot be inferred from the drama; what can, however, be inferred is that he was a great deal more interested in political forces than Marlowe was.

One particular emphasis does, however, suggest a genuine fear of anarchy on the dramatist's part. When Cade confronts the Lord Say, he charges him with two crimes: 'Thou hast most traitorously corrupted the youth of the realm in erecting a grammar school; and, whereas before, our forefathers had no other books but the score and the tally, thou hast caused printing to be used, and contrary to the King his crown and dignity, thou hast built a paper-mill.' There is some purposeful anachronism at work here: the first printing-press in England was established by William Caxton in 1477, twenty-seven years after Cade's rebellion, and the first paper-mill was new at the time of the play (it was built in 1588). The Lord Say may have established a grammar school (that at Sevenoaks in Cade's native Kent), but the great expansion of grammar schools belongs to the mid-sixteenth century. The corruption which Cade alludes to is really the enfranchisement from which Shakespeare benefited in his own youth. His father signed his name with a mark and almost certainly did not go to school. Shakespeare owed his reading, his writing, his ticket out of Stratford, and his new profession as a dramatist to exactly those innovations which Cade condemns: education and print.

Cade's attitude to literacy is dramatized a few scenes earlier in a moment of terrifying violence. He is sounding off about lawyers when one of his rabble brings in the Clerk of Chatham. The man can 'write and read'; he is therefore, Cade says, a 'conjuror'. He can sign his name instead of merely making a mark 'like an honest plain-dealing man'. This is regarded by the rabble as a confession of crime. Cade pronounces the sentence: 'Away with him, I say! Hang him with his pen and inkhorn about his neck' (4.2.85–110). The possibility that Shakespeare was a lawyer's clerk in his 'lost years' of the mid-1580s (the plays reveal a fair knowledge of legal matters) raises the fleeting idea that the Clerk is a kind of self-portrait. Even if we reject this, it must be highly significant that a young author who has forwarded himself by virtue of his literacy should portray a man being lynched by the vulgar for no other reason than that he is literate.

The clerk of Chatham is called a 'conjuror'. Earlier in *The First Part of the Contention* the witch Margery Jordan has conjured up a spirit to predict the fates of the King and the Dukes of Suffolk and Somerset. There has been a bit of spectacular stage business: '*Here do the ceremonies belonging, and make the circle. Southwell reads 'Conjuro te', etc. It thunders and lightens terribly; then the spirit Asnath riseth*' (1.4.23). This scene is not integral to the structure of the play; it has the air of being included because there was a theatrical fashion at the time for scenes in which spirits and devils are conjured up. This, surely, is Shakespeare's first – fairly lame – step in the footprints of *Dr Faustus*. The conjunction of the act of conjuring and the naming of the Clerk as a conjurer suggests that two aspects of Faustus are being split: his spectacle into Margery, his learning into the Clerk. The Clerk may thus be read as an image not only of Shakespeare himself, but also of Marlovian drama.

A similar attempt to challenge Marlowe through *splitting* may be seen in *Henry VI Part One*. By 1592, when that play had made Shakespeare's name sufficient of a threat to incur the notice of the university wits, Marlowe was pre-eminent upon the London stage. In the same dying breath, Robert Greene called Shakespeare an upstart crow and Marlowe a famous gracer of tragedians. Marlowe's plays were noted above all for two kinds of character and one kind of action. The characters were the military overreacher (Tamburlaine the exemplar) and the scheming machiavel (the exemplar being Barabas in *The Jew of Malta*, but with the Guise in *The Massacre at Paris* following close behind). The action was the magical spectacle of *Dr Faustus*. Shakespeare responded. He created the first military hero on the Elizabethan stage who was not an overreacher but a true Englishman: brave Talbot. And he matched this character against a figure who was both Faustus-like conjuror and cunning schemer: Joan la Pucelle.

By dramatizing the war between Talbot and Joan, Shakespeare showed that he could split the Marlovian achievement into halves which could be joined together into a new dramatic whole. He thus overcame the central weakness of all Marlowe's plays: their imbalance. In Marlowe until this point, the overreacher or machiavel or conjuror is so strong a presence, both linguistically and dramatically, that no one else in the plays has a chance of being fully realized.

The result of this breakthrough was that, for the first time, Shakespeare was pushing ahead in the game. If Thomas Nashe is to be believed, more than ten thousand spectators thronged to witness the Talbot–Joan clash. Marlowe responded in the manner of an elder brother who realizes that his sibling has the capacity to outstrip him. He began to be influenced by Shakespeare. His *Edward II* was almost certainly new when performed at court by the acting company of Pembroke's Men around Christmas 1592; it was thus his last surviving play.

Here Marlowe reined in his mighty line and resisted the temptation to let a single character dominate the action. He followed Shakespeare's example and turned to an English historical subject. He followed the Henry VI plays and made his central character a weak king, instead of the strong man who had been at the heart of all his previous dramas. He also followed the example of Shakespearean history in introducing a bevy of schéming barons. But because, unlike Shakespeare, he was not really interested in political questions – the clash between the need for legitimacy and the dire consequences of royal weakness – he couldn't stop the play trying to turn itself into the kind of drama he had written previously.

He thought that the danger man would be Gaveston, a thrilling machiavellian schemer who could easily have dominated the action. Marlowe overcame this potential problem by copying Shakespeare's device of *splitting*. Where Shakespeare had split Talbot and Joan, Marlowe split the single figure of the machiavel who trades on the king's proclivities. He killed off Gaveston halfway through and brought him back in the figure of Spencer. (Shakespeare made a note of the technique: if a character is getting out of hand and threatens to upset the balance of your play, kill him off halfway through – Mercutio in *Romeo and Juliet*.) But in concentrating on the problem of Gaveston, Marlowe didn't notice that the real danger man was Mortimer: *he* was the potential Tamburlaine or Barabas. The result is that there is a shadow of a play called 'the rise and fall of Mortimer' obscuring the tragedy of the fall of Edward II. The title-page to the 1593 quarto tried to accommodate it in the subtitle: *The troublesome Reign and lamentable Death of Edward the Second, King of England, with the tragical Fall of proud Mortimer.*

Shakespeare saw what Marlowe failed to see. In order to focus on the fall of the weak king, to make him the absolute centre of tragic interest, you must push the strong man all the way to the margins. In *Richard II*, which was Shakespeare's reply to *Edward II*, Bolingbroke is never given enough space to command attention. The consequence of this is that analysis of his rise has to be postponed and given retrospective attention in the context of its results – the civil broils after he has been crowned as King Henry IV. And the consequence of this is that the analysis becomes bound up with his wayward son, Prince Hal. Henry IV regards the riotous behaviour of his son as punishment for his own pursuit of a crooked path to the crown. In moving from Bolingbroke to his son, Shakespeare reverses the Marlovian pattern of rise and fall into a new pattern of fall and rise, charted in Hal's progress from a prince to a prentice to a king. And the consequence of this is that the Marlovian two-part structure could finally be overcome in the triumphant three-part structure of *Henry IV/Henry V*.

Richard II's relationship to *Edward II* is so obvious that it is not very interesting. The structure of the two plays is identical: the King is surrounded by flatterers and pitted against an assemblage of nobles with vested interests of their own, then isolated and uncrowned, stripped of his royal identity, thus forced to discover his inner self by means of a supple, reflective soliloquy delivered whilst humiliatingly in prison. In each play the Queen is pushed to the margins in part because of the king's homoerotic leanings. Marlowe is bolder than Shakespeare in his explicit portrayal of the homosexuality and his neat device of joining the Queen with the rebels in revenge.

The more interesting cross-dramatic relationship is that suggested in the mirror-scene which is the pivot of *Richard II*. The shattered mirror is a brilliant symbol of the splitting of the king's two bodies that is effected by the de-coronation. Once the glass is broken, Richard is himself alone, no longer both himself and the embodiment of the state. But when he calls for the mirror and looks in it, the face he sees is neither his own nor Edward's:

> Was this face the face
> That every day under his household roof
> Did keep ten thousand men? Was this the face
> That like the sun did make beholders wink?
> Is this the face which faced so many follies,
> That was at last out-faced by Bolingbroke?
> A brittle glory shineth in this face.
> As brittle as the glory is the face
> > *He shatters the glass.*
> For there it is, cracked in an hundred shivers.
> > (4.1.271–9)

This is one of the occasions on which we must speak of a *quotation*, not a mere verbal parallel. The relentless reiteration of the word 'face' and the interrogative form cannot but evoke some of Marlowe's most famous lines:

> Was this the face that launch'd a thousand ships,
> And burnt the topless towers of Ilium?
> Sweet Helen, make me immortal with a kiss:
> Her lips suck forth my soul, see where it flies.
> Come, Helen, come, give me my soul again.
> Here will I dwell, for heaven is in these lips,
> And all is dross that is not Helena.

What is going on here? Is the multiplication of Marlowe's thousand ships into ten thousand men an overgoing? Or an undercutting, since men are lesser things than ships and a 'household roof' is a poor thing in comparison to 'the topless towers of Ilium'? Either way, the quotation is a sign of Shakespeare's anxiety. It is as if he cannot help seeing his dramatic elder brother in his own poetic mirror.

Faustus imagines he is finding heaven in Helen's lips, but this is a poetic illusion, for 'Helen' is but a succubus and both his body and his soul will very soon be on their way down to hell. Richard's claim at his moment of death is another splitting: 'Mount, mount, my soul! thy seat is up on high, / Whilst my gross flesh sinks downward, here to die' (5.5.111–12). The distinction suggests that where Faustus follows the flesh and pays the price, Richard learns first to abandon the flesh (the shattering of the glass being a symbol for the rejection of worldly vanity) and then to educate his spirit into mortification, with the result that his soul can rise. If that is the case, then Shakespeare's conclusion looks tamely orthodox. Marlowe imposed orthodoxy on the end of *Dr Faustus*, perhaps in order to please the censor, but whilst his poetic energy remains at full charge in Faustus' final soliloquy, the challenge of the irreligious overreacher is maintained at full force.

In boldness of both language and plot, *Dr Faustus* remains far out in front of *Richard II*. Shakespeare has reclaimed the debt of *Edward II* to his own history plays, but in pure tragedy he is not yet ready to tackle *Faustus*. His first encounters with that play were the localized conjuring scenes in the *Henry VI* plays. Now he has moved towards a linguistic challenge, but he does not seem able to stretch himself beyond a gesture of homage and mild adaptation. The acid test, as always, is endurance. Dozens of Shakespearean speeches survive in the popular imagination, but Richard's address to his own face is not one of them. One of Marlowe's speeches survives in the popular imagination: it is Faustus' address to the image of Helen's face. The Marlovian glass has not yet been smashed to shivers.

Shakespeare the overreacher

There had been other developments prior to *Richard II*. Shakespeare tried out two versions of the Marlovian overreacher in his first major tragedies, plays which I attach to the period of his reemergence as a dramatist after the plague closures which led him down the bypath of non-dramatic writing. In the first of those plays, *Titus Andronicus*, he performed a *double splitting* of Marlowe.

He took *The Jew of Malta* as his prime model. It gave him one of the play's structures: a sequence of revenges and counter-revenges is brought to a climax with an invitation to a meal in which an ambush is sprung and bloody revenge is executed. By a nice twist, where Barabas ends up falling into a giant cooking-pot, Tamora Queen of Goths ends up eating something very nasty which comes out of Titus' kitchen: the heads of her own two sons, baked in a pasty. *The Jew of Malta* also gave Shakespeare key ideas for his villains. The remark which begins innocuously but has a stinging aside in the tail, the tendency to pun and stab in the same breath, the sheer delight in villainy: these are learnt from Marlowe. More specifically, Aaron the Moor's catalogue of villainous misdeeds, spoken with relish towards the end of *Titus Andronicus*, is closely modelled on an exchange between Barabas and his slave Ithamore in which they outdo each other in outrageous ill-doing.

But Shakespeare also recognized that the Marlovian villain is a kind of hero, an extreme embodiment of the Renaissance self-made man. An outsider, he aspires to unimaginable heights before he tumbles to his fall; the theatre audience delights in his energy and inventiveness, especially when he confides in us through soliloquy or aside. Morally, we know that we should condemn him, but dramatically we are mesmerized by him, especially when his language takes poetic flight. Aaron's first soliloquy – a trial run for that of the villainous Edmund early in *King Lear* ('Thou, Nature, art my goddess') – is in just this mode. 'Now climbeth Tamora Olympus' top ... Then, Aaron, ...

mount aloft with thy imperial mistress' has the distinct smack of
Tamburlaine's 'scale the icy mountains' lofty tops' or Faustus' heights:

> Learned Faustus . . .
> Did mount him up to scale Olympus top,
> Where, sitting in a chariot burning bright
> Drawn by the strength of yoked dragons' necks,
> He views the clouds, the planets, and the stars.

Aaron the Moor's speech is one of the first great villain's soliloquies in
Shakespeare. A direct line passes from Marlowe via the scheming Moor
to Iago, the schemer who brings down the noble Moor, to Edmund in
Lear.

Shakespeare's double splitting of a Marlovian model occurs through
the dual invention of Aaron the Moor and Tamora Queen of Goths.
They are both Marlovian overreachers. One of them is a Moor, an
outsider to match Marlowe's Jew, but the other is a woman. The
importance of Tamora is that she is Shakespeare's first powerfully active
woman – Queen Margaret, the dominant female in the *Henry VI* plays,
was more prophet than performer, more voice than actor. Marlowe's
women were never active, were hardly realized at all. The transformation of the Marlovian overreacher into a woman gave Shakespeare the
idea for two of his greatest female characters: the ambitious Lady
Macbeth and the magnificent Cleopatra.

Tamora and Aaron are not only overreachers, they are also machiavels. Yet they are also both sufferers: they both have their children
ripped from them. They elicit a measure of audience sympathy. Barabas
in Marlowe's *Jew of Malta* does not really love his daughter – he always
puts his wealth before her. The humanizing of Tamora and Aaron in
Titus Andronicus is a key development away from Marlowe which
prepares the way for the moral complexity of Shakespeare's later
tragedies. Edmund in *King Lear* is not only a scheming machiavel, but
also a victim of his lowly status as both a younger and an illegitimate
son. To judge from the opening scene of the play, his father has
neglected him. And in the closing scene, when Edmund takes comfort
in the belief that he was beloved by both Regan and Goneril, we begin
to wonder whether all his villainy was but the consequence of his not
having been loved.

Shakespeare's other combined machiavel/overreacher is Richard of

Gloucester, who becomes Richard III. The character first makes his mark in *The True Tragedy of Richard Duke of York*. He is instantly established as a Marlovian figure:

> Therefore to arms! And, father, do but think
> How sweet a thing it is to wear a crown,
> Within whose circuit is Elysium
> And all that poets feign of bliss and joy.
>
> (1.2.28–31)

This is very nearly a direct allusion to Marlowe. The poet who most famously feigned of the sweetness of wearing a crown was the author of *Tamburlaine*:

> The thirst of reign and sweetness of a crown . . .
> Mov'd me to manage arms against thy state. . . .
> Our souls, whose faculties can comprehend
> The wondrous architecture of the world,
> And measure every wand'ring planet's course,
> Still climbing after knowledge infinite,
> And always moving as the restless spheres,
> Wills us to wear ourselves and never rest
> Until we reach the ripest fruit of all,
> That perfect bliss and sole felicity,
> The sweet fruition of an earthly crown.

These lines constitute one of Tamburlaine's most magnificent blasphemies: the rhetorical ladder sets up the expectation of an ascent towards heavenly bliss, but by a brilliant twist the speech ends up with the sweetness of the earthly crown with which it began. Marlowe's greatest blasphemy is to bring Tamburlaine's aspirations crashing down not when he subdues a Christian kingdom or massacres the innocent virgins of Damascus, but when he insults a holy book – which turns out to be not the Bible, but the Koran, which Marlowe's audience would have regarded as an infidel text. It is Mahomet, not the Christian God, who seems to strike down the self-styled scourge of God.

Tamburlaine really seems to believe that he is God's scourge. Shakespeare's Richard takes a different view. For Tamburlaine, unbending physical strength is the prerequisite for military conquest; that is why he is so incensed by his effete son, Calyphas. For Richard, pursuit of the crown is compensation for physical deformity. It is also a self-conscious performance. At the climax of his first long soliloquy in *The True Tragedy* (3.2.188–95), he announces that he will 'play the orator', 'add colours to the chameleon', and 'Change shapes with Proteus for advantage': each image is of the art of the actor, with his persuasive tongue and power of self-transformation.

Richard adds that he will 'set the murderous Machiavel to school'. In *The Jew of Malta*, Marlowe had brought on a representation of the politic Machiavelli to speak the prologue. As soon as the Prologue leaves the stage, Barabas the Jew is revealed, speaking his opening soliloquy. The audience thus makes the equation that Barabas is a machiavellian schemer. Shakespeare made a bold advance in *Richard III*. He dispensed with the prologue and began the action with Richard's riveting soliloquy, 'Now is the winter of our discontent'. Where Marlowe had cast Barabas in the role of the machiavel by means of a pointed structural device, Shakespeare's Richard casts himself. He announces that since his crookback prevents him from playing the role of a stage-lover, he will self-consciously adopt that of a stage-villain.

For good measure, he goes on in the second scene to show that he *can* in fact play the lover – with such accomplishment that he successfully woos Lady Anne over the corpse of the father of her first husband, both of whom he has killed. As promised, he plays the orator to supreme effect. By the third act, he is changing shapes with Proteus and appearing between two bishops in the colour of a holy man. By means of the orator's art of saying the opposite of what he means – 'I cannot, nor I will not' accept the crown – he wins over the mayor and citizens of London.

The character of Richard III is Shakespeare's overstepping of the Marlovian (anti-)hero. Tamburlaine, Barabas and Faustus fashion their identities by assuming roles – scourge of God, machiavel, conjuror. They do not stop to think that such roles are precisely that: flimsy theatrical impersonations. If they did stop, the whole Marlovian house of cards would come tumbling down. But Shakespeare began from a different place. *He was an actor himself.* This was the one trump card which was unavailable to Marlowe. Richard is quintessentially Shakespearean, supremely charismatic in the theatre, because he knows that he is a role-player. He revels, and makes the audience revel, in play-

acting. He is the first full embodiment of a Shakespearean obsession
which culminates in Macbeth's 'poor player' and Prospero's 'These our
actors'.

It is Iago who says 'I am not what I am' (*Othello*, 1.1.65). But
Richard could have said it too. And so, as the critic Lionel Trilling has
remarked, could almost every one of Shakespeare's most memorable
characters:

> Hamlet has no sooner heard out the Ghost than he resolves to be
> what he is not, a madman. Rosalind is not a boy, Portia is not a
> doctor of law, Juliet is not a corpse, the Duke Vincentio is not a friar,
> Edgar is not Tom o' Bedlam, Hermione is neither dead nor a statue.
> Helena is not Diana, Mariana is not Isabella.

Marlowe's characters invest everything in their aspirations; Shakespeare's are more flexible. They are not what they are. That is surely
because Shakespeare was an actor and Marlowe was not; it is also one
reason why Shakespeare's characters have a richer, more varied and
continuous stage afterlife than Marlowe's.

Only in his dreams does Richard stop acting. And when that
happens, his identity collapses:

> Richard loves Richard; that is, I am I;
> Is there a murderer here? No. Yes, I am. . . .
> I am a villain. Yet I lie: I am not.
> (*Richard III*, 5.5.136–7, 145)

Since he has forged his identity through acting, Richard denies the
possibility of an essential being that is anterior to performance. He
cannot sustain a language of being – 'I am', 'I am not' – because he
keeps coming back to particular roles ('villain') and actions (murdering).
The moment when an authentic self ought to be asserted, as in a
deathbed repentance, becomes that when the self collapses. This is an
actor-dramatist's way of looking at the nature of human being.

The ghosts who appear to him in his dream the night before the last
battle make him realize that actions have consequences: murder will
bring him 'to the bar' and a verdict of 'guilty' will be pronounced. This
final emphasis upon guilt is the pragmatic Shakespeare's correction of
the blasphemous Marlowe towards religious and moral orthodoxy.
Having been granted his earthly crown, Richard is defeated by Henry

of Richmond, who has spent the night before the battle of Bosworth
Field in pious prayer to the Christian God: 'O Thou whose captain I
account myself, / Look on my forces with a gracious eye' (*Richard III*,
5.5.61–2). The fall of the overreacher is thus yoked to the Tudor myth
of that providential scheme of history which combined the houses of
York and Lancaster and established the dynasty which brought unity,
then Reformation and imperial glory to the nation.

Richmond's prayer prepares for King Harry's similar words of piety
on the night before the battle of Agincourt in *Henry V*. It was with the
trilogy of Prince Hal/King Harry plays that Shakespeare finally
triumphed over both Marlowe's two-part structure and his character-
type of the bold and ambitious aspirer after power or knowledge.
Several critics have noted the structural similarity between *Tamburlaine*
and *Henry V*: the winning of battles with a small number of brave
followers fighting against apparently impossible odds; the prologues
(and in the case of *Henry V*, the choruses throughout) directing the
audience's response; the hero as military leader who regards his troops
as brothers one moment and followers the next; the marriage to a
defeated king's daughter (the woman having no choice in the matter,
simply doing the best she can to salvage her father); the irony of the
warrior king not being able to sustain his conquests for long, since he
has a weak son (Calyphas in *Tamburlaine*, the forward reference to
Henry VI at the end of *Henry V*, which circles us back to the plays in
which Shakespeare first took on *Tamburlaine*).

A simple reading of *Henry V* would propose that Shakespeare has
simply inverted the character of Tamburlaine: where the Scythian
Shepherd's conquests are made for his own glory, King Harry's are for
the glory of God. But Shakespeare was more sophisticated than this.
He recognized that military victory cannot be achieved without cruelty.
Whilst remaining a threat rather than a performed action, Harry's words
in the third act about spiking the infants of Harfleur and 'mowing like
grass / Your fresh fair virgins' clearly echo Tamburlaine's most appalling
deed, the killing of the virgins of Damascus. And King Harry does kill
the French prisoners, expressly against the law of arms. Furthermore, in
the context of the trilogy as a whole we know that Harry is following
his father's advice about how to avoid the civil broils which afflicted
his own reign:

> Therefore, my Harry,
> Be it thy course to busy giddy minds
> With foreign quarrels, that action hence borne out
> May waste the memory of the former days.
>   (*2 Henry IV*, 4.3.341–4)

If this is what Harry is doing in France, then he is risking the lives of his men for a pretty machiavellian cause.

Harry also has a rival for the mantle of Tamburlaine. The most famous moment in *Tamburlaine* is that in the second part when the protagonist enters in a chariot drawn by two kings with bits in their mouths. He cries, 'Holla, ye pampered jades of Asia! / What, can ye draw but twenty miles a day?' (4.3.1–2). These words are equally famously parodied by Ancient Pistol in *Henry IV Part Two*: 'hollow pampered jades of Asia, / Which cannot go but thirty mile a day' (2.4.161–2). The point of all Pistol's quotations is that they are poetic old hat. Tamburlaine's rhetoric is implied to be linguistically *hollow* because it is horribly stuffed with bombast, is associated with the strut and rant of that outdated style of acting which Hamlet also makes a point of mocking. The Pistol who follows Harry to France is Tamburlaine's ghost, always ready to pop up and discompose the king, a reminder that fine rhetoric – rousing speeches about bands of brothers, for instance – is sometimes mere vaunt, motivated by self-promotion.

Pistol is, however, a double ghost. He is the trace not only of Tamburlaine, but also of Falstaff. At the end of *Henry IV Part Two*, Shakespeare had promised his audience that he would take Sir John Falstaff to France with the fifth Harry. But when he sat down to write *Henry V*, he realized that he could not do so. The *Henry IV* plays throve on that balance between high and low, noble and vulgar, verse and prose, which had been initiated in *The First Part of the Contention*. But the lesson of the Marlovian overreacher was that he could have no rival, no distracting force.

If Shakespeare was to transform the Marlovian warrior-antihero into the mirror of all Christian kings, he had to retain the same structure: Hal had defeated a rival Tamburlaine-figure in the form of Hotspur in *Henry IV Part One*, but his other rival, the wholly un-Marlovian Falstaff, bounced back in *Part Two* and proved a great deal more difficult to lay to rest. If Falstaff had been allowed to France, he might well have overshadowed Harry. He therefore had to be killed off. Only his Page and some of his friends survive.

The biggest of these survivors is Pistol. His language is the nearest Shakespeare allows himself in *Henry V* to a Falstaffian voice; his actions on the battlefield of Agincourt (the capture of Monsieur le Fer) are shadows of Falstaff's actions on the battlefield of Gaultree (the capture of Sir John Colvile of the Dale). Pistol is a constant reminder that the price of Harry's greatness is the rejection of Falstaff.

Great reckonings

Shakespeare does not only remind us of the rejection of Falstaff. He also includes in *Henry V* a detailed narrative of the *death* of Falstaff. We hear how Sir John died, his heart killed by the king, in a (presumably small) room in Hostess Quickly's tavern.

We can date the composition of *Henry V* with unusual precision because the Chorus makes an allusion to the Earl of Essex's Irish expedition: the play almost certainly belongs to the year 1599. Two years earlier, in 1597, Thomas Beard had included in his book *The Theatre of God's Judgements* the first published account of Christopher Marlowe's gruesome death. Then in 1598 Meres published his *Palladis Tamia*, with its remark about Marlowe being killed by a rival for his lewd love. Meres described the rival as a 'bawdy servingman', implicitly locating the crime in a tavern. Also in 1598, Marlowe's unfinished erotic narrative poem, *Hero and Leander*, reached print for the first time, with a continuation by George Chapman. And it was in 1599 that 'The Passionate Shepherd to his Love', the most celebrated of Marlowe's poetic works, already widely known in manuscript, was published for the first time, albeit in a poor quality text:

> Live with me and be my love,
> And we will all the pleasures prove
> That hills and valleys, dales and fields,
> And all the craggy mountains yield . . .

The book in which this lyric appeared was entitled *The Passionate Pilgrim*. That would seem to be an obvious enough home for the 'passionate shepherd', save that, as we saw in chapter two, the title-page announced that it was 'by W. Shakespeare'. Shakespeare could not but have been mildly embarrassed to have a book in print – going through two editions within a matter of months – with his name on the title-page but with its major highlight being the most famous poem of his dead contemporary.

I suspect that it was with this conjunction of affairs on his mind that in *As You Like It*, probably also written in 1599, Shakespeare made his most explicit allusions to Marlowe. Phoebe, on seeing Rosalind (dressed as the boy Ganymede), proclaims 'Dead shepherd, now I find thy saw of might: "Who ever loved that loved not at first sight?"' Marlowe is called a shepherd because he was the author of 'The Passionate Shepherd to his Love'. Phoebe's quotation is a celebrated line from *Hero and Leander*. In the very next scene, Rosalind alludes to the same poem, playfully denigrating it by saying that when Leander drowned as he swam across the Hellespont, it was of the cramps, not as a result of his love for the lovely Hero. 'Men have died', says Rosalind knowingly, 'from time to time, and worms have eaten them, but not for love' (4.1.100). Could this even be a quiet reply to Meres: when the reckoning was drawn up at Deptford, the death was not for Marlowe's *love*?

Many critics have heard an allusion to Marlowe's death, precipitated by a quarrel over a 'reckoning', in a remark of Touchstone's a couple of scenes before the explicit allusion to Marlowe as 'dead shepherd': 'it strikes a man more dead than a great reckoning in a little room'. This seems to combine the ill-fated Deptford bill with a famous Marlovian line about money in Barabas' dazzling opening soliloquy in *The Jew of Malta*: 'Infinite riches in a little room'. There is, then, a cluster of Marlovian allusions at this point in *As You Like It*.

I have suggested that the murdered Clerk in *The First Part of the Contention* was Shakespeare's first portrait of the artist as a young man. Marlowe made the idea of the murdered writer more explicit in *The Massacre at Paris*, his play about the slaughter of French Protestants at the hands of the Duke of Guise on St Bartholomew's Day 1572.

Few of the victims of the massacre initiated by the Guise are individualized, but one is a historically identifiable figure. In the play's ninth scene, the famous rhetorician Peter Ramus is discovered in his study. He is doing no harm; rather than conjuring, Faustus-like, he is quietly reading upon a book. The Guise has him stabbed to death for a crime no greater than his modernization of logic and rhetoric, his attack on Aristotelian scholasticism. From Marlowe's point of view, Aristotelianism here stands for benighted medieval Catholicism, whereas Ramus is a representative of the Reformation. Retes, one of the Guise's followers, spares Ramus' companion Taleus because 'he is a Catholic' – the clear implication is that Ramus will not be allowed to escape because he is an embodiment of Protestantism.

But, interestingly, Taleus is also described as 'Ramus' bedfellow'. Rather as the barons in *Edward II* despise Gaveston not because of his homosexuality but because of his base birth, Ramus is not killed for having a male bedfellow. As it was tempting to see a Shakespearean self-portrait in the lawyer's clerk, so it is tempting to see a Marlovian self-portrait in Taleus. Imagine the character turning against Catholicism as a result of the assassination of his lover – he then becomes the homosexual who slips away from a near-encounter with death and lives on to witness in his drama against the barbarities of Catholicism (and in his life to assist in the suppression of Catholicism by means of his participation in Sir Thomas Walsingham's secret service).

The figure of the murdered writer is reclaimed by Shakespeare in *Julius Caesar*. And this time it is explicitly a poet. Cinna the Poet is torn to pieces by the crowd solely because of a word, the name which he happens to share with one of the conspirators. When he distinguishes himself from Cinna the conspirator, he is told that he will be torn to pieces for his bad verses. At one level, Cinna the Poet is Shakespeare himself and all poets who make their living out of literacy and patronage, whether private or public. Shakespeare knows instinctively that civil war is not good news if you are a poet. At such a time, aristocrats have other things on their minds than accepting poetic dedications, while citizens have other things to do than paying pennies to go to plays. It would not have surprised Shakespeare to learn that the theatres would be closed when civil war broke out in England in 1642. But at another level, I do not think it is coincidental that the figure of the murdered writer which first emerged with the Clerk and Ramus reappears in a play written around the time that Shakespeare explicitly referred to Marlowe's death in *As You Like It.*

In 1599, Shakespeare wrote of two great reckonings with death in little tavern rooms: Marlowe's and Falstaff's. If, as I suggested in chapter one, one source for the death of Falstaff was the death of Robert Greene, then there is a further link with the 'university wits' and their deaths. Pistol's parodies are generally reminiscent of the drama of the late 1580s and early 1590s, when the stage was dominated by the university wits. Marlowe may then have served as shorthand – rhetorically speaking, as synecdoche – for the whole of the generation of dramatists whom Shakespeare overcame on his rise to theatrical pre-eminence.

Internally within Shakespeare's dramatic world, Pistol is a reminder of the down-to-earth tavern milieu associated with the dead Falstaff. Externally within Shakespeare's theatrical world, Pistol is a reminder of the heaven-ringing Tamburlainean verse associated with the dead Marlowe. What, then, is the relationship between Falstaff and Marlowe? In a wonderful essay in his book *Some Versions of Pastoral*, the critic William Empson noted the similarity between the language applied to the 'fair youth' in sonnet 94 and the language of Hal's first soliloquy, in which the rejection of Falstaff is foreshadowed. Empson suggested in passing that at a deep imaginative level – not the level of crude biographical correspondence – Hal might be Harry Wriothesley and Shakespeare might therefore be Falstaff.

Pursuing this intuition – for who would deny that Shakespeare is linguistically his most magnificent self in Falstaff? – I propose that in order to create a 'good overreacher' in the character of Henry V, and thus to kill off the legacy of Tamburlaine, Shakespeare also had to kill off some part of himself. The Falstaff part which he denied was precisely that part which was most himself, which had its origins in Cade, and which owed nothing to Marlowe.

Harry the Fifth clambers to greatness over the bodies of both Marlowe's mighty verse line, as epitomized by the dead Shepherd, Tamburlaine, and Shakespeare's own mighty wit, as epitomized by the dead Falstaff who is a genius of one kind of language which Marlowe never managed: living vernacular prose. King Harry's verse is glorious – Marlovian without being bombastic – but his wit, as witnessed in his feeble attempt to laugh Kate into acceptance of her forced marriage, is a poor thing indeed. The Marlovian overreacher could only be overreached at the cost of a denial of the most *distinctive* aspect of Shakespeare's own genius.

If Falstaff is Shakespeare's most distinctive creation, an idea to which

I will return in chapter seven, then there is a deep paradox about Shakespeare's work. His first hallmarked contribution to the art of the history play was Jack Cade; his wit's ultimate allegiance must have been to Falstaff. Yet Cade and Falstaff are anarchic forces, hardly compatible with Shakespeare's own upward mobility. He was becoming a gentleman just around the time his audiences were revelling in Falstaff's ungentlemanly conduct.

This, I suspect, is why Shakespeare paradoxically feared the vernacular that was his strength, and why he dramatized that fear in the lynching of the Clerk of Chatham and Cinna the Poet. Shakespeare was the 'upstart crow', the parvenu without a university degree, who drove the university wits out of the repertoire. His achievement prepared the way for other non-university dramatists, most notably Ben Jonson and John Webster. Remember this, and one begins to see another splitting: the *poet* in Shakespeare, who learnt his verse from Marlowe, is split from the *upstart wit* in him. The upstart wit's challenge to the university wits is enacted in the murder of the Clerk and Cinna, in Falstaff's challenge to the reformed Tamburlaine who is King Harry. And so we see why the two reckonings with death in little tavern rooms come into conjunction with each other. There is a Marlowe in Shakespeare: he kills Falstaff. There is a Cade in Shakespeare: he cannot avoid projecting himself into the role of Ingram Frizer, the murderer of Marlowe.

That affable familiar ghost

This, then, is how Shakespeare dealt with the legacy of the Tamburlainean overreacher. What did he do about the figure of the machiavel? Here we see a classic pattern of influence which leads to the complete triumph of the inheritor, the absorption and thus obliteration of the precursor.

Aaron in *Titus Andronicus* was the first step on the way, Richard III the second: as combined overreacher and machiavel, the latter outdid both Barabas the Jew and the massacring Guise. The figure of the Jew was further, and comprehensively, absorbed in *The Merchant of Venice*. The structural parallels are as clear as those between *Edward II* and *Richard II*. Marlowe's Barabas and Shakespeare's Shylock are both Jews who are usurers, are treacherous, are tricked out of their money and their daughter, are roundly defeated but remain figures of some sympathy because the Christians are no better than they are. Shakespeare was extraordinarily confident in his overgoing of *The Jew of Malta* in *The Merchant of Venice*. He took Barabas the usurer, a figure who absolutely dominated the action of what billed itself as a tragedy, and converted him into the traditional *senex* of comedy (the father who is reluctant for his daughter to marry and is therefore gulled out of her). He gave his version of the rich Jew a role in a mere five scenes of the play, and yet he made him into one of the most memorable characters in all literature. Again, the test of endurance is all-revealing: *The Merchant of Venice* has remained one of the most popular plays in the repertoire, a maker of reputations for actors such as Charles Macklin in the eighteenth century and Edmund Kean in the nineteenth, whilst *The Jew of Malta* has only ever been given a handful of revivals.

Having absorbed Barabas in Shylock, Shakespeare went on to create his greatest machiavels, who are no longer directly derivative from Marlowe: Iago in *Othello* and Edmund in *King Lear*. Since *The Merchant* is a comedy, Shylock could be described as a *parody* of Barabas. The pattern of first imitation, then parody, then free independent creation is typical of Shakespeare's relationship with Marlowe. We may see this at work in several different areas.

Consider the matter of desire. *The Two Gentlemen of Verona* begins with some banter about the nature of love. Proteus says that he will pray for Valentine's success in love 'upon some book' that he loves. I would wager that the book in question is Marlowe's *Hero and Leander*.

> VALENTINE That's on some shallow story of deep love –
> How young Leander crossed the Hellespont.
> PROTEUS That's a deep story of a deeper love,
> For he was more than over-shoes in love.
>
> (1.1.21–4)

This is the first phase: mere imitation. *Hero and Leander* is a crisper, more memorable, anatomy of desire than is *The Two Gentlemen of Verona*.

Shakespeare's next move is to write his own poem in the style of *Hero and Leander*. If Shakespeare knew his rival's poem in manuscript, and not merely by reputation, he would have noticed that Hero's garment depicted the story of Venus and Adonis. That could have been the starting point for his own choice of erotic subject out of Ovid's *Metamorphoses*. *Venus and Adonis* is a comic version of Marlowe's tale of a lovely boy — except that the lad Adonis is in love with himself and out of love with the idea of love. Where Marlowe's Hero was Venus' Nun, Shakespeare's female character is not a virgin girl but a very unchaste Venus herself. This is the second phase of Shakespeare's treatment of Marlovian love-writing: parody. As such, it perforce underestimates the strength of the precursor work, the way in which *Hero and Leander* is simultaneously a moving love-elegy and itself a wickedly comic parody.

Then a couple of years later, Shakespeare returns to the theme and writes *Romeo and Juliet*, a tragedy of love which — whilst its quick bright language still has a profoundly Marlovian tonality — owes none of its matter to Marlowe. This is the third phase: free independent creation.

Again, consider the matter of Troy. Marlowe, probably in collaboration with Nashe, writes *Dido Queen of Carthage*, at the centre of which is Aeneas' narration of the Fall of Troy. Shakespeare first portrays static pictures of Troy in his rhetorically top-heavy poem, *The Rape of Lucrece*: mere imitation. Then some years later, the player in *Hamlet* closely imitates the descriptive language of Aeneas in Marlowe's play. Aeneas in *Dido* incants, 'At last came Pyrrhus, fell and full of ire, / His harness dropping blood, and on his spear / The mangled head of Priam's youngest son'. The player in *Hamlet* hams, 'The rugged Pyrrhus . . . Now is he total gules, horribly tricked / With blood of fathers, mothers, daughters, sons'. This is not mere imitation, for Marlowe's language is being parodied, set up as an old-fashioned, inflated idiom that contrasts with the fresh, supple inwardness of Hamlet's own discourse. Having passed through this phase, Shakespeare is then able to advance to the third one, in which he converts the Dido and Aeneas story into the Antony and Cleopatra story without any recourse to Marlowe.

As a third example, consider Faustus' magic. First Shakespeare imitates it with Margery Jordan in *The First Part of the Contention*. Then he parodies it in a comic conjuring scene in *Henry VI Part One*, in which Joan la Pucelle summons up a bevy of fiends only to find them obstinately refusing to obey her will, hanging and shaking their heads in response to her demands. Then he independently creates his own play of black magic and incantation in *Macbeth*.

But for once this is not the end of the story. By the time we reach the Jacobean years, Shakespeare has triumphantly overcome *Tamburlaine, Dido, The Jew of Malta, The Massacre at Paris* and *Edward II*. The measure of his triumph is, again, that none of these plays have endured in the repertoire, save for isolated revivals. *Hero and Leander* has, I suspect, continued to find readers because Shakespeare never bettered it in its own form; he only did so through the shift of medium represented by *Romeo and Juliet*. But *Macbeth* did not put an end to the anxiety of *Faustus'* influence.

It was not until his very last solo-authored play that Shakespeare came to final grips with *Dr Faustus*. Unable to surpass its representation of black magic, he created a white magician instead. But the way in which Prospero cannot quite differentiate his own powers from those of Sycorax – the way in which he has to acknowledge Sycorax's child as his own thing of darkness – suggests that the battle is not wholly lost and won. When Prospero says 'I'll drown my book', he is clearly echoing Faustus' last unfulfilled promise, 'I'll burn my books'. The fact that the quotation bobs up to the surface of *The Tempest* shows that Shakespeare is still haunted by Marlowe. The one play he was unable to drown was *Dr Faustus*. And, sure enough, that is the one pre-Shakespearean play to endure in the theatrical repertoire. For a very long time now, the core of English Renaissance drama has been regarded as Shakespeare's works, a handful of post-Shakespearean achievements (by Jonson in comedy, Webster and Middleton in tragedy), and Marlowe's *Dr Faustus*.

As we saw in chapter two, interpreters of Shakespeare's Sonnets divide themselves into two camps. There are those who regard the poems as autobiographical and therefore seek for the 'originals' of the fair youth, the dark lady and the rival poet. And there are those who regard them as brilliant rhetorical exercises in the conventions of sonnet-matter, who point out that virtually every situation imagined in the sequence's narrative has its parallels in prior sequences. The trope of the rival poet stealing the poet's love, and by implication clientage, is no exception to this. I argued in chapter two that the truth lies between the two camps, that the Sonnets are best regarded as *imaginings of potential situations which might have grown* from the initial Southampton situation. It is in this way that I think we should read the identity of the chief rival poet.

There is no evidence that Marlowe sought Southampton's patronage in the last months of his life. There is some evidence that others did, Tom Nashe and Barnabe Barnes for instance. The 'rival poets' sequence – sonnets 78 to 86 – begins with several rivals. Shakespeare writes of *every* alien pen and of *others'* works. Suppose that these initial rivals were, say, Nashe, Barnes, and Florio. But then Shakespeare *imagines* a more powerful rival coming on the scene. In sonnet 80, he calls him 'a better spirit'. A 'spirit'? Could he conceivably be a dead poet?

This great rival writes verse in mighty lines which have the stately motion of a great ship at full sail. It is the poet of the mighty line who comes to dominate the sequence and to triumph in sonnet 86:

> Was it the proud full sail of his great verse
> Bound for the prize of all-too-precious you
> That did my ripe thoughts in my brain inhearse,
> Making their tomb the womb wherein they grew?
> Was it his spirit, by spirits taught to write
> Above a mortal pitch, that struck me dead?
> No, neither he, nor his compeers by night
> Giving him aid, my verse astonishèd.
> He, nor that affable familiar ghost
> Which nightly gulls him with intelligence,
> As victors, of my silence cannot boast;
> I was not sick of any fear from thence
> > But when your countenance filled up his line,
> > Then lacked I matter; that enfeebled mine.

The power of this rival is so great that Shakespeare imagines himself silenced. He seems to be saying: I am not afraid of my rival's inherent poetic art, but I am struck dumb by the thought of his powers of expression in conjunction with the beauty of the patron/lover.

For biographical interpreters, the two most plausible candidates for this character are George Chapman and Christopher Marlowe. 'Compeers by night' has been linked to Chapman's poem *The Shadow of Night*, and the 'full sail' to the ample fourteen-syllable line of Chapman's translation of Homer. The 'spirit' has been supposed to be that of Homer himself, under whose guidance Chapman claimed to have undertaken his translation. If we assume that Shakespeare's eighty-sixth sonnet was written late in the 1590s, such a reading is plausible.

If Homer is the spirit in line five, then who is the affable familiar ghost in line nine? Could the word *intelligence* be significant here? Could there have been gossip and rumour in the London theatrical world concerning writers who crossed over into the murky world of espionage? If so, then the affable ghost begins to take on the shape of the dead poet and intelligence agent, Christopher Marlowe. Perhaps he is to be imagined feeding *Hero and Leander* to Chapman, gulling him into supposing that he could complete the poem. Shakespeare need not have been sick of any fear from thence: he knew that Chapman's completion of Marlowe's unfinished poem, published with it in 1598, was a heavy-handed thing indeed. In its playful sprightliness, his own *Venus and Adonis* was a far truer continuation of *Hero and Leander.*

If we suppose an earlier date for this sonnet, a time of composition closer to the original involvement with the house of Southampton, the rival poet has to be Marlowe himself. In the mid-1590s he remained synonymous with the mighty line, the proud full sail of the iambic pentameter. According to this reading, the spirits are those conjured up by Faustus and the affable familiar ghost is the character of Mephistophilis.

We do not have to suppose Marlowe or Chapman actually seeking the patronage or love of Shakespeare's patron or lover. We do not have to choose between Marlowe and Chapman as the 'he' of the poem. We do not have to decide whether Marlowe was alive or dead when the poem was written. Whatever the precise circumstances of composition, one can feel that the driving-force of the sonnet is Shakespeare's anxiety at the idea of a more powerful poet than himself addressing the fair youth.

Whether he is there from line one or there as the intelligencer beyond the grave, or both, Marlowe has to be there as the ghost in the machine of this sonnet. And what he is doing is striking Shakespeare dumb, *inhearsing* him, burying him. He is there because Shakespeare knew that, alive or dead, he had no rival but Marlowe. His only way of proving himself was through the conceit of pretending that Marlowe's influence on the youth has struck him poetically dumb, has metaphorically killed him. But since it is Shakespeare who is writing the poem, we know that this is only a conceit and that in fact it is Shakespeare who is metaphorically killing Marlowe. As Harold Bloom would say, the poem is not *about* Shakespeare's anxiety regarding Marlowe. Rather, it *is* that anxiety.

William Gleason Zeigler and Calvin Hoffman thought that Shakespeare was nothing but Marlowe's ghost writer. They were wrong. But in a more profound way they were right. Marlowe did come back from the dead after the Deptford stabbing: his ghost astonishes us even as we read and hear the verse of Shakespeare.

5

SHAKESPEARE'S PECULIARITY

'Great men are more distinguished by range and extent,
than by originality. . . . The greatest genius is the most
indebted man.'

      – Ralph Waldo Emerson, 'Shakspeare'

Inheriting the repertoire

A good poet's made as well as born. All creative artists have to learn
their craft. What makes a writer, apart from innate talent? School is the
place where most writers begin. It was there that Shakespeare learnt to
read and write; to write, moreover, in a particular way, with an
emphasis on linguistic virtuosity and copiousness. At some point after
school comes the decision to try to make a career out of writing.
Usually at this stage, the young writer falls under the influence of an
admired exemplar. One of the principal stories of any writer's early
career is the attempt to throw off that influence, to pass beyond
imitation and to find a distinctive voice. I proposed in the last chapter
that for the young Shakespeare the admired exemplar was Christopher
Marlowe.

No writer's life is, however, solely the story of a battle with a single
master. Shakespeare began his career as an actor. He would thus have
gained an intimate knowledge of the theatrical repertoire of his time.
Day after day, he would have acted in plays, old and new. One can
imagine the writer in him thinking, 'I could have done that better, I
could rework this scene more interestingly.'

Anti-Stratfordians like to represent Elizabethan Stratford-upon-Avon
as a rural backwater that was wholly devoid of culture. We have already
seen that this was not the case as far as schooling was concerned. Nor
was it the case when it came to public entertainment. In 1568, John

Shakespeare was elected high bailiff – effectively mayor – of Stratford. During his tenure, two companies of travelling players, the Queen's Men and the Earl of Worcester's Servants, performed in the town Guildhall. After his tenure expired, Shakespeare's father became high alderman, and deputy to the new bailiff, his friend Adrian Quiney. (It was Quiney's son, Richard, who in 1598 wrote the only surviving letter addressed to William Shakespeare, a request for a financial loan.) During Adrian Quiney's tenure as bailiff, another company, the Earl of Leicester's Men, played in Stratford. As high alderman, John Shakespeare would certainly have been entitled to good seats for himself and his family, so the performance by Leicester's Men may well have been the nine-year-old William's first trip to see a play. By a neat coincidence, the leading player was James Burbage, whose son Richard was to become Shakespeare's closest theatrical colleague.

During the 1580s, the Queen's Men were reconstituted and became the most celebrated acting company in the land. Their brightest star was Richard Tarlton, the age's greatest comedian. Stratford remained on their touring itinerary. They visited in 1586 and 1587. In 1587, the company played in Oxfordshire before going on to Warwickshire. Disaster struck them at Thame: William Knell, one of their leading actors, died of a sword wound to his throat. It is a pleasing fantasy to suppose that the company consequently arrived in Stratford one player short and departed a few days later with a new recruit, a lad with the same name as the dead actor: William. The timing is propitious, for it would give Shakespeare a couple of seasons – 1587 to 1589, say – to have learnt his trade as an actor, in exactly the period when Marlowe and his contemporaries were revitalizing the theatre, before making his own first attempts as a writer.

Even if this possible route to the London theatrical world is discounted, it may be assumed with some degree of assurance that the Stratford visits of the Queen's Men would have given Shakespeare the opportunity to see some of the latest new plays of the period immediately before the advent of Marlowe and the university wits.

The repertoire of the Queen's Men at this time included a set of thematically linked one-act dramas produced under the title *Five Plays in One*. One of the five was a dramatization of Ovid's story of the rape of Philomel and the bloody revenge in which the sons of Tereus, her rapist, are dished up in a pie. Is it a coincidence that one of Shakespeare's early plays, *Titus Andronicus*, was a dramatization of the same plot?

Another drama which the company may well have brought to Stratford was one which they played at court in January 1585, *The History of Felix and Feliomena*. This work is lost, but its title suggests that it was a dramatization of a story in Jorge de Montemayor's Spanish romance, *Diana Enamorada*. The story tells of a girl called Felismena and her beloved, Don Felix. He leaves home and she follows him, disguised in male apparel. She overhears him wooing another woman, Celia. Felismena, calling herself Valerius, gains employment as Don Felix's page; he uses her as emissary in his courtship of Celia. An exchange of letters plays a central role in the development of the affair. Celia asks about Don Felix's former love; Felismena-dressed-as-Valerius thus finds herself talking movingly about herself. The result is that Celia promptly falls in love with him/her. After a variety of further twists, Felismena is restored to her identity and reunited with Felix in a forest.

The main plot of Shakespeare's early comedy *The Two Gentlemen of Verona* tells of a girl called Julia and her beloved, Proteus. He leaves home and she follows him, disguised in male apparel. She overhears him wooing another woman, Silvia. Julia, calling herself Sebastian, gains employment as Proteus' page; he uses her as emissary in his courtship of Silvia. A letter plays a central role in the development of the affair. Silvia asks about Proteus' former love; Julia-dressed-as-Sebastian thus finds herself talking movingly about herself. The result is that Silvia is encouraged in her determination to remain constant to her beloved, Valentine, and not to give in to the advances of either Proteus or the foolish Thurio, who is also wooing her. After a variety of twists, Julia is restored to her identity and reunited with Proteus in a forest.

We cannot exactly praise Shakespeare for the originality of his invention in this play. *The Two Gentlemen of Verona* establishes the pattern for Shakespeare's mature comedies, with their twists and turns of courtship, their marvellous sympathy for a leading female character – Rosalind, Viola – who spends much of the time cross-dressed in boy's apparel. And yet the pattern is manifestly taken from the story of Felismena and Felix. Just how deeply the influence penetrated may be seen from the fact that Shakespeare omitted from *Two Gentlemen* the sub-plot in which Celia falls in love with Felismena-dressed-as-Valerius, but stored it in his mind and reverted to it several years later in *Twelfth Night*, when Olivia falls in love with Viola-dressed-as-Cesario.

Since the old play of Felismena and Felix is lost, we cannot be sure what dramatic context was created for their story, but the title of that play carries no suggestion that the male–female encounters were intermingled with a narrative of male–male rivalry. Shakespeare's play, on the other hand, is not called *Julia and Proteus*. Although Julia is the most engaging character, the title and the opening scenes give the dominant emphasis to the two male friends, Proteus and Valentine. For purposes of dramatic unity, the problem with the Felismena and Felix story is Celia. What is one to do with her once Felismena and Felix are reunited? Montemayor simply got rid of her by having her die of her unrequited love for the page who is not really a boy at all. That is all very well in a tale written to be read – there are so many miniature sub-narratives in *Diana* that we may pass over Celia's end without a tear or even a second thought. Killing off a character in a stage-play, especially a comedy, is a much more serious matter. I suspect that it was in rethinking the role of Celia that Shakespeare saw his opportunity. Instead of having Silvia fall in love with the page, he makes her remain constant to her beloved. And instead of making her a character who appears from nowhere for no particular reason, he makes her the girlfriend of Proteus' best friend. With this move, the love-plot is wedded to the friendship-plot. The name Proteus means 'change' and the character is made much more despicably changeable than Montemayor's Don Felix by the manner in which he is simultaneously unfaithful to his girlfriend Julia and his best friend Valentine.

Looking forward through Shakespeare's career, we see that he returns again and again to the pattern of close male friendship disrupted by rivalry over a woman: think of the sonnets, of *The Winter's Tale*, or of his last play, *The Two Noble Kinsmen*, a dramatization of Chaucer's 'Knight's Tale' which replays *The Two Gentlemen of Verona* in a tragic key. So is this pattern Shakespeare's great original insight? I think not: the most fashionable reading-matter of the 1580s was John Lyly's prose romance *Euphues*, a tale concerning a pair of close male friends who are split apart by rivalry over a woman.

When Shakespeare arrived in London, Lyly was the leading writer of comedies, as admired in that kind of drama as Marlowe was in tragedy and history. Shakespearean comedy grew from – and eventually outgrew – Lyly, just as Shakespearean tragedy and history grew from – and eventually outgrew – Marlowe. A description of the world of Lyly's best plays, his *Gallathea* and *Endimion*, will sound uncannily like a prescription for that of Shakespeare's pastoral comedies: being in love is the principal comic situation, witty banter between lovers – courtship as flirtation – the principal substance of dialogue; the plot is of a mingled kind, with elements of farce, with clowns in the sub-plot who echo the concerns of the higher characters; different social worlds – courtiers, shepherds, artisans, forest nymphs – are drawn together and thrown into confusion; girls are dressed as boys; father–daughter relationships are a source of dramatic tension that is finally released with the triumph of the younger generation, comedy thus taking the form tragedy averted; the action is forwarded, and emotional transformation wrought, by means of a journey into a forest; characters narrate their dreams; there are dances, fights, banquets, mood-setting songs woven into the action; many of the scenes are written in a virtuoso prose spangled with light-fingered allusions to classical mythology.

Love's Labour's Lost has never been among Shakespeare's more popular works. It was the only one of the plays never staged in the eighteenth century. Revivals remain comparatively infrequent. Audiences find the elaborate wordplay difficult; the characters are less engaging and the plot less gripping than those of such favourite comedies as *Twelfth Night*. But there is one scene which always works in the theatre.

The King of Navarre and his three courtiers, Biron, Longueville, and Dumaine, have forsworn love in the name of academic study. The arrival of the Princess of France and her three charming attendant ladies is proving something of an inconvenience for this plan. Each of the four men has fallen in love, but none of them wants the others to know that he has been the first to break the vow of austerity. Biron comes on, clutching a poem he has written for the lady to whom he has taken a fancy; he hears the King coming, so hides himself. The King enters with a paper; he reads out the (clichéd) love poem he has written for the Princess; then he hears Longueville coming, so he hides himself. Longueville reads the rhetorically ornate love sonnet he has written for another of the ladies; hearing Dumaine, he steps aside. No surprise for the audience here: Dumaine reads out a lyric addressed to his 'most divine Kate'. When the King was on stage, seemingly alone, Biron crowed in an aside; Longueville's outburst provoked asides from both Biron and the King, in their respective hiding-places; Dumaine's love-babble, needless to say, is punctuated by asides from all three of the others.

We await the turnaround with delicious anticipation: Longueville comes forward and chides Dumaine for breaking the vow. The King emerges and does not spare Longueville's blushes. Then it is Biron's turn to step forth and whip hypocrisy: 'You found his mote, the King your mote did see, / But I a beam do find in each of three' (4.3.159–60). Just when it seems that Biron has triumphed, on come Jaquenetta the country wench and Costard the clown with a letter that has gone astray – which just happens to be a love-epistle written by Biron.

In every production I have attended, the atmosphere in the theatre feels special in this scene. Until this moment, one often gets a sense of the audience struggling to tune themselves in to the wavelength of the play. With the comedy of overhearing, the dramatic voice suddenly takes on absolute clarity. We recognize it as something we know and love: 'Shakespearean comedy'. The novice who has been wondering why people make so much fuss about Shakespeare begins to understand. The experienced playgoer who is familiar with the more frequently performed comedies, but is seeing *Love's Labour's Lost* for the first time, feels the thrill of recognition that is so special to theatre. Memories click: this is like Sir Toby and company peeping out from behind the box tree as Malvolio reads the letter, it is like Benedick being set up to overhear the conversation about how Beatrice is supposedly in love with him and Beatrice set up to overhear the conversation about how Benedick is supposedly in love with her. This, we say, is comic genius in action.

Love's Labour's Lost is unusual among Shakespeare's work in apparently having no direct source. It seems to be an 'original', not a dramatization of an existing story in the manner of *Two Gentlemen*. Yet this scene, surely the best in the play, is not original. In Lyly's comedy *Gallathea*, there is a scene in which first one, then another, then another character is caught falling into the love-trap she has forsworn. Paradoxically, then, in *Love's Labour's Lost* the scene of greatest genius is that of least originality. Thematically, in respect of the tension between friendship and sexual desire, structurally, in the shapes of multiple plot and pastoral diversion, and technically, in the exploitation of a comedy in which actions expose the hypocrisy of words, Lyly was more of an original than Shakespeare. What is peculiar to the younger dramatist must be found elsewhere.

The weakness of the invented plot of *Love's Labour's Lost* suggests that the invention of plot was not our dramatist's greatest strength. Shakespeare knew, as Ralph Waldo Emerson put it, that 'tradition supplies a better fable than any invention can'. Emerson suggests in his essay on Shakespeare as exemplary poet that valuable originality does not consist in unlikeness to other men. A good story is likely to resemble other good stories; a wholly original plot may well have no merit save that most ephemeral of qualities, novelty. Stories survive because they seem true to the experience of successive generations of readers and spectators; that is why the oldest stories are usually the best. A remarkable proportion of Shakespeare's comic matter – whether patterns of action like the exposure of hypocrisy or set piece devices like the choice between three caskets – has antecedents extending far back into the traditions of comedy and folklore. Because he makes old truths new, he himself can always be made new.

The device of *overhearing* is a stroke of comic genius because it dramatizes one of the chief processes through which comic satisfaction is constituted: *dramatic irony*, whereby we in the audience know more than the character on stage. The brilliance of the scene in *Love's Labour's Lost* stems not just from the way in which Biron knows more than the King knows and the King knows more than Longueville knows and Longueville knows more than Dumaine knows. The punchline is that *we* know more than Biron knows. He says

> All hid, all hid – an old infant play.
> Like a demigod here sit I in the sky,
> And wretched fools' secrets heedfully o'er-eye.
>
> (4.3.75–7)

But it is we in the audience who are really in the position of the gods. We know how things are going to turn out. That is one of the reasons why we like comedies: we know that, give or take a few loose ends, they will work out as we would want them to. Which is not something we can say about our own lives.

The genius of the overhearing scene in *Love's Labour's Lost* is a function of its complication and its self-consciousness, not its originality. Where Lyly drops three characters into the trap, Shakespeare goes one better with four. And there is no equivalent in Lyly for the *timing* of embarrassment upon embarrassment, culminating in the master stroke of Jaquenetta's arrival. Nor does Lyly self-consciously explore the relationship between the dramatic narrative and the theatrical experience; it is Shakespeare, with his allusion to 'an old infant play', who introduces the extra layer of the audience's overhearing of the action.

By the same account, the idea of writing a comedy about twins and mistaken identity is by no means original to Shakespeare. The situation in *The Comedy of Errors* is lifted from the *Menaechmi* of the Roman comic dramatist Plautus. But what *is* original to Shakespeare is the doubling device, whereby the Antipholus twins have in tow a pair of slaves, the Dromios, who are themselves identical twins. There's complication, there's a need for the timing of the deftest *farceur*. And when in *Twelfth Night* Shakespeare reunites another pair of twins, Viola and Sebastian, he uses the old comic plot for a new purpose: Orsino describes the resemblance between brother and sister as 'A natural perspective, that is and is not' – a phrase which perfectly describes the relationship of theatre to life.

Narrative into drama

The Two Gentlemen of Verona is the earliest play in which Shakespeare combines two of his favourite comic devices, the journey into the wood and the cross-dressing of the heroine. He returned to the wood in *A Midsummer Night's Dream* and to the cross-dressed heroine in *The Merchant of Venice*. Then in *As You Like It* he perfected the combination. It is the most elegantly constructed, most finely finished of his comedies. But from the point of view of plot and character, it is among his least original.

Before praising Shakespeare as an 'original genius', we had better read Thomas Lodge's novella, *Rosalynd*, published in 1590. It begins with the legacy of a gentleman to his three sons and the ill-treatment of the youngest at the hands of the eldest. The latter plans to do away with his brother by having him killed in a bout with a supposedly invincible wrestler at court; amazingly, though, the youth wins the wrestling match and in so doing attracts the eye of Rosalynd, daughter of the rightful king who has been forced into exile by a usurper. Further schemes against the hero, Rosader, force him to leave home; he goes to the forest of Arden, in company with his faithful retainer, Adam Spencer; there he meets up with the exiled king and his courtiers. Meanwhile, Rosalynd is banished. Alinda, the daughter of the usurping king, determines to go with her. Since two women travelling alone would be vulnerable, the tall Rosalynd dresses as a boy and pretends to be Alinda's page; they call themselves Ganymede and Aliena.

In the forest, they encounter an old shepherd and a young one, the latter complaining about his unrequited love for a shepherdess named Phoebe. The princesses in disguise give financial help to the shepherds; the court-in-exile gives civil welcome to young Rosader and hungry old Adam. The princesses meet up with Rosader, who has been busy writing love poems in praise of Rosalynd. Ganymede pretends to be Rosalynd, so that Rosader can rehearse his wooing of the real Rosalynd; after their 'courting-eclogue', Aliena plays the priest at a mock-wedding. Ganymede approaches Phoebe on the shepherd's behalf and Phoebe promptly falls in love with the lovely boy who is really a girl. Rosader sees a man in danger from a lion, recognizing him as his brother; despite having been wronged, he saves him. The brother and Aliena fall in love with each other. Phoebe agrees that if she can't have Ganymede, she'll settle for the shepherd. Rosalynd reveals her identity, multiple marriages are celebrated and we may assume that they all live happily ever after.

Lodge's tale has a distinctly dramatic quality. There is a high proportion of dialogue; characters soliloquize at moments of intense passion. The plot is less important than the rhetorical articulation of emotion arising from each new situation. *Rosalynd* is also marked by a notable degree of self-consciousness on the part of the major characters; as the story's most recent editor puts it, 'Rosalynd and Alinda watch themselves having their emotions and control at least the moment and the way in which they will disclose them'. We cannot, then, say that Lodge merely provides the plot, while all the depth of emotional development is Shakespeare's. Much that we would wish to praise in *As You Like It* must be attributed to *Rosalynd*.

Having acknowledged this, we might then ask a cross-section of playgoers what they regard as the three most memorable aspects of *As You Like It*. My experience in asking this question is of a general consensus which singles out Jaques, Touchstone and Rosalind-playing-Ganymede-playing-Rosalind. Lodge's Adam Spencer has a speech in which he complains about the fickleness of fortune, but, this hint apart, there is no equivalent in *Rosalynd* for the melancholy Jaques. The content of the famous oration on the seven ages of man was Renaissance commonplace; the placing of it in the dramatic context of the entrance of young Orlando and old Adam is uniquely Shakespearean. In Lodge, all the loose ends are tied up in the closing paragraphs. The refusal of Jaques to join the party at the end of *As You Like It* has no source save Shakespeare's own habitual tough-mindedness, which never allows a complete comic resolution, always recognizes that some human temperaments will never be pleased, or will take pleasure in being displeased. Malvolio, another character for whom there is no precedent in his play's source, is the finest example of such a temperament.

There is no equivalent at all in *Rosalynd* for the clowning Touchstone. His dialogue with Corin on the relative merits of the court and the country gives dramatic life to a debate about custom which on the page could all too easily become sterile. His wooing of Audrey gives the audience four marriages instead of three, but also pricks any illusions we may have about all marriages being romantic, all attachments lasting – as Jaques recognizes, the 'loving voyage' of the clown and the goatherd is 'but for two months victualled' (5.4.189–90).

Shakespeare complicates Lodge for purposes of critique. He introduces the foppish Le Beau in the first act in order to mock at the pretensions of the court. He introduces Jaques in the second in order to mock at the pretensions of pastoral idealization. Duke Senior regards the forest of Arden as untainted, redolent of the Golden Age; Jaques points out that whilst the wicked Duke Frederick has usurped his brother's place at court, Duke Senior and his men have usurped the stag's place in the forest. Shakespeare introduces the loutish William and Audrey in order to juxtapose a realistic view of country people against the literary view provided by the shepherd-in-love he inherits from Lodge. As for Touchstone, he is introduced in order to mock at everybody – yet his sophisticated court mockery is itself mocked by the dignity with which Corin speaks for honest country values.

The characters invented by Shakespeare may be described as

'counter-voices'. Lodge's story is controlled by a narratorial voice which leads the reader to make discriminations and moral judgements. Shakespeare's dramatic form means that there is no single authorial voice; the play's succession of mockings, ironic juxtapositions and unresolved debates render its world 'open'. Even when 'closure' is reached with the multiple marriages, Jaques stands off against the resolution. This openness means that ample space is left for the intervention of the audience. We step in to continue the unresolved debates: that is one of the things which makes Shakespeare so performable, so discussable.

Performance means trying on different identities. When Lodge's Rosalynd dresses in man's clothing, she starts adopting a male point of view:

> 'You may see,' quoth Ganymede, 'what mad cattle you women be, whose hearts sometimes are made of adamant that will touch no impression, and sometime of wax that is fit for every form. They delight to be courted, and then they glory to seem coy, and when they are most desired then they freeze with disdain, and this fault is so common to the sex that you see it painted in the shepherd's passions, who found his mistress as froward as he was enamoured.'

It was from such touches as this that Shakespeare created his Rosalind, who reaches into the depths of womanhood at the time when she is on the surface a man, and who finds a strong way of expressing what it is like to be in love by pretending to be someone who is not in love, and who is scornful of love, when in fact she really is in love all along. Lodge's 'wooing eclogue' between Rosader and Ganymede-as-Rosalynd does not reach beyond the conventional sentiments of courtly love — beauty, female pity, male loyalty. Shakespeare's dramatization of the dialogue imagines a testing of what remains in a relationship once the fond illusions of courtly love are stripped away.

> ROSALIND Now tell me how long you would have her after you have possessed her?
> ORLANDO For ever and a day.
> ROSALIND Say a day without the ever. No, no, Orlando; men are April when they woo, December when they wed. Maids are May when they are maids, but the sky changes when they are wives.
>
> (4.1.135–41)

Our peculiar pleasure in this exchange derives in large measure from its quality as performance. Ganymede is playing at being Rosalind. But we know that Ganymede is really Rosalind. But we also know that Rosalind is really a stage-player. 'In fact she really is in love all along', I wrote in the previous paragraph. The watching of a play depends upon the operation of what Samuel Taylor Coleridge called 'that willing suspension of disbelief for the moment, which constitutes poetic faith'. So it is that in normal circumstances, terms such as 'in fact' and 'really' are held in suspension when we go to the theatre. In a scene like the mock wooing, such terms are thrown into peculiar relief. When it is Ganymede doing the acting, instead of simply suspending our disbelief that Rosalind is but an actor too, we enter a delicious spiral of confusion. As in Borges' fable of Shakespeare, 'existing, dreaming and acting' begin to dissolve into one another.

In the epilogue, Rosalind addresses the audience directly. 'If I were a woman', she says, reminding us that, like all Shakespeare's female parts, the role was originally written for a young male actor. This is another aspect of Shakespeare's complication of Lodge: in the story we read of a woman playing a man playing a woman, whereas in the theatre we witness a man playing a woman playing a man playing a woman. The actual presence of the original performer on the stage of the Globe in 1599 was more Ganymede than Rosalind. By capitalizing on a technical limitation inherent in his profession – the prohibition of women from the Elizabethan public stage – Shakespeare makes us consider the possibility that gender is a role we put on, a social performance, not a condition inherent in human nature.

When Lodge's Rosalynd compares women to mad cows, Aliena replies to the effect that she would not be so satirical against her sex were she dressed in her own petticoat again. Shakespeare's Rosalind is a more complicated and elusive, hence a more fascinating, creation because in the theatre she has no 'original' dress. She *is* what she wears, what she says. That is why her origin in Lodge's Rosalynd is not a limitation; her true originality is that she improvises her own identity. And that is why actors, audiences, readers have kept on coming back to her for four hundred years.

Tolstoy's error

There were six of us gathered one evening in winter at the house of an old university friend. The conversation turned to Shakespeare and his types and how they were taken profoundly and truly from the very depths of human nature. We marvelled particularly at their truth to life and their everyday normality; each of us could name Hamlets, Othellos and Falstaffs, even Richard IIIs and Macbeths (these last, true, only in potential) whom we'd come across.

'But I, gentlemen,' exclaimed our host, a man already elderly, 'I've known a King Lear!'

'How so?' we asked him.

'Yes, just so. Would you like me to tell you?'

'Please.'

And our friend immediately set about telling his story.

— Ivan Turgenev, 'King Lear of the Steppes'

When Viola lands in Illyria early in *Twelfth Night*, she is assisted by a kindly sea-captain. In the novella which gave Shakespeare his main plot for the play, the equivalent character is less well meaning. Whilst on board ship, he offers his cabin to Silla, the story's Viola-figure. He then attempts to rape her. She is only saved by the breaking of the storm. The ship is wrecked, but Silla survives by clinging to a chest that was in the captain's cabin. On opening it when she is washed up alone on shore, she finds some of the captain's clothing. Knowing at first hand the dangers attendant upon a woman travelling alone, she takes the opportunity to dress as a man.

At the beginning of *The Winter's Tale*, Leontes conceives a sudden, inexplicable jealousy towards Polixenes. In Robert Greene's *Pandosto*, the novella of which Shakespeare's play is a dramatization, the Hermione-figure does not hesitate to go to the bedroom of the Polixenes-figure in order to check that he is comfortable; the married queen and the visiting king also frequently walk together in the garden 'where they two in private and pleasant devices would pass away the time to both their contents'. In these circumstances, Pandosto, the original for Leontes, is not unreasonable to have his suspicions.

The first writer to attend in detail to Shakespeare's use of his sources was the eighteenth-century novelist Charlotte Lennox. In the 1750s, she published a collection called *Shakespear Illustrated: or the Novels and Histories, on which the Plays of Shakespear are Founded*. She generally took a dim view of the dramatist's treatment of his materials. To the provocation of the literary establishment, in which Bardolatry was growing by the year, she argued that in almost every case the source was superior to Shakespeare's version of it. As far as *Twelfth Night* was concerned, she thought that there was insufficient motivation for Viola's decision to dress herself in boy's apparel. The near-rape in the source provided a genuine rationale, yet Shakespeare chose to omit it.

As for *The Winter's Tale*, the story was 'much less absurd and ridiculous' in Greene's *Pandosto*. The jealousy of Leontes is the foundation for all that follows; Lennox regarded it as extravagant in both versions, but better accounted for in the novella. For Lennox, the most ridiculous thing of all in *The Winter's Tale* was the bringing to life of Hermione's statue. Since this incident was unique to the play (in Greene, the queen remains stone dead), Lennox took it as proof that Shakespeare was bad when dramatizing his sources, but much worse when going his own way.

Ill-tempered as these criticisms are, there is some perception in them. One of the major characteristics of Shakespeare's handling of his sources is a removal of obvious motivation. Examples could be multiplied well beyond *Twelfth Night* and *The Winter's Tale*. In Lodge's *Rosalynd*, Aliena falls in love with the previously villainous older brother because he heroically rescues her and Ganymede from the assault of some ruffians. In *As You Like It*, she falls in love with him for no apparent reason. In the story that is the source for *Othello*, the Iago-figure is motivated by his own desire for Desdemona; in Shakespeare's play, his lack of sufficient motive is a notorious critical debating-point.

Lennox was a novelist. Her preference for the brief novels on which most of Shakespeare's comedies were based stemmed from a desire to promote her own trade – which in the eighteenth century was still new and far from fully established. Logical plot development and long-term psychological motivation are two of the glories of the novel; Charlotte Lennox looked for them in Shakespeare and found them wanting. But a play is not a novel. Theatre audiences care not a hoot about Viola's reasons for dressing as a boy; they are too busy watching her lose and find herself in the guise of Cesario. Iago and Leontes are compelling stage presences exactly because we cannot pin a single motive upon them. They make us work harder than that. Like the absence of moralization at the end of the plays, the absence of motivation at the beginning forces us to concentrate on the unfolding action, on character as a *process*. Shakespearean character is not a recipe, it is a meal.

One hundred and fifty years after Mrs Lennox, a more distinguished novelist launched a similar attack on Shakespeare. Near the end of his long life, some thirty years after completing *Anna Karenina*, Leo Tolstoy recorded that he was astonished when he first read Shakespeare. His first impression of these 'works regarded as the summit of perfection by the whole of the civilized world' was that they were 'trivial and positively bad'. Over a period of fifty years, he read and reread Shakespeare – in his own Russian, in the original English, in Schlegel's admired German translation – but each time he came to the same conclusion. Before sitting down in 1906, now in his late seventies, to write his essay on 'Shakespeare and the Drama', he reread all the plays yet once more. This time, however, he felt not bewilderment but 'a firm, indubitable conviction that the unquestionable glory of a great genius which Shakespeare enjoys, and which compels writers of our time to imitate him and readers and spectators to discover in him nonexistent merits – thereby distorting their aesthetic and ethical understanding – is a great evil'.

Like Charlotte Lennox before him, Tolstoy was especially vexed by Shakespeare's missing motives. This time Iago is singled out. The character has a variety of vague, implausible motives: his failure to win promotion is insufficient cause to destroy Desdemona, his profession that both Othello and Cassio have bedded Emilia is incredible. In the source, on the other hand, 'there is but one simple and clear motive: Iago's passionate love for Desdemona, transmuted into hatred toward her and Othello after she had preferred the Moor to him and had resolutely repulsed him'.

Tolstoy devoted the major part of his essay to *King Lear*. The insufficiency of motivation is the marshalling point of his attack. 'Lear has no necessity or motive for his abdication; also, having lived all his life with his daughters, he has no reason to believe the words of the two elder and not the truthful statement of the youngest; yet upon this is built the whole tragedy of his position.' Similarly, Gloucester has no reason to believe the false Edmund and not the true Edgar. Edgar has no reason to withhold disclosure of his identity from his father for as long as he does.

According to Tolstoy, Shakespeare took all his most celebrated characters – Lear, Cordelia, Othello, Desdemona, Falstaff, Hamlet – from old plays, romances, and chronicles. Contrary to the received wisdom that he rendered them more powerful, Tolstoy thought that 'in most cases, they are weakened and spoiled'. Especially lamentable was the adaptation of the anonymous play of *King Leir* into *King Lear*. In the old play, Leir abdicates because his wife has just died and he therefore wants to prepare his own soul for death. The test of his daughters' love is also clearly motivated. Leir does not want Cordella, his most beloved daughter, to marry a foreign potentate and live abroad; he will therefore demand an absolute profession of love, in response to which he will tell Cordella that if she loves him as much as she says, then she will do him one last favour and marry the man of his choice (i.e., a prince from Britain, not overseas). In Shakespeare's play, by contrast, neither the abdication nor the staging of the love-test are properly justified.

Tolstoy fails to see that it is the very folly of arbitrarily linking the division of the kingdoms to the rhetorical profession of love that is the root of Shakespeare's tragedy. He spends much of his essay complaining about the grandiloquent, pretentious language of all Shakespeare's characters, whilst praising the simplicity and Christian piety of the language in the old *Leir* play. He fails to see that Shakespeare's play is itself highly critical of the inflated court language of Goneril, Regan and Lear himself before his humbling in the storm and through his madness.

Shakespeare's most sustained alteration of his source was the removal of nearly all its Christian references. The anonymous *True Chronicle History of King Leir* is a drama steeped in piety: God rules the world of this play from Leir's initial decision to renounce the court for the sake of his soul, through the Gallian King's journey to Britain as a pilgrim (in which guise he woos and wins Cordella), to the divine intervention of a thunderclap at the moment when Leir's life is in greatest danger, to the touching reunion of father and daughter, to the eventual triumph of virtue. Shakespeare removes the action to a pagan setting. He has his characters call on the gods, but receive no sign from them in response.

Because Albany gives voice to pious sentiments, he is the only character for whom Tolstoy has any admiration, but Albany's vision of how the world goes is utterly flawed by his hapless optimism – 'the gods defend her!', he says of Cordelia, only to see her borne in dead or dying in Lear's arms; 'we will resign / During the life of this old majesty / To him our absolute power', he says, only to see his old Majesty drop dead.

'Human life', wrote Tolstoy near the end of his essay on Shakespeare, 'is perfected solely through the development of the religious conscious-ness, the only element which permanently unites men.' *King Lear* was unbearable to Tolstoy because it was stripped of the religious conscious-ness that pervaded *King Leir*, because it replaced humble submission to the divine will with rage against the dying of the light. The play's paganism blinded Tolstoy to those moments in it when human beings are united in care, in kindness, in love. He says nothing about the selflessness of Kent, about the servants who tend to Gloucester's bleeding eye-sockets. At the beginning of the fourth act, Gloucester gives his purse to the disguised Edgar as a practical token of the maxim that 'distribution should undo excess, / And each man have enough' (4.1.63–4). Shakespeare's play does not recognize this action as divinely sanctioned charity; a few lines earlier, Gloucester's opinion of the gods has been unremitting – 'They kill us for their sport', as wanton boys kill flies. The good deed is purely human. Because it is not linked to Christian mercy, Tolstoy has no time for Gloucester's principle of equal distribution. The words about undoing excess are said to be 'strange'.

Yet they could hardly be more late-Tolstoyan words. In his final years, Count Tolstoy renounced his title and his estate. He espoused the principle that distribution should undo excess, and each man have enough. Like Lear in the storm, he exposed himself to feel what wretches feel. He eventually fled across the Russian wastes, accom-panied only by a single faithful daughter. He died at a railway station, which makes him a little like his own Anna Karenina, but, since he was fourscore years and upward, a very foolish fond old man, with white hair and a long white beard, it makes him even more like the protagonist of that despised play *King Lear*.

The main difference between the old *King Leir* play and Shake-speare's *King Lear* is that in the former the old king is restored to his daughter and his throne. Shakespeare turned this happy ending into the most painful of his tragic endings – his Lear is granted a brief reunion with Cordelia only for her to be hanged a couple of scenes later. The old play granted Tolstoy the romance of a happy ending; perhaps the Shakespearean revision was unbearable to him because he somehow intuited that it foreshadowed his own tragic ending.

Since Tolstoy had become King Lear, he was bound to resent Shakespeare for having created King Lear – or rather metamorphosed the romance-figure King Leir into the tragic titan King Lear – without himself having gone through any of the sufferings which make King Lear what he is. Tolstoy wrote in his essay that the most important factor in the creation of great art is

> Sincerity, i.e., that the author should himself keenly feel what he expresses. Without this condition there can be no work of art, as the essence of art consists in the contemplator of the work of art being infected with the author's feeling. If the author does not actually feel what he expresses, then the recipient cannot become infected with the feeling of the author, he does not experience any feeling, and the production can no longer be classified as a work of art.

The complete absence of sincerity from all the plays is the primary indictment in Tolstoy's case against Shakespeare.

The demand for sincerity was Tolstoy's error. The genius of *King Lear* is that it was written by a man who was totally unlike his creation. The poetry of a teenager in love is sincere: that is what makes it bad. The key to dramatic art is Insincerity, i.e., that the author should only pretend keenly to feel what he expresses. That way, he can pretend equally keenly to feel the opposite things which he also expresses. He can infect the spectator with the feeling of what it is like to be Goneril as well as that of what it is like to be Lear.

Tolstoy's diagnosis of Shakespeare was extraordinarily accurate, his prognosis wildly askew. He was right about the missing motives, the irreligiousness, the pervasive insincerity. He was wrong in his conclusion that Bardolatry would prove but a passing fad like the inflated price of tulips in seventeenth-century Holland. Compared with their prototypes in the sources, Shakespeare's characters *are* curiously lacking in clear motivation. That is why they are so endlessly fascinating. Compared with the old anonymous play, Shakespeare's version of the Lear story *is* worryingly lacking in religious sentiment and moral order.

That is why it is endlessly translatable to cultures alien from the religious and moral world in which it was written. Had *King Lear* been tamely Christian like *King Leir*, the film director Akira Kurosawa would not have been able to remake it in the harsh, bright light of the Samurai warrior code. Compared with the Romantic artist who keenly feels what he expresses, Shakespeare is wantonly insincere. He does not project himself into his heroes. That is why so much room remains for his spectators and readers to project themselves into the world of the plays. Because Shakespeare did not sincerely become King Lear, Turgenev could imagine a Russian landowner becoming what Tolstoy himself also became: a King Lear of the Steppes.

By what peculiarity is it the case that Shakespeare's characters were inherited from his sources, yet have seemed to generations of playgoers and readers as they seemed to Turgenev: uniquely Shakespearean and also uniquely true to our experience of human behaviour?

Just over halfway through his diatribe, Tolstoy pauses and offers Shakespeare a single paragraph of praise. He suggests that it is an illusion that Shakespeare was good at depicting character. The illusion came from his actually possessing a 'peculiarity' which consisted in 'the capacity of representing scenes expressing the play of emotion':

> However unnatural the positions may be in which he places his characters, however improper to them the language which he makes them speak, however featureless they are, the very play of emotion, its increase and alteration and the combination of many contrary feelings expressed correctly and powerfully in some of Shakespeare's scenes, and in the play of good actors, evokes, even if only for a time, sympathy with the persons represented. Shakespeare, himself an actor, and an intelligent man, knew how to express by the means not only of speech, but of exclamation, gesture, and the repetition of words, states of mind and developments or changes of feeling taking place in the persons represented.

This is a wonderful insight. Shakespeare's characters are not the fixed entities they tend to be in his sources. Rather, they are embodiments of the fluidity, the *play*, of emotion. That same mobility which characterized the dramatist's social life is the gift which animates his drama.

'Shakespeare, himself an actor': the life of his personages is less in their origins, motives and sentiments than in their actions. Tolstoy pinpoints this peculiar art with great precision:

> in many instances, Shakespeare's characters, instead of speaking, merely make an exclamation, or weep, or in the middle of a monologue, by means of gestures, demonstrate the pain of their position (just as Lear asks someone to unbutton him) or in moments of great agitation, repeat a question several times, or several times demand the repetition of a word which has particularly struck them, as do Othello, Macduff, Cleopatra, and others.

Shakespeare is most Shakespeare not when some character is philosophizing or moralizing or talking politics, but when Lear says, 'Pray you, undo this button' or Macduff hears Ross's 'Wife, children, servants, all / That could be found' and cannot get the word 'all' out of his head: 'All my pretty ones? / Did you say all? O hell-kite! All?' The peculiar immediacy of the plays comes from such details as these. As far as the philosophizing, the moralizing and politics are concerned, they are mostly inherited. Shakespeare's works are great stores of second-hand sense. It is the art of immediacy which memorably impresses that sense upon our sensibilities.

We should not, however, underestimate the work and the 'intelligence' — Tolstoy's surprising word — that went into the gathering of the store. The greatest man, said Ralph Waldo Emerson, does not set out to be great. Rather, 'he finds himself in the river of thoughts and events, forced onward by the ideas and necessities of his contemporaries.' Shakespeare emerged at a time when audiences were hungry for theatre. Audience and arena were ready. A rich body of source material was to hand: Plutarch for Roman history, the chronicles for English; Italian romances and old plays for both comedy and tragedy. Shakespeare regarded the existing repertoire as so much waste stock on which he could try experiments of his own.

Paradoxically, then, 'Great genial power, one would almost say, consists in not being original at all; in being altogether receptive'. Shakespeare was receptive to every mood, every position and disposition: hence the intermingling, the layering and counterpoint, which is one of his stylistic hallmarks. He was receptive to everything but reductive singularity: hence his stripping of unitary motive from such characters as Leontes and Lear. We praise writers for being receptive to all experience; so too should we praise them for being altogether receptive to their reading, save when that reading closes the mind rather than opens it. The range and extent of Shakespeare's indebtedness is a badge of his genius, not a blemish upon it.

PART TWO

THE SHAKESPEARE EFFECT

I remember your saying that you had notions of a good
Genius presiding over you – I have of late had the same
thought. for things which [I] do half at Random are
afterwards confirmed by my judgment in a dozen features
of Propriety – Is it too daring to Fancy Shakspeare this
Presider?
                    – John Keats to Benjamin Haydon, 10 May 1817

6

THE ORIGINAL GENIUS

The idea of genius

Consider the statement 'Shakespeare was a genius'. Is this a fact or an opinion?

Judgements about the quality of works of art begin in opinion. But for the last two hundred years only the wilfully perverse (and Tolstoy) have denied the validity of the opinion that Shakespeare was a genius. It has become as close to a fact as we are ever likely to get in aesthetics. Why has the opinion become so fixed? What would an argument against it sound like? And what exactly do we mean by the statement?

Presumably we mean that there is something out of the ordinary about Shakespeare's plays. That his powers of invention were astonishingly wide and quick. We think of the range of his vocabulary – over fifteen thousand different words. We find memorable quotations flashing into our minds – 'To be or not to be', 'Tomorrow and tomorrow and tomorrow', 'All the world's a stage', 'Our revels now are ended'. We marvel at the process whereby the characters have taken on lives of their own: even someone who has never seen or read a Shakespeare play will almost certainly have images of Hamlet, Cleopatra, Romeo and Juliet, and may well have conceptions of Falstaff, Lady Macbeth, Othello, and Caliban. The plays have held the stage, the poetry is held in our minds, the characters have become archetypes. These phenomena, we will say, are proof of Shakespeare's genius.

The origins of Shakespeare's art are to be found in the rhetorical training he received at school, in his reading, his reshaping of inherited materials and traditions, above all in his theatrical environment, his creative engagement with the tragedies of Marlowe and the comedies of John Lyly. But to explain the origins of his art cannot fully account for his genius. Other dramatists – the prolific Thomas Heywood, for instance – had very much the same inheritance. Though Heywood wrote some very serviceable plays, he was not Shakespeare. His *Woman Killed with Kindness* is a moving tragedy of marital breakdown, but no one would rank it on the level of *Othello*. Shakespeare's environment did much to make his plays, but in the end what made Shakespeare uniquely Shakespeare was something indefinable, some peculiar alchemy of genes and circumstances. 'Genius' is the word we reach for in order to connote this alchemy.

To use the word 'genius' thus is to give it two senses. Each of us is uniquely ourself by virtue of that peculiar alchemy of genes and circumstances: this is the old sense of 'genius' as meaning 'characteristic disposition'. But with only a tiny handful of human beings does the alchemy turn base metals to gold in such a way that others mark them out as 'great', 'inspired', or somehow 'superhuman'. In the first sense, we may say 'each of us has a genius'; in the second sense, it is only of a few that we say '(s)he is a genius'. My subject in this chapter is Shakespeare's special relationship to this second sense.

How do we decide whether or not a work of art is 'good' or even 'great'? The question has been debated ever since Western art took shape in ancient Greece. Among the traditional answers are the following:

(1) A great work of art is true to nature.
(2) A great work of art stirs strong emotions in us.
(3) A great work of art is wise; it makes us think.
(4) A great work of art has formal beauty.
(5) The greatness of a work of art may be judged by the extent to which it measures up to the standards of the universally acknowledged great works of the past.

The last of these answers is the least likely to be given today, but it has a venerable pedigree. For the ancient Greeks, Homer was the father of poetry, so later poetry could be judged by means of comparison with Homer. Homer was true to nature; truth to nature must therefore be commensurate with truth to Homer. Since the Homeric corpus provided the Greek tragedians with most of their source material, this argument from commensurability worked well in classical times, despite the formal differences between Homer's epic and the tragedies of Aeschylus, Sophocles, and Euripides.

When Ben Jonson collected his plays in his Folio volume of 1616 and entitled it *Works*, he was making a very bold implicit claim: that contemporary, secular, vernacular drama was worthy of the serious aesthetic attention previously accorded only to the classics. Previously the notion of 'Collected Works' (Latin *Opera*) had been reserved for editions of the ancients and of elevated Latinate authors such as Sir Thomas More. The dedicatory poem which Jonson wrote for the Shakespeare Folio seven years later aggrandized the contemporary drama still further. As we saw in chapter one, it went so far as to claim that Shakespeare was a greater dramatist than Aeschylus, Sophocles, and Euripides, and, for good measure, that he also surpassed the greatest comic writers of ancient times, Aristophanes, Terence, and Plautus.

How, then, does Shakespeare match up to our five classical criteria of aesthetic excellence? Let us take each in turn.

(1) From his own time to ours, almost everyone has agreed that his plays are remarkably true to nature. *Romeo and Juliet* has seemed true to the experience of being in love, *Othello* to the experience of jealousy, *Macbeth* to the pressure of ambition, *Hamlet* to the difficulty of translating intention into action, and so on.

(2) From his own time to ours, his plays have roused strong emotions in their spectators and readers. Through generation upon generation, men and women have been drained by the end of *Lear*, have felt good at the end of *Twelfth Night* and *As You Like It*, have been moved to pity by Desdemona's willow song and to wonder by the animation of Hermione's statue.

(3) If wisdom is a matter of moral and political precepts, we can certainly find plenty of it in the plays. *Coriolanus*, for instance, shows that what a state needs in time of war is not the same as what it needs in time of peace; *The Merchant of Venice* and *Measure for Measure* make us think about the conflicting demands of mercy and justice. But 'matter' of this kind was usually derived by Shakespeare from his sources. He was not a moral philosopher or a deliverer of homilies. His interest was in *dramatizing* 'matter' and if there is a principal 'moral' to be drawn from his work it is the one which follows from his mastery of dramatic form – that any position may be answered by a counter-position and that actions are worth more attention than opinions.

(4) This is where one begins to run into difficulties. Western criteria for formal beauty were first laid out in ancient Greece. The Parthenon is beautiful because of its symmetry, clarity, and economy of design. By the same account, there is a beauty about the drama of Sophocles, with its balance between choric song and dialogic speech, its economy of vocabulary and verse-forms, its singleness of tragic purpose and clear line of dramatic argument (typically, there are only two principal characters on stage at any one time, each of them standing for an opposing set of values and actions). Such formal beauty is not matched by the Shakespearean drama, with its loose and episodic scenic form, its multiple plots, its vertiginous course from tragedy to comedy and back again, its motley assemblages of character, its profligacy of vocabulary and speech idiom, its jumble of verse and prose.

(5) This is another way of putting (4). If we are to judge Shakespeare by the standard of Sophocles, he will fail lamentably.

Ben Jonson regarded a writer's truth to nature as coordinate with his keeping of the company of the classics. When he said that 'Shakespeare wanted Art', he meant that due to ignorance of the example of Sophocles and the *Poetics* of Aristotle, Shakespeare's plays failed to achieve greatness according to criteria (4) and (5). As I suggested in chapter one, Jonson's poem for the First Folio attempted to get round this problem by proposing that Shakespeare was nevertheless an artful poet who was capable of striking the second heat upon the muses' anvil. But, as I also suggested in that chapter, Jonson's offering of equal praise for original endowment and the work of revision did not take hold. For Leonard Digges in his eulogy published in 1640, Shakespeare was born, not made. Shakespeare was the poet of nature, not art.

Digges was not the first to make this move. Within ten years of the publication of the First Folio, John Milton was praising Shakespeare by splitting nature apart from art. In 1630 he wrote a sonnet in memory of Shakespeare which was printed in both the Second Folio of 1632 and the 1640 edition of Shakespeare's *Poems*, as well as in Milton's own *Poems* of 1645. Milton writes that Shakespeare's 'easy numbers' – his natural poetic facility – put to shame the 'slow-endeavouring Art' of other writers. Shakespeare's lines are said to be Delphic, which is to say inspired, coming straight from Apollo, god of poetry; the lines of poets who think too much, who have too much art, are by contrast marmoreal, which is to say dead. A few years later, Milton made the same kind of distinction in his poem 'L'Allegro':

> Then to the well-trod stage anon,
> If Jonson's learned sock be on,
> Or sweetest Shakespeare fancy's child
> Warble his native wood-notes wild.

Here 'learning', and by implication the classical tradition, is given to Jonson, while Shakespeare is a natural child of the imagination. Milton's imagery makes Shakespeare into a bird singing in a wood.

'*Native* wood-notes' suggests not only naturalness and innate – as opposed to learned – brilliance, but also 'rooted in a national tradition' and 'belonging to the place of birth'. The artful poet is cosmopolitan, able to draw skill from Greece or Rome and translate it to Paris or London. The natural poet, by contrast, is 'native'. He could therefore be made into a symbol of what were imagined to be the distinctive characteristics of his nation. The Shakespearean temperament was seen to match the English temperament: empirical, sceptical, unsystematic, ironic. Shakespeare's rural origins proved invaluable to this process whereby he was reconstituted as the national poet. In the eighteenth century the Bard was seen as a country boy, a genius of the English earth, not a city man. The enshrining of Stratford-upon-Avon as a site of pilgrimage had causes in aesthetic theory as well as effects in the emergent economy of tourism.

I am fairly sure that Shakespeare was the first writer in Western high culture to be praised specifically for his supposed artlessness. The effect of this move was drastic: it is no exaggeration to say that it altered the entire course of Western art.

In the classical aesthetic system, criterion (5) circled back to criterion (1). It was agreed that a writer most certainly needed native ability, the capacity for invention (Latin *ingenium*); but it was also agreed that the true end of writing, namely the imitation of nature, could only be reached by means of the imitation of the great writing of the past. To imitate nature and to imitate Homer, the father of poetry, were regarded as one and the same thing. The praise of Shakespeare for *not* imitating classical dramatic form established an *opposition* between criterion (1) and criterion (5). The history of eighteenth-century aesthetics was in large measure the history of the hardening of that opposition. Its culmination was that reconfiguration of values and practices in all the arts which we call Romanticism.

Once the split between nature and art was established, a fresh term was needed for the kind of poet who was supposed to work from artless inspiration alone. What emerged was not a new word, but a new meaning for that old word 'genius'.

When Ferdinand speaks in *The Tempest* of 'our worser genius' (4.1.27), he does not mean what we mean by 'genius'. He is alluding to the ancient Christian idea that we each have a good and a bad angel watching over us, as in Marlowe's *Dr Faustus*. The word *genius* is derived from Latin, where it refers to 'the tutelary god or attendant spirit allotted to every person at his birth, to govern his fortunes and determine his character, and finally to conduct him out of the world'. We still speak of 'the spirit of a place', an idea derived from the Latin *genius loci*; what we have lost is the sense of genius as 'the spirit of a person'.

That sense has been replaced by the new one. When someone says 'genius' now, the images that press upon our mind are of the artist or scientist undergoing a flash of inspiration, Shakespeare or Mozart in the heat of composition, Einstein formulating the General Theory of Relativity or Wittgenstein dissolving a complex philosophical problem. The association of this sense of genius with science and philosophy is a later development; its first emergence was specifically bound up with 'natural' artistic inspiration.

In the course of the seventeenth century, *genius* in the sense of 'native endowment' was frequently contrasted with the *art* which could be achieved by study. This contrast became central to aesthetic theory primarily because of the example of Shakespeare. The classical meaning of 'genius' as a tutelary deity suggested, as *The Oxford English Dictionary* puts it, 'that the word had an especial fitness to denote that particular kind of intellectual power which has the appearance of proceeding from a supernatural inspiration or possession, and which seems to arrive at its results in an inexplicable and miraculous manner.' The analogy with the spirit of a place strengthened the association: where the artful poet draws his knowledge from books, the genius goes to a natural source – the Castalian spring, the banks of Avon.

So it was that the French word *génie*, the German *Genie*, and the

English *genius* all took on that new sense which *The Oxford English Dictionary* defines as 'instinctive and extraordinary capacity for imaginative creation, original thought, invention, or discovery'. The concept of 'original genius' as the essence of poetry became widespread by the mid-eighteenth century. We will see that the reasons for this were bound up with particular conditions in the national and social history of polite letters, but the results went far beyond those conditions. The concept was at the heart of the 'Romantic' aesthetic which dominated the following century. Shakespeare was the cardinal exemplar of 'original genius' since it was above all because of his supposed 'artlessness' that the concept was developed and became so widely accepted.

He was the cardinal but not the unique exemplar. Homer also played a paternal role; instead of being a model for technical imitation, he became the prototypical blind seer, the ideal for emulation. Other 'bardic' poetry was also brought forward: the ancient Greek odes of Pindar, the sublime Hebrew psalmody of the Old Testament prophets. In the 1760s a 'newly discovered' Bard, the legendary Gaelic Ossian, was hailed as the archetypal original genius. That which Shakespeare was reckoned to have in common with Homer and Ossian was central to his influence in Germany in the later eighteenth century: all three were supposed to have been original geniuses because they had written when their national culture was in its infancy. German national culture was in its infancy; therefore, the argument went, the time was ripe for the emergence of an equivalent German national genius. Thus did Herder present Goethe in the '*Sturm und Drang*' ('Storm and Stress') period of the 1770s, the first full flowering of European Romanticism. That age was also known as the *Genieperiode*.

Some answers to my initial questions now become apparent. Why is 'Shakespeare was a genius' as near as we are likely to get to a fact as opposed to an opinion in matters of aesthetic judgement? *Because 'genius' was a category invented in order to account for what was peculiar about Shakespeare.*

The only reasoned argument against Shakespeare is the neoclassical one premised on the assumption that all great art must be like the art of the ancients. The Greeks considered that the serious subject matter of tragedy required an elevated form: tragedies should therefore be written exclusively in verse. They assumed that the concentration of emotion required by tragedy necessitated the exclusion of any comedy: artistic lucidity was therefore dependent upon the separation of genres and restriction to a single plot line. Concentration and clear organization also necessitated limitation to a small number of dramatic parts – a maximum of seven or eight, as in Racine, not the thirty or forty we get in *Macbeth* and *Richard III*. Tragedy, said the Greeks, should not descend to a prurient gaping upon gruesome detail: its concern should be the *emotional response* to violence and suffering; violent events should therefore take place not in on-stage chaos, but off stage, so that they can be ordered in reported speech and our attention drawn to the *reactions* of other characters. When Shakespeare was attacked by French or French-influenced critics in the late seventeenth and eighteenth centuries, it was on the grounds that out of either ignorance or wantonness he disregarded every recommendation of the Greeks, broke every decorum in the classical book.

But even those who launched such attacks still acknowledged Shakespeare's genius. The classic case is that of Voltaire. On the one hand, he was the first to tell the French reading public of Shakespeare's greatness. On the other hand, he was the bugbear of all Bardolaters. The reason for this paradox is abundantly clear from what he wrote about Shakespeare in the eighteenth of his *Philosophic Letters* on English culture, published in 1734: 'he created the [English] drama, he had a genius full of force and fecundity, of the natural and the sublime, without the least glimmer of good taste and without the least knowledge of the rules'. Praise of the genius is balanced against damnation for failure to follow the example of the classics. In the next sentence, the damnation wins out: Shakespeare, says Voltaire, has ruined the English theatrical tradition because 'there are such fine scenes, such grand and terrible parts interspersed in those monstrous farces called tragedies, that his plays have always been acted with great success'.

Patriotic Englishmen were deaf to the urbane irony by which Voltaire says here that the reason why Shakespeare is so bad is that he is so good. What they heard was France's leading intellectual complaining that their beloved Shakespeare was little more than an inspired idiot, a fairground clown. For them, Voltaire was the man who could not stomach drunken, singing, quipping gravediggers intruding upon a tragedy. At this point, questions of genius are overtaken by those of nationalism. In 1769, Elizabeth Montagu, whom Dr Johnson dubbed Queen of the Bluestockings, published a book which made the link with national pride quite explicit: *An Essay on the Writings and Genius of Shakespear, compared with the Greek and French Dramatic Poets. With some Remarks upon the Misrepresentations of Mons. de Voltaire.* Seven years later, in reaction against Pierre Le Tourneur's translation of Shakespeare into French, Voltaire described the plays as a heap of dung. Elizabeth Montagu stood in the French Academy and defended her National Genius. Much had changed since Milton's apparently innocuous poetic conceit of the 1630s.

The English genius

In 1642 the London theatres were closed down by the Puritans. When they reopened with the Restoration of the monarchy in 1660, the available repertoire consisted principally of the three bodies of work which had been collected in Folio editions: the plays of Ben Jonson (*Works*, 1616), of William Shakespeare (*Comedies, Histories, and Trage-dies*, 1623), and of Francis Beaumount and John Fletcher (*Plays*, 1647). During the first forty years of the new theatrical regime, the plays of Beaumont and Fletcher were performed twice as often as those of William Shakespeare. The 'heroic' and 'sentimental' dramas of the age emulated Fletcherian romance to a far greater extent than Shakespear-ean tragedy. Restoration comedy, with its city settings and emblematic names, its Foppingtons and Lovewits, owed more to Jonson than to Shakespeare.

Meanwhile in literary criticism, opinion-makers were under the influence of the neoclassical aesthetic ideology of the French court, where the English aristocracy had waited in exile during the Cromwel-lian years. From a neoclassical point of view, Shakespeare's verbal inventiveness and his mingling of kings with clowns were unforgivable 'irregularities'. For this reason, of the three bodies of pre-Civil War verse-drama, his was the one which required most 'modernization'. The Restoration was the great age of Shakespearean adaptation. The law of 'poetic justice' dictated that those who die at the end of a tragedy must have done at least something to deserve their fate; the innocent Cordelia cannot therefore die, so Nahum Tate ends his version by marrying her off to Edgar. In so doing, he also makes *King Lear* more like a Fletcherian romance than a Shakespearean tragedy.

John Dryden, in his 1668 *Essay of Dramatic Poesy*, expressed an instinctive admiration for Shakespeare, but his intellectual allegiance was to the learned and 'correct' Jonson. One hundred and one years later, at David Garrick's Jubilee in Stratford-upon-Avon, there were no such equivocations: Shakespeare was now 'the god of our idolatry'. In 1700, Shakespeare was an admired dramatist, but no more admired than Jonson or Beaumont and Fletcher; by 1800 he had become England's chief cultural icon. It was in the course of the eighteenth century that he rose through the ranks of poets and assumed his status as supreme 'genius'. This journey – which was, as I have suggested, a typically eighteenth-century ascent from humble origins to great exaltation – is the most important sub-narrative within the overall plot of his afterlife. Once Shakespeare was identified as a genius, he became infinitely exportable, infinitely reappropriable.

The first book with a title asserting the genius of its subject was *An Essay on the Genius and Writings of Shakespear* by John Dennis, a pamphlet of seventy pages published in 1712 at the cost of one shilling. It consisted of a series of letters to the editor of *The Spectator*, which Dennis had written the previous year to accompany his adaptation of *Coriolanus*. In them, Dennis asserts that '*Shakespear* was one of the greatest Genius's that the world e'er saw for the Tragick Stage'. The plays are praised for their supreme representation of character and passion. But Dennis weighs their greatness against their deficiencies: 'If *Shakespear* had these great Qualities by Nature, what would he not have been if he had join'd to so happy a Genius Learning and the Poetical Art?' The problem was that Shakespeare was ignorant of the best models. Had he known the tragedies of ancient Greece, he would not have polluted the purity of *Julius Caesar* and *Coriolanus* by bringing a rabble on stage. He would have had a clearer conception of that 'poetic justice' which demanded that the good should end happily and the bad unhappily. Dennis had therefore taken it upon himself to 'improve' *Coriolanus* so that it conformed to the 'rules' of art.

For Dennis, then, 'genius' is that which comes from nature. Because Shakespeare 'wanted Art', in the sense in which art had been practised by Sophocles, anatomized in the *Poetics* of Aristotle, and revived in

French high culture, 'genius' came to be defined as artless but also as un-French.

In *The Spectator* of 3 September 1711 Joseph Addison laid out all the essentials of the conception. For Addison, the first class of geniuses were those 'who by the mere Strength of natural Parts, and without any assistance of Art or Learning, have produced Works that were the Delight of their own Times, and the Wonder of Posterity'. Addison assumes that genius is a term most fittingly used to praise *writers*, especially poets, and above all those poets whose strength comes from nature rather than art or learning: 'There appears something nobly wild and extravagant in these great natural Genius's, that is infinitely more beautiful than all the Turn and Polishing of what the French call a Bel Esprit.' This dissociation from the French term 'esprit', at a time when French thinking dominated literary theory, implicitly makes genius into a distinctively English category.

This was a crucial move in the making of Shakespeare as a national poet. English criticism of the late seventeenth and early eighteenth centuries set up an opposition between genius and those rules of art which were associated with French neoclassicism. Throughout the eighteenth century, English theorists glossed over the variety of French criticism, homogenizing it into an identifiable 'other' that was taken to be tied rigidly to neoclassical precepts such as the three unities, which prescribed that plays should have a single plot-line, a single location and a timescale for the action not exceeding twenty-four hours.

In reality, Boileau, the high priest of seventeenth-century French neoclassicism, was an apologist not only for poetic *art*, but also for sublimity: he praised Homer in the same language that would be used by later writers on original genius, revelling in the power of poetry to elevate, ravish, and transport the soul of the listener. A hundred years later the great French Enlightenment intellectual Denis Diderot also expressed admiration for the genius of Shakespeare. It had become a standard anti-classical move, typical of English and German criticism, to compare Shakespeare to a Gothic cathedral as opposed to a Greek temple. But this was precisely the move which Diderot made: Shakespeare, he said, did not have the poise of classical art, he was not the *Apollo Belvedere*, but he was nevertheless a colossus, comparable to Notre-Dame's great Gothic *St Christopher*. Diderot was as scornful of the shackling prescriptions of academicism, as committed to the idea that strong natural passion was the true source of creative genius, as any English theorist ever was. He would not have quarrelled with the sentiments of Pierre Le Tourneur in the dedicatory epistle to the first complete French translation of Shakespeare, published in 1776: 'Never did a man of genius penetrate more deeply into the abysses of the human heart nor cause passions to speak the language of nature with greater truth'. Yet, for all this, English critics from Addison to Coleridge insisted that the French met Shakespeare with nothing but abuse.

No exemplary Frenchman is to be found in Addison's first class of geniuses, in which Shakespeare is an English representative occupying a privileged place beside Homer, Pindar, and the Old Testament prophets. An integral part of the elevation of Shakespeare into this sublime company was the rejection of what was seen as stultifying French strictness – a rejection that would subsequently be repeated in Germany, when the writers of the '*Sturm und Drang*' deployed Shakespeare in a battle against French cultural domination.

Addison was but the most influential of many writers in the early eighteenth century who yoked Shakespeare, genius, and originality or naturalness. Again and again, we come across remarks such as the following, which is from a little *Dissertation on Reading the Classics* written in 1709 by one Henry Felton: 'Shakespeare is a wonderful Genius, a single Instance of the Force of Nature, and the Strength of Wit'. To say that a writer *is* a genius rather than that he *has* a genius is not merely to make a small change in customary linguistic usage; it is also to begin to elevate the artist into the special kind of man he became in Romanticism. It was exactly because of such moves that Shakespeare came to matter, and to be argued over, more and more profoundly as the eighteenth century went on.

In the same year as the *Spectator* paper we find Elijah Fenton making a link with the sense of genius as a 'presiding deity' when he describes Shakespeare as 'the Genius of our Isle'. Here the patriotic impulse is at work, as Shakespeare is used to make French critical principles look deficient; his transgression of those principles is a synecdoche for England's independence from the continental aesthetic mainstream. And aesthetic independence had its corollary in national independence.

For most of the eighteenth century England was at war with France or overshadowed by the memory of the last such war or the prospect of the next one. The 1712 *Essay on the Genius and Writings of Shakespear* was dedicated to George Granville, not because he had improved *The Merchant of Venice* for the stage, but because he was Secretary of War in the Cabinet. Several of Addison's *Spectator* papers were of the first importance in the growth of Bardolatry – they were written during the war with France that lasted from 1702 to 1712. Dr Johnson's 1765 edition of the Works of Shakespeare and David Garrick's Shakespeare Jubilee four years later were long-prepared milestones in the history of the Bard's reputation – they were planned during the Seven Years War against France. The 1808 lectures of August Wilhelm von Schlegel in Vienna and Samuel Taylor Coleridge in London might be said to constitute the arrival of Shakespearean appreciation at its high-water mark – they were delivered during the Napoleonic Wars.

Emergent English nationalism in the period throve on popular Francophobia, together with disdain for aristocratic Francophilia. In a classic analysis of nationalism, Isaiah Berlin suggested that 'It may be true that nationalism, as distinct from mere national consciousness – the sense of belonging to a nation – is in the first place a response to a patronizing or disparaging attitude towards the traditional values of a society, the result of wounded pride and a sense of humiliation in its most socially conscious members, which in due course produce anger and self-assertion.' Nationalism is a cultural phenomenon and one of its places of birth is therefore cultural tradition; the creation of an English literary history was a typical manifestation of mid-eighteenth century national (and anti-Gallic) consciousness. Berlin's statement may therefore be turned to literary historical account: the veneration of Shakespeare as English national poet was in the first place a response to a patronizing and disparaging attitude towards his works on the part of French critics and a Francophile court taste. That response emerged among eighteenth-century England's 'most socially conscious' groups, which is to say in anti-Jacobite, Whig circles, among what Marxist analysts have dubbed the incipient bourgeoisie.

In *The Spectator* no. 419 Addison argued that the imagination is particularly pleased by what Dryden had called 'the Fairie Way of Writing', that is to say, writing which comes from invention and fancy, not the observation of everyday reality. The English are said to be especially attuned to this sort of poetry, being 'naturally Fanciful' and 'disposed to Gloominess and Melancholy of Temper'. Here we have one of the seeds of the cult of the Gothic, which became widespread later in the century. Again, Shakespeare is the exemplar:

> Among the English, Shakespear has incomparably excelled all others. That noble Extravagance of Fancy which he had in so great Perfection, thoroughly qualified him to touch this weak superstitious Part of his Reader's Imagination; and made him capable of succeeding, where he had nothing to support him besides the Strength of his own Genius.

Addison was thinking of Shakespeare's 'Ghosts, Fairies, Witches and the like Imaginary Persons'; the first act of *Hamlet*, *A Midsummer Night's Dream*, *Macbeth*, and *The Tempest* thus came to be seen as his most characteristic achievements. The point had already been made in paper 279: 'It shows a greater Genius in *Shakespear* to have drawn his *Calyban*, than his *Hotspur* or *Julius Caesar*. The one was to be supplied out of his own Imagination, whereas the other might have been formed upon Tradition, History and Observation.' The originality of Shakespeare's supernatural characters, the way in which they seemed to embody the creative power of imagination, was perhaps the largest single factor in the English rejection of neoclassical theory. Caliban and Ariel, the fairies and the witches, are an affront to the creed of mimesis, of art's duty to be true to nature; in the second half of the eighteenth century they would provoke the extreme anti-classical claim that 'True Poesy is magic, not nature'. The way is prepared for the Romantic image of Shakespeare himself as Prospero, conjuring up magical spirits out of his own fertile imagination.

The Spectator belongs to a period when Addison was out of office after one of the Whigs' very few electoral setbacks in the first half of the century. Several essays in proximity to those on Shakespeare's imaginative originality express opposition to Tory negotiations for peace with France. Given this context, any reference such as that in paper 419 to a national genius stemming from the racial temperament of the English must be acknowledged to have had its origin in high political anti-French sentiment. But effects are not bound by their causes. Although Addison's views on Shakespeare were shaped by his own immersion in – and contribution to the formation of – a Whig-dominated public sphere for 'polite', gentlemanly literary discourse in the early eighteenth century, aesthetic positions are not determined wholly by the contingencies of the historical moment at which they emerge. A recognizably modern conception of the 'creative imagination' was first formulated in detail in Addison's series of eleven *Spectator* papers (nos. 411–21) on the pleasures of the imagination; the influence of that conception has far outlasted the coffee-house clique in which it emerged. The *Spectator* papers were highly formative in the very different cultural context of Germany, and during the 1740s they took on renewed life in England as a result of the popularization of some of their principal ideas in *The Pleasures of Imagination*, a much-reprinted poem by Mark Akenside, who came from lower middle-class northern Presbyterian stock – his father was a butcher in Newcastle-upon-Tyne – and thus wrote from well outside the dominant London literary culture.

A big idea like the 'creative imagination' can serve many masters; it provides a way of thinking and a language for talking about art which are extremely 'translatable'. Indeed, this particular idea offers a theoretical ground for the possibility of cultural translation: what is meant by the creative imagination is exactly the capacity to inhabit mentally places one has not experienced physically. By reading or watching a play we can imagine what it would be like to be Julius Caesar; the highest form of imagination, the argument goes, is that which conceives not just another person or another age but something unimaginable within the normal experience of nature. The extreme 'otherness' of Ariel and Caliban is the most authentic token of Shakespeare's strong imagination. In chapter eight we will see how a character such as Caliban has continued to exercise fascination and to perform cultural work in environments utterly different from that in which he was conceived by Shakespeare and praised by Addison. The afterlife of such characters demonstrates that the underlying general principles of Addison's papers on the imagination cannot be contained within their original political context. Those principles go on working in other contexts, they are reshaped in other traditions. Furthermore, a Shakespeare who is admired more for his Caliban than his Hotspur and his Julius Caesar is difficult to fit into a model of art that emphasizes its service to heroic patriotism and good government. Shakespeare's variety and mobility are impediments to any match between political and aesthetic partisanship.

There is notable restraint in Addison's phrase in the 419th *Spectator*, 'this weak superstitious Part of his Reader's Imagination'. While positing a link between imagination, genius, and the supernatural, Addison viewed the association with an air of detachment and superiority. His own poetic works, such as his tragedy *Cato*, widely admired in its own time but utterly moribund within a generation, are in a vein of high classicism that bears none of the marks of the Shakespearean supernatural. They are also more closely tied to the values of the polity within which they were composed: if one is seeking for an Addisonian production that is firmly locked in its own historical moment, one would do much better to look to *Cato* than to the papers on imagination. What is striking about the latter is how they were out of step with the dominant aesthetic values of their time: Addison sowed the seeds of the cult of imagination, but the fruit was not born in poetic practice until the 1740s.

Formally speaking, the poetry of Alexander Pope is perhaps the most artful, ordered, and 'French', the most un-Shakespearean, in the English language. Yet Pope edited Shakespeare's plays, and wrote of their author's originality and inspiration. It was principally with Shakespeare in mind that he asserted in his *Essay on Criticism* that

> Great Wits sometimes may *gloriously offend*,
> And rise to Faults true Criticks *dare not mend*;
> From *Vulgar Bounds* with *brave Disorder* part
> And *snatch* a *Grace* beyond the Reach of Art.

Whereas Shakespearean verse is characterized by '*brave Disorder*', Pope's couplets spring confusion into order. As with Addison, the perception of Shakespeare prevents Frenchified classicism from taking full hold. And again as with Addison, the genius of Shakespeare elicits ideas that are not so much locked in their own historical moment as proleptic of future literary revolutions. Later in the century a Shakespearean '*brave Disorder*' would be unleashed in both poetry and politics: radical commentators on the 'Romantic revolution', such as William Hazlitt and Leigh Hunt, linked the overthrow of the school of Pope with the ending of the French *ancien régime*. As will be seen in the case of Hector Berlioz, when an argument in favour of the Shakespearean grace beyond the reach of Racinean art finally gained ground in France in the 1820s, it too was driven by a revolutionary impulse.

The poet of nature

The split between theory and practice in Addison and Pope goes back to John Dryden's twin roles as father of both English literary criticism and English heroic verse. In Dr Johnson's words, Dryden 'refined the language, improved the sentiments, and tuned the numbers of English poetry'. He instituted a poetry in which, as Thomas Warton put it, 'imagination gave way to correctness, sublimity of description to delicacy of sentiment, and majestic imagery to conceit and epigram.' In crude terms, Dryden replaced Shakespearean imagination and original-ity with French art and learning. Yet in his poetic theory, he could not go along with a French-style condemnation of Shakespeare for breaking the rules of art. Restoration high culture found itself lodged on the horns of a dilemma: formed in exile in France during the Interregnum, it owed a debt to French precepts, but once transposed back to England it had to celebrate a native tradition which was not assimilable to French models.

In 1692 Thomas Rymer launched his arch-classical attack on Shake-spearean tragedy. For Rymer, it was a preposterous breach of decorum that the tragedy of Othello should turn on something so banal as a lost handkerchief. The play teaches us nothing but that ladies should look to their linen, he scoffed. Dryden responded by claiming that Shake-speare's genius outweighed his deficiencies:

> we know, in spite of Mr. R——, that genius alone is a greater virtue (if I may so call it) than all other qualifications put together. You see what success this learned critic has found in the world, after his blaspheming Shakespeare. Almost all the faults which he has dis-covered are truly there; yet who will read Mr. Rym[er] or not read Shakespeare? For my own part, I reverence Mr. Rym[er]'s learning, but I detest his ill nature and arrogance. I indeed, and such as I, have reason to be afraid of him, but Shakespeare has not.

Dryden's own learning and concern for decorum led him to acknowl-edge the truth of Rymer's Frenchified claims, but at the same time the metaphor of blasphemy implicitly makes Shakespeare into a god. Rymer established his credentials with the translation of a work of high neoclassicism, René Rapin's *Reflections on Aristotle's Treatise of Poesy*; he ended his career as the king's historiographer: Shakespeare could only be an obstacle on his path from French theory to the English court. More directly, what he saw as the vulgar theatrical taste for Shakespeare's hybrid dramas was an obstacle in getting his own heroic drama, *Edgar, or the English Monarch*, into the repertoire. This play – which obeyed the neoclassical unity of time so exactly that the entire action took place between noon and ten p.m. on a single day – never reached the stage, a fate bound to fuel its author's animus against plays like *Othello* which held the stage despite their gross indecorums and wanton breaches of the precept that the action of a play should be confined to a single day and a single location.

After the Glorious Revolution of 1688 and with the Whig ascendancy in the new century, court and French values became increasingly unpopular. The school of Rymer never constituted more than an embattled minority; instead, the seed of Bardolatry sown by Dryden took root. Subsequent French-influenced English theorists such as Charles Gildon had to perform a delicate balancing act: 'Those scatter'd Sparks of a great Genius, which shou'd shine with united Glory, are in the huddle of Ignorance or want of Art so dissipated and divided, and so blended with Contraries, that they are extremely obscur'd, if not entirely extinguish'd.' In judgements such as this, there is an uneasy attempt to value both 'French' polish and native 'English' Genius.

That Shakespeare became England's supreme culture hero in the eighteenth century caused great difficulty for the *ancien régime* aesthetics associated with theorists like Gildon and John Dennis. To characterize Shakespeare by way of his native genius made it impossible to sustain arguments about the need for refinement and control. But then the dangerous thing about genius is that it is no respecter of rank. Fear of a *vulgar* Bard gaining too much ground was one cause of the vigour of Edmond Malone's attempts to co-opt Shakespeare in the name of tradition after 1789, and hence his hostility to the Ireland forgeries, discussed in chapter three.

The tension between literary theory and dramatic-poetic practice in the English neoclassical tradition is seen most obviously in Dryden's *All for Love*, his reworking of *Antony and Cleopatra*. In the preface to that play Dryden wrote, 'In my style I have professed to imitate the divine Shakespeare [who] by the force of his own genius perform[ed] so much that in a manner he has left no praise for any who come after him'.

Shakespeare is the exemplar of original genius and divine inspiration; Dryden's desire to imitate him was so great that for once he disencumbered himself of rhyme and wrote a tragedy in blank verse. Yet when we read *All for Love* we cannot conceive of it as Shakespearean.

T. S. Eliot tried to account for this in a radio talk. He compared the dying words of Shakespeare's Charmian,

> It is well done, and fitting for a princess
> Descended of so many royal kings.
> Ah, soldier!
>
> (5.2.321–3)

with those of her counterpart in *All for Love*: 'Yes, 'tis well done, and like a queen, the last / Of her great race: I follow her' (5.1.505–6). For Eliot, the key to the superiority of Shakespeare's lines was the last two words, which Shakespeare added to the description of Charmian's death in his source, North's Plutarch. In its very mysteriousness, 'Ah, soldier!' gives Shakespeare's Charmian a kind of life that Dryden's equivalent lacks. We cannot know what she is thinking as she addresses the Roman soldier and dies, but the fact that she addresses him in this way makes us believe that she is thinking something – perhaps 'if you only knew', or 'you would not understand', or 'my mistress is the true soldier', or even 'you gorgeous man, if only I weren't dying, I might make you mine as Cleopatra made Antony hers'. The illusion is created that Charmian has a rich interior life and it is this that makes her into a truly 'dramatic' creation. 'Ah, soldier!' is one of those touches that are definitive of what Tolstoy called Shakespeare's 'peculiarity'.

In undertaking an analysis of this sort, T. S. Eliot was following in the tracks of William Hazlitt who, together with Coleridge, was among the first to argue that the essence of Shakespeare's genius lay in such details as this. Thus in his essay on *Antony and Cleopatra* in *Characters of Shakespear's Plays* (1817), Hazlitt wrote, 'Few things in Shakespear (and we know of nothing in any other author like them) have more of that local truth of imagination and character than the passage in which Cleopatra is presented conjecturing what were the employments of Antony in his absence – "He's speaking now, or murmuring – *Where's my serpent of old Nile?*"' You could not imagine one of Voltaire's tragic characters descending to such fancies. Hazlitt's emphasis on the particular in imagery – 'that *local* truth of imagination' – and, concomitantly, on local observation in analysis, are further marks of a distinctively anti-French, anti-systematic, empirical inflection of both creativity and criticism.

Cleopatra's image of herself as the serpent of the Nile prepares the way for her suicide with a serpent of the Nile, an asp, at her breast. That serpent is brought to her by a clown. The intrusion into tragedy of clowns, with their prose vulgarities and colloquialisms, was widely regarded by neoclassical theorists as Shakespeare's worst breach of decorum. In the course of the eighteenth century, the custom of 'improving' Shakespeare's poetic language for theatrical representation was gradually abandoned – but it was not until 1838 that his most remarkable clown, the Fool in *King Lear*, was restored to the stage.

Literary theory usually lags behind theatrical practice, but in the recognition that truth to nature meant the mingling of high and low, tragedy and comedy, it was for once ahead. In 1765, long before the restoration of the Fool, Dr Johnson's magnificent Preface to his edition of Shakespeare demolished the neoclassical theory that verisimilitude demanded the separation of dramatic kinds:

> Shakespeare is above all writers, at least above all modern writers, the poet of nature ... Shakespeare's plays are not in the rigorous and critical sense either tragedies or comedies, but compositions of a distinct kind; exhibiting the real state of sublunary nature, which partakes of good and evil, joy and sorrow, mingled with endless variety of proportion and innumerable modes of combination; and expressing the course of the world, in which the loss of one is the gain of another; in which, at the same time, the reveller is hasting to his wine, and the mourner burying his friend; in which the malignity of one is sometimes defeated by the frolick of another; and many mischiefs and many benefits are done and hindered without design.

Nor was Johnson by any means the first to argue that the mingling of tragedy and comedy, the interplay of moods and the sheer range of characters, was the quintessence of Shakespeare's genius. A hundred years before the 1765 preface, Margaret Cavendish, Duchess of Newcastle, had said something very similar. Beginning from a defence of Shakespeare's taste for 'Clowns, Fools, Watchmen, and the like', she argued that it required as much art to represent low characters as high ones, drunken ones as politic ones, and that Shakespeare's 'wit' consisted in his power to express in his plays 'all Sorts of Persons, as one would think he had been Transformed into every one' of them.

Someone's gain is always another's loss; nature knows no moment of pure tragic mourning or unalloyed comic festivity. Johnson's perception of the movement of Shakespearean drama is reminiscent of the pair of buckets ascending and descending a well to which King Richard II compares himself and Bolingbroke: the triumph of one is dependent on the decline of the other (*Richard II*, 4.1.184–9). Margaret Cavendish understood that Shakespeare's genius was, so to speak, to pour himself equally into each bucket: 'Who would not think he had been such a man as his Sir *John Falstaff*? and who would not think he had been *Harry* the Fifth?' She also believed that there was no distinction of sex in his character-filling capacity: 'one would think that he had been Metamorphosed from a Man to a Woman, for who could Describe *Cleopatra* Better than he hath done, and many other Females of his own Creating?' But, as in the cases of her contemporary Dryden and her successor Johnson, the Duchess of Newcastle's admiration for Shakespeare's mingling of styles and characters did not spill over into dramatic practice – her own witty and urbane plays are monovocal; they do not attempt to weave together tragedy and comedy, or elevated verse and vernacular prose.

Origin and originality

From the mid-eighteenth century onwards, Shakespeare as 'poet of nature' was increasingly associated not only with broad truth to the course of the world, but also with 'nature' in the sense of the country as opposed to the city. Joseph Warton's poem *The Enthusiast: or the Lover of Nature* was a typical production of the 1740s. English rural locations are regarded as the source of poetic inspiration or 'enthusiasm'. Warton's image of Shakespeare revives and elaborates the native woodnotes of Milton's 'L'Allegro':

> What are the Lays of artful *Addison*,
> Coldly correct, to *Shakespeare*'s Warblings wild?
> Whom on the winding *Avon*'s willow'd Banks
> Fair Fancy found, and bore the smiling Babe

>   To a close Cavern. (Still the Shepherds shew
>   The sacred Place, whence with religious Awe
>   They hear, returning from the Field at Eve,
>   Strange Whisperings of sweet Music thro' the Air.)

Nature is given a local habitation and a name through the siting of Shakespeare in Stratford-upon-Avon. The notion that Shakespeare's inspiration has a divine origin has here led to an almost outrageous identification with Christ, achieved through the juxtaposition of shepherds and birthplace, and the equation of The Tempest's music in the air with the angels heralding the Incarnation.

In his Pindaric ode, The Progress of Poesy, written a few years later, Thomas Gray identified Shakespeare as 'Nature's darling' and planted him firmly on the banks of the Avon. William Blake illustrated the stanza in question (Fig. 6) with the infant Shakespeare – his profile uncannily like that of Blake himself – crooked in the arms of a mother Nature who unveils her face and hands him the key to the golden gate of joy which opens onto the realm of the imagination. In the foreground a female figure representing Sympathy empties a bowl of tears into the 'lucid Avon'. The river which runs through Stratford is thus made into England's equivalent of the springs of Mount Helicon from which classical poets traditionally drew inspiration. The mingling of waters symbolizes both the full flow of Shakespeare's sympathetic imagining of the passions and the poet's oneness with the powers of Nature.

In The Pleasures of Imagination, one of the most widely read poems of the mid-eighteenth century, Mark Akenside conceived of the moment of imaginative creation by way of a Shakespearean allusion that would be reiterated countless times in the following eighty years. The poet is called 'The child of Fancy': the phrase signals that Shakespeare is the exemplar, for in 'L'Allegro' Milton had famously called him 'fancy's child'. But then there is a more direct quotation:

>   By degrees, the mind
>   Feels her young nerves dilate: the plastic powers
>   Labour for action: blind emotions heave
>   His bosom; and with loveliest frenzy caught,
>   From earth to heaven he rolls his daring eye,
>   From heaven to earth.

This is an attempt to poeticize a theory of associative mental activity that is based on the ideas of John Locke, but it is also an image of poetic creation that is based on Shakespeare's own:

> The poet's eye, in a fine frenzy rolling,
> Doth glance from heaven to earth, from earth to heaven,
> And as imagination bodies forth
> The forms of things unknown, the poet's pen
> Turns them to shapes, and gives to airy nothing
> A local habitation and a name.
>
> (*A Midsummer Night's Dream*, 5.1.12–17)

In the context of *A Midsummer Night's Dream*, these lines spoken by Theseus are a critique of the imagination's delusive power, but in the second half of the eighteenth century they were almost universally treated as Shakespeare's own, and therefore the authoritative, definition of poetic creativity. This idea that creativity is to do with the embodying of airy nothings rather than verisimilitude to a commonly perceptible 'general nature' would have been anathema to Voltaire.

Perhaps the most concentrated manifesto for original genius as against French neoclassical imitativeness was Edward Young's *Conjectures on Original Composition* of 1759. Dr Johnson was characteristically tetchy about this little book: 'he was surprized to find Young receive as novelties, what he [Johnson] thought very common maxims. . . . he believed Young was not a great scholar, nor had studied regularly the art of writing.' They thought differently of this matter in Germany: there, where Young's *Night Thoughts on Life, Death, and Immortality* was already well known, his essay's concerns chimed with those of the nascent '*Sturm und Drang*' and within a year two translations had appeared. Together with other English-language works of the same period and tenor, such as Lord Kames' *Elements of Criticism* (1762), the *Conjectures* played a significant role in shaping the aesthetics of Herder, and in particular his essay on Shakespeare.

Johnson's reaction to Young and that of the Germans are not as aberrant from each other as they seem: both are accounted for by the pithiness of the *Conjectures*. Young achieved his effect through the establishment of rigid dichotomies: 'Learning we thank, Genius we revere; That gives us pleasure, This gives us rapture; That informs, This inspires; and is itself inspired; for genius is from heaven, learning from man'. The phrases are held in balance, but genius is always given the stronger epithet; the scale is tipped through the addition of 'and is itself inspired'. Where others were beginning to produce philosophical and psychological tracts about genius, Young crystallized a number of key ideas into maxims that were at once lucid and provocative.

In classical poetics, the imitation of ancient authors had gone hand in hand with the imitation of nature; Young, in contrast, divided the two practices, confined the term imitation to the imitation of previous authors, and extolled as originals those writers who had direct access to nature. '*Originals* can arise from genius only,' he asserted. Johnson saw both genius and learning as qualities; Young argued that 'To neglect of learning, genius sometimes owes its greater glory'. Dennis had suggested that Shakespeare would have been even greater if he had added learning to his genius; for Young, he would have been diminished – 'Who knows whether *Shakespeare* might not have thought less, if he had read more?', '*Shakespeare* mingled no water with his wine, lower'd his genius by no vapid imitation'.

Young's metaphors include that of the genius as magician: 'A *Genius* differs from a *good understanding*, as a magician from a good architect; *that* raises his structure by means invisible; *this* by the skilful use of common tools. Hence Genius has ever been supposed to partake of something Divine.' The two very different concepts of poetry bequeathed to the modern world by the ancients, imitation and inspiration, are no longer viewed as complementary. The second is now pre-eminent. Young makes Shakespeare into the archetypal genius by reading him as exemplar of the second without the first.

The German national poet

The popularity in Germany of Young's work was the result of a need to find an alternative aesthetic to the French model. The two principal features of German political and cultural life in the middle of the eighteenth century were that the language of the nobility was French and that a unified nation as such did not exist, since the German-speaking territories were divided into an array of independent sover-eignties. Faced with these divisions, men and women of letters began to argue for the forging of a 'polite literature' in the German language.

Potentially, this was a means of both breaking free from Francophone domination and unifying the nation. Even if the different states retained political autonomy, it would become possible to speak of a German national culture.

In the 1730s and '40s, a manifesto for a new German literature was set down by Johann Christoph Gottsched. He argued that a national culture must be based on a national theatre and that the best model for a German theatre would be French neoclassical drama. This position was contested by Johann Elias Schlegel in his *Vergleichung Shakespears und Andreas Gryphs*, the first extended German treatise on Shakespeare, published in 1741 in the wake of the first translation of a complete Shakespearean play into the German language, Caspar Wilhelm von Borck's version of *Julius Caesar*. J. E. Schlegel argued that Shakespeare had to be judged by different standards from those of neoclassical drama; he thus opened up the possibility that the model for a new German literature might not be the French one. It was at exactly this time that *The Spectator* was appearing in German translation. In sketching the nature of Shakespeare's genius, Johann Schlegel referred to those essays of Addison which emphasized his imagination and the special power of his supernatural creations.

The desire of the emergent German bourgeoisie to cut free from the Francophone aristocracy and forge their own cultural identity meant that Johann Schlegel's position came to look more attractive than Gottsched's. So it was that a group of critical theorists based in Berlin was able to press home the case for Shakespeare. In the seventeenth of his *Literaturbriefe*, published in 1759, G. E. Lessing argued that Gottsched's reliance on French models was misguided because it emphasized the pretty, the tender, and the amorous, whereas the German temperament was more suited to the characteristics of the English, and in particular the Shakespearean, drama: the grand, the terrible, the melancholy. Shakespeare thus became the presiding genius – in theory, though not initially in terms of actual stage repertoire – of the attempt to establish a German national theatre in Hamburg. In the eleventh and twelfth papers of Lessing's manifesto for that theatre, the *Hamburgische Dramaturgie*, the ghost in *Hamlet* was praised above that in Voltaire's *Sémiramis*. Lessing's analysis marks Germany's decisive break from the most influential figure of French Enlightenment letters.

This was the context, then, in which Young's *Conjectures* were received into Germany. It was under their influence that Heinrich von Gerstenberg set learning against genius and claimed Shakespeare, in language identical to that of Warton and Gray, as 'the darling genius of mother nature'. In the eyes of Johann Georg Hamann, it was Young who had shown once and for all that the essence of art was inspiration, not imitation, that poetry was born from divine fury, not made through neoclassical craft.

Hamann's disciple, Johann Gottfried Herder, saw the key application to literary practice in Germany: Young had demonstrated that what was needed was not imitation of Shakespeare, but rather emulation of him. Foreign models, and especially French ones, should be thrown off; the ground would then be clear for native genius to grow, as it had done in Shakespeare's England. This native genius would be characterized by spontaneity and enthusiasm; through it, German culture would be regenerated. The new culture would share in the spirit of Shakespeare, but be distinctively national in its identity. Herder was expressing these ideas contemporaneously with the young Goethe's discovery of Shakespeare, which was again characterized – as in his 'Shakespeare's Birthday' oration of 1771 – by praise of the English poet's truth to nature as opposed to the restrictions of French art.

Herder wrote that the aim of his essay on Shakespeare was 'to explain him, feel him as he is, use him, and – if possible – make him alive for us in Germany'. For Herder and his successors, Shakespeare's creation of a drama that showed no concern for the so-called rules of Aristotle served as the prime precedent for their own artistic principles and practice. The drama of Elizabethan England was exemplary because it was created out of the nation's 'own history, the spirit of its age, customs, views, language, national attitudes, traditions, and pastimes'. A programme for a new national drama was raised upon the claim that Shakespeare's plays were deeply rooted in the traditions of the people (*das Volk*) and the exultation of history as the substance of the drama ('every play is History in the widest sense'). Herder's hopes for German culture were amply realized in the next thirty years, principally through the great historical tragedies of Goethe and Schiller.

That Herder's essay on Shakespeare was intimately linked to contemporary cultural nationalism is demonstrable from the context in which it was first published, an anonymous collection of five essays, actually edited by Herder himself, which appeared in Hamburg in 1773 under the title 'On German Character and Art' (*Von deutscher Art und Kunst*). Shakespeare was brought into the company of the Gaelic bard Ossian (praised in Herder's second contribution as another un-French, 'folk' poet), of Gothic – again unclassical – architecture (the subject of two essays, including one by Goethe in praise of Strasbourg Cathedral), and of German history (the subject of the fifth essay, by Justus Möser). Shakespeare had for some time been established as the English national poet; now he was the German one too. For both nationalities he served as a weapon against the hegemonic tendencies of French neoclassical culture. This was the most significant sense in which he was 'used' and 'made alive' in the eighteenth and nineteenth centuries.

'Classical' German literature, we may then say, had its origins in a combination of anti-French sentiment, Shakespearean inspiration, Young's articulation of the divisibility of genius and imitation, Herder's theory of national culture expressing itself in untrammelled poetry, and Goethe's own innate genius.

In the following century, German writers turned again and again to Shakespeare for their inspiration. They found a perfect mirror of themselves in the character of Hamlet. Did he not attend a German university at Wittenberg? Is not his problem that being a German intellectual has not prepared him for the great political task that has been laid upon his shoulders? This reading of *Hamlet* had its origins in Goethe's *Wilhelm Meister's Apprenticeship*, which I will discuss in chapter nine. It eventually led to the anguished cry of the ardently democratic and nationalist poet, Ferdinand Freiligrath: '*Deutschland ist Hamlet*' – Germany *is* Hamlet, when will it stop agonizing and philosophizing, when will it rouse itself to action? Freiligrath's poem of 1844, which begins with this identification, proceeds to an allegorical reading of the play. The ghost symbolizes the Freedom that Germany lacks; he summons Hamlet, at once a representative of both the diseased body-politic and the paralysed intellectual, to bring revolution, freedom from French influence, and new national vigour.

The first detailed retrospective treatment of Shakespeare and the birth of German literature was Friedrich Gundolf's *Shakespeare und der Deutsche Geist* ('Shakespeare and the German Spirit'), published in Berlin in 1911. By then Germany was ready to flex its national muscles. Under Kaiser Wilhelm II, the nation was no longer Hamlet but Coriolanus. That Gundolf wrote the history of Shakespeare as

Germany's national poet shortly before Germany went to war with England has a certain irony. As will be seen in the next chapter, one impulse behind the English patriotic praise of Shakespeare in the Great War was the desire to reclaim him from the Germans.

The uses of genius

Shakespeare and Mozart are the archetypal Original Geniuses because the idea of original genius emerged as a way of explaining the phenomenon of Shakespeare and because Mozart appeared as a child prodigy at the precise historical moment – the late eighteenth century – when pure native endowment was becoming the vital test of true creative greatness.

The history I have sketched in this chapter reveals the capacity of Shakespeare to effect long-term cultural change. The qualities that distinguished his works from those admired by 'French' taste required the creation of a new descriptive literary-critical language. That language – of imagination, genius, originality – led to changes in aesthetic practice. Literary historical shorthand has a word for those changes: Romanticism. With Romanticism, poetry was elevated into a form of secular scripture, Shakespeare into God.

It has been suggested that genius became a Romantic obsession because it was a conception that seemed to guarantee individuality. It was, according to the scholar Thomas McFarland, 'an analogue of the unduplicatibility, always hoped for even if only precariously real, of the individual'. Hamlet may be the archetype of the individual consciousness, but Shakespeare was not Hamlet. If anything, he was the genius of community, not individuality. He lived and lives in a community of artists, or, in William Hazlitt's term, in 'the commonwealth of letters'. The cultural commentator David Bromwich has written of the difference between Wordsworth and Coleridge over the question of the poet's individuality or communality. Where Coleridge set store by 'the creative, and self-sufficing power of absolute *Genius*', Wordsworth argued that without poets no community is fully human, for the poet is the representative instance of 'a man speaking to men'. Coleridge's solitary Romantic genius is the inheritor of Hamlet, Wordsworth's voice of the community is the inheritor of Shakespeare.

For by 'Shakespeare' we mean not an individual, but a body of work, and that body was, I argued in part one, shaped by many individuals — by the dramatist's education and his precursors, by the actors of his company, by the audience without whom no play can be completed. Furthermore, because of what happened in the eighteenth century, the meaning of 'Shakespeare' cannot be restricted to William Shakespeare's lifetime: it also has to embrace his afterlife as the 'presiding genius' of later cultures. His friend Jonson claimed that he was 'Not of an age, but for all time'. The eighteenth-century elevation of him to the very image of creative genius fulfilled this prophecy. It allowed his communality to extend to his influence on the lives of subsequent readers, writers, and playgoers.

When Shakespeare died, he did not know that in a later century he would come back to life as midwife assisting at the birth of a new and powerfully enduring conception of 'Literature' as a special kind of writing, marked above all by intensity of imagination. He did not know that in the eighteenth century he would become an icon for the height of human creativity and the possibility of secular immortality — 'the god', in the famous phrase of Garrick's Jubilee ode, 'of our idolatry'. In all this, through the very process of shaping a new sense for the word 'genius', Shakespeare forced it back to its oldest sense, that of a tutelar deity. Once claimed as the national poet, he was identified as 'the Genius of our Isle'. It has been argued that nationalism developed in the eighteenth century because religion and monarchy ceased to exercise the spiritual and temporal power they had held until then. By this account, Shakespeare took over from God and King and became the deity of the secular Enlightenment and the guarantor of the new 'imagined community' of the nation-state.

But he also became the tutelar deity of a panoply of cultural communities. Though his cult first grew on native ground and drew strength from opposition to the cosmopolitanism of French intellectuals such as Voltaire, that cult itself became a new vehicle for international exchange. The deification of Shakespeare was partly a function of emergent nationalisms associated with rising middle-classes. But the emergent discourse of genius also created a language of cultural *emancipation*. 'A foreign greatness', wrote Emerson in 'Uses of Great Men', 'is the antidote for cabalism'. Hazlitt recognized that the 'aristocracy of letters' is a very different thing from the 'aristocracy of rank'. To speak of Shakespeare as boundless and wild, to characterize genius in terms of enthusiasm and excess, is to reinvent the poet as revolutionary man, free from restraints of decorum and rank. Paradoxically, in their 'anti-French' promulgation of Shakespeare's genius, Addison and his followers prepared the ground for an identification between the poetry of inspiration and the principles of the French Revolution. They let, we might say, the genius out of the bottle.

1. That domed forehead:
the Droeshout engraving
in the First Folio of
Shakespeare

2. Shakespeare's patron:
Henry Wriothesley, third
Earl of Southampton

3. *Above left:* John Florio: Italian tutor, household spy (?), cuckold (??)

4. *Above right:* Samuel Daniel: sonneteer, brother of a possible dark lady

5. *Left:* Bacon writes Shakespeare: caricature by Max Beerbohm

6. Shakespeare and nature: illustration by William Blake to Thomas Gray's *The Progress of Poesy*

7. Character as icon: *David Garrick as Richard III*, engraving after William Hogarth

8. *Left:* Laurence Olivier as Hamlet: the influence of Goethe

9. *Below:* Hamlet and Gertrude: the influence of Freud

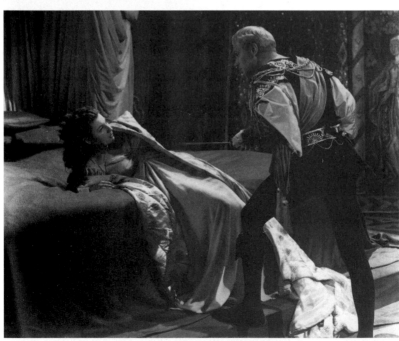

10. The Pre-Raphaelite Ophelia in Olivier's *Hamlet*

11. Ophelia, by J. E. Millais

12. Theatrical representation: *Garrick and Mrs Pritchard as Macbeth and Lady Macbeth after the murder of Duncan*, by J. H. Fuseli, now in the Kunsthaus, Zürich

13. Imaginative vision: *Garrick and Mrs Pritchard in Macbeth*, by J. H. Fuseli

14. Seeing things: *The Apparition of the Ghost*, engraving after J. H. Fuseli

15. Dreaming: *Titania and Bottom*, by J. H. Fuseli

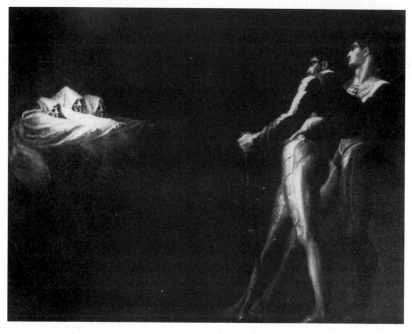

16. A vision across the abyss: *The Witches appear to Macbeth and Banquo,*
engraving after J. H. Fuseli

17. 'Confronting him with self-comparisons': *Macbeth consulting the vision of the Armed Head*, by J. H. Fuseli

18. Romeo (Charles Kemble) 'snatches the beloved body' of Juliet (Harriet
Smithson) 'and brings it to the front of the stage where he holds it upright
in his arms': engraving from performance at the Odeón, Paris, 1827

19. 'A certain moral grandeur, a saintly grace, something of vestal dignity and purity': *Isabella appearing to Angelo*, by William Hamilton

20. The concentration of the reader: *John Keats*, by Joseph Severn, Shakespeare
(engraving from the 'Chandos' portrait) presiding on the wall

7

THE NATIONAL POET

Back to basics

Imagine a country in which Shakespeare is made compulsory in the national curriculum in secondary schools and where an 'official' interpretation transforms him into the guardian of the value system of the established powers. Such a country might be England, where a set Shakespeare play is a key element of the nationally prescribed tests in English for fourteen-year-olds and where the official interpretation is heard in the mouths of government ministers.

In January 1994, the British Conservative government, in its fifteenth year of uninterrupted power, had a particularly bad month. Just as it was embracing a new leading idea of a return to 'basic' values, stories broke concerning ministerial adultery which made pious pronouncements about traditional morality look hypocritical. Then an independent auditor produced a mass of evidence that Westminster City Council, hailed by successive Conservative prime ministers as the party's 'flagship' authority in local government, had been engaged in gerrymandering, selling publicly owned housing to private individuals in return for the expectation of their votes. The day after the publication of these findings, Michael Portillo, the Chief Secretary to the Treasury, made a speech to the annual dinner of Conservative Way Forward, a grouping within the party devoted to the fostering of a strongly right-wing agenda. It was a speech which marked him out as the right's candidate for the prime ministerial succession. In it he argued that the greatest danger facing the nation was lack of respect for institutions:

> The relations which hold society together stretch from top to bottom. If Crown, Parliament, and Church are not respected, neither will be law, judges, or policemen, nor professors nor teachers nor

social workers, nor bosses, managers, or foremen. Social disorder
follows when respect breaks down. A society in which people hold
those in authority in contempt, and don't even think much of
themselves, is set upon the road to disintegration.

He then went on to support this claim by means of a substantial
quotation:

> In Shakespeare's *Troilus and Cressida*, Ulysses explains how order in
> society depends upon a series of relationships of respect and duty
> from top to bottom.

> > When degree is shaked,
> > Which is the ladder to all high designs,
> > The enterprise is sick. How could communities,
> > Degrees in schools, and brotherhoods in cities,
> > Peaceful commerce from dividable shores,
> > The primogenity and due of birth,
> > Prerogative of age, crown, sceptres, laurels,
> > But by degree stand in authentic place?
> > Take but degree away, untune that string,
> > And hark what discord follows . . .
> > Strength should be lord of imbecility.
> > And the rude son should strike his father dead;
> > Force should be right, or rather right and wrong . . .
> > Should lose their names, and so should justice too.

Shakespeare, it seems, was a good Tory, a believer in rank and
institutions and the established order. The ellipsis in the quotation after
'right and wrong' indicates that Portillo omitted an awkward parenthesis
in which Ulysses says that 'justice resides' in what seems to be a rather
grey area 'between' the 'endless jar' of 'right and wrong'. Such a
complication did not serve the quoter's purpose, so it was quietly
suppressed. Quotation was as ever used selectively to support a
particular position; for Portillo and his audience, it was comforting to
see the national poet promulgating the values in which they believed
and by which they sought to govern.

Shakespeare put some persuasive political rhetoric into the mouth of
Ulysses in *Troilus and Cressida*, but this is not to say that Ulysses'
argument is the argument of the whole play, let alone an expression of
the personal political beliefs of its author. A good test of the worth of a

character's opinions is their relation to that character's actions, and by this account Ulysses looks distinctly questionable. He identifies as one of the causes of the untuning of degree in the Greek camp the fact that their best soldier, Achilles, is sulking in his tent when he should be in the appropriate place for the best soldier, namely on the battlefield. But the method Ulysses then proposes by which Achilles can be restored to his proper place is itself a disruption of degree: Hector, the top Trojan warrior, has challenged the top Greek to single combat; degree should dictate that Achilles will be put forward, but Ulysses proposes the blockish Ajax instead, thus snubbing Achilles and provoking him to rejoin the army. For Ulysses, 'degree' is but rhetoric in the service of machiavellian 'policy'. Given the proximity in time of Portillo's speech to the revelations about gerrymandering by Westminster Tories, there is a certain piquancy in the fact that a few minutes after delivering his apology for 'degree', Ulysses rigs an election.

Portillo's speech was directed against those who had become 'cynical' about Britain's ancient institutions and traditional values. Ironically, there could be no better word than 'cynical' for Shakespeare's representation in *Troilus and Cressida* of traditional codes and values. It was exactly for that reason that the legitimate theatre hardly ever staged the play in the eighteenth and nineteenth century; this deeply ironic drama only came into its own in the aftermath of the First World War, when it was successful for the very reason that its cynicism about military top brass caught the public mood as the nation reflected on what General Haig and his colleagues had inflicted upon the common soldier on the Somme and at Ypres. The case of *Troilus and Cressida* demonstrates that Shakespeare has been made to speak against the Establishment as well as for it.

As was shown in the last chapter, Shakespeare's eighteenth-century emergence as England's genius was in part a manifestation of cultural nationalism. But the nation and the Establishment are by no means one and the same thing. This is something which the Establishment has a tendency to forget. Oddly, though, it is something which the anti-Establishment also has a tendency to forget.

At exactly the time when the British government was prescribing Shakespeare as the centre of the national secondary school curriculum in English studies, some college and university English departments began following an American lead and removing him from the centre of the higher level curriculum, so as to give space instead to those who had previously been on the margins of culture – women and blacks. In 1992, the arch-conservative newspaper *The Sunday Telegraph* was apoplectic at the news of a survey which claimed that the black American woman novelist Alice Walker had become a compulsory author in more institutions of higher education than was Shakespeare.

It was in the name of the national heritage that the Conservative government gave Shakespeare his honorific place in the school curriculum. In the late twentieth century, advanced literary theory was out of sympathy with Toryism and very uncomfortable with the idea of a national heritage. The *Sunday Telegraph* article made Shakespeare synonymous with 'our cultural inheritance' – radical theorists wanted nothing to do with that 'our'. During the 1980s literary studies became more openly politicized than they had ever been before. Demographic and cultural changes in the United States meant that there was a mounting challenge to the canons of taste which placed Dead White European Males at the centre of the literature curriculum. The idea of 'England's Heritage' became so associated with Conservative hegemony that independent-minded academics wished to detach themselves from anything tainted by association with it. Because of these developments, a new story began to be told about Shakespeare's status as National Poet, Bard of Bards, genius not of an age but for all time.

The argument goes something like this. Shakespeare's extraordinary reputation and continuing prestige are a function not of his poetic genius but of his political servility, his adaptability to Establishment values. He rose to pre-eminence in the period 1660–1830 on the back of the British Empire, the strength of the middle class and the reaction against the French Revolution. The guardians and propagators of Shakespeare's reputation in the early twentieth century – men like A. C. Bradley, Sir Walter Raleigh, John Dover Wilson, T. S. Eliot and G. Wilson Knight – were all compromised by either Romantic idealism (pretending that Shakespeare wasn't political when in fact he was) or right-wing fanaticism. By the middle of the twentieth century, Shakespeare had become an apologist for order and hierarchy as embodied in a value-structure that was best summed up by Ulysses' speech on degree. The shorthand term for this value-structure was 'The Elizabethan World Picture', and so it was that sniping at a small book so named, written in the 1940s by E. M. W. Tillyard, became the most easily recognizable badge of those whom I shall call the New Iconoclasts in Shakespeare studies.

I do not wish to nail this story as a complete lie, because I do not believe that it is one. But I do believe that it offers nothing like the whole truth and that there is a real danger of other parts of the Shakespeare story being forgotten. My next two chapters sketch some of those other parts. It is my argument that, confining it to its socio-political dimension alone, the story of Shakespeare's extraordinary reputation and continuing prestige is a function not only of the impulses variously labelled by the New Iconoclasts as 'reactionary', 'hegemonic', and 'nationalistic', but also of counter-readings which could variously be labelled 'radical', 'anti-Establishment', and 'supranational'.

The aim of the chapters is, if one may adapt a rousing phrase of the historian E. P. Thompson, to rescue some of Shakespeare's past admirers from the enormous condescension of current academic criticism. My quarrel with the New Iconoclasm is that it seems to have a vested interest in ignoring the contribution which Shakespeare has made to the lives and works of people whom 'radical' critics ought to care about – people like the Chartist Thomas Cooper and the poet of *négritude* Aimé Césaire, people whose radicalism brought about real historical change.

Many of those whose passion for Shakespeare I wish to resuscitate were either anti-Establishment or not English. A persistent feature of the Establishment or Tory or English nationalist construction of Shakespeare during the last two and a half centuries has been the attempt to wrest him away from foreigners (especially Germans) and those regarded as subversive (such as William Hazlitt, whose vital engagement with the plays I have discussed in my book *Shakespearean Constitutions*). The supreme irony of the Anglo-American New Iconoclasm is that it too contrived to exclude foreigners and subversives from the province of Shakespeare. If these chapters do a little to restore them there, they will have done their work.

This England

The two most influential books on Shakespeare written in the early years of the twentieth century were A. C. Bradley's *Shakespearean*

Tragedy of 1904 and Walter Raleigh's *William Shakespeare* of 1907, the latter being the capstone to the best-selling series of primers, 'English Men of Letters'. In two essays which represent the New Iconoclasm in Shakespeare studies at its wittiest and most irreverent, Terence Hawkes has reconstructed and deconstructed the ideological circumstances in which these books were written. The academic careers of Bradley and Raleigh ran curiously in parallel: from Oxford to Liverpool to Glasgow and back to Oxford. Each time Bradley vacated a Chair, Raleigh stepped in to fill it. Hawkes might say that Raleigh was always there as the overtly ideological, chauvinistic shadow of Bradley's apparently supraideological idealism. I begin in the same place as Hawkes, but do so in order to reach a different destination.

In 1889, Andrew Cecil Bradley, first holder of the University of Liverpool's King Alfred Chair in English Literature, and still the first name of which many people think when 'Shakespearean Criticism' is mentioned, departed for the Regius Chair at Glasgow. He was succeeded by the twenty-eight-year-old Walter Raleigh, a man furnished with an auspicious name for the study of the 'golden' period of English literature, the age of Queen Elizabeth. When translated to Oxford early in the new century, Raleigh would gain a knighthood and complete his name, becoming Sir Walter. It was from Oxford that Raleigh had gone to Liverpool, so it is not unexpected that he said the city was drab and the people provincial.

But he was initially enthusiastic about the job. University departments of English literature were new things in the 1890s and he relished the opportunity of leading one in the investigation of a large question: 'Is Literature gossip, or philosophy, or waxworks, or homiletics?' At Oxford high tables it had been largely gossip, though in the hands of Matthew Arnold it had become homiletics. At Liverpool, Raleigh initially followed his predecessor, the Hegel-influenced Bradley, and treated it as philosophy – his inaugural lecture defined poetry as 'Life in the process of transmutation into Metaphysic', or, with nice circularity, 'Metaphysic in the process of transmutation into Life'. This high view of the subject, which had its roots in the Romantic poetics of the early nineteenth century, was still an advanced, not to say an avant-garde, one, in the 1890s. It would perhaps have surprised Raleigh that a hundred years later, the literary critical avant-garde tended towards one of his other alternatives, namely the view that the canon of English Literature is nothing more than a collection of waxworks.

The reasons for this strange reversal begin to be apparent if we turn to a letter which Raleigh wrote later in his tenure of the Liverpool Chair: 'I have just been asked to examine for the Indian Civil Service (which pleases me well) in English Literature. I have to examine on a special period, Shakespeare to Dryden. If only one could do a little towards helping to keep a crock or two away from the Service – but they are hard to recognize in writing, and often impossible to refuse marks to.' Literature has become neither philosophy nor homiletics, not even gossip, but rather a device for keeping crocks out of the Indian Civil Service. As Raleigh recognized, it was not a very satisfactory method of recruitment – the correlation between mugging up on the Bard and administering the Empire was inexact – but it was a necessary one, given that the demand for junior administrators outstripped the supply of Oxbridge men trained in the classical languages, the traditional source of recruitment for the service.

Modern historians of the discipline of English studies have seized upon this development and argued from it that the content was defined by the function: a test in 'English Literature' was invented in order to create a ruling class, so the canon of English Literature was constructed out of a body of material which propped up the value-structure of that ruling class. The primal scene of instruction becomes the colonizing Prospero oppressing the native Caliban by teaching him the English language from which his only profit is slavery and the ability to curse. Never mind that Shakespeare gave a voice to Caliban, gave him the best poetry in the play. Nor indeed that – as will be shown in my next chapter – identification with him has been a liberating resource for modern West Indian writers.

The New Iconoclasm regards Shakespeare as the prize waxwork in the museum of the national heritage. It has been given more ammunition by Sir Walter Raleigh than anyone else – for instance, by his 1918 British Academy lecture on 'Shakespeare and England', which fulminated against the perversion of Shakespeare on the part of German philologists. Raleigh celebrated the National Bard as the guardian of all that England was fighting for against the philistine Hun. Terence Hawkes quotes with relish a passage in which Sir Walter reconstructs

Caliban as a cowering German infantryman in no man's land, Trinculo and Stephano as (somewhat unlikely) noble-hearted English Tommies:

> A small British expeditionary force, bound on an international mission, finds itself stranded in an unknown country. The force is composed of men very various in rank and profession. Two of them, whom we may call a non-commissioned officer and a private, go exploring by themselves, and take one of the natives of the place prisoner. This native is an ugly low-born creature, of great physical strength and violent criminal tendencies, a liar, and ready at any time for theft, rape, and murder. He is a child of Nature, a lover of music, slavish in his devotion to power and rank, and very easily imposed upon by authority. His captors do not fear him, and which is more, do not dislike him. They found him lying out in a kind of no man's land, drenched to the skin, so they determine to keep him as a souvenir, and to take him home with them. They nickname him, in friendly fashion, the monster, and the mooncalf, as who should say Fritz, or the Boche. But their first care is to give him a drink, and to make him swear an allegiance upon the bottle. 'Where the devil should he learn our language?' says the non-commissioned officer.

In time of war, the dominant Shakespeare will always be the Bard as Britannia ruling the waves. The routine patriotic construction had its origins in such remakings as *Harlequin's Invasion*, David Garrick's wartime pantomime of 1759, in which the forces of King Shakespeare stave off the threat of French Harlequin to a rousing chorus of Boyce's 'Heart of Oak'. It reached a zenith in the Laurence Olivier film of *Henry V*, with its opening frame dedicating the film to the airborne and seaborne commandos who spearheaded the D-Day landings of 1944.

There are plenty of examples from the First World War too. In 1916, the Clarendon Press of the University of Oxford published two handsome volumes entitled *Shakespeare's England: An Account of the Life and Manners of his Age*. The purpose of the book was to describe the habits of the English people during Shakespeare's lifetime. Here one could read L. G. Carr Laughton on the subject of the Elizabethan navy, Lionel Cust, CVO, Litt.D., FSA, on the fine arts in the period, the Hon. Gerald Lascelles, Deputy Surveyor of the New Forest, on falconry, and so on. But the lead essay, a general account of the age of Elizabeth, was by Sir Walter Raleigh. It begins:

The Age of Elizabeth is the most glorious, and in some ways the
most significant, period of English history. To be an Englishman is to
be the fellow countryman of Cromwell and Milton, of Chatham and
Johnson. Yet not a few Englishmen would renounce even these high
titles before they would renounce their fellowship with Drake and
Sidney, Bacon and Ralegh, Spenser and Shakespeare. If these names
could pass into oblivion, half the national pride would go with them.
They are ours more completely than the great men of a later time.
They express the national temper . . . their figures are illuminated by
the flood of light which suddenly revealed to Englishmen that
England was a great nation, and was to bear a hand in shaping the
destinies of the world.

The post-Elizabethan names are nicely balanced: Cromwell and Milton
stand for republicanism and radical religion, whereas Chatham and
Johnson evoke Whig oligarchy and Tory Anglicanism. But there is no
ambivalence in the portrayal of the Elizabethan age: it is triumphant in
glory and national pride, thanks to the defeat of Spain and the
beginnings of empire. To publish this in 1916 was to use the past as an
exhortation for the defeat of Germany and the defence of empire in
the present.

Raleigh's essay did not stand alone. It was preceded in *Shakespeare's
England* by an 'Ode on the Tercentenary Commemoration of Shakespeare by Robert Bridges, Poet Laureate'. Bridges's ode is the quintessence of apostrophic laureate poetry:

> Thee, SHAKESPEARE, to-day we honour; and evermore,
> Since England bore thee, the master of human song,
>   Thy folk are we, children of thee,
>   Who, knitting in one her realm
> And strengthening with pride her sea-borne clans,
> Scorn'st in the grave the bruize of death.
> All thy later-laurel'd choir
>   Laud thee in thy world-shrine:
>   London's laughter is thine;
>   One with thee is our temper in melancholy or might,
> And in thy book Great-Britain's rule readeth her right.

Shakespeare was born in the region that the Tourist Board now calls
the Heart of England. From here he pumps out the lifeblood of the

realm, so that the stanza which begins with England ends with Great Britain. But the outward expansion does not stop there. Shakespeare becomes a universal conqueror: the couplet 'Laud thee in thy world-shrine: / London's laughter is thine' simultaneously roots him in the London theatre, implicitly imagined as a place where the nation is united, lords rubbing shoulders with groundlings, and elevates him into a world-spirit. His empire is made to parallel Great Britain's. Thus the next stanza of the ode moves from the male poet to the female nation:

> Her chains are chains of Freedom, and her bright arms
> Honour, Justice and Truth and Love to man.
> > Though first from a pirate ancestry
> > > She took her home on the wave,
> > Her gentler spirit arose disdainful,
> > And, smiting the fetters of slavery,
> > Made the high seaways safe and free.
> > > In wisdom bidding aloud
> > > To world-wide brotherhood,
> > Till her flag was hail'd as the ensign of Liberty,
> And the boom of her guns went round the earth in salvos of peace.

As in Raleigh's essay, Shakespeare's genius is made coordinate with Elizabethan naval power. If one did not know better, it would be easy to imagine from this that the Bard had written a play in celebration of Sir Francis Drake. The oxymoronic last line of the stanza then performs the truly astonishing feat of making an ode on Shakespeare the pretext for a justification of gunboat diplomacy.

Bridges's image of Shakespeare's world-conquest did not extend to a magnanimous recognition of his creative influence on German culture. Ironically, Shakespeare had been so fully naturalized by Goethe, Schlegel, and their successors that he was used in German propaganda against England during the First World War, as well as vice-versa. Bridges's ode, however, equates the folly of submitting Shakespeare to pedantry (for which read 'German scholarship') with the 'arrogant arms' of a devastator (for which read 'Germany') who murders and maims mankind, 'batters and burns some loveliest dearest shrine, / Laugheth in ire and boasteth aloud his brazen god'. In the hands of the Laureate in time of war, literature becomes patriotism of the crudest and most bellicose kind.

The occasion of Bridges's writing of the ode was the tercentenary of Shakespeare's death, celebrated in April 1916. The anniversary was marked in schools and other institutions throughout the country by a quasi-religious ceremony involving a reading of the passage in Ecclesiasticus, 'Let us now praise famous men', the singing of a Shakespeare song, a discourse on Shakespeare, another Shakespeare song, the recitation of scenes or passages from Shakespeare, another Shakespeare song, and 'God Save the King'. The Board of Education gave general sanction to the necessary departures from the timetables of Public Elementary Schools in England and Wales for the purpose of observing Shakespeare Day, so special application to His Majesty's Inspector of Schools, which was normally required for any variation from the national school timetable, was not necessary. As far as the discourse on Shakespeare was concerned, the secretary of the Tercentenary Committee, Israel Gollancz, provided the requisite material in some 'Notes on Shakespeare the Patriot' included in the Tercentenary Observance pamphlet (the first page of which carried an epigraph from Sydney Dobell, leader of the so-called Spasmodic School of Victorian poetry, which began 'Children brave and free / Of the great mother-tongue – and ye shall be / Lords of an empire wide as Shakespeare's soul').

Gollancz had an exalted sense of duty: 'While all the world acclaims him, those who are privileged to be his fellow-countrymen owe to themselves the high duty of gratefully recalling, on this occasion of the Tercentenary of his death, some of the lessons he has left us, and, especially at the present time, how it behoves us as patriots to strive to play our part in war as in peace, and how best to maintain our faith in the ultimate triumph of a noble humanity.' He also had a predictable taste in Shakespeare. His quotations included 'the never-to-be-forgotten words' which close *King John* ('This England, never did, nor never shall, / Lie at the proud foot of a conqueror, / But when it first did help to wound itself'), the 'imperishable' praise of England from the lips of the dying John of Gaunt in *Richard II*, and a succession of passages, most notably the Crispin's Day oration, from *Henry V*, the play in which 'Shakespeare gives us, in the person of the King, his ideal Patriot-Englishman'.

Suppose that Raleigh or Gollancz had been asked to put together an anthology for incorporation into the national timetable in schools. Suppose that their brief had been to produce a narrative of English history illustrated by suitable passages from the poets. How would Shakespeare have been represented in such an anthology? The key passages would surely have been the three just mentioned, as included in Gollancz's 'Notes on Shakespeare the Patriot': 'This England' from *King John*, 'this England' from *Richard II*, and 'we band of brothers' from *Henry V*. It would also have been necessary to give a more conceptual sense of Shakespeare's political position, so a fourth speech would have been added. It would almost certainly have been the one that Raleigh quoted in full in his essay on the age of Elizabeth in support of his contention that Shakespeare 'believed in rank and order and subordination', for 'his speeches in favour of these things have nothing ironical about them, and are never answered by equally good speeches on the other side'. The greatest of these speeches, says Raleigh, 'is put into the mouth of Ulysses, the wisest of the Greeks' – it is the oft-cited oration on 'degree' in *Troilus and Cressida*.

What sort of commentary would Raleigh or Gollancz have provided to accompany these passages in their hypothetical anthology? Something like the following, I would imagine: after the deposition of Richard II, 'The House of Lancaster had started its reign and Shakespeare was to be its retrospective Poet Laureate'; to go with Crispin's Day, 'the prince acceded to the throne as Henry V, cast off his old friends, and became a national hero – or so the genius of Shakespeare would have it'; and to go with Ulysses on degree, 'Shakespeare emphasizes to his Jacobean audience the importance of an authority which is divinely ordained and which is maintained by the hierarchical nature of society. He offers a clear warning of what would happen should the state of things be undermined.' Ulysses' speech might have been juxtaposed in the anthology with 'Let us now praise famous men' from the Book of Ecclesiasticus in the Authorized Version; this would have illustrated how 'the plays of Shakespeare and the King James Bible established the English language as the greatest glory of Western civilization'.

The anthology which represents Shakespeare by these passages and with these comments was not produced by Gollancz or Raleigh as educational propaganda during the Great War. It was published in 1988 under the title *The Faber Book of English History in Verse*. Its editor was the Right Honourable Kenneth Baker, at that time Her Majesty's Secretary of State for Education. It was not the only substantial text which Baker oversaw in 1988. He was also responsible that year for the

Great Education Reform Bill, which imposed a new National Curriculum upon English state schools. The exact content of that curriculum
went through several mutations after Baker departed from the Department of Education, but his desire for Shakespeare to be one of the
jewels in its crown was fulfilled to the extent that it was decreed
that every fourteen-year-old in the land should be tested on a set
Shakespeare play. According to a press release from the Department
of Education, dated 30 June 1992, headlined 'SHAKESPEARE AND
GRAMMAR TESTS FOR ALL 14 YEAR OLDS', that was what John Patten,
the then minister, saw as 'real education'.

The decree had its local origins in arguments about supposedly
declining standards in schools: there was a widespread perception,
particularly among Tory backbenchers and their middle-class constitu-
ents, that trendy teachers had given up on 'proper' English literature in
favour of the easy option of showing videos of soap operas or setting
the novels of Frederick Forsyth as examination texts. The avant-garde's
theory of canonical literature as waxworks added fuel to this perception.

But there was a grander design as well as the local one. The most
culturally revealing political development of 1992 was the formation of
a Department of National Heritage. In any other country, this would
have been called a Ministry of Culture. But in Britain, the arts and
related activities had to be seen to support the nation, to come under
the banner of that guarantor of the nation's sense of its own greatness,
its heritage. And Shakespeare is the epicentre of that heritage. Baker's
mind-boggling claim that 'the plays of Shakespeare and the King James
Bible established the English language as the greatest glory of Western
civilization' was the ultimate justification for Shakespeare's central
position in the National Curriculum.

As well as his notes on Shakespeare the Patriot, Israel Gollancz
contributed to the Tercentenary Observance pamphlet some 'Brief
Annals of Shakespeare'. They include the entry, '1616–1916: During
three centuries Shakespeare's fame has grown until his sovereignty has
become well-nigh universal – England's most cherished possession,
shared and adored by all the world.' It is no coincidence that those
same three centuries marked the growth across the world of the
'sovereignty' of the British Empire.

Just under ten weeks after Gollancz's Shakespeare Day, twenty
thousand British soldiers lost their lives in the first few hours of the

battle of the Somme. A. J. P. Taylor has described the following year, 1917, as the moment of birth for our contemporary world. The Russian Revolution and the entry of America into the war brought the end of European history in the old sense and the beginning of a new world history. These events of 1916–17 marked the end of England, of the congratulatory self-image that stretched back to Elizabethan times. There is a pathos about the dedication of Laurence Olivier's D-Day film: standing in for Harry, England, and St George were General Eisenhower and Uncle Sam. It was as solace in the face of this decline that modern Toryism turned to the national heritage; the world-sovereignty of Shakespeare and the English language represented the last dominion. They would endure after Hong Kong and even the Falkland Islands were gone.

Arthur's bosom

A certain inconsistency of British Conservative government policy in the period which began with Margaret Thatcher's assumption of power in 1979 has often been remarked upon: while economic policy was driven by privatization, deregulation, and market forces, education policy was driven by nationalization (of the curriculum), regulation (of university statutes, teachers' performance, and so on), and government forces (at the expense of local education authorities). If market forces were to prevail in the reading curriculum, Frederick Forsyth would prevail over Shakespeare. Thatcher, who once confessed to her taste for re-reading the thrillers of Forsyth, would probably have been perfectly happy with this; but after her removal from power, the regulation of what was to be studied in schools was determined less by her laissez-faire ideology than by an old-style One Nation Toryism. Education Ministers like Kenneth Baker and John Patten really did believe that heritage – that Shakespeare – could be the glue to bind the nation together and make it feel good about itself. Michael Portillo's reading of Ulysses' speech in relation to the defence of established institutions was of a piece with their vision.

But what service did it do to Shakespeare to nationalize him in this way? What warrant was there for the interpretations propagated by Baker's anthology? The first thing that needs to be said is that the chauvinistic readings are risible simplifications of the plays, neglecting as they do the cardinal principle that dramatic speeches must be read in the context of character and action. Gaunt in *Richard II* and the Bastard who speaks the closing speech of *King John* are not disinterested apologists for England – they have agendas of their own. As I have already pointed out, the Ulysses of *Troilus and Cressida* is not so much the wisest of the Greeks as the slyest of the Greeks. Henry V's justification for being in France on Crispin's Day is distinctly questionable: as William Hazlitt put it, 'Henry, because he did not know how to govern his own kingdom, determined to make war upon his neighbours; because his own title to the crown was doubtful, he laid claim to that of France'.

That said, there is no denying that Shakespeare was interested in creating a myth of England. He was the only dramatist of the age who returned repeatedly to that foundation-text of Tudor ideology, Holinshed's *Chronicles*. But in the canon of his works as a whole, and even in the plays based on Holinshed, the England he created has a much more complex identity than that proposed by Raleigh, Gollancz, and Baker. The patriotic Bardolaters slip easily from England to Britain. Raleigh seems to have no difficulty in forgetting the years he spent as a professor in Glasgow; Israel Gollancz glosses over the uneasiness of his position as an English Jew; Baker has nothing to say about the oddity of his 'National' school curriculum applying to England and Wales, but not to Scotland and Northern Ireland. For Shakespeare, on the other hand, national identity is ragged about the edges. He is fascinated by outsiders: most drastically, Shylock and Othello, but in the history plays such figures as the Welshman Owain Glyndŵr, the Scottish Douglas, the Irish MacMorris, and the Northumbrian Percy family, who may well have put members of Shakespeare's original audience in mind of the northern earls who in 1569 had rebelled against the Anglican regime. In the first scene of *Henry IV Part One*, Westmorland speaks disdainfully of 'the irregular and wild Glyndŵr' (1.1.40). But, as neoclassical critics were again and again to complain, irregularity and wildness are the energizing forces of Shakespearean genius. To illustrate the complexity of Shakespeare's sense of the nation, I want to show how he was used in another anthology, this time one which *was* commissioned during the First World War but which adopted a very different tone from that of the flag-waving Baker.

Published in 1915, it was called *This England: An Anthology from her Writers compiled by Edward Thomas*. It carried an unassuming prefatory note:

> This is an anthology from the work of English writers rather strictly so called. Building round a few most English poems like 'When icicles hang by the wall', – excluding professedly patriotic writing because it is generally bad and because indirect praise is sweeter and more profound, – never aiming at what a committee from Great Britain and Ireland might call complete, – I wished to make a book as full of English character and country as an egg is of meat. If I have reminded others, as I did myself continually, of some of the echoes called up by the name of England, I am satisfied.

There is nothing here of kings and queens, empire and war. Edward Thomas's idea of England was rooted in place – his anthology has a preponderance of rural writing, but also a section on London – and in home. For Thomas, England was not a set of institutions, a heritage, but 'a system of vast circumferences circling round the minute neighbouring points of home'.

The longest complete poem in the anthology is Samuel Taylor Coleridge's 'Fears in Solitude', a troubled meditation in time of war which differentiates sharply between Britain in the sense of its political institutions, which is dismissed as 'One Benefit-Club for mutual flattery', and the 'mother Isle' in the sense of a synecdochic representation of the local community and landscape which have nurtured the poet. Coleridge's poem is a reworking of Gaunt's 'this England' oration, which was itself simultaneously a panegyric of the land and a denunciation of governmental mismanagement.

In Edward Thomas's anthology, insofar as the name of England means a history, it means the defence of liberty. The collection begins with three passages from Milton's prose and part of a speech by Cromwell. Edmund Burke on tradition is represented, but is balanced by a splendid extract from Hazlitt: 'It always struck me as a singular proof of good taste, good sense and liberal thinking, in an old friend, who had Paine's *Rights of Man* and Burke's *Reflections on the French Revolution* bound up in one volume, and who said, that, both together, they made a very good book.' It was Hazlitt who said that a viewing of *Coriolanus* would save one the trouble of reading both Burke attacking

the French Revolution and Paine defending it because Shakespeare
gave both sides of the argument. It was also Hazlitt who, in a passage
concerning Charles James Fox, gave Edward Thomas's anthology its
definition of patriotism: 'his love of his country did not consist in his
hatred of the rest of mankind'.

Patriotism has always been a troublesome concept, as *Chambers
Dictionary* recognizes through the two-handedness with which it defines
a patriot: 'one who truly, or ostentatiously and injudiciously, loves and
serves his fatherland'. Coleridge in 'Fears in Solitude', Hazlitt in many
of his essays, and Edward Thomas in his anthology reject ostentatious
and injudicious patriotism, discovering instead a quieter and more
profound love of their native land. Shakespeare is one of their paths to
that discovery.

Contrary to the expectation established by his title, Thomas omitted
the 'this England' speeches from *King John* and *Richard II*. The reader
of *This England* first encounters Shakespeare in the form of the song of
winter from *Love's Labour's Lost*, Falstaff in praise of sack, and the tale
of Herne the Hunter from *The Merry Wives of Windsor*. The tone for
the whole is set by the claim in the prefatory note that the 'most
English' kind of writing is 'When icicles hang by the wall', a song about
rural labour in which the burden is 'While greasy Joan doth keel the
pot'. At the climax of the anthology is a substantial section called 'The
Vital Commoners'. England is defined by its people, not its monarchs,
by greasy Joan and not Queen Elizabeth. In a subtle move, Thomas
includes in his final section the 'up to the mountains!' address of
Belarius to Guiderius and Arviragus in *Cymbeline*, a speech in which
true nobility finds itself not at court but in nature, and in which
national identity is complicated because the location is Wales. Edward
Thomas himself was able to negotiate between Englishness and Britain
precisely because his origins were mainly Welsh; the difficulty of that
negotiation is acknowledged by the prefatory note's careful rider, 'never
aiming at what a committee from Great Britain and Ireland might call
complete'.

The anthology does embrace the Crispin's Day oration, but the
King's pep talk is not presented in isolation. In the 'Vital Commoners'
section, Thomas also included Michael Williams's unanswerable argument against Harry Le Roy, 'But if the cause be not good, the king
himself hath a heavy reckoning to make, when all those legs and arms

and heads, chopped off in a battle, shall join together at the latter day'
– the publication of this in a wartime anthology which soldiers could
carry in their knapsacks was typically brave of Thomas. And on the
page opposite Harry's address to his men before Agincourt, we find
Falstaff's address to himself in the Boar's Head Tavern: 'Go thy ways,
old Jack; die when thou wilt, if manhood, good manhood, be not
forgot upon the face of the earth, then am I shotten herring. There live
not three good men unhanged in England; and one of them is fat and
grows old'. Thomas forces us to consider the possibility that Shakespeare
gives us his ideal Patriot-Englishman not in Henry V, as Gollancz had
it, but in old Jack Falstaff.

Consider what it would mean to make Falstaff into the true
embodiment of England. Sir Walter Raleigh would have found the
idea inconceivable. He was of the view that 'a clear stage was needed
for the patriotic and warlike exploits of King Harry; here was to be no
place for critics and philosophers', so 'in the name of the public safety,
Falstaff must be put to death'. The sinister overtones of the Committee
of Public Safety in Robespierre's Terror are wholly unintended, but
revelatory of exactly what is troubling about King Harry.

By including more of Falstaff than of Harry in his anthology, Edward
Thomas unobtrusively reveals his allegiance to a long tradition of
liberal, dissenting Englishness. In 1817 Hazlitt's abhorrence of kings, of
empire, and of war was registered by his remark that 'we never could
forgive the Prince's treatment of Falstaff'. In 1774 Maurice Morgann
defended Falstaff's courage by reading the character as an active
opponent of the absurd and tyrannical code of honour. It is a reading
which must be seen in the context of Morgann's public career: as
Under-Secretary of State in charge of American affairs, he argued
against taxation of the colony; as special envoy of the Privy Council to
Canada, he argued for the retention of French law there and laid the
ground for the enshrining of civil and religious liberty in the Quebec
Act of 1774; he also published a *Plan for the Abolition of Slavery in the
West Indies*. Supporting Falstaff against war and king in the 1770s was a
political act. Given Morgann's knowledge of the colonies, it is to be
regretted that his essay on the character of Caliban does not survive
beside that on Falstaff.

As Sir John, Falstaff is a symptom of the corruption of the patronage
system, but as plain Jack he represents those irrepressible forces of life

itself – wit, companionship, thirst – over which governments legislate at their peril. There is no more tender moment in Shakespeare's history plays than that in *Henry IV Part Two* at which Falstaff parts from the blubbered Doll Tearsheet and the forgiving Mistress Quickly: 'Well, fare thee well: I have known thee these twenty-nine years, come peascod-time, but an honester and truer-hearted man – well, fare thee well.' The first public act of King Henry V's reign is the arrest and beating of these two women. We are told that they are accessories to a manslaughter, but we have seen that they are accessories to love.

'In the name of the public safety, Falstaff must be put to death': to put him to death is to suppress English liberty. In Spenser's *Faerie Queene*, Prince Arthur rode through Gloriana's land, fighting for truth and justice. Is it Henry V who reanimates Arthur, England's patron king? No: it is Falstaff who gives us a running Arthurian commentary. His is an earthy England, not a chivalric one like Spenser's: '"When Arthur first in court" – empty the jordan! – "And was a worthy king."' But it offers nonetheless the play's deepest myth of England, a myth that becomes comically religious in the inspired malapropism of Nell Quickly, or Nell Pistol as she has by then become: 'Nay, sure he's not in hell; he's in Arthur's bosom, if ever man went to Arthur's bosom.'

The rhythm of Prince Hal's life is that of providential history, leading to his 'reformation' and his assumption of the roles which attracted Queen Elizabeth to him: unifier of the body-politic, victor over a rival kingdom, heroic leader of a great and independent nation. The rhythm of Falstaff's life is that of the body and the seasons. In *Henry IV Part Two* he journeys into deep England; on his deathbed he babbles of green fields. Justice Shallow's orchard is in the Gloucestershire which First World War poets like Edward Thomas and Ivor Gurney regarded as the quintessence of the green England for which they were fighting. The immemorial quality of the rural world animated by Shallow's ramblings – his talk that is strangely profound in its very triviality – summons up an England that is older and more stable than anything possible in the court-world of intrigue, innovation, and reversal.

We learn from Shallow that Falstaff began his career as page to Thomas Mowbray, Duke of Norfolk. This appears to be a Shakespearean fancy without source: it is true of neither the historical Sir John Fastolf, who flees the battlefield in *Henry VI Part One*, nor the historical

Sir John Oldcastle, of whom the character of Falstaff was originally an irreverent portrait. Why did Shakespeare give Falstaff a past that began thus? At one level, it links him with opposition to the Lancastrian ascendancy represented by King Henry IV and his son. Mowbray was Henry IV's opponent when the latter was still Bolingbroke, back at the beginning of *Richard II*. Like father, like son: as Bolingbroke's accusation of treachery was instrumental in the banishment of Mowbray from the land, so Hal will banish Falstaff from his presence.

Mowbray departs with a moving farewell to his native land and language; the effect of his words is to suggest that love of the English earth and the English word goes deeper than dynastic difference. We do not hear similar patriotic sentiments in the mouth of the self-interested Bolingbroke. In the *Henry IV* plays, he reveals himself to be more concerned with the cares of kingship than those of the land over which he rules; he does nothing to bring back the old England idealized in the deathbed speech of his father, John of Gaunt (whose name and whose England are also remembered by Shallow). The association between Mowbray and Falstaff calls into question the capacity of Bolingbroke's son to turn England back into Eden. King Harry will temporarily restore the nation to greatness by means of foreign conquest, but, in the words of the epilogue to *Henry V*, 'the world's best garden' will soon fall into decay again in the time of his son, the child-king Henry VI, of 'Whose state so many had the managing, / That they lost France, and made his England bleed'.

In Shakespeare's own time those who suffered banishment because of ideological difference, but who claimed that they were nevertheless loyal to England, were predominantly Catholics. And this suggests another level to the allusion which binds Falstaff to the Duke of Norfolk. To an Elizabethan audience, the name of Norfolk – the only surviving dukedom in the land – was synonymous with overt or suspected Catholic sympathy. The old Catholic ways persisted in the country long after the official change of religion inaugurated by Henry VIII's break from Rome. The Catholic liturgy's integral relationship with the agricultural calendar and the cycles of human biology could not be shattered overnight. There may, then, be a sense in which Falstaff's journey into deep England is also a journey into the old religion of Shakespeare's father and maternal grandfather. One wonders if it is a coincidence that in fleshing out the skeletal character of the prince's riotous companion which he inherited from the old play of *The Famous Victories of Henry the Fifth*, Shakespeare retained and made much of his own (Catholic) father's name of John.

It is ironic that Falstaff's original surname, Oldcastle, had to be changed because the character was regarded as an insult to the memory of the proto-Protestant Lollard of that name: 'for Oldcastle died martyr', says the epilogue to part two, 'and this is not the man'. Indeed it is not the man, for Falstaff is if anything an embodiment of those ancient Catholic rhythms which were suppressed in the name of Reformation. At the beginning of *Henry IV Part One*, Prince Hal announces the argument of the story: it will concern his 'reformation' (1.2.210). At the beginning of *Henry V*, the Archbishop of Canterbury announces that the process was completed with the rejection of Falstaff: 'Never came reformation in such a flood' (1.1.34). If there is a proto-Protestant or embryonic Puritan in the plays, it is King Harry the Fifth, newly washed of his past, casting off his old companions, turning away England's former self.

Even as he uses Hal for his own advancement, Falstaff is always a truer father than the cold and politic King Henry IV can ever be. The point is made with beautiful clarity by the contrast between Falstaff's warmth in the scene in which he and Hal act out the prodigal prince's forthcoming interview with his father and the king's chilliness in the interview itself. The complexity and the pain of the end of *Henry IV Part Two* stem from the way in which, by casting himself as the prodigal son and coming home to his politic heritage, Hal tears into the heart of old England. According to Holinshed's *Chronicles*, King Henry V left no friendship unrewarded. This cannot be said of Shakespeare's version of history.

The rejection of Falstaff has the exact effect which Hal has said it will have way back in his first soliloquy in part one: the fact of his youthful waywardness brings him extra credit when he reforms himself. 'I like this fair proceeding of the King's', says his machiavellian brother Prince John to the Lord Chief Justice, Hal's new surrogate father, in reaction to the turning away of Falstaff. But in the audience our sympathies are with Sir John, the impolitic but loving father-figure. 'Master Shallow, I owe you a thousand pound', he says immediately after he has been publicly denounced by his 'sweet boy', and we remember an earlier exchange:

PRINCE Sirrah, do I owe you a thousand pound?
FALSTAFF A thousand pound, Hal? A million, thy love is worth a
    million; thou owest me thy love.

                                          (*Part One*, 3.3.135–8)

A. C. Bradley, writing under the influence of Morgann and Hazlitt, picked up Nell Quickly's image of Falstaff in Arthur's bosom: 'We wish Henry a glorious reign and much joy of his crew of hypocritical politicians, lay and clerical; but our hearts go with Falstaff to the Fleet, or, if necessary, to Arthur's bosom or wheresomever he is.' According to Bradley, the essence of Falstaff is 'the bliss of freedom gained in humour'. As always with Bradley, the essay takes on an other-worldly tone: instead of assimilating Shakespeare to his own late Victorian liberalism, the critic makes Falstaff's freedom a 'freedom of soul', an escape from the tawdry world of day-to-day politics into the infinity to which Bradley's distinctive brand of Christianized Hegelianism gives access. He really wants Falstaff to be in heaven, to be in Abraham's bosom. But the point about Arthur's bosom is that it is an earthly, an English, and a temporary resting place: the conceit is that Falstaff will rest with Arthur under Glastonbury Tor not for all eternity but until the land has need of him again, when he will return.

In *Henry V*, his spirit has no sooner left than it does return, reanimated in his friends who follow the wars in France. Throughout the *Henry* plays there is a counter-movement to Hal's growth into the bellicose kind of patriot-Englishman: a confused but vibrant prose voice is counterpointed against the polished verse of law, order, and military glory. Harry spurs 'you noblest English' on to the breach, but seconds later we hear the sanity of the boy who was Falstaff's page: 'Would I were in an alehouse in London. I would give all my fame for a pot of ale, and safety.' Justice Shallow remembers when Sir John himself was a page; this boy who yearns for ale and safety is a pint-sized Falstaff already out from under Arthur's bosom. After Agincourt, the King thanks God that fewer than thirty English have been killed in the battle. In his listing of the dead, he does not mention Falstaff's proxies, yet they are the ones whom the audience mourns most: Bardolph and Nym, hanged; the boy, killed with the luggage; Nell, dead in the spital of a malady of France. They have died not for Harry's but for Falstaff's

England, not for a palace or parliament in Westminster but for an alehouse in Eastcheap.

As prime embodiment of the Eastcheap crowd, Falstaff is Shakespeare's primary means of access to those whom Edward Thomas called 'the vital commoners' and it is in this sense that he is England. He has somehow won himself a knighthood, but he has decayed from the gentry and is back among the commoners. His language is a living vernacular prose, richer in metaphor and invention than the verse of any of the plays' noble speakers. He possesses no property, is always in debt, on the run from the law. If he has a home and a family, it is in the alehouse among his drinking companions: as Maurice Morgann put it, 'he dies where he lived, in a Tavern'.

His voice of ale and safety belongs to the common foot soldier in every age. It does not care for the rhetoric of fame with which kings and officers exhort their men. One must stress again that there is a distinction, gestured towards by Justice Shallow, between Jack Falstaff and Sir John. As a recruiting officer, Sir John sends lesser men to their deaths without even the compunction of Harry in the night before Agincourt. But in the tavern Falstaff is always Jack, and this Jack is a generic name for the vital commoners. In *Richard III*, a Jack is the opposite of a gentleman. In a pamphlet dedicated to the fishmongers and butchers of England, John Taylor the Water-poet, himself a sometime pressed man in the Elizabethan navy, saluted Jack of Newbury, Jack Drum, Jack Dog, Jack of Dover, Jack Herring, Jack Sprat, Jack Straw, Jack Cade and any number of other common-or-garden Jacks. So does Shakespeare salute Jack Falstaff.

Her privates we

In 1915, when he compiled *This England*, Edward Thomas also composed his most innovative poem, 'Lob'. Robert Frost wrote to him in a letter, 'The goodness is in Lob. You are a poet or you are nothing . . . I never saw anything like you for English'. Frost was thinking here especially of the speech-rhythms of Thomas's fluid verse-paragraphs – had he been looking for precedents in the literary representation of colloquial English speech, he might well have found it in the prose of Falstaff and Co. – but he could just as well have said, 'I never saw anything like you for Englishness'. For Lob, like Falstaff, is the spirit of England – England 'rather strictly so called', that is.

Lob is an old man travelling, a repository of country lore, landless but of the land. His first words are an assertion of public right of way, a challenge to the landowners' threat to trespassers: 'Nobody can't stop 'ee. It's / A footpath, right enough'. He is both a series of particularized agricultural labourers – biographically, he is partly based on Thomas's poacher friend, 'Dad' Uzzell – and a literary archetype. 'Lob' is a name for the hobgoblin or Robin Goodfellow: Puck in *A Midsummer Night's Dream* is addressed as 'thou lob of spirits', and it is with this in mind that Thomas guesses that his Lob 'Christened one flower Love-in-idleness'.

Some subsequent lines push the connection with Shakespeare further: 'This is tall Tom that bore / The logs in, and with Shakespeare in the hall / Once talked, when icicles hung by the wall'. The allusion is to that 'most English' song at the end of *Love's Labour's Lost*: 'When icicles hang by the wall / And Dick the shepherd blows his nail / And Tom bears logs into the hall'. Shakespeare is brought into his own work, imagined conversing with Tom. He is made a poet of the people, deriving his idiom from the folk tradition. Lob is also Herne the Hunter, a figure impersonated by Jack Falstaff. And he is 'Jack Cade, / Jack Smith, Jack Moon, poor Jack of every trade, / Young Jack, or old Jack, or Jack what-d'ye-call'. In the poem 'Words', published together with 'Lob' on 1 April 1916, Thomas asked to be chosen by 'You English words', to make poetry from the names and things of England. The names he means are those not only of the places but also of the people, the poor Jacks of every trade.

The Jacks of Lob are the Toms, Dicks, and Francises with whom Prince Hal swears brotherhood in Eastcheap, studying their language in order to be able to command them in the future – and in particular to make them glad to die for him on the battlefield. The scene before Agincourt with Michael Williams, in which the foot soldier asks some awkward questions about his duty to die, suggests that the Prince's plan hasn't fully worked. The debate with Williams forces the king to recognize in his subsequent soliloquy that kings have nothing 'that privates have not too' save the 'idol Ceremony'.

Edward Thomas remembers the battlefield but ignores the king altogether:

> One of the lords of No Man's Land, good Lob, –
> Although he was seen dying at Waterloo,
> Hastings, Agincourt, and Sedgemoor too, –
> Lives yet.

Lob has the resilience of Falstaff, who was seen dying at Shrewsbury but rises to live again. But he is also what Falstaff turns his ragged troop into – food for powder. What he is dying for is not the nation as embodied in the king or the constitution: he is on both sides in the Battle of Sedgemoor, fought in the 1680s when the future of the monarchy, parliament, and the national religion hung in the balance. What he is dying for is the land which he inhabits but does not own and the vital commoners who work that land. As the poem was being written, Lob in the incarnation of Tommy Atkins was bogged down in the no man's land of First Ypres. Within three months, Edward Thomas himself had decided to enlist, out of loyalty to Lob not to Kitchener.

Lob is what Thomas understood by England. Versions of him appear throughout his prose writings and poetry. Here he is in an essay of April 1915 which Thomas called 'England':

> One man said to me that he felt it, that he felt England very strongly, one evening at Stogumber under the Quantocks. His train stopped at the station which was quite silent, and only an old old man got in, bent, gnarled, and gross, a Caliban; 'but somehow he fitted in with the darkness and the quietness and the smell of burning wood, and it was all something I loved being part of.' We feel it in war-time or coming from abroad, though we may be far from home: the whole land is suddenly home.

Stogumber station is not the rural idyll of Thomas's most famous poem, 'Adlestrop', which also belongs to 1915, because Lob is there, this time more as Caliban than Falstaff. 'Adlestrop' is a soft pastoral and many of Thomas's other poems mediating between the English land and the war in France, for instance 'As the team's head-brass', suggest parallels with pastoralist memoir-writers like Siegfried Sassoon and Edmund Blunden. But 'Lob', with its robust and unsentimental claiming of acquaintance with every Tom, Dick, and Jack, has a different companion-piece.

I think that we should set the poem beside what is in the strict sense the most vulgar of the major novels by those who fought in the Great

War. It was published privately in 1929 as *The Middle Parts of Fortune* and publicly the following year, stripped of the swear words which give authenticity to its soldiers' language, as *Her Privates We*.

Both titles are allusions to Rosencrantz and Guildenstern's image of themselves as pawns in a power-game over which they have no control. Though it belongs to the expurgated version, *Her Privates We* is the more fitting of the two titles, since this is a book written from the private soldier's point of view. Indeed, the author's name was given on the title-page simply as 'Private 19022'. A prefatory note describes the novel as 'a record of experience on the Somme and Ancre fronts, with an interval behind the lines, during the latter half of the year 1916'. Lawrence of Arabia was the first to identify the author as the Australian writer Frederic Manning.

The novel's focus on the common soldier's daily life behind the lines might tempt us to view it as a genre-piece, as just one of the scores of retrospectives on 1916 which were published between 1928 and 1930. But like Homer's *Iliad* and Shakespeare's *Henry* plays, it is not ultimately a war book. War unaccommodates man. The literature of war transcends its occasion when it asks whether or not man is found wanting when his superfluities are stripped away. In *Troilus and Cressida* Shakespeare tested the language of honour and heroism until it cracked into cynicism. In the *Henry* plays he was more measured, giving a space to the military code but also a voice, heroic in its honesty, to those who are the pawns of war: to Feeble, with his 'By my troth, I care not; a man can die but once . . . and let it go which way it will, he that dies this year is quit for the next', and to John Bates, with his 'He may show what outward courage he will; but I believe as cold a night as 'tis, he could wish himself in Thames up to the neck; and so would I he were, and I by him, at all adventures, so we were quit here'.

These are the prose voices of the privates. They give Manning's novel its chapter epigraphs, all of which are from Shakespeare, most from the vulgar tongue of the *Henry* plays. Shakespeare privatized – not sold off to those who can afford him, but given over to the private soldier – tells of the regiment of the appetites, of what Manning calls 'the fundamental necessities of [man's] nature'. These are Falstaff's needs: for food, for shelter, for companionship, for occasional sexual indulgence, and whenever possible for drink. Manning's protagonist, Bourne, drinks heavily and, like Falstaff, can hold it – unlike the author himself, who fought as a private on the Somme because he was found unfit for a commission due to drunkenness. As a private, he shared the experience of the ordinary soldier more intimately than did any other major writer who came through the Great War.

Bourne is eventually killed on a raid in no man's land, and his body is carried back by Weeper Smart, the most Shakespearean of all the privates. Weeper is a version of John Bates or Falstaff's boy:

> 'All that a says is, if a man's dead it don't matter no more to 'im 'oo wins the bloody war,' said Weeper. 'We're 'ere, there's no gettin' away from that, Corporal. 'Ere we are, an' since we're 'ere, we're just fightin' for ourselves, an' for each other.'

As the Tommies' song had it, 'We're 'ere because we're 'ere because we're 'ere'. But Bourne discovers in his final moments that Weeper's comrades can always rely upon him:

> no one could have had a greater horror and dread of war than Weeper had. It was a continuous misery to him, and yet he endured it. Living with him, one felt instinctively that in any emergency he would not let one down, that he had in him, curiously enough, an heroic strain.

He is a hero not for king and country, but 'for ourselves, an' for each other'. So too in the novel is Bourne for his friends, Martlow and Shem; so too at the Beaurains Observation Post in Flanders, where he lost his life, was Edward Thomas for the Tom, Dick, and Jacks of 'Lob'.

The allusive practice of Thomas in 'Lob' and Manning in *Her Privates We* was calculated to give Shakespeare over to the 'privates', the 'vital commoners'. It participates in a tradition which we may call Popular Shakespeare. That tradition had its origins in the dissenting culture of the eighteenth century; it offers an explicit challenge to Establishment Shakespeare. When William Hazlitt caps an argument with a quotation from Shakespeare, or when he lectures on Shakespeare at the Nonconformist Surrey Institution, he is deliberately affronting two characteristics of Establishment culture: its use of urbane quotations from the Latin classics and its complacent assumption that Shakespeare speaks for its own values, its own understanding of England. Classical quotations are among the most polished badges of the elite; most obviously, they bespeak an expensive education. Hazlitt makes Shakespeare his classic as a way of fostering a counter-tradition, one nurtured in the dissenting academies in which those excluded from the old universities found an educational community.

Shakespeare has survived and has been made to matter as a voice of radical culture, not just of established culture. Consider the case of Thomas Cooper, born in 1805 of Quaker stock and brought up by his widowed mother, who worked as a dyer in Lincolnshire. He had no opportunity to enter the official culture, to attend Oxford or Cambridge. He was largely self-taught, initially courtesy of one Mrs Trevor's circulating library. 'I say *self*-educated, so far as I was educated,' he writes in his autobiography. 'Mine has been almost entirely self-education, all the way through life'. By the age of fifteen, acquainted, thanks to Mrs Trevor, with some 'odd plays of Shakspeare', he gained employment as a shoemaker. His employer, Joseph Clark, was also self-taught. The latter, recalls Cooper,

> rehearsed to me what he had seen and heard of London actors, and repeated the criticisms of the Londoners on the personations of Shakspeare's characters by Kemble and Young and Mrs Siddons, and later performers. All this directed me to a more intelligent reading of Shakspeare for myself; though I did not yet feel the due impression of his greatness.

Cooper and some friends established a 'Mutual Improvement Society' for reading and discussion. Gradually he developed his literary capacities and broadened his circle of dissenting and working acquaintance. Shakespeare and Milton were now committed to memory. He became an early and highly active member of the Mechanics' Institute which was established in Lincoln in the 1830s for the improvement of young working men in the city; similar Institutes were springing up in towns and cities across the country.

Out of dissent and self-education came Chartism. In 1840, Cooper heard his first Chartist lecture and discovered his 'destiny': to be a radical activist. He became the leader of the Chartists in Leicester, where he 'proposed that we should take a new name; and, as we now held our meetings in the "Shaksperean Room," we styled ourselves "The Shaksperean Association of Leicester Chartists."' This is a rallying to Shakespeare about which neither the Right Honourable Kenneth Baker nor the New Iconoclast tells us.

Cooper and his friends collected radical anthems in their 'Shaksper-ean Chartist Hymn Book'. He gave lectures on contemporary politics, but also on Shakespeare: to do so was to reclaim a heritage for the people. When Cooper was arrested for fomenting riot and on a false charge of arson, he raised money for the legal expenses of himself and his fellow-accused by putting on a production of *Hamlet*: 'I took the part of Hamlet – as I knew the whole play by heart.' The case went against him, so his next encounter with Shakespeare was as solace while in prison. After his release, he published a series of papers under the Hazlittian title *The Plain Speaker*; these included his widely disseminated 'Eight Letters to the Young Men of the Working Classes'. A favourite device in these letters was the use of quotations from the plays to illustrate an argument. Shakespeare was explicitly cited as a master-teacher of the anatomy of society.

In 1850 Cooper launched a weekly penny periodical called *Cooper's Journal: or, Unfettered Thinker and Plain Speaker for Truth, Freedom, and Progress*. The first number sold nine thousand copies. Here are some lines from a poem by William Whitmore published in that journal. They may serve as a foil to Robert Bridges's Tercentenary Ode:

> The young spring morn breaks brightly on a scene
>   Of festival outstretching far and wide:
> Toil is respited, mute the town's huge din,
>   And throngs of freemen, consciously allied
> To England's Shakspere, hail with soul-felt pride
>   This glorious natal day!

The poem goes on to imagine free theatrical performances for all, and, in a spirit of free thought, proposes the abolition of holidays in celebration of saints and military heroes such as Wellington. Instead there should be a holiday in celebration of the birthday 'Of him whose sole name beams more sovereignty / Than all kings, nobles, joined, that strut o'er earth!'.

But the poem is called 'Shakspere's Birthday – in the Future'. The truly popular Shakespeare has not yet come into his own: the ambition of realizing him is an integral part of the Chartist and working-man's struggle.

Shakespeare has been regarded for a long time as retrospective poet laureate of the House of Lancaster, his works as the book in which

'Great-Britain's rule readeth her right'. But another aspect of his genius – his creation of Feeble, of Bates, of Falstaff and his boy – gave a voice to plain men and women, whether activists like Thomas Cooper or common soldiers like Private 19022 and Second Lieutenant Philip Edward Thomas, killed by a stray shell near Arras early on the morning of Easter Monday 1917, the copy of Shakespeare's sonnets that was in his pocket remaining intact but strangely creased by the pressure of the blast.

Edward Thomas was held in special esteem by his men. Is it fanciful to suppose that his bond with them owed something to what he had learnt from Shakespeare? Only someone who has understood the *Henry* plays could focus a war poem in an English pub and make it funny as well as tender. It is called 'A Private':

> This ploughman dead in battle slept out of doors
> Many a frozen night, and merrily
> Answered staid drinkers, good bedmen, and all bores:
> 'At Mrs Greenland's Hawthorn Bush,' said he,
> 'I slept.' None knew which bush. Above the town,
> Beyond 'The Drover', a hundred spot the down
> In Wiltshire. And where now at last he sleeps
> More sound in France – that, too, he secret keeps.

8

ALL THE WORLD HIS STAGE

What ish my nation?

In the summer of 1605, King James, still new to the English throne, visited the University of Oxford. At the gates of St John's College, three undergraduates cross-dressed in the female garb of sibyls emerged from an arbour of ivy. The first hailed him as King of Scotland, the second as King of England, and the third as King of Ireland. The first also reminded the King that three prophesying sisters had told the ancient Scottish Thane Banquo that, though he would not be king himself, his descendants would one day rule an immortal empire. (S)he explained that since King James claimed descent from Banquo, the sisters were now reconfirming their prophecy.

Tradition has it that Shakespeare stopped off in Oxford whenever he returned from London to Stratford. His godson, William Davenant, was the son of an innkeeper there. The King's visit was Oxford's hottest gossip of 1605. It is pleasing to suppose that Shakespeare was told about the little dramatic spectacle of the three prophetic sisters over a pint of ale as he refreshed himself from his journey, and that this gave him the idea of dramatizing the story of Banquo, Duncan, and Macbeth which he could read in Holinshed's *Chronicles*. His company had recently become the 'King's Men': what more flattering play to perform before the King than one which included a procession of Banquo and his royal descendants? *Macbeth* can be assigned with some certainty to 1606, when it may well have been played at court.

But to make the play 'topical' in this way is purely suppositious. To read it thus depends on phrases such as 'tradition has it', 'to suppose that Shakespeare was told', and 'may well have been played'. Besides, *Macbeth* is not fundamentally about King James's descent from Banquo, persuasive as it is to see connections with his interest in witchcraft and to hear allusions in the Porter's monologue to the 'equivocation' of the

Jesuit Father Garnet in his trial following the Gunpowder Plot against the King's life. The play is called *Macbeth*, not *Banquo*, and Macbeth had no place in the Oxford students' sycophantic *tableau vivant*.

Topicality in Shakespeare is rare, enigmatic, and incidental. An allusion to a 'fair vestal thronèd by the west' in *A Midsummer Night's Dream* seems to be a compliment to Queen Elizabeth, but the precise nature of the compliment is so elusive that it took nearly twenty closely printed pages in the Variorum edition to elucidate all the possible interpretations of it that were put forward in the eighteenth and nineteenth centuries alone. In *The Merry Wives of Windsor* there seems to be a reference to the Order of the Garter investiture celebrations, but the comedy of Falstaff in love hardly constitutes a major political statement. The issue of corn prices with which the action of *Coriolanus* begins was a matter of concern when the play was written, but if Shakespeare was thinking about the Midland Rising of 1607 he was careful to be indirect about it. Cranmer's prophecy at the very end of *Henry VIII* certainly praises Queen Elizabeth and her successor, but it is by no means certain that Shakespeare wrote the speech, for the final scene seems to be part of John Fletcher's contribution to the play.

There is only one explicit, pointedly focused, uncontrovertible contemporary political allusion in the whole of Shakespeare. In the chorus at the beginning of the fifth act of *Henry V* we hear the following lines:

> Were now the General of our gracious Empress –
> As in good time he may – from Ireland coming,
> Bringing rebellion broachèd on his sword,
> How many would the peaceful city quit
> To welcome him!
>
> (*Henry V*, 5.1.30–34)

Any audience member at the Globe theatre with the remotest knowledge of contemporary affairs would have identified the General as the Earl of Essex and 'our Empress' as Queen Elizabeth.

On 27 March 1599 Elizabeth sent Essex on one of England's many expeditions to quell the rebellious Irish. The play must have been performed in the version preserved in the First Folio some time in the next six months. Shakespeare expresses the hope that Essex will complete his bloody work with success and return in triumph. But in

September the Earl returned in disgrace; he embarrassed the Queen by bursting into her chamber while she had her hair about her face. He was banished from the court. In February 1601 he made the boldest possible attempt at a return to the centre of power: together with a small group of other disaffected aristocrats, including Shakespeare's former patron the Earl of Southampton, he launched a disastrous attempt at a *coup d'état*.

And it was here that the first recorded political appropriation of Shakespeare took place. Essex's faction commissioned the Chamberlain's Men to stage a performance of *Richard II* the afternoon before the planned coup. That play included a scene in which an English monarch was deposed from the throne. This was dangerous matter. The scene in question had been censored out of the printed text of the play. The intention of the Essex faction must have been to use the theatre to prepare the people for the removal of a monarch. After the failure of the coup, Sir Gilly Meyrick was sentenced to death for, among other things, commissioning the performance. Shakespeare's company managed to persuade the court that they had been used, that they had had no knowledge of the coup. They got away with a reprimand.

As for Shakespeare himself, it may be that he showed characteristic wiliness in soon writing *Troilus and Cressida*, a play which debunks the epic idiom of George Chapman's translation of Homer's *Iliad*. Chapman had dedicated his translation to Essex; it carried a preface claiming that the Earl was a reincarnation of Achilles. Essex's hallmark was the chivalric code, the cult of honour. Shakespeare's *Troilus and Cressida* tears that code to shreds and makes Achilles into a figure more interested in sharing camp theatricals with his gay lover Patroclus than performing heroically on the battlefield. This looks like quite a good way of brushing off any association with the Essex who, at the probable date of *Troilus'* composition, was languishing in the Tower awaiting execution.

But in making this link I am indulging in unsubstantiated speculation, looking for nudges and winks on Shakespeare's part. All we can say for sure about the dramatist's political affiliations is that he once flattered Essex and that one of his plays was used by the Essex faction.

It would also be foolhardy to try to extract a committed vision of the nation from the plays in question. *Richard II* may have appealed to the followers of Essex because it seemed to give good reasons for the deposition of an ineffective, vacillating monarch, and because it appeared to lament the decline of chivalric England. But the *Henry IV* plays which follow bring no peace to the nation during the reign of the usurper, only further disintegration. And not even the final play in the sequence, *Henry V*, so frequently read as an unalloyed celebration of the English nation as conqueror, is sure about the identity of the nation.

Where *Henry IV Part One* began with rebellion coming from Scotland (the Douglas) and Wales (Owain Glendŵr), *Henry V* brings the whole of the British Isles together in the fight against France. Included in King Henry's army is a quartet representing England (Gower), Wales (Fluellen), Scotland (Jamie), and Ireland (MacMorris). But we cannot say for sure that the play is celebrating the unification of the four nations into one, for during the campaign against France, King Harry's army is by no means united. The Irish MacMorris, in particular, is an odd man out, not even at peace with the affable Fluellen:

> FLUELLEN Captain MacMorris, I think, look you, under your
> correction, there is not many of your nation –
> MACMORRIS Of my nation? What ish my nation? Ish a villain and a
> bastard and a knave and a rascal? What ish my nation? Who talks
> of my nation?
>
> (*Henry V*, 3.3.64–8)

In the chorus to the fifth act, Essex is celebrated because as the audience is watching the play in London he is broaching the Irish on his sword. Yet here in the body of the third act, Shakespeare gives a voice to Ireland. Or rather, he questions England's – for the Welsh Fluellen, in his loyalty to Harry of Monmouth, once Prince of Wales and now King of England, speaks for England – he questions England's right to speak for Ireland. What Englishman or Anglicized Welshman dare talk of MacMorris's nation? What kind of a nation can Ireland be when the Irish are construed by the English as villains and bastards and knaves and rascals? And that is how the dominant voice of Elizabethan England's national poet, Edmund Spenser, did construe them in his dialogue of the mid-1590s, *A View of the Present State of Ireland*. But even Spenser had his counter-voices. *A View* is written in the form of a *dialogue* and it is more sharply critical of the 'Old English' settlers in Ireland than the Irish themselves, while in *The Faerie Queene* there is a Salvage Nation resembling Ireland, but also a Salvage Man who is the noblest man. As for Shakespeare, he is all counter-voice. When MacMorris says 'What ish my nation?', Ireland in all its anguish is allowed to speak, just as in *The Tempest* Shakespeare's most beautiful poetry is put into the mouth of a salvage and deformed slave whose name evokes Carib and Cannibal.

The sole function of the Oxford interlude was to flatter King James. That is why it has never been performed again. Flattery of King James is marginal to the dramatic life of *Macbeth*. That is one reason why the play has been performed again and again. Because he was hardly ever narrowly topical in his own age and culture, Shakespeare has remained topical in other ages and cultures. Because he addresses great political issues rather than local political circumstances, his plays speak to such perennial problems as tyranny and aggressive nationalism. Because his own positions are so elusive, because every one of his voices has its counter-voice – Fluellen his MacMorris, King Harry his Michael Williams, Prospero his Caliban – he has become the voice of many positions.

'What ish my nation?' What if Shakespeare asked that question now? I would reply that his has been many nations and can potentially be every nation, and that is why he matters more than any other writer there has ever been.

The central point in world literature

Imagine a country in which Shakespeare is made compulsory in the national curriculum in secondary schools and where an 'official' interpretation transforms him into the guardian of the value-system of the established powers. Such a country might be Britain, as we saw in the last chapter. But it need not necessarily be. It might, for instance, be Bulgaria, where *Hamlet* is read by every fifteen-year-old in the land.

There, however, for forty years the 'official' state interpretation of Shakespeare went rather differently from the English Tory line. It claimed that Shakespeare was a card-carrying Marxist-Leninist. The Romantic image of Hamlet as an effete melancholy intellectual was castigated as a bourgeois fabrication; instead the Prince of Denmark was a man of destiny whose task was to solve the problem of the world social order in the transition from feudalism to capitalism. He was the embodiment of the progressive historical will of his age, tragically doomed because he was born before his time, before the working masses were ready to rise with him.

Throughout Eastern Europe the story is the same. In the former Soviet Union, in Poland, in former East Germany, in Romania, Shakespeare's plays were co-opted by state ideology in the name of official 'socialist realist' aesthetics. But in each country the same thing happened: starved by censorship of new plays critical of the Stalinist regimes, theatre companies turned to Shakespeare as a way of staging subtly oppositional performances. His canonical status exempted him from restrictions and he became the voice of liberty. Production after production implicitly read the corrupt court of Claudius in *Hamlet*, with its Polonian surveillance apparatus and its petty bureaucratic Osrics, as an allegory of the courts of Brezhnev, Ceauşescu, Zhivkov.

And after the fall of the dictators? Like the fittest organisms in the biological world, the greatest artworks survive by mutating and adapting themselves to new conditions. After 1989, another Hamlet stalked the stage of Eastern Europe. Alexander Morfov's version in Sofia in 1993 was one in which the consequence of freedom was disorientation, while Heiner Müller describes his production, the first that was staged in Berlin after the Wall came down, as 'a play that deals with crises in the state, with two epochs, and with the fissure between them. This fissure is straddled by an intellectual who is no longer certain how to behave and what to do: the old things don't work any more, but the new ways aren't to his taste.'

Shakespeare's tragedies of state are obvious material for strong political readings. But even an apparently light-hearted comedy such as *A Midsummer Night's Dream* may yield similar results. Central to Erich Honecker's cultural policy in East Germany was a progression towards *harmony* in the form of a socialist Brotherhood of Man ('*Menschenge-meinschaft*'). The movement from disharmony to harmony is very much that of Shakespeare's *Dream*. But in Werner Freese's production in Magdeburg in the 1970s, which reached large and youthful audiences, the lovers' reintegration into society at the end of the play was viewed cynically. There was no Brotherhood between them and the rude mechanicals. The production deliberately broke individual fulfilment apart from social integration, instead of unifying the two processes. Something similar happened at the other end of Europe and the other end of the political spectrum: in Spain, anti-Franco productions of *A Midsummer Night's Dream* and *As You Like It* emphasized the power of youth to go against oppressive parental will and achieve freedom in the magical world of the forest.

In chapter six, we saw how the elevation of Shakespeare to the rank of supreme 'original genius' was bound up with British and German cultural identity in the eighteenth century. In chapter seven, we heard a babble of voices in which Shakespeare has been made to speak for a variety of conceptions of England. But it is clear from the above examples that he has also spoken to other nations.

Let us return for a moment to the Tercentenary celebrations of 1916. *Shakespeare's England*, discussed in the last chapter, marked the occasion in scholarly fashion, but for pure Bardolatry another multi-author volume – even larger and more handsomely produced – was offered by the Oxford University Press: *A Book of Homage to Shakespeare*, edited by Israel Gollancz of the Tercentenary Committee.

It offers an unstoppable flow of praise in verse and prose. We learn, for example, that when God rested on the seventh day it was so that he could concentrate on creating Shakespeare. The *Book of Homage* includes more than its measure of predictably English and war-provoked sentiments, typified by these lines of G. C. Moore Smith:

> When to dark doubts our England would resign,
> Thy patriot-voice recalls her from her fears;
> Shakespeare of England, still thy country rears
> Thy pillar and with treasure loads thy shrine!

There is also ample bluster about the shared greatness and influence of Shakespeare and the British Empire.

Yet the book as a whole does not represent a triumph of Englishness or a colonization of other cultures. It is an extraordinarily polyglot production. Its homages to Shakespeare include contributions in Gaelic, Welsh, Hebrew, Sanskrit, Bengali (a panegyric by Rabindranath Tagore), Urdu, Burmese, Arabic, Setswana, Spanish, Greek, Italian, Portuguese, Romanian, Flemish, Dutch, Icelandic, Danish, Swedish, Russian, Serbo-Croat, Polish, Finnish, Japanese, Chinese, Persian, and finally Armenian ('To me Armenia seems thy home . . . What token shall my poor Armenia bring? . . . She lays upon thy shrine her Crown of Thorns'). Ananda Coomaraswany reflected on 'Intellectual

Fraternity'; Nicholas Velimirovic found a Slav soul in Shakespeare; Maung Tin detected a Buddhist strain in him; Rudyard Kipling contributed a reading of *The Tempest* in which the 'otherness' of Prospero's island was solely the function of an English voyager's fantastic projection whilst under the influence of drink; William Tsikinya-Chaka, a black South African, argued that Shakespeare's dramas show how 'nobility and valour' (he is thinking of Othello) 'are not the monopoly of any colour', whereas 'I have become suspicious of the cinema and acquired a scepticism which is not diminished by a gorgeous [contemporary film] which shows, side by side with the nobility of the white race, a highly coloured exaggeration of the depravity of the blacks' (he was thinking of D. W. Griffith's *Birth of a Nation*).

It would take more than a lifetime's work to tell the story of Shakespeare's assimilation into all these cultures, to demonstrate that he can truly be described – as he was by one contributor to the *Book of Homage* – as 'the central point in world literature'. In accordance with my practice throughout this book, rather than give a superficial sketch of a vast subject I shall concentrate in detail on a small number of case histories. In the first of them, Shakespeare assists a nationhood that comes into being retrospectively, the form in which he is used is structural and the ideology which he supports is conservative; in the second, he assists in a process of artistic liberation from a dominant national culture, the form in which he is used is rhetorical and the ideology which he supports is universalist; in the third, he assists a nationhood as it comes into being for the first time, the form in which he is used is revisionary and the ideology which he supports is that of racial liberation.

Shakespeare invents the historical novel

In what sense does Shakespeare take on new nationalities? One way in which he may do so is through topical productions, such as those in Eastern Europe before the revolutions of 1989 which gave political theatre the means to circumvent the censor's control of new plays. But another way is through an inspiriting influence upon writers who themselves become recognized as 'national poets'. Shakespeare lends his voice to an aftercomer who is hailed as the voice of a nation. The example of Shakespeare as historical dramatist inspired the historical drama of Schiller and the young Goethe, which exercised a formative influence upon German national identity.

My first example fits this German paradigm well, though with the modification that the national identity in question was constructed not at birth but at death. Though Shakespeare might be regarded as an honorary Scotsman by virtue of his writing of *Macbeth* and King James' patronage of his acting company, his elevation to the status of national poet in the very century during which England effectively absorbed Scotland through the 1707 Act of Union was potentially galling to Scotsmen. That is one reason why Scottish Enlightenment literary theorists such as Lord Kames, Alexander Gerard, and William Duff extolled Shakespeare as an exemplar of original genius but also made a case for a figure from their own ancient national tradition, the legendary Gaelic Bard Ossian. But the possibility that the Ossianic poetic corpus was forged in modern times by James Macpherson made that case difficult to sustain. In the nineteenth century, there were two candidates for the title of Scottish national bard: Robert Burns and Sir Walter Scott. The claim for Scott was nearly always made on the grounds that he was 'the Scottish Shakespeare'.

Sir Walter Scott concluded his first novel, *Waverley*, with 'A Postscript, which should have been a Preface'. In it, he lamented the decline of the old Scotland:

There is no European nation which, within the course of half a century, or little more, has undergone so complete a change as this kingdom of Scotland. The effect of the insurrection of 1745, − the destruction of the patriarchal power of the Highland chiefs, − the abolition of the heritable jurisdictions of the Lowland nobility and barons, − the total eradication of the Jacobite party, which, averse to intermingle with the English, or adopt their customs, long continued to pride themselves upon maintaining ancient Scottish manners and customs, commenced this innovation. The gradual influx of wealth, and extension of commerce, have since united to render the present people of Scotland a class of beings as different from their grandfathers, as the existing English are from those of Queen Elizabeth's time.

The purpose of the novel, says Scott, is to use imaginary scenes to preserve some idea of the 'ancient manners' of which he has 'witnessed the almost total extinction'.

The Waverley Novels are the foundation of the historical novel in its high form, that is to say as a literary genre which seeks to recover the manners of the past and a sense of its difference from the present, often with a tone of explicit or implicit nostalgia. Typically, the historical novel concerns itself with forces of change and key historical moments at which a new order becomes dominant.

Waverley itself is the archetype for the rest of Scott's long sequence of 'Scotch' novels. Its subtitle, *'Tis Sixty Years Since*, locates it specifically at the transitional moment of the insurrection of 1745, while its structure dramatizes a journey into the old Scotland, as the young Englishman Waverley travels from the Hanoverian army first to Lowland feudalism, embodied in the Baron of Bradwardine, and then to Highland Jacobitism, embodied in Fergus and Flora Mac-Ivor. Romance draws the protagonist to the Jacobite cause, but the march of history dictates that it will be defeated and new England will take over old Scotland. Waverley takes Bradwardine's house and daughter. It is through the fictional characters that 'the ancient manners' are brought to life, but the factuality of the underlying history is stressed by the constant presence at the edges of the action – and occasionally at its centre – of 'real' historical figures, most notably the Young Pretender, Charles Edward.

Scott's method here is profoundly indebted to that of Shakespeare's history plays and in particular to *Henry IV* and *Henry V*. *Richard II* is focused entirely on 'high' historical figures; even the socially low figures such as the gardeners and the loyal groom speak in verse – the garden scene is in the high old-fashioned style of allegory. The *Henry IV* plays introduce a 'low' prose voice, the voice of Eastcheap which is maintained in *Henry V*, where it merges with the voice of the common soldier (MacMorris, Michael Williams); in *Henry IV Part Two*, in place of the Queen's allegorical garden there is Justice Shallow's rural estate, one of the most densely realized locations in Shakespeare. The plays continue to foreground high history, but in opening up the space of Eastcheap, of the rural estate, of the foot soldier, they make possible Scott's telling of history from below.

According to the Hungarian Marxist critic Georg Lukács, in his influential account of the Waverley series as the primary historical novels,

> Scott's greatness lies in his capacity to give living human embodiment to historical-social types. The typically human terms in which great historical trends become tangible had never before been so superbly, straightforwardly, and pregnantly portrayed. And above all, never before had this kind of portrayal been consciously set at the centre of the representation of reality.

This seems to me as good an account of Shakespeare's history plays as of Scott's historical novels. The processes of history are given human embodiment through character; at the centre is 'the representation of reality' achieved through an accumulation of minute details, whether a question about the cost of bullocks at Stamford fair or an ancient tun-bellied pigeon-house on a Scottish laird's estate.

H. J. C. Grierson was a great editor of John Donne, but a terrible poet. Bad poems can, however, contain simple but telling truths, as in this couplet in the poem of Grierson's that was Scotland's contribution to the 1916 *Book of Homage to Shakespeare*: 'From Shakespeare Scott the inspiration drew / Peopled his page with such a motley crew'.

The relationship between historical change and character development is of the essence. On the title-page of *Waverley*, we read the epigraph: '"Under which King, Bezonian? speak, or die!" *Henry IV, Part II*'. The voice is that of Pistol at the transitional moment when Prince Hal becomes King Harry. The course of history is measured by the development of Hal's character. So too with Edward Waverley. He spends the novel wavering between loyalty to the Hanoverian King and to the Jacobite Pretender; that choice is effectively between greater England and Scottish nationalism. The king under which the novel ends is the king of greater England, of Union, of the end of feudalism in Scotland.

Scott reads the triumph of English modernity as progress, and in so doing he is in the mainstream of Enlightenment historiography, but he also recognizes that a place must be kept for Scottish national pride. This is his reason for casting a retrospective glow of romance upon the Highland world. It was to Scott that the nineteenth century owed the nostalgic reinvention of Scotland in the form of tartan plaids and the like. It was also because of their rich texture of national characteristics that the Waverley novels became so popular throughout post-Napoleonic Europe; since the most far-reaching realization of Enlightenment 'progress' had seemed to be Napoleon's extinction of small nations, the reaction of post-1814 legitimacy was a nationalistic atavism which found its spokesman in Scott. William Hazlitt, writing from the opposite political pole, saw exactly what Scott was doing: 'Through some odd process of *servile* logic, it should seem, that in restoring the claims of the Stuarts by the courtesy of romance, the House of Brunswick are more firmly seated in point of fact, and the Bourbons, by collateral reasoning, become legitimate!'

History for ever repeats itself in its ebb and flow; it never repeats itself in its particular configuration. So whilst post-Napoleonic and post-Soviet Europe cannot be mapped onto each other with any precision, it may be seen that Scott's reshaping of Shakespearean historiography in the name of atavistic 'legitimacy' suggests that the resurgence of nationalism in the Europe of the 1990s was only to be expected.

The romance of the past on which nationalism thrives is to be found above all in the chivalric code. It is already possible from *Waverley* to see that when Scott turned to English history he would write *Ivanhoe*. In the *Henry* plays the chivalric code belongs to the defeated. Richard's fall begins with his attempt to resolve the dispute between Mowbray and Bolingbroke by means of chivalric ritual; Hotspur is the quintessence of chivalry. So it is that Scott's Prince Charles Edward is a Richard-figure and Fergus MacIvor, the Highland chieftain who achieves his greatest dignity in defeat and death, is a Hotspur.

These identifications are seen most clearly in the sequence of *Waverley* which follows the march of the Jacobite army into England. Fergus is described as 'confident against the world in arms', an allusion to Hal's lines just before the battle of Shrewsbury, 'The Douglas and the Hotspur both together / Are confident against the world in arms'. Fergus combines the Douglas' Scottishness with Hotspur's chivalric ambition; but just to remind us that he will be on the losing side, Scott also describes him as 'all air and fire', a phrase which another defeated prince, the Dauphin in *Henry V*, applies to his supposedly invincible horse. As for the Chevalier Charles Edward himself, when the name of the Jacobite King is proclaimed by the army as it marches through the towns of northern England, Waverley cannot help noticing that '"no

man cried, God bless him"'. The allusion here is to the first major
public turning point in the *Henry* plays, when Bolingbroke rides into
London in triumph and the deposed Richard follows along behind:

> Even so, or with much more contempt, men's eyes
> Did scowl on gentle Richard. No man cried 'God save him!'
> No joyful tongue gave him his welcome home;
> But dust was thrown upon his sacred head.
>
> (*Richard II*, 5.2.27–30)

The allusion functions as an anticipatory signal of the coming collapse
of the Jacobite enterprise.

Here we should consider the reading of the *Henry* plays implied
by Scott's allusive structure. As *Waverley* is set at the historical turning point represented by the '45 rebellion, so the *Henry* plays are set
at the turning point represented by the establishment of the House
of Lancaster. The parallel suggests that Scott viewed Shakespeare as,
like himself, a supporter of the status quo. At the time of the Essex
rising, Queen Elizabeth might have feared that she was being read as
Richard II, but her more positive self-image was as Henry V, defeating
Spain where he had defeated France. Henry V is read as a monarch
who keeps the peace at home and achieves success abroad. He is a
pragmatist more than a chivalric hero: Hotspur would not have
threatened to spike the babies of Harfleur, would not have killed the
prisoners expressly against the law of arms or entered into a convenient
dynastic liaison (as opposed to the lively love-match he has with his
Kate).

For Scott, chivalry, as embodied in Hotspur and Fergus MacIvor and
as praised in his own time by Burke, is a necessary romance, but it must
ultimately give way to the pragmatism of Queen Elizabeth, of Colonel
Talbot in *Waverley*, of prime minister William Pitt the Younger. The
future belongs to them: according to Scott's implied reading, the *Henry*
plays as a whole, despite the explicit flattering allusion to 'our general'
in *Henry V*, proposes that Essex's quest for a renewed chivalric England
was as doomed and misguided as the Jacobite adventure a century and
a half later.

Scott's reading of Shakespearean historiography is a central part of
his revision of honour from an active into a passive virtue. As Alexander
Welsh, one of the best readers of the Waverley Novels, notes,

the modern sense of honor (modern in 1814) is strictly defensive –
just as the doctrine of private property is defensive. . . . By the early
nineteenth century the modern concept of honor is a standard
implicit, and sometimes explicit, in British political thinking. Honor
means self-imposed restraint; orderly government and the preser-
vation of property depend upon the restraint of individuals.

Scott's novel ultimately rejects the old kind of active honour embodied
in Fergus Mac-Ivor because it is associated with Hotspur-like *ambition*.
Shakespeare is thus co-opted in the name of stability, passivity, and a
defence of property that is in the tradition of Edmund Burke's attack
on the French Revolution. Scott's Shakespeare thus becomes a spokesman for nationhood in its most conservative form.

Shakespeare without a muzzle

As we saw in chapter six, the eighteenth-century deification of
Shakespeare was premissed upon a demonization of classical French
culture. Romanticism and Shakespeare idolatry were the two sides of
the same anti-Gallic coin. For that reason, both phenomena came late
to France itself.

In July 1822 a performance of *Othello* in Paris was curtailed amidst
cries from the audience of '*à bas Shakespeare! C'est un lieutenant de
Wellington!*' – down with Shakespeare, he's part of the Duke of
Wellington's military campaign against the French. 'English drama',
writes the critic Peter Raby, 'had been irrevocably identified with
military invasion and the slogan was now "Out with the English, no
foreigners in France"'. A cavalry charge was needed to disperse the
anti-Shakespearean crowd.

But that October, scandalized by the treatment of the English actors,
Stendhal published an article in the *Paris Monthly Review*. The following
year it was reprinted as the first chapter of his polemical pamphlet,
Racine and Shakespeare. Stendhal asks, 'To write tragedies which can
interest the public in 1823, is it necessary to follow the ways of Racine
or those of Shakespeare?' Having worked through the argument in the
pamphlet and its sequel of 1825, Stendhal came down on the side of
the flexibility and modernity of Shakespeare. In a deeply subversive

move, he had produced a Romantic manifesto in Paris, the very capital of classicism. 'What is Romanticism?' he asks in the third chapter of the 1823 pamphlet: it is the art that gives people most pleasure. 'What is classicism?': it is the art that gave most pleasure to their great-grandparents. The clear implication is that contemporary drama must reject the traditions of Racine and model itself on the Romanticism of Shakespeare, with its disregard for the unities and its energetic combination of verse and prose, of the heroic and the quotidian. Stendhal went on to write historical novels on the Shakespearean model of Sir Walter Scott: in *Le Rouge et le Noir* and *La Chartreuse de Parme* fictional stories of ordinary people's lives and loves are played out against the backdrop of real historical events.

In 1827, Victor Hugo pushed Stendhal's argument home in the preface to his historical drama *Cromwell*, and attempted to put it into practice in that play itself: 'Shakespeare *is* drama; and drama, which is based on the grotesque and the sublime in the same breath, tragedy and comedy, such drama is the appropriate form for the third period of poetry, the literature of the present'. '*Shakespeare, c'est le Drame*': to the French Academy, the effrontery of this was nothing short of revolutionary. Hugo did not merely claim that Shakespeare rather than Racine represented the summit of modern poetry, he praised and set up as models precisely those aspects of Shakespeare which French neoclassicism had condemned: the mixed genre, the indecorous but realistic mingling of high and low, tragedy and comedy, sublime and grotesque. He especially commended the gravediggers whose presence in *Hamlet* had provoked some of Voltaire's most excoriating remarks. Among the 'Personnages' of *Cromwell* were numbered Trick, Giraff, Gramadoch, and Elespuru, 'the four Fools of Lord Protector Cromwell' – it is as if French high drama had gone so long without Fools that Hugo decided to make up for lost time by including four of them in one play.

Parisians in late 1827 not only had the opportunity to read Hugo's homage to Shakespeare in *Cromwell*. They were also given the chance to revise their opinions of the plays in the theatre. Charles Kemble and Harriet Smithson played in *Hamlet* and *Romeo and Juliet* at the Odéon. Reactions were as positive as those to the *Othello* of 1822 had been negative. These performances – cried up by an extraordinary circle of young artists including Delacroix, Dumas, Gautier, Hugo, Sainte-Beuve, and Alfred de Vigny – were the trigger for the explosion of

French Romanticism. The eventual success of Hugo's Romantic historical tragedy *Hernani* in 1830 was a direct consequence of the transformation of the aesthetics of the Parisian theatre brought about by the English company in 1827. The first performance of *Hernani* was marked by violent disputes between traditionalists and the new Romantic faction in the auditorium; the triumph of the Romantics demonstrated that an aesthetic revolution was possible, that the barricades of the Academy could be stormed. This was a precedent for the political revolution later in 1830: that July, rioting in a theatre spread to the streets, and as a result of the ensuing three days of violence Charles X abdicated and fled the country. Whereas Shakespeare had been used in England and Germany as a bulwark against French revolutionary and Napoleonic influence, when he eventually reached France he was in the vanguard of a republican and Bonapartist revolution.

Two vignettes from the *Mémoires* of Hector Berlioz bring these events marvellously to life. First, the advent of Shakespeare in 1827:

> I come now to the supreme drama of my life. I shall not recount all its sad vicissitudes. I will say only this: an English company came over to Paris to give a season of Shakespeare at the Odéon, with a repertory of plays then quite unknown in France. I was at the first night of *Hamlet*. In the role of Ophelia I saw Henriette Smithson, who five years later became my wife. The impression made on my heart and mind by her extraordinary talent, nay her dramatic genius, was equalled only by the havoc wrought in me by the poet she so nobly interpreted. That is all I can say.
>
> Shakespeare, coming upon me unawares, struck me like a thunderbolt. The lightning flash of that discovery revealed to me at a stroke the whole heaven of art, illuminating it to its remotest corners. I recognized the meaning of grandeur, beauty, dramatic truth, and I could measure the utter absurdity of the French view of Shakespeare which derives from Voltaire – 'That ape of genius, sent / By Satan among men to do his work' – and the pitiful narrowness of our own worn-out academic, cloistered traditions of poetry. I saw, I understood, I felt . . . that I was alive and that I must arise and walk.

The quotation is from Hugo's *Chants du crépuscule*; the final image casts the young artist as someone who has been miraculously brought to fullness of life by Shakespeare's Christlike intervention. Berlioz's exaggerations – *Hamlet* was not 'quite unknown' in France – are part and parcel of his Romantic rhetoric. The language closely echoes that of Goethe's oration on his discovery of Shakespeare nearly sixty years earlier:

> The first page of his that I read made me his for life; and when I had finished a single play, I stood like one born blind, on whom a miraculous hand bestows sight in a moment. I saw, I felt, in the most vivid manner, that my existence was infinitely expanded ... I did not hesitate for a moment about renouncing the classical drama. The unity of place seemed to me irksome as a prison, the unities of action and of time burthensome fetters to our imagination; I sprang into the open air, and felt for the first time that I had hands and feet.

In France in the 1820s, as in Germany in the 1770s, Shakespeare is imagined as not just an antidote to the prescriptions of Voltaire's classicism, but a saviour of the artistic spirit, a bringer of sight, feeling and freedom – a freedom that is linked to political emancipation.

The intersection between Romantic art and revolutionary activity in 1830 is apparent in this second passage from Berlioz's memoirs:

> I was finishing my cantata when the Revolution broke out.... Grapeshot rattled on the barricaded doors, cannon-balls thudded against the façade, women screamed, and in the brief lulls in the firing, the swallows filled the air with their shrill sweet cry. I dashed off the final pages of my orchestral score to the sound of stray bullets coming over the roofs and pattering on the wall outside my window. On the 29th I had finished and was free to go out and roam about Paris till morning, pistol in hand, with [the] 'blessed rabble'.

A day or two later, Berlioz joins a group who are singing in the streets a battle-hymn of his own composition with words translated from the Irish Romantic poet Tom Moore.

Berlioz's self-analysis suggests that the supreme event of his life is not the moment when he joins in the Revolution, when he discovers that his own art is inspiring the activists in the street, but the advent of Harriet Smithson and Shakespeare. Although art is used to further the Revolution, the Romantic artist is ultimately a man of feeling and not a man of action. Even at the height of the Revolution, his attention is drawn to nature, to the music of the swallows. The composer at work as violence flares around, *having* to finish his creation before he can take up his pistol and join the crowd: it is an archetypal Romantic image. In Berlioz's *Mémoires*, revolutionary language is removed from the streets and applied to the artist's intimate feelings. He is more concerned with the upheaval within, brought upon him by Shakespeare, than the political revolution without. His most impassioned assaults are not on the narrowness and intransigence of Charles X but on the anti-Shakespearean prejudices of the Academy, the classicists, and the arbiters of taste. Shakespeare was the instigator of a sustained artistic revolution in France: his form of history-writing exercised a powerful influence on the novels of Hugo and Stendhal; his plays inspired much of Berlioz's best work, most notably the *Roméo et Juliette* symphony, which I discuss in the next chapter. His directly political influence was, however, spasmodic.

On 9 December 1832, Harriet Smithson was in the audience for the first performance of the revised version of the *Symphonie fantastique* which she had unwittingly inspired, together with its sequel. Also present at the Conservatoire were Dumas, Gautier, Hugo, George Sand, and de Vigny, not to mention Chopin, Liszt, and Paganini. As at *Hamlet* in 1827 and *Hernani* in 1830, the cohorts of Romanticism were out in force. The new work performed was ' *"Le retour à la vie"*, *monodrame qui est le complément de cette oeuvre, et forme la seconde partie de l' "Épisode de la vie d'un artiste"* ': *The Return to Life*, a lyric monodrama conceived as a sequel to the *Symphonie*, forming the second part of *Episode in the Life of an Artist*. Later entitled *Lélio*, it consisted of several previously written compositions linked by the spoken monologue of the 'Artist'. The 'episode' in his life is his obsessive love for an actress, not his participation in a revolution. *The Return to Life* begins with the Artist awaking from the opium-induced nightmare of the final two movements of the symphony. Having imagined his own execution in the previous work, he now recollects 'the scaffold, the judges, hang-men, soldiers, the screaming mob'. The language here is that of revolutionary tribunal and revolutionary crowd, but the Artist, far from going into the streets to join the masses, is alone and in full flight from them. Later in the work he apostrophizes Shakespeare and denominates as blasphemers Voltaire and the priests of classicism. For the true artist a society ruled by tradition and the Academy is worse than hell. But the Artist's response is not to call for an aesthetic revolution, to change the regimen of society by storming the barricades of the Academy as Hugo had done a few years earlier; instead, it is to escape to the hills: 'I want to go away to the mountains of Italy, to some banditti-chief, even if I have to do humble service there'. This is Romantic primitivism and escapism at its most extreme.

The Artist's final decision, however, is to dedicate himself to his work. Hamlet-like, he chides himself for his reflectiveness: 'Why reflect? I have no more mortal enemy than reflection, I must distance myself from it. Action, action, and it will fly'. The action he decides on is the performance of a composition presided over by Shakespeare: he prepares himself '*avec un accent religieux*', like a priest before the sacrament, with the invocation 'may SHAKESPEARE protect me!'. Like Hamlet, he gives advice to the players on how to perform his work; musical technicalities are substituted for Hamlet's theatrical ones. But this is a *Mousetrap* without a mouse to trap: where Hamlet puts on his play in order to establish the guilt of the King and to proceed towards the act that will set right the rotting state, Berlioz's Artist puts on his performance solely in order to console himself and find inner peace. What, then, is the work that is played? It is a fantasia on *The Tempest* in the form of a blessing on Miranda sung by airy spirits as she leaves the island. It is a version of *The Tempest* stripped of political content: there is nothing of usurpation and power politics, only the beauty and harmony of music and love. At the very end of his *Mémoires*, Berlioz said that these two things were the two wings of the soul, and ultimately his Shakespeare was the source of them. Romantic Shakespeare is for a while emptied of politics and removed from society. He becomes instead the bringer of music and love.

His political force was rekindled later in the century. Asked who was the great French writer of the nineteenth century, André Gide replied, '*Victor Hugo, hélas.*' We tend to endorse that '*hélas*', forgetting the extraordinarily high regard in which Hugo was held by the end of his life. When he returned to France in 1870 after the fall of the Second Empire, Hugo was greeted as a national hero. André Maurois reminds us of his funeral fifteen years later: 'For the first time in the history of mankind a whole nation was rendering to a poet the honours usually reserved for sovereigns and military leaders.'

As we have seen, Hugo's first encounter with Shakespeare, albeit an indirect one since he knew no English, was in the 1820s; it led to his

Romantic manifesto, the preface to *Cromwell*. After 1850, having been exiled by Louis Napoleon, he again made Shakespeare the pretext for a manifesto that was at once both aesthetic and political. According to his own recollection, when he took up residence in Guernsey, his son asked him how would spend his exile; he replied that he would gaze at the ocean and asked his son what he would do. '"I," said the son, "I shall translate Shakespeare."' To which Hugo adds that the two activities are one and the same, for there are indeed men 'whose souls are like the sea'. Hugo's Shakespeare is like the sea, a force of nature transcending national boundaries.

He originally intended to contribute a preface to his son's translation, but it grew into a book called *William Shakespeare* which summed up his thoughts on genius, on art, and on politics. It was published in 1864, three hundred years after Shakespeare's birth and two years after the other *chef d'oeuvre* of Hugo's exile, *Les Misérables*. The publisher's announcement, which Hugo oversaw, makes some grand claims:

> the poet of England [is here] judged by the poet of France . . . Taking off from Shakespeare, Victor Hugo has embarked upon all the complex questions of art and civilization. Grand as the title is, the book surpasses it. It is not a purely literary book, it is a humanitarian, a social, even a political book, which addresses itself to all the emotions of the present, to all the pending questions, and to all living interests. Speaking of all countries, it is directly relevant to all peoples. It will be the literary manifesto of the nineteenth century. The book will carry on the philosophical and social uproar caused by *Les Misérables*.

The grand aesthetic scheme is taken up in Hugo's own preface: 'In contemplating Shakespeare, all the questions relating to art have arisen in the Author's mind. To deal with these questions is to set forth the mission of art; to deal with these questions is to set forth the duty of human thought toward man'.

As for the book's political effect, it was immediate. Hugo was invited to a banquet to celebrate both its publication and the tercentenary of Shakespeare's birth. The event was promptly banned by the authorities out of fear at the mere prospect of the exiled writer setting foot on French soil. Most reviews of the book were highly partisan, with pro-government journals condemning it and oppositional ones praising it to the skies. Always for Hugo the literary revolution and the political revolution were one and the same; he made a virtue of his enemies' accusation that Romanticism was dangerous because it was the same thing as socialism.

It cannot be denied that Hugo's vatic style is frequently overblown, nor, as one reviewer wryly noted, that the book is an egotistic performance: 'The great Greek is Aeschylus, the great Hebrew is Isaiah, the great Roman is Juvenal, the great Englishman is Shakespeare, the great German is Beethoven. And the great Frenchman? What? There isn't one? Rabelais? No! Molière? No! You're making it difficult! Montesquieu? Still no! Voltaire? Fie! – Well then? Well: Hugo!' And yet the passion and the energy make the book a magnificent call to arms for a new literature.

For Hugo, whereas classical French literature had been polished and elite, the plays of Shakespeare were characterized by their excess, their impropriety, their drunkenness, all those qualities which classicism and moralism abhorred: 'He strides over proprieties, he overthrows Aristotle, he spreads havoc among the Jesuits, the Methodists, the Purists, and the Puritans; he puts Loyola to disorderly rout, and upsets Wesley . . . He does not keep Lent. He overflows like vegetation, like germination, like light, like flame.'

Hugo's attack on the literary establishment, the Academy with its obsessive regulation, was inextricable from his political position. 'This race of writers' – the race of recalcitrant geniuses, he means,

> requires repression; it is useful to have recourse to the secular arm . . . Good taste is a precaution taken to keep the peace. Sober writers are the counterpart of prudent electors. Inspiration is suspected of love of liberty. Poetry is rather outside of legality; there is, therefore, an official art, the offspring of official criticism.

In the face of the liberty of genius, official culture sometimes resorts to banishment (Aeschylus, Voltaire, implicitly Hugo himself), but sometimes it relies on a lighter weapon, namely 'a state criticism' written by 'literary policemen'. The neoclassical La Harpe accused Shakespeare of pandering to the mob, describing him as '*Ce courtisan grossier du profane vulgaire*' – this gross courtesan of the ungodly masses. That is why the plays were hated by what Hugo called '*l'école*' and we would call the Establishment.

'*L'école*' is the Academy, which is compromised not only by its pedantry but also by its link to the police; it is the 'intellectual mandarinship governing in the various authorized and official teachings, either of the press or of the state': 'The school hates Shakespeare. It detects him in the very act of mingling with the people, going to and fro in public thoroughfares ... The drama of Shakespeare is for the people; the school is indignant, and says, "*Odi profanum vulgus.*" There is demagogy in this poetry roaming at large.'

Shakespeare, writes Hugo, has been policed for too long in France, reined in not least by Le Tourneur's wholly prose translation, the only complete rendering of the plays into French. The new version of Hugo junior will bring to France 'Shakespeare without a muzzle'. The translation will educate and thus liberate the masses: 'Let it not be forgotten that true Socialism has for its end the elevation of the masses to the civic dignity, and that, therefore, its principal care is for moral and intellectual cultivation ... That is why Shakespeare must be translated in France.'

For Hugo, Shakespeare is an artist of and for the people; he touches the contrary poles of Olympus and the fairground. He must be given back to the people, must become – together with Hugo himself, of course – the basis of a 'popular literature'. He must be disseminated by means of state-provided mass education: 'Teach! learn! All the revolutions of the future are enclosed and engulfed in this phrase: Gratuitous and obligatory instruction.'

Hugo's refusal to condescend to the masses is one of his great strengths at this point. Will the people understand the literature they are taught? Of course they will, he replies. We know of nothing too high for them:

> The soul of the people is great. Have you ever gone, of a holiday, to a theatre open gratuitously to all? What do you think of that audience. Do you know of any other more spontaneous and intelligent? Do you know, even in the forest, a vibration more profound? ... The multitude – and in this lies their grandeur – are profoundly open to the ideal. When they come in contact with lofty art they are pleased, they palpitate. Not a detail escapes them. The crowd is one liquid and living expanse capable of vibration. A mob is a sensitive plant. Contact with the beautiful stirs ecstatically the surface of multitudes, – a sure sign that the deeps are sounded.

The forest, the deeps of the sea, the sensitive plant, Shakespeare, the crowd in Hugo's own novels: all are inexorable forces which will triumph over petty state power.

As Scott found in Shakespeare a precedent for his own politics of the status quo, so Hugo finds in the plays a demagogic art that is his own. 'He drops his eyes and looks at the people. There in the depths of shadow, well-nigh invisible by reason of its submersion in darkness, is that fatal crowd, that vast and mournful heap of suffering, that venerable populace of the tattered and of the ignorant,– a chaos of souls': such passages have the uncanny effect of making Shakespeare sound as if he were the author of *Les Misérables*.

Like Scott, Hugo valued Shakespeare for writing history from below as well as above, and thus making way for a new kind of historical novel which overturned the many centuries during which 'history has been a courtier'. But Hugo went much further than Scott, who in the dramatic opening scene of his novel *The Heart of Midlothian* revealed his fear of the mob. Hugo attempted to wrest Shakespeare away from the dominant critical tradition which proposed that he held the mob in contempt for its fickleness. This had been the position of the leading Romantic critics of the earlier nineteenth century, A. W. Schlegel and S. T. Coleridge; even the liberal-minded William Hazlitt had reluctantly concluded that Shakespeare ultimately admired Coriolanus more than the citizens. At the same time, Hugo sought to wrest the plays away from nationalism, arguing that Shakespeare was the one redeeming feature of the insular English mind because he was himself far from insular and because 'in that prudish nation he is the free poet'.

Hugo's *William Shakespeare* is a book of slogans as much as an act of literary criticism. Perhaps the most memorable of all its arresting claims is the following: 'A little more, and Shakespeare would be European'. Hugo was a passionate advocate of a United States of Europe, conceived in socialist and republican terms, not imperial Napoleonic ones. In his will he left his books to the Bibliothèque Nationale in Paris, which he said would one day be the library of the United States of Europe. If he had been asked who would be the poet of the United States of Europe, he would doubtless have hoped that it would be himself, but he would unhesitatingly have replied: Shakespeare.

The Prospero complex

Scott became a baronet, Hugo was the son of a count. Though the former gave a voice to the disinherited Highlands and the latter became a republican and an oppositional icon during the French Second Empire, they both remained loyal to what may properly be called the high bourgeois phase of European culture. As the Marxist literary theorist Georg Lukács demonstrated, the literary form in which they were pre-eminent, the historical novel, was the quintessential expressive medium of that culture. Hazlitt saw that the nostalgic nationalism of the Scotsman was really a means of propping up the English establishment. And even the Romantic internationalism of the Frenchman, conceived as an ideal in opposition to the dominant culture of Bonapartism, was – at what we might now call the 'macro' level – an expression of a deeper dominant culture. There is a limitation, potentially a complacency, about the way in which Scott and Hugo make Shakespeare a spokesman for certain disenfranchised groups, since they always keep him within a pale in which education, rational discourse, freedom of imagination, the prizing of the individual artistic genius, and the other basic values of European 'civilization' remain sacrosanct.

It was these values which increasingly came under attack in the work of British and American academics of a left-wing persuasion during the Thatcher–Reagan decade. Since Shakespeare is commonly regarded as the apex of the high culture of the West – since he is Dead White European Male in chief – he was a focal point of many of these attacks. The rise of Shakespeare and the rise of the British Empire were viewed as twin phenomena; the implication was that since one had fallen, the other would have to fall soon.

Empire and colonization are at the heart of the matter. For three hundred years, the new critical radicalism claimed, critics and adapters had assumed that Shakespeare's final play, *The Tempest*, was a summation of his art and his reflections upon art; but this is an illusion, as airy as Prospero's pageant – the ugly truth which late twentieth-century criticism could exclusively reveal was that the play is in fact a text reeking of the discourse of colonialism. *The Tempest* must bear the blame for the Atlantic slave trade.

It is no coincidence that the now hugely influential reading of *The Tempest* in these terms began for the purposes of the Anglo-American academy with Stephen Greenblatt's essay 'Learning to Curse', published in 1976, in a book called *First Images of America: The Impact of the New World on the Old*, which explicitly marked – in troubled fashion – the bicentenary of the American Declaration of Independence. As was the case some years later in Australia, official celebrations of a young nation's coming to the age of two hundred released an anguished cry from the liberal intelligentsia as they came to full realization of the exploitation and oppression on which their nation was built. The task of literary theory became to assuage the guilt of empire by making the author of *The Tempest* a scapegoat.

Ironically, though, very few of the 'radical' critics of the 1970s and 1980s who read *The Tempest* in the context of 'the discourse of imperialism' acknowledged that a revisionary reading of the play had already been undertaken in the 1950s and 1960s by non-white non-Europeans. I have to admit to my shame that I have been much longer familiar with the 'new historicist' readings of rebellious American Stephanos like Stephen Greenblatt and Stephen Orgel than with the remarkable creative work done a generation before them by self-proclaimed West Indian Calibans like George Lamming, Edward Kamau Brathwaite, Aimé Césaire, and Roberto Fernández Retamar.

What I mean by a revisionary reading is one that brushes against the grain of the dominant interpretation of a canonical work. In the case of *The Tempest*, that means a reading that is more sympathetic to Caliban than to Prospero. But the West Indian born writers whom I shall be considering were not only reacting against a long critical orthodoxy which failed to appreciate the critique of Prospero that is built into the play. They were also undertaking a more local task of revision.

In 1950, Octave Mannoni's *Psychology of Colonisation* was published in Paris. At the centre of the book was the argument that colonization functioned by means of a pair of reciprocal neuroses: the 'Prospero complex' on the part of the colonizer and the 'Caliban complex' on the part of the colonized.

According to Mannoni, the African races are psychologically predisposed to subservience. Before the white man came, they were subservient to the shades of their ancestors; after he came, they were subservient to him. This complex, the argument goes, has its archetypal representation in the Caliban who compulsively submits first to Prospero and then to Stephano and Trinculo. As for the colonizer, he will always be the kind of person who has failed in his own community – as Prospero has failed in his role as Duke. In the heyday of empire he was the younger son or black sheep of the family dispatched to the colonies. The key to his behaviour is a projection of his own neuroses onto the colonized.

The archetypal representation is again provided by *The Tempest*, in the form of Prospero's accusation that Caliban has attempted to rape Miranda. 'You tried to violate Miranda, *therefore* you shall chop wood': by a process that Mannoni sees as the root of colonial racism, Prospero justifies his hatred on grounds of sexual guilt. According to Mannoni, 'the "inferior being" always serves as scapegoat; our own evil intentions can be projected onto him. This applies especially to incestuous intentions.' In other words, Prospero projects his own incestuous desire for Miranda into an accusation which becomes the pretext for his oppression of Caliban:

> The 'Prospero complex', which draws from the inside, as it were, a picture of the paternalist colonial, with his pride, his neurotic impatience, and his desire to dominate, at the same time portrays the racialist whose daughter has suffered an attempted rape at the hands of an inferior being . . . These rapes allegedly perpetrated by members of one race on those of another are pure projections of the unconscious.

Mannoni was, I think, the first to read the rape accusation in this way. An immediate hostile response came from Frantz Fanon. His influential *Peau noire, masques blancs* ('Black Skin, White Masks') was published in 1952. It is a refutation of the idea of the Caliban complex. Against Mannoni, Fanon argues that 'it is the racist who creates his inferior'. Inferiority is not a predisposition in certain races; indeed, racial identity itself only comes into being through the recognition of otherness. But having denied one complex, Fanon accepts the other: 'what is interesting in this part of his book is the intensity with which M. Mannoni makes us feel the ill-resolved conflicts that seem to be at the root of the colonial vocation'. He reads the rape fantasy as the core of the Prospero complex: 'Toward Caliban, Prospero assumes an attitude that is well known to Americans in the southern United States.

Are they not forever saying that the niggers are just waiting for the chance to jump on white women?'

This reading was further developed by George Lamming in his *The Pleasures of Exile* (1960), an autobiographical meditation which made use of *The Tempest* as 'a way of presenting a certain state of feeling which is the heritage of the exiled and colonial writer from the British Caribbean'. For Lamming, 'it is Shakespeare's capacity for experience which leads me to feel that *The Tempest* was also prophetic of a political future which is our present. Moreover, the circumstances of my life, both as a colonial and exiled descendant of Caliban in the twentieth century, is an example of that prophecy.'

Just as the Prospero and Caliban complexes are at the centre of Mannoni's treatise on colonization, so at the centre of Lamming's reflection on being colonized is a chapter called 'A Monster, A Child, A Slave'. The monster is Prospero, who projects onto Caliban the darkness that is within himself: 'Prospero is afraid of Caliban. He is afraid because he knows that his encounter with Caliban is, largely, his encounter with himself'. The rape accusation is central. 'Did Caliban really try to lay her?' asks Lamming. We would only know if Miranda gave birth to a black child. Prospero's fear is of something that is not his: 'It would be Miranda's and Caliban's child. It would be *theirs*: the result and expression of some fusion both physical and other than physical: a fusion which, within himself, Prospero needs and dreads!' Again, there is a suggestion of perverse sexual desire on Prospero's part. Lamming extends this idea further into the play than Mannoni had done. Why is Prospero so angry whenever Sycorax is mentioned and why does he feel it necessary to reassure Miranda of her dead mother's sexual fidelity? 'The tone suggests an intimacy of involvement and concern which encourages speculation. But we could not speak with authority on the possibilities of this defect until we had heard from Sycorax and Miranda's mother.'

History is not only a courtier, as Hugo had it, but also a colonizer. It is Prospero who has written the history of the play's imaginary past – and what might he be suppressing or distorting when he tells that history in the first act of the play? Lamming hints, though he is too subtle openly to assert, that Miranda may not be Prospero's child. He developed this hint in his 1971 novel, *Water with Berries*, in which he casts himself as a Caliban-figure who has become an immigrant in 1950s

London. The Old Dowager, his landlady, turns out to be Prospero's wife. Her secret is that she had a lover: her husband's brother, the Antonio figure. Miranda is their child. One day some theatre director will create a skewed production of *The Tempest* in which Miranda is Antonio's child by Prospero's wife, while Caliban is Prospero's by Sycorax.

What does the text of *The Tempest* actually tell us about the events which occurred when Prospero first arrived on the island? The exposition of the past history of the characters is unusually laboured, which suggests that the matter was important to the dramatist. Typically, the mature Shakespeare will begin a play with a couple of courtiers – Gloucester and Kent in *Lear*, Philo and Demetrius in *Antony and Cleopatra*, Camillo and Archidamus in *The Winter's Tale* – sketching in the background to the story. But such opening scenes usually last no more than a few minutes; Shakespeare then gets on with the action of the play, only providing additional information about the imagined 'pre-action' in passing when required. In *The Tempest*, however, having grabbed his audience's attention with the storm, he proceeds with an expository scene of some five hundred lines, easily the longest in the play. First Prospero tells Miranda the story of her life, then he tells Ariel the story of his, then Caliban his. That Prospero keeps accusing Miranda of not listening to his narrative suggests that Shakespeare was aware that his audience might not be listening – there is nothing more boring in the theatre than detailed exposition of the lives of characters whom we have not yet got to know.

Prospero's version of the story goes as follows. Twelve years before the action of the play begins, he was exiled from Milan when his brother Antonio usurped his crown, with the assistance of King Alonso of Naples. He admits that he was himself partly to blame for his overthrow, since he spent all his time in 'secret studies' in his library, leaving the business of government to his brother. His retirement 'awaked an evil nature' in Antonio (1.1.92). The implication here is that ambition and treachery lay dormant in Antonio until they were stimulated by the opportunity which Prospero created by retreating to his library and leaving a power vacuum in Milan.

Prospero and the infant Miranda were washed up on the shores of the island. He was not the first person to find haven there. Twelve years before, an Algerian woman named Sycorax was found guilty of witchcraft; she would have been executed, save for the fact that she was pregnant; she was therefore exiled and she too landed on the island. She used her magical powers to conjure up the spirits of the isle. One of them, Ariel, was 'too delicate / To act her earthy and abhorred commands' (1.2.274–5), so, with the assistance of other spirits, she confined him in a cloven pine tree. He remained there for twelve years, until Prospero arrived and, by means of his own magic, released him. Meanwhile, Sycorax had died, leaving her child Caliban alone on the island.

Prospero calls Caliban 'my slave, who never / Yields us kind answer' (1.2.311–12). But Caliban claims that his first encounter with Prospero was characterized by mutual kindness:

> When thou cam'st first,
> Thou strok'st me and made much of me, wouldst give me
> Water with berries in't, and teach me how
> To name the bigger light, and how the less,
> That burn by day and night; and then I loved thee,
> And showed thee all the qualities o'th' isle,
> The fresh springs, brine-pits, barren place and fertile.
>
> (1.2.334–41)

Initially, then, there was an exchange of affection and linguistic education for tips on where to find food and drink. Caliban would have offered Prospero what he offers Trinculo and Stephano later in the play:

> I'll show thee the best springs; I'll pluck thee berries;
> I'll fish for thee . . .
> I prithee, let me bring thee where crabs grow,
> And I with my long nails will dig thee pig-nuts,
> Show thee a jay's nest, and instruct thee how
> To snare the nimble marmoset. I'll bring thee
> To clust'ring filberts, and sometimes I'll get thee
> Young seamews from the rocks.
>
> (2.2.159–71)

Caliban is an instructor in the arts of survival. He has lived alone on the island without any assistance from Prospero. Prospero, on the other hand, cannot survive without the assistance of Caliban.

In order to win that help, he offers Caliban 'water with berries'. Most editors of the play remain silent on the meaning of this phrase. Those who do comment on it merely point to a parallel in William Strachey's narrative of the Bermuda tempest of 1609, from which Shakespeare drew a number of details in his descriptions of the storm and the island. Strachey noted that the shipwrecked party had to face the problem that there was no fresh water on the island; they survived thanks to the local cedar trees, 'the berries whereof, our men seething, straining, and letting stand some three or four days, made a kind of pleasant drink'. But this is not a parallel case. There *are* 'fresh springs' on Caliban's island, and he knows perfectly well how to pluck berries for himself. Caliban's speech turns on the division between the natural resources of the island, which are his expertise, and the knowledge brought to the island, which is Prospero's. 'Water with berries' cannot be a distillation from local fruit; it must be something that Prospero *brings to* the island, together with his books and his language.

It sounds like Caliban's attempt to find words for some fruity-tasting drink with which he has previously been unfamiliar. In Elizabethan English, 'berry' was synonymous with 'grape'. Europeans had a magical-seeming art of turning grapes into something more pleasurable to drink than plain water. Is it not reasonable to suppose that wine was among the 'stuffs and necessaries' which Gonzalo packed for Prospero, together with his rich garments, linens, chess-set, and books? Prospero tells Miranda that Gonzalo's supplies have been very valuable, 'have steaded much' (1.2.166). The 'water with berries' seems to have been particularly useful: Caliban enjoyed drinking it so much that in return he showed Prospero the way to fresh water and edible food.

If 'water with berries' means wine, there is a remarkably close correspondence between Prospero's first exchange with Caliban and that of Stephano and Trinculo: in each case, intoxication is a means of eliciting subservience. It is a familiar story of colonization. But Gonzalo would not have been able to pack a very large supply of wine. What would have happened when it ran out? At that point, the book replaced the bottle. The link is made explicit in the scene with Trinculo and Stephano: Caliban emphasizes that Prospero's power comes from the book, while Stephano describes his bottle as a book (2.2.141). The alcohol that comes out of the bottle makes Caliban follow his master's will. The lesson that comes out of the book has the same effect. Prospero teaches his pupil about hierarchy: to call the sun the 'bigger light' and the moon 'the less' is to take a first step towards a cosmological justification of the theory of the divine right of kings. As the sun is above the moon, so the man is above the woman, the master above the slave, and so on.

Mannoni took Caliban's subservience first to Prospero, then to Stephano and Trinculo, as evidence of a psychological predisposition or complex. Fanon and Lamming argued to the contrary that it was a condition created by the colonizer's act of oppression. As soon as Prospero sets himself up as master and Caliban as pupil, he creates the conditions for Caliban's rebellion. Once the initial kind 'strokes' are replaced by the 'stripes' of the master's whip, Caliban will begin to feel put upon. Call a man 'filth' (1.2.349) and he will start behaving like filth. Once Caliban is taught about hierarchy and property, he will begin to articulate arguments for his own rights: 'This island's mine, by Sycorax my mother, / Which thou tak'st from me' (1.2.334–5). He will then think about repossessing the isle for his own people – which will mean begetting a child upon Miranda.

Antonio, in league with the Neapolitan court, rebelled against Prospero: but Prospero had created the conditions which made the rebellion inevitable. Caliban, in league with Neapolitan commoners, rebels against Prospero: but Prospero has created the conditions which make the rebellion inevitable. That may be why at the end of the play he comes to acknowledge Caliban as his own 'thing of darkness' (5.1.278). As Sycorax used spirits to torment Ariel, so Prospero uses spirits to torment Caliban. The fact that Caliban has been on the island for twelve years before Prospero's arrival means that Caliban cannot literally be his child, but the parallels between the magical powers of dead mother and those of the surrogate father make him his symbolic child. A 'Prosperian' reading of the play locates darkness in Caliban's rough nature; a 'Calibanesque' reading finds it in Prospero's art of nurture which is a means to mastery.

It is a defining characteristic of Shakespeare's Caliban that he hears the music of the isle, 'Sounds and sweet airs that give delight and hurt not' (3.2.138–46). Prospero's failure to appreciate Caliban's ear for music vitiates any purely 'Prosperian' reading of the play. Shakespeare's decision to represent Caliban as a poet as well as a rebel (something which sets him apart from the vulgar, prosaic Stephano and Trinculo) opened a space for the voices of rebellious Caribbean poets.

As a reader of *The Tempest*, Frantz Fanon was Caliban to Mannoni's Prospero. He was able to liberate the Calibanesque reading that has always been latent in the play because his own master was no colonizer. Born in Martinique, Fanon was a student of Aimé Césaire, whom Lamming described as 'perhaps the greatest of all Caribbean poets'. Lamming quotes Césaire's description of the shack where he was born: 'a tiny house stinking in the narrow street, a miniature house which lodges in its guts of rotten wood dozens of rats . . . a tiny, cruel house . . . the thinned roof, patched with tin from petrol cans . . . And the bed of boards which brought forth my race, the bed with feet of kerosene rags . . . with kid-skin cover, and dried banana leaves, its rags.' When Shakespeare speaks to a man born in such a place, we witness a cultural translation far beyond those undertaken by Scott and Hugo.

Perhaps the most astonishing thing about Shakespeare's achievement is that it contained enough for him to become not just an icon of various European nationhoods but a voice of what we now call multiculturalism. Fanon's *Black Skin, White Masks* was a foundation stone of the multicultural project; in a more limited way, Lamming's *Pleasures of Exile* was a manifesto for British West Indian writing. That these two works should have taken off from a revisionary reading of Mannoni's reading of *The Tempest* is testimony to Shakespeare's continuing centrality to cultural understanding even as the dominant Eurocentric tradition comes under attack.

Césaire, the mentor of Fanon and the inventor of the term 'négritude', for many years Mayor of Fort-de-France and subsequently President of the Progressive Party of Martinique, has claims to be the 'national poet' not just of his own island but of the whole disparate Afro-Caribbean nation. His rewriting of *The Tempest* from the point of view of Caliban reconstitutes Shakespeare in a theatre of négritude.

Une tempète ('A Tempest'), first published in the journal *Présence africaine* in 1968, then performed in Paris and elsewhere in 1969, is one of the great creative revisions of our time. Linguistically, it smuggles into the language of the European tradition the voice of Caliban. The character's first word is 'Uhuru!', which is Swahili for 'freedom'; his last utterance is a triumphant repetition of that word in French, 'La liberté, ohe la liberté'. The cry of 'freedom' is in Shakespeare's original, but there it is an illusion – Caliban is at that moment enslaved to the bottle – whilst here it has force, not least because it is spoken by a black actor.

Mannoni's reading of the rape of Miranda is now given a dramatic inflexion: 'Rape! rape!' says Caliban to Prospero, 'Look here, you old goat, you're attributing *your* libidinous ideas to me.' And the profound kinship between Caliban and Miranda is emphasized by Césaire's giving over to the girl a speech of welcome to the isle, an induction to its natural riches – a speech which in Shakespeare is twice given to Caliban, first with Prospero, then with Stephano and Trinculo. The play is full of clever modernizing twists: the infected grotto in which Caliban is lodged becomes by a small linguistic slippage 'le ghetto'; Gonzalo's Utopian vision of the isle becomes a desire for it to be developed as a kind of Rousseauistic holiday resort for well-to-do Europeans (which seems prophetic of what has happened to the West Indies in the years since the play was written).

'To me', wrote Césaire, 'Prospero is the complete totalitarian. I am always surprised when others consider him the wise man who "forgives". What is most obvious, even in Shakespeare's version, is the man's absolute will to power'. The question for the writer of 'négritude' is how to break the white man's totalitarian grip on power. Césaire rewrites the play with this question in mind.

For most of the time, he follows the action of the original, but one crucial scene is an innovation. Ariel is reimagined as a mulatto slave. In the added scene, he debates with Caliban, who is a negro slave, as to whether liberation is best achieved by cooperation with the authorities or by outright revolution. In *The Pleasures of Exile*, Lamming had read Ariel negatively as a collaborator: 'For Ariel, like Caliban, serves Prospero; but Ariel is not a slave. Ariel has been emancipated to the status of a privileged servant. In other words: a lackey. Ariel is Prospero's source of information; the archetypal spy, the embodiment – when and if made flesh – of the perfect and unspeakable secret police.' Césaire reads Ariel more generously, seeing his method of achieving freedom as a legitimate one. When Césaire was commissioned to work on *The Tempest*, he was contemplating writing a play about the civil rights movement in the United States. With this in mind, we may see that Ariel is a figuration of the 'moderate' Martin Luther King.

Who then is Caliban? At one point he says to Ariel – in English – 'Freedom now!', the slogan of the Black Power movement. And his identity is made even clearer in an exchange about naming which Césaire added to the text published in 1969 (it is not in the original *Présence africaine* version):

CALIBAN Well, there we are: I've decided that I will no longer be Caliban.

PROSPERO What's this nonsense? I don't understand.

CALIBAN Let me explain: I'm saying to you that from now on I'm not going to answer to the name of Caliban.

PROSPERO Where do you get that idea?

CALIBAN It's that Caliban isn't my name. It's simple.

PROSPERO Perhaps it's my name, then?

CALIBAN It's the nickname which your hate has pressed upon me and which insults me every time it's used.

PROSPERO Devil! You're becoming cheeky. So what are you proposing? I've got to call you something. What's it going to be? *Cannibal* would suit you well, but I'm sure you wouldn't like that either. Let's see – Hannibal. That'll do nicely. Why not? Everybody likes historical names.

CALIBAN Call me X. That would be more appropriate. As you call a man without a name. More exactly, a man whose name has been stolen. You speak of history. Well, that's history – a famous history. Each time you call to me, it brings back to me the fundamental fact that you've stolen everything from me, right down to my identity. Uhuru!

The representation of Caliban as popular demagogue and revolutionary has a long history, going back via Ernest Renan to the Jacobinism of the 1790s. But this reinvention of him as Malcolm X makes Shakespeare into something new: the voice of a recovered black identity.

9

FROM CHARACTER TO ICON

Visible representation

The ancient Chinese maxim tells us that a picture does the work of many words. The computer software designer knows that we find it easier to remember images than word-strings: instead of typing a precisely worded instruction to delete the file named such-and-such, we use the mouse to drag a picture representing the file across the screen to a picture of a trash receptacle. In computer jargon, these pictures are called 'icons'. The word goes back to the ancient Greek *eikon*, meaning a 'likeness'.

In *The Art of English Poesy*, published in 1589, around the beginning of Shakespeare's career, George Puttenham described a particular kind of verbal similitude as '*Resemblance* by Portrait or Imagery, which the Greeks call *Icon* . . . alluding to the painter's term, who yieldeth to the eye a visible representation of the thing he describes'. The allusion reminds us that verse-drama has the potential to combine the arts of the poet and the painter. Shakespeare did not only write memorable language. He also created memorable stage images, visible representations of the things he describes.

Three related developments in the eighteenth century were of particular importance for the history of Shakespeare's visual memorability. First, the acting style of the period had a tendency to emphasize key 'points', powerful dramatic moments over which the actor paused for emphasis and applause, or in which the performers froze in picturesque tableau. Secondly, printed editions of the plays began to include illustrations of key scenes. Frequently, the moments chosen for illustration were those which were celebrated in the theatre. Nicholas Rowe's edition of 1709 was the first illustrated Shakespeare; several of the engravings in it – for instance, Macbeth and the witches, Hamlet and the Ghost in Gertrude's chamber – draw on the memory of highly praised tableaux in Thomas Betterton's theatrical performances.

Soon painters began to produce free-standing Shakespearean images, to be sold separately from the printed texts. This was the third development. Initially, paintings were again of famous theatrical moments. William Hogarth's image of David Garrick as Richard III startled by the ghosts on the night before the Battle of Bosworth Field was the most frequently engraved and widely disseminated dramatic image of the eighteenth century (Fig. 7). But by the end of the century painters were no longer dependent on the theatre. In the 1790s John Boydell commissioned the leading artists of the day to paint scenes for his Shakespeare Gallery in Pall Mall. Conceived as the foundation of a British school of 'history painting', the Boydell paintings were intended to offer a more idealized and heroic repertoire of Shakespearean images than that available in the theatre.

There is a paradox here: Garrick's histrionic power did more than anything else to fix certain images of Richard III, Hamlet, Romeo, Macbeth, and Lear in the popular imagination, but within a generation of Garrick's death Shakespeare-worshippers were beginning to argue that those characters were too great for the stage. Characters such as Hamlet, Macbeth, Romeo, and Juliet took on a mythic force. They no longer needed their plays, they were recreated in other media – first painting, then forms as diverse as the novel and music.

Shakespearean 'character-criticism' assumed new sophistication in the second half of the eighteenth century. Books began to appear under such titles as *A Philosophical Analysis and Illustration of some of Shakespeare's Remarkable Characters*. The original aim of such studies was to explain the workings of the characters in relation to the plays in which they appeared, and thus to vindicate Shakespeare from neoclassical scepticism regarding his artistic and organizational capabilities. But frequently the authors of these books became so interested in the characters they were writing about that they lost sight of the plays.

In his *Essay on the Dramatic Character of Sir John Falstaff*, published in 1777, Maurice Morgann set out with the apparently quixotic ambition of proving that Falstaff was not a coward. Before long, he found himself giving Sir John a complete life-history. The character becomes at the very least more like someone in a novel than a play. By the end of the essay, Morgann has almost convinced both himself and his reader that

Falstaff is a real person whom we have come to know and love. Character-criticism thus shades off into myth-making. Falstaff transcends the plays in which he appears and is seen instead as the archetype of a set of human characteristics. He ceases to be a character and becomes an icon. This transformation, wrought upon a whole range of characters, was the chief gift to Shakespeare of the Romantic movement. It is my subject in this chapter.

When we say 'Shakespeare', we think immediately of certain characters. Hamlet comes first. Then a host of others: Macbeth and Lady Macbeth, Cleopatra, Falstaff, Richard III, Shylock, Malvolio, Romeo and Juliet, Iago and Othello. You don't need to know the plays to have images of Falstaff's fatness, Richard's crookback, Cleopatra's infinite variety, Shylock and his pound of flesh. These characters are as easily recognizable as the icons on our computer screens.

They are *iconic* in another sense, too. In the Eastern Churches, an icon is a painting, mosaic, or other representation of a sacred person which is itself regarded as sacred. To the Orthodox, Christ has real presence in an icon of Christ, as to the Catholic He has a real presence in the bread and wine of the Eucharist. To speak of a movie or rock star as an icon is to give a secular inflection to this belief. The worshipper attributes divinity to the performer on stage or screen. The connection with the sacred origin of the idea is deliberately exploited by Madonna in her choice of a name for herself. But in the case of Shakespeare's plays something remarkable has happened. Although Shakespearean actors – Garrick, Sarah Siddons, Henry Irving, Laurence Olivier – have frequently been revered as stars, it is the characters who are the icons. With a movie star, the presence is in the performer: we remember Marilyn Monroe as Marilyn Monroe, we forget the names of most of the characters she played. With Shakespeare, the presence is in the performed: the iconic power belongs to Hamlet, Macbeth, Iago, and the rest. What, then, is this real presence which the Romantic believes to be immanent in Shakespearean character?

The skull and the book

When Hamlet addresses the skull of Yorick, the audience observes an icon, a memorable visible representation, of mortality. Whether Clown, like Yorick and Gravedigger (a role played by the company clown), or Prince, like Hamlet, Alexander the Great, and Caesar, we all return to the same dust. The idea is simple and potent. Hamlet's accompanying words are unusually plain; he speaks in prose of Alexander, in doggerel couplets of 'Imperial Caesar, dead and turned to clay'. It is not the words that stick in the spectator's mind, but the visual image that is made possible by the stage prop of the skull. An iconic moment such as this endures in the popular imagination because it means the same thing in 1600, in 1800, in 2000. It will only lose its power when we find a way of cheating death.

Now consider another iconic image of Hamlet: the slender, melancholy prince, clad in black, holding a book (Fig. 8). Where the skull was an icon of the body, the book is an icon of the intellect. Only when Hamlet has put down the book and picked up the skull, when he has stopped philosophizing about death ('To be, or not to be; that is the question') and looked death in the face, is he ready to carry out his task and go to his own death. Once he has held the skull, Hamlet can say of death,

If it be now, 'tis not to come. If it be not to come, it will be now. If it be not now, yet it will come. The readiness is all.

(5.2.165–8)

The book is less easily read than the skull. It is multiply iconic. 'What do you read, my lord?' asks Polonius. 'Words, words, words', replies Hamlet (2.2.192–4). The difficulty comes in the passage from words to matter, from thoughts to actions. The holding of the book iconically represents Hamlet's isolation, his difference from everyone else in the court of Elsinore. Claudius is a man of action; in the first act, we have seen him conducting a great variety of court business. Hamlet is a man of words. His very facility in words – that restless punning apparent from his first utterance, 'A little more than kin and less than kind' (1.2.65) – seems an impediment to action. He contrasts 'actions that a man might play' to his own possession of 'that within which passeth show' (1.2.85). The bookish Hamlet of the first four acts of the play thus becomes an icon of the gap between visible appearance and 'that within'. Where Yorick's skull reminds us of the bodily mortality which humankind shares with the beasts, Hamlet's philosophizing reminds us of those less tangible qualities in which we are different from the rest of created nature: our powers of reasoning and of speech, our self-consciousness.

Whereas the icon of the youthful Prince holding the skull endures because audiences project onto it the same thing at all times, that of Hamlet reading his book endures because audiences project onto it both the same thing and very different things. The same thing because all thinking people desire to be more than quintessence of dust, to be 'noble in reason' and 'infinite in faculty' (2.2.305). Different things because different individuals and different ages have divergent conceptions of what nobility in reason and infinity in faculty might mean. The elusiveness of these conceptions gives the book-icon a complexity that is lacking in the skull-icon. The skull is a straightforward figure; it would be a misreading to associate it with anything other than death. The book is susceptible to many layers of reading; we cannot say precisely what it signifies and it is quite possible that we will be able to say mutually contradictory things about it.

Hamlet tells Polonius that his book contains some satirical moralizing about old men. He could of course be making this up: he is the one who is satirizing the old spy Polonius. The content of the particular book is immaterial. Hamlet has been to university at Wittenberg. In Shakespeare's time, that place name had an iconic quality: because of its association with Martin Luther, it was synonymous with the Reformation. Hamlet's book is therefore an icon of reformed reading. To read as a Protestant meant to probe one's books – the Bible above all – for spiritual and moral edification, whilst simultaneously examining one's own conscience. Historically speaking, Hamlet as reader is an icon of conscience.

At the end of his most celebrated soliloquy, Hamlet says

> Thus conscience does make cowards of us all,
> And thus the native hue of resolution
> Is sickled o'er with the pale cast of thought,
> And enterprises of great pith and moment
> With this regard their currents turn awry,
> And lose the name of action.
>
> (3.1.85–90)

For an audience in 1600, dieted on revenge drama in the tradition of Kyd's *Spanish Tragedy* and Shakespeare's own *Titus Andronicus*, one of the main respects in which Hamlet was a visible representation of 'nobility in reason' would have been his moral scruple, that Christian conscience which makes him aware that the revenger may all too easily descend to the barbarity of his antagonist. At the beginning of the play, Hamlet is a good Christian. He accepts that, however sickened he may be by the flesh, he must not break God's law against 'self-slaughter'. Horatio regards him as a 'sweet prince'; to Ophelia, he was once the all-round Renaissance man, soldier, scholar and courtier. These are roles which can only be performed well by a man with a clear conscience.

Hamlet's task is to will himself into the very different role of the revenger. He has some success. In casting off Ophelia and publicly humiliating her, he says farewell to all courtliness. In his shortest soliloquy, after he has been fired up by the play-within-the-play, he momentarily finds the style of the traditional stage-revenger:

> Now could I drink hot blood,
> And do such bitter business as the day
> Would quake to look on.
>
> (3.2.379–81)

He is as capable of violent action as any other revenger – witness his casual lugging of Polonius' guts into the neighbouring room. Nor does he delay nearly so much as he tells us that he is delaying: he has to establish the authenticity of the ghost, to ensure that it is not a devil sent to tempt him into evil action, and as soon as he has done this by watching Claudius' reaction to the play, he goes off to kill him; he doesn't kill him at prayer because that would be 'hire and salary, not revenge', would send him to heaven not to hell; he then thinks that he has killed him in Gertrude's chamber; it turns out that he has killed Polonius instead, and as a result he is packed off to England; as soon as he has tricked and despatched Rosencrantz and Guildenstern, effected his daring escape via the pirate ship, and returned to Denmark, he is in a state of 'readiness' and the revenge duly takes place during the duel.

But the style of the 'hot blood' soliloquy is completely unlike that of the Prince's other solo speeches, which are all much longer and more introspective. It is from them that we derive our image of the intellectual Hamlet: in the first act, so disgusted by his mother's hasty remarriage that he wishes he were dead; in the second, moved to self-disgust by the way in which the player can work himself into a frenzy for the fictional sorrows of Hecuba, while he himself has not yet done anything about his father's murder; in the third, meditating on the afterlife; and in the fourth, still chiding himself when he compares his own inaction with the military activity of Fortinbras and his army ('How all occasions do inform against me / And spur my dull revenge!'). Hamlet's self-analysis leads us to wonder whether his failure to kill the praying Claudius might be the result of procrastination, even mental paralysis, not calculation about whether he would be sending him to heaven or hell. The soliloquies present such a convincing picture of irresolution and inaction that even when it comes to the final scene we cannot help noticing that the killing of the King seems to happen by chance, to be not so much the climax of Hamlet's plans as an incidental consequence of Laertes' quest for revenge for the deaths of his father and sister.

The word 'conscience' in Elizabethan English did not only mean internal acknowledgement of the moral qualities of one's motives and actions. An older usage of the word was still audible: it could also refer to the mere presence of inward knowledge. 'Conscience' was 'consciousness'. It is Hamlet's extreme self-consciousness which sets him apart from the traditional revenger. When alone on stage, reflecting on his own situation, he seems to embody the very nature of human *being*; it is consciousness that forms his sense of self, his 'character', and in so doing makes it agonizingly difficult for him to perform the action that is demanded of him.

For this reason, the philosophizing Hamlet has remained an iconic figure long after the particular issue upon which he tests his conscience (the morality and the consequences of blood-revenge) has lost the immediacy it had when the play was first performed. Hamlet has become a universal dramatic character because he is an icon of human consciousness.

Yorick's skull remains the same, but Hamlet changes as conceptions of consciousness change.

Dr Johnson, annotating the play for his edition of 1765, took the word 'conscience' in the 'To be, or not to be' soliloquy merely to refer to the way in which criminal action may be checked by fear of eternal damnation in the hereafter. Johnson regarded Hamlet as a reluctant and ultimately unwitting instrument of divine providence – after all, the

Prince is not the one who poisons the cup, and the rapiers are exchanged by chance. 'Hamlet is, through the whole play, rather an instrument than an agent'.

By the time we reach Laurence Olivier's 1948 film of the play, from which I have taken my visual representation of the intellectual Hamlet, there has been a radical change. At the beginning of the film, a voice-over imposes an interpretation upon the play: 'This is the tragedy of a man who could not make up his mind.' This, in other words, is a tragedy of consciousness. Johnson regarded Hamlet as a blind instrument; Olivier reads the play in terms of the character's agency, his growth from irresolution to action. '*In scuffling they change Rapiers*', reads the original Folio stage-direction. Hamlet is not consciously trying to get hold of the poisoned foil; it is providence, not the Prince, who hoists Laertes with the petard of his own envenomed point. But Olivier's Hamlet is self-consciously in control: angry at being pricked with an unbated point, he flicks the rapier out of Laertes' hand, traps it beneath his foot, refuses to return it to his opponent, and picks it up for himself.

The nineteenth century, whose speculative genius is a sort of living Hamlet

Olivier's reading, from the assertion of Hamlet's indecision in the opening voice-over to the staging of agency in the closing duel, was made possible by a shift in emphasis from 'conscience' to 'consciousness' that occurred in the intellectual life of late-eighteenth-century Europe. Olivier's Hamlet was the Romantic Hamlet, the nineteenth-century Hamlet. 'It was not until the nineteenth century,' wrote Ralph Waldo Emerson, 'whose speculative genius is a sort of living Hamlet, that the tragedy of Hamlet could find such wondering readers. Now, literature, philosophy, and thought are Shakspearized. His mind is the horizon beyond which at present we do not see.'

In 1765, Johnson correctly maintained that for Shakespeare 'conscience' referred primarily to moral scruple; in 1904, A. C. Bradley categorically denied that this was the meaning of the word. Steeped in the poetry and philosophy of Romantic idealism, Bradley could only hear the sense of 'consciousness'; he made 'conscience' synonymous with what Hamlet in a later soliloquy calls 'thinking too precisely on the event'.

Dr Johnson began from the design of the play, in which he saw an echo of God's providential design for the world. Such a reading corresponds with Hamlet's own development towards the view that 'There's a special providence in the fall of a sparrow' (5.2.165). Laurence Olivier began at the other end, seeking for a germ of characterization which would explain Hamlet. To proceed thus is to rewrite a dramatic structure as a psychological novel.

A few years after Johnson completed his edition of Shakespeare, Johann Wolfgang von Goethe began work on a novel to be called 'Wilhelm Meister's Theatrical Mission'. The heart of that mission was to be a performance of *Hamlet*. Goethe did not publish this first draft, but he incorporated his protagonist's reading of the character of Hamlet in the revised version of the novel that was published in 1795–6 under the title *Wilhelm Meister's Apprenticeship* (*Wilhelm Meisters Lehrjahre*). Goethe's book is the classic example of what became one of the nineteenth century's most popular literary forms, the *Bildungsroman*. A literal translation of the German term would be 'growth-novel': the narrative follows a young man or woman through their formative years; he or she makes a number of wrong decisions, but undergoes a spiritual education and eventually matures into a well-balanced adult who fits into society.

Wilhelm's family are in business; he escapes from their dull world into the exciting realm of the drama. His love for the theatre, together with the romantic conception of passion which he discovers there, leads him to fall in love with an actress, Mariane. Then he becomes convinced that she has been unfaithful to him, so he rejects the life of the imagination and settles down to business. But whilst on his way to visit some clients, he falls in with a troupe of actors and his passion for the theatre is rekindled. He joins the actors when they are invited to perform at the house of a count. Previously Wilhelm's taste has been for classical French drama, but now he is introduced to the works of Shakespeare. A new world is opened to him: he finds in Shakespeare everything he has ever thought about human nature, and much more. He decides that he will devote his life to the transmission of Shakespearean wisdom to the German people.

He moves on to a more elevated theatrical company, led by an actor-manager called Serlo. They plan a performance of *Hamlet*, preparing for it by means of a lengthy debate on the character of the Prince. Their opening night is a success, but the next evening a fire breaks out. During the fire it is hinted that a child who travels with the acting company is actually Wilhelm's own son. After a number of further twists, Wilhelm discovers that he was mistaken about Mariane's fidelity, that she had borne him a son and then died. Through bitter experience, he has come to maturity; he begins the novel as an 'apprentice' and ends it as a 'master'. The fire effects a structural break in the novel; after it, Wilhelm rejects the theatre for the sake of direct action and personal experience. But the theatre has been formative in his education. Hamlet's inaction serves as the negative example from which Wilhelm learns to take his own positive course of action. Goethe creates a successful 'Bildungs-hero' by reading Hamlet as a failed one.

In the novel, Goethe writes about his characters as if they are real people in the real world. By the same account, Wilhelm analyses the character of Hamlet as if he were a real person. He begins – as the *Bildungsroman* begins – with the character's childhood. He reconstructs Hamlet's youth: a student and thinker, a good companion and conversationalist, a tender lover. He proceeds – as the *Bildungsroman* proceeds – to the moment of crisis: the father's death, the uncle's succession to the throne, the mother's over-hasty remarriage. He then finds the 'key' to the tragedy in the disjunction between Hamlet's internal nature and the external task he is called upon to perform:

> It is clear to me what Shakespeare set out to portray: a heavy deed placed on a soul which is not adequate to cope with it. And it is in this sense that I find the whole play constructed. An oak tree planted in a precious pot which should only have held delicate flowers. The roots spread out, the vessel is shattered.
>
> A fine, pure, noble and highly moral person, but devoid of that emotional strength that characterizes a hero, goes to pieces beneath a burden that it can neither support nor cast off. Every obligation is sacred to him, but this one is too heavy. The impossible is demanded of him – not the impossible in any absolute sense, but what is impossible for him. How he twists and turns, trembles, advances and retreats, always being reminded, always reminding himself, and finally almost losing sight of his goal, yet without ever regaining happiness!

This is the 'Romantic' reading of Hamlet which was reiterated by Samuel Taylor Coleridge and A. C. Bradley, then fixed on celluloid in Olivier's film.

In order to write a novel about a man who does finally make up his mind, Goethe reinvented Hamlet as a man who could not do so. In his discussions with Serlo, Wilhelm expresses doubt as to whether *Hamlet* can be represented adequately on the stage; the conclusion is reached that the play must be performed in adapted form. The 'true' Hamlet can only be *read*, as a novel is read: the Shakespearean essence is relocated within the mind. Wilhelm's rejection of the theatre and his psychological approach to the character of Hamlet are typical of the Romantic internalization of Shakespeare. Hamlet comes to represent the opposition between thought and action, mind and world. An icon of pure consciousness, unwilling to enter the fallen world of grubby political intrigue, he becomes the spirit of Romantic idealism. For Coleridge, Hamlet *was* 'the prevalence of the abstracting and generalizing habit over the practical'. 'I have a smack of Hamlet myself, if I may say so,' he is reported to have added.

Immanuel Kant argued that we cannot know *things-in-themselves*. We can only know *the idea of things* in our own minds. The Kantian revolution made consciousness itself the starting point of philosophy. Hamlet became the perfect exemplar of the distinction: 'He persists in the inactivity of a beautiful inner soul which cannot make itself actual or engage in the relationships of his present world'. Thus G. W. F. Hegel.

The effect of such a reading is that the aesthetic is placed in opposition to the quotidian and the political. For Hegel, this was the difference between classical and Romantic tragedy. Ancient Greek tragedy turned upon the clash of ethical imperatives, notably that between duty to the state ('ethical life in its *spiritual* universality') and duty to the family ('*natural* ethical life'). The *Antigone* of Sophocles was regarded as the greatest of all classical tragedies because it so fully embodied this conflict in its principal characters: Creon speaks for 'public life and social welfare', while Antigone speaks for 'the bond of kinship'. Shakespeare, by contrast, is held up by Hegel as the great exponent of Romantic tragedy. Romantic tragedy does not concern itself with ethical collisions; it locates crisis in the disjunction between external circumstance and inner character. According to the Romantic view, a Shakespearean tragedy is the tracing of the 'progress and history of a great soul, its inner development, the picture of its self-destructive struggle against circumstances, events, and their consequences'.

For Hegel, the accidents of the final act of *Hamlet* are an irrelevance. The important thing is that Hamlet wanted to die anyway. This means that there is aesthetic satisfaction, a sense of reconciliation, at the end of the play. A Hamlet who is pure spirit can only be himself when he is freed from the imperatives of the body and the world. That is to say, when he is dead:

> Looked at from the outside, Hamlet's death seems to be brought about accidentally owing to the fight with Laertes and the exchange of rapiers. But death lay from the beginning in the background of Hamlet's mind. The sands of time do not content him. In his melancholy and weakness, his worry, his disgust at all the affairs of life, we sense from the start that in all his terrible surroundings he is a lost man, almost consumed already by inner disgust before death comes to him from outside.

With this reading, we return full circle to Yorick. The skull and the book become icons of one and the same world-weariness.

But where does Hamlet's self-consuming disgust come from? Hegel followed Goethe in regarding it as a given: the noble soul is not made for this world. Subsequent interpreters have sought a more specific cause.

Olivier found a visual representation of a possible source in a piece of furniture, on which his camera dwells both early in the film and in its very closing sequence: Gertrude's bed. The first we hear of Hamlet's disgust with life is the first soliloquy, 'O that this too too solid [or 'sallied'/soiled] flesh would melt'. That soliloquy dwells more on Gertrude's remarriage than on old Hamlet's death, more on the frailty of woman than the fickleness of political fortune. At the very centre of the play is Hamlet's lacerating confrontation with his mother in her bedchamber (Fig. 9). In this iconic moment, Hamlet is forcing Gertrude back on to the bed; he seems on the verge of piercing not just her ear but her body. Earlier we have heard him say 'Words, words, words'; now he says 'Mother, mother, mother!' (3.4.6).

The opening voice-over in Olivier's *Hamlet* is a crystallization of a reading which was first articulated at the end of the eighteenth century.

The image of the bed is a crystallization of an interpretation which was first worked out at the end of the nineteenth. In a long footnote to the first edition of *The Interpretation of Dreams*, Sigmund Freud proposed a new key to the mystery of Hamlet's character:

> The play is built up on Hamlet's hesitations over fulfilling the task of revenge that is assigned to him; but its text offers no reasons or motives for these hesitations and an immense variety of attempts at interpreting them have failed to produce a result. According to the view which was originated by Goethe and is still the prevailing one today, Hamlet represents the type of man whose power of direct action is paralysed by an excessive development of intellect. (He is 'sicklied o'er with the pale cast of thought'.) ... The plot of the drama shows us, however, that Hamlet is far from being represented as a person incapable of taking any action. We see him doing so on two occasions: first in a sudden outburst of temper, when he runs his sword through the eavesdropper behind the arras, and secondly in a premeditated and even crafty fashion, when, with all the callousness of a Renaissance prince, he sends the two courtiers [Rosencrantz and Guildenstern] to the death that had been planned for himself. What is it, then, that inhibits him in fulfilling the task set him by his father's ghost? The answer, once again [as in the case of *Oedipus Rex*, which has just been discussed], is that it is the peculiar nature of the task. Hamlet is able to do anything – except take vengeance on the man who did away with his father and took that father's place with his mother, the man who shows him the repressed wishes of his own childhood realized. Thus the loathing which should drive him on to revenge is replaced in him by self-reproaches, by scruples of conscience, which remind him that he himself is literally no better than the sinner whom he is to punish.

Hegel regarded *Antigone* and *Hamlet* as the greatest tragedies of ancient and modern times. Freud gave the palm to *Oedipus Rex* and *Hamlet*. For him, it was not a coincidence that both plays were about the murder of a father and the sexual activity of a mother. Hamlet can do anything save kill Claudius because Claudius has done the one thing he unconsciously wants to do himself: kill his father and sleep with his mother.

We have come a long way from Dr Johnson and Hamlet's Christian 'conscience'. With Goethe's reading, the old sense of the word as meaning 'thought' itself was revived and secularized. With Hegel's, it was translated into the philosophical idea of 'consciousness' that is the post-Kantian Idealist's highest principle of human existence. Now with Freud, it is relocated in the dark *un*conscious which is supposed to drive our deepest desires.

Freud qualifies his interpretation by saying 'Here I have translated into conscious terms what was bound to remain unconscious in Hamlet's mind'. The novelistic method of treating Shakespeare's characters as if they were real people reaches its apogee here. Hamlet is given an unconscious. Coordinate with this move is the Romantic tendency to read biographically. Freud's note went on to suggest that the character of Hamlet was developed under the impact of the death of Shakespeare's father and with the memory of the death of his son, Hamnet, and that 'Just as *Hamlet* deals with the relation of a son to his parents, so *Macbeth* (written at approximately the same period) is concerned with the subject of childlessness'. In the 1930 edition of *The Interpretation of Dreams*, this biographical reading was given a bizarre twist by a new footnote announcing Freud's conversion to the Oxfordian cause, which I discussed in chapter three: 'Incidentally, I have in the meantime ceased to believe that the author of Shakespeare's works was the man from Stratford'.

Had he been charged that it was anachronistic to back-project modern psychoanalytical theory onto Shakespeare, Freud would have maintained that all he was doing with his theory of the Oedipus complex was redescribing in more scientific terms a dynamic which is essential to human nature and which the poets, notably Sophocles and Shakespeare, had already identified and explored by means of dramatic narrative. The conception of character and motive which Freudian reading brings to Shakespeare is anachronistic, but it cannot be denied that for thousands of readers there has been a mystery about the character of Hamlet. What is explicitly written in the text has somehow not been enough; reader after reader has been impelled to propose some 'new solution' – or, as in the case of T. S. Eliot, to give up in exasperation and say that the play is a failure because it lacks the necessary 'objective correlative' to make sense of Hamlet's motivation.

The problem with Freud's reading is that it is not verifiable. You cannot confute it by saying that there is no textual evidence for it, since repression is the very premiss of the theory. Try to deny that you have a desire and the Freudian will reply that your conscious denial is confirmation that your unconscious really does have the desire. This is frustrating. But frustration is exactly the fate of the interpreter of Hamlet. In this respect an approach in terms of the unconscious is the most elegant possible, since it is built upon that very elusiveness which is the prime source of the play's enduring fascination. Hamlet's apparent under-motivation keeps him alive long after the more obviously motivated revengers of the Elizabethan drama have become moribund.

The value of Freud's reading stems, then, from its interrogative form, not its Oedipal substance. It is true to the play's opening watchwords:

BARNARDO Who's there?
FRANCISCO Nay, answer me.

Freud has seen that the play refuses to give its own answers. The phenomenon is similar to that of the sonnets' refusal to tell us to what extent they are autobiographical and to what extent they are fictive. If there is a key to Hamlet, it is the fact that so many people have tried to find a key. Generation upon generation of new interpreters – directors, actors, readers, critics – feel compelled to have their say about the mystery. That is what keeps Hamlet alive. More than any other work of Western literature, the Prince's play is both iconic and elusive.

Shakespeare's painter

Icon, said Puttenham, is a painter-like figure.

At the end of act four of *Hamlet*, Gertrude describes the body of the drowned Ophelia, dressed in garlands of flowers, her clothes spread wide and bearing her on the surface of the water a little while before she is dragged down to muddy death. This is not something we see on stage, but the precision and evocativeness of the description make us see it in our imagination, in what Hamlet calls 'the mind's eye'.

In Olivier's film, however, we *do* see it. The technology of film achieves what the Elizabethan theatre could not. As we hear Gertrude's words, we see Ophelia floating down the brook (Fig. 10). Once again,

Olivier is drawing on the Romantic tradition: his image is based on a famous painting by the Pre-Raphaelite John Everett Millais (Fig. 11).

In Millais' painting, Ophelia's palms are upturned, a detail absent from Gertrude's description. She looks as if she is gladly offering herself to death. She thus comes to resemble Hegel's death-desiring Hamlet. This is an idealized reading of Ophelia, which has nothing to say about the snatches of sexually-charged song which characterize her mad scene. In Millais, she is beautifully dead rather than sordidly mad. A feminist might argue that such a treatment is blind to the realities of sexual oppression. In order to make his painting convincing, Millais placed his model, Lizzie Siddall, fully clothed in a bathtub full of water. Considerately, he lit oil lamps under the tub to keep the water warm. But in the final session he became so absorbed in the work of painting that he kept her in the water for five hours, failing to notice that the lamps had burnt themselves out. Lizzie caught pneumonia and her father threatened to sue Millais for damages to the tune of £150. Millais paid the doctor's bill instead, but the woman's health remained poor for the rest of her life. The story is a fine allegory of Romantic idealism's lack of concern for worldly practicalities.

The painting transforms a complex dramatic character into a simple but memorable icon. It fixes *an* Ophelia in the imagination, with the result that for several generations after it was painted in 1852 critics found very little else to say about the character. A. C. Bradley's *Shakespearean Tragedy* devoted seventy-one pages to Hamlet, six to Ophelia.

Yet a Romantic painting need not necessarily achieve its iconic memorability at the expense of imaginative complexity. It may itself offer a strong reading of Shakespeare.

In May 1774 Johann Herder wrote in a letter to his mentor, Johann Hamann: 'There is living in Rome a noble German from Zurich, Henry Fuseli, a genius like a mountain torrent, a worshipper of Shakespeare, and now, Shakespeare's painter.' An artistic genius is compared to a force of nature. Shakespeare is idolized. Herder's tone is unmistakably that of *Sturm und Drang* ('Storm and Stress'), the first phase of European Romanticism. This was the period when *sublimity* – awe-inspiring vastness – became an ideal in both poetry and painting. This was the period when the most fashionable new novels partook of the cult of the Gothic (dark deeds amidst the mountains, supernatural solicitings, medieval atmosphere) or that of Sensibility (exquisitely heightened emotion, frequent swooning).

What is iconized Shakespeare like? There is no better place to *see* the phenomenon than Johann Heinrich Fuseli's paintings. Although Fuseli was in many technical respects a neoclassical artist, his vision of the plays is the quintessence of Romantic passion and Gothic sublimity. The archetypal novel of the period was Goethe's *The Sorrows of Young Werther* – a tale of love and loss which supposedly caused ardent young men across Europe to commit suicide in imitation of its hero. A. W. Schlegel splendidly described the book as a declaration of the rights of feeling. Fuseli's paintings are declarations of the power of feeling in Shakespeare's plays.

The artist wrote in one of his *Aphorisms* that the most powerful scenes spring from the strongest passions – in the face of them we weep, we tremble, we laugh. But in order to elicit passion in others the artist must live through the passion himself: 'Consider it as the unalterable law of Nature that all your power upon others depends on your own emotions'. Shakespeare, therefore, was stale when he did not write from his own emotions. This is the extreme Romantic view that authentic artistic creation comes only from a massive investment of personal feeling.

The Romantic way of looking at the world invests passion in nature itself. Fuseli believed that Shakespeare was 'the supreme master of passions and the ruler of our hearts' by virtue of his unique intuition into 'the spontaneous ebullitions of nature'. Shakespeare's power to dramatize those moments when the raw affective force of nature suddenly bursts forth was at its height in *Macbeth*: 'by this he made Banquo see the weird sisters bubble up from earth, and in their own air vanish; this is the hand that struck upon the bell when Macbeth's drink was ready, and from her chamber pushed his dreaming wife, once more to methodize the murder of her guest.' Being 'Shakespeare's painter' meant capturing such scenes on canvas.

The *spontaneity* of passion was at the heart of Romantic poetics. It was in one of his lectures on painting delivered in London in 1801 that Fuseli spoke of the spontaneous ebullitions of nature in Shakespeare; the previous year, William Wordsworth had written in the preface to the second edition of *Lyrical Ballads* that 'all good poetry is the spontaneous overflow of powerful feelings'.

The Romantic way of looking at Shakespeare produced a heightened concentration upon those moments when the poetic language seems to change gear and a character is charged with new intensity of passion. This way of looking had an ambivalent relationship with the theatre. In conception, it was very much influenced by the acting style which had been pioneered by David Garrick: key 'points' in Garrick's reading of a Shakespearean lead character would be emphasized by sudden modulations of voice or turns of stage business. The Romantic actor Edmund Kean carried this technique to an extreme in the Regency period. Samuel Taylor Coleridge said that watching Kean act was like reading Shakespeare by flashes of lightning. He meant that at certain moments of intense electrical energy – Fuseli's 'spontaneous ebullitions of nature' – Kean illuminated a character as no one had ever done before, but that between these moments there were long passages of complete darkness. Coleridge's desire to understand the evolving shape and the organic unity of a Shakespearean drama set him at odds with Romantic acting's emphasis upon 'moments', and he was accordingly doubtful about the capacity of stage performance to do justice to Shakespeare. The stronger the claim for Shakespeare's unique truth to the pure passion of nature, the more doubtful the claimant becomes as to an actor's capacity to reproduce that truth.

Throughout his life (1741–1825), Fuseli was obsessed with Shakespeare. He supposedly had the works so completely in his memory as to be able to recollect any passage that was quoted. As a teenager he translated *Macbeth* into German. As a student in Zurich he fell under the influence of J. J. Bodmer and J. J. Breitinger, pioneers of the aesthetics of the sublime and the European idolatry of Shakespeare.

In London in the 1760s, he succumbed to the power of Garrick's acting. A watercolour executed at this time is an attempt to immortalize one of the most memorable moments in one of Garrick's most celebrated roles: his re-entry as Macbeth after the murder of Duncan (Fig. 12). An inscription on the floor gives the relevant lines from the play: Lady Macbeth's 'My husband!', Macbeth's 'I have done the deed'. Fuseli captures not just the single moment but the whole scene: the wide-eyed horror and backward stagger of Garrick's Macbeth as he recollects the voice which cries 'Sleep no more', the firm posture and imperious manner of Hannah Pritchard's Lady Macbeth as she silences her husband so as not to wake Donalbain in the second chamber and, stretching out her other hand towards the bloody daggers, chastises him for bringing the murder weapons from the place.

Over forty years later Fuseli, now Professor of Painting at the Royal Academy, returned to the scene in an oil painting (Fig. 13, exhibited 1812). This time, though, he stripped the characters of the encumbrances of eighteenth-century costume. Macbeth has become one of the primal, sinewy figures characteristic of the mature Fuseli's representation of the human body; Lady Macbeth leans forward, suggesting motion instead of stillness, and she is lit from behind in a way that imparts a ghostly pallor to her figure. Where the early watercolour, following Mrs Pritchard's performance, renders the force of the character at this point in the play, the late oil painting does what a stage performance cannot do: it simultaneously evokes Lady Macbeth's controlled energy here and her subsequent hollow ghostliness in the sleepwalking scene. Fuseli's chiaroscuro becomes a visual analogue for Shakespeare's poetic imagery, in which Lady Macbeth's dismissive 'A little water clears us of this deed' in this scene is transformed into her anguished 'What, will these hands ne'er be clean? . . . All the perfumes of Arabia will not sweeten this little hand' in the fifth act.

Fuseli, then, begins from the stage, but moves towards an idealized representation. The first painting is of Garrick and Mrs Pritchard *as* Macbeth and Lady Macbeth, the second can be viewed as Macbeth and Lady Macbeth *themselves*. Yet at the same time, Fuseli's art of shadows makes us question the idea that Macbeth and Lady Macbeth have fixed selves, for it suggest that the characters are inherently shadows, not solid substances, in accordance with Macbeth's own vision of life as 'but a walking shadow'. In high Romantic manner, Fuseli goes beyond stage representation and seeks to take Shakespeare directly into the imagination, translating character into icon.

Walking shadows

The actor moving across the stage is already in another dimension. It alters his bearing, gives his movements an unnatural emphasis, and makes his voice resound unnaturally. It is precisely this artificiality that excludes him from nature. He stands alone in front of the dark, crowded

auditorium in the same way that man in Kierkegaard's
vision stands alone before God. His only authentic existence is therefore the ritual of make-believe ... What
Fuseli really discovered in Shakespeare, apart from his
immense dramatic variety, was the mysterious, secretive,
Orphic nature of the theatre.

In translating *Macbeth* from the moving stage to the still canvas and the
excited imagination of the spectator, Fuseli remains true to the
dramatist's own dissolution of any ready distinction between being,
acting, and dreaming. The paradox of the actor is also the paradox
of Fuseli's painted figures. The player does not walk across the stage:
he stalks. It is this exaggeration which Fuseli catches in the seeming
motion of his Macbeth, daggers in hand. Such motion is 'unnatural'
in the sense that it is not how we move in everyday life. But it would
be wrong to say that it is 'less than natural'; rather, it is more than
natural.

A rationalist would say that the supernatural is by definition unnatural; Shakespeare and Fuseli would reply that when men and women
feel and imagine at full stretch they see apparitions. Our ambition may
lead us to see a group of mysterious female figures who will tell us what
we want to hear but dare not say ourselves: 'All hail, Macbeth, that
shalt be king hereafter!' Our sense that something was not right about
our father's death may lead us to meet his ghost (Fig. 14). Our feeling
for the magical enchantment of a moonlit midsummer night in a wood
may lead us to dream that we are waited upon by fairies and made love
to by their queen, even though we ourselves are but an ass (Fig. 15).
Macbeth, Hamlet, and Bottom are the characters of strongest imagination in their respective plays; if we look at the play or the painting
with strong imagination, we will not dismiss their visions as illusions, as
false creations 'Proceeding from the heat-oppressèd brain'.

Who is to say that waking life is 'real' and dreaming an illusion? In
the second half of their play, the Macbeths of waking life are a king and
a queen. This is the illusion. The reality is what they experience in the
terrible dreams that shake them nightly. The illusion is that a little
water has cleared them of the deed; the reality is that they cannot ever
get the blood off their hands.

Macbeth knows that he is only playing the role of a king. Increasingly, as the play moves inexorably to its end, others realize that it is a role which does not fit him: 'Now does he feel his title / Hang loose about him, like a giant's robe / Upon a dwarfish thief' (5.2.20–22). Warrior Thane, King, husband, childless man: they are all roles. More directly and terrifyingly than any other character in Shakespeare, Macbeth voices the thought that we are all actors improvising our roles in a play of unknown authorship – and that we do not know when or in what manner our personal part will end. He hears the cry of women and is told that his wife and queen is dead:

> She should have died hereafter.
> There would have been a time for such a word.
> Tomorrow, and tomorrow, and tomorrow
> Creeps in this petty pace from day to day
> To the last syllable of recorded time,
> And all our yesterdays have lighted fools
> The way to dusty death. Out, out, brief candle.
> Life's but a walking shadow, a poor player
> That struts and frets his hour upon the stage,
> And then is heard no more. It is a tale
> Told by an idiot, full of sound and fury,
> Signifying nothing.
>
> (5.5.16–27)

Fuseli's late – ghastly, ghostly – image of Macbeth with the daggers is also an image of human life as a walking shadow. Viewed thus, the figure which began as Garrick and then departed from him into a Macbeth of the imagination becomes an actor again. Not, however, a specific actor, but rather the poor player who is all of us.

Fuseli's figures from *Macbeth* are always surrounded by blackness. He painted several versions of the first encounter between Macbeth, Banquo, and the three weird sisters; in the most extraordinary of them, the canvas is completely dark save for the two armed warriors on one side, the three shrouded sisters on the other (Fig. 16). The sisters represent destiny: Macbeth and Banquo stand before them, as Kierkegaardian man stands before God. The confrontation is sublime, awe-inspiring, for Macbeth is one step away from the absolute abyss. The equally compelled but more cautious Banquo holds back.

An image like this could be realized within the frame of a

proscenium-arch stage and with the benefit of artificial lighting. Because Fuseli witnessed performances of Shakespeare within a picture-frame stage, he saw the possibility of developing an English school of history painting which framed moments of high drama from the plays within the analogous rectangular space of a canvas on the wall of a picture gallery. The power of his images makes us temporarily forget that the original Shakespearean stage was something very different: an open platform thrust out into a yard, with an audience standing on three sides. In Shakespeare's Globe there was no proscenium arch, no artificial lighting. Plays were performed by daylight in the afternoon. The crowded auditorium is not dark. Watching Shakespeare in his own time would have been a communal experience; watching and reading him romantically becomes a solitary affair. The Elizabethan theatregoer always sees the faces of his or her fellow audience members; the Romantic Shakespearean projects him or herself into the play with piercing concentration and exclusive focus. The ideal for which the Romantic strives is a pure encounter in the imagination – we meet with the play in the surrounding darkness, as Macbeth and Banquo meet with the weird sisters.

Fuseli's most powerful Shakespearean illustrations are of scenes from *Macbeth* and *A Midsummer Night's Dream*. The peculiar technical achievement of those two plays is their sustained evocation of night on a bare, daylit stage. Conjure into your mind the poor player in Macbeth's speech. Is he not on a dim, barely lit stage? That would not have been the condition of Richard Burbage as he spoke the lines in the first public production of the play. It is a condition created by the language – by 'tomorrow', to which we turn our minds as the day ends; by 'creeps', with its suggestion of the careful tread necessary in the dark; by 'lighted', which implies surrounding darkness; by 'dusty', by 'shadow', and, above all, by 'Out, out, brief candle'. It is also a condition created by contextual resonance: the last we have seen of Lady Macbeth, who is here being mourned, is as a shadow of her former self, walking in the dark, bearing a taper, watched from the shadows by the doctor and the gentlewoman.

The technical challenge of representing night in *Macbeth* stretched Shakespeare to some of his very greatest poetry. Darkness is made visible before our ears:

> Light thickens, and the crow
> Makes wing to th' rooky wood.
> Good things of day begin to droop and drowse,
> Whiles night's black agents to their preys do rouse.
>
> (3.2.51–4)

The actor is on a bare stage, yet we follow his gaze out through a non-existent window and see in our mind's eye a black bird flying home to a dusky wood.

Fuseli is the painter of night's black agents. He returned again and again to the weird sisters. The eighteenth-century theatre had made them spectacular. During the Restoration, Sir William Davenant had reworked *Macbeth* with a full chorus of singing and dancing witches; productions over the next hundred years introduced more and more elaborate stage-machinery to assist their business. Fuseli sought instead to make the sisters sublime. 'All apparatus', he wrote, 'destroys grandeur: the minute catalogue of the cauldron's ingredients in *Macbeth* destroys the terror attendant on mysterious darkness'. For Fuseli, a painting could render the ineffability of the sisters and the sublimity of Macbeth on the edge of the abyss in a way that the stage could not:

> It is not by the accumulation of infernal or magical machinery, distinctly seen, by the introduction of Hecate and a chorus of female demons and witches, by surrounding him with successive apparitions at once, and a range of shadows moving above or before him, that Macbeth can be made an object of terror, – to render him so you must place him on a ridge, his down-dashed eye absorbed by the murky abyss; surround the horrid vision with darkness, exclude its limits, and shear its light to glimpses.

In *Macbeth consulting the vision of the Armed Head* (Fig. 17), painted for the Shakespeare Gallery which opened in Dublin in 1793, Macbeth's front foot is lodged on the rocky brink of a precipice. In opening up the abyss, the space of blackness, Fuseli simultaneously draws the eye to the human body. Look at Macbeth's right leg and the sisters' choppy fingers. They are in one sense unnatural in their extension and their taut muscularity; but in another sense they are the purest possible representations of human *embodiment*. Stare at the painting for long enough and the leg, the hands, the heads become detached from the whole person.

From his earliest work in tragedy, *Titus Andronicus*, Shakespeare was fascinated by the fragility of the body as a whole thing, by the possibilities of dismemberment and disembodiment. In *Titus*, Lavinia has her hands chopped off and her tongue cut out, Titus chops off his own hand, the severed heads of two of his sons are brought onto the stage, and the severed heads of two of Tamora's sons are baked in a pie which is consumed on stage. In *Richard III*, the head of Hastings is brought on stage and a procession of ghosts – disembodied bodies – appears to round off the action in the fifth act on the night before the battle in which Richard finally loses his life. The same preoccupations recur in the later tragedies: the most appalling act of onstage dismemberment is the plucking out of Gloucester's eyes in *King Lear*, while the most powerful ghostly presence is that of the father in *Hamlet*. Coriolanus thinks of his body as a machine, a sword in the hands of Rome; he is then made to stand in the public market-place and display the scars on his wounded body. The language of *Macbeth* also reveals an obsession with the body and body-parts: a soldier unseamed from the crotch to the jaw, a sailor's thumb, a woman's breast with milk turned to gall, the dashed-out brains of a suckling infant, a hand grasping a dagger and then stained with unwashable blood, a slit throat, the liver of a Jew, the finger of a birth-strangled babe, an armed head, a bloody Caesarean-sectioned child, the severed head of Macbeth.

Each of the weird sisters points with her right hand. The index finger of each left (sinister) hand is raised to the lips. Macbeth's finger is in the same position – as was Lady Macbeth's in the painting of the night of the murder. The gesture connotes the unspeakable, the deed without a name, the dark theme of the drama. Fuseli reads the whole play through Banquo's

> Live you, or are you aught
> That man may question? You seem to understand me
> By each at once her choppy finger laying
> Upon her skinny lips.
>
> (1.3.40–43)

The power and the paradox, the fairness and the foulness, of the weird sisters is that at one and the same time they answer Macbeth's questions and leave the question of his ending unanswered. It is only at the moment of ending itself that he discovers the meaning of their riddles.

As is only appropriate in this equivocal play, the answers come in reverse order. First, the third riddle: the boy King Malcolm bearing the branch of Birnam Wood. Second, the second: that Macduff was born of a doctor's knife, not a woman's pains. And third, the first: that what Macbeth has to fear the most is a man in armour.

> Though Birnam Wood be come to Dunsinane,
> And thou opposed being of no woman born,
> Yet I will try the last. Before my body
> I throw my warlike shield. Lay on, Macduff,
> And damned be him that first cries 'Hold, enough!'
>   (5.10.30–33)

Macbeth's soul has long been damned; as the Porter scene suggests, his castle is already a kind of hell. It is his body for which he fights. This, it seems to me, is the genius of Fuseli as *Macbeth*'s painter: he has understood that it is a play not so much about good and evil as about the imagination and the body. Macbeth is the only one to see the air-drawn dagger and the ghost of Banquo. His strength is his imagination. His weakness is that the imagination cannot lead him anywhere, for as soon as he acts out his desires he imagines some dire consequence and has to act again, killing Banquo, killing Macduff's family. But some Fleance always scapes. Macbeth would only be content if his body could survive. The Shakespeare of sonnets one to seventeen could have told him the obvious answer to his problem: beget a son. But he has no bodily children, only the children of his fertile mind – his self-consuming thoughts.

This is the most brilliant insight of Fuseli's painting. At one level, the armed head is Macduff. It is also Macbeth's guilty remembrance of his murder of his brother in arms, for the helmet is identical to that worn by Banquo in the painting of *Macbeth, Banquo and the Witches* which Fuseli produced as a companion-piece for the Irish Shakespeare Gallery. At a deeper level, though, the armed head is *Macbeth himself*. Quiff, eyebrows, eyes, and nose, it is a mirror image across the diagonal of the canvas. The only differences between the heads are that Macbeth's is pale and the Other is dark, Macbeth's mouth is closed and the Other's is open.

The first we have heard of Macbeth is in the Thane of Ross's account of his contribution to the battle against the combined army of Norwegians and traitors. Macbeth fights in single combat with the traitorous Thane of Cawdor:

> Confronting him with self-comparisons,
> Point against point, rebellious arm 'gainst arm,
> Curbing his lavish spirit.
>
> (1.2.55–7)

Macbeth wins and is rewarded with Cawdor's name. He makes his first appearance in the King's presence at the exact moment when Duncan is saying of Cawdor,

> There's no art
> To find the mind's construction in the face.
> He was a gentleman on whom I built
> An absolute trust.
>
> (1.4.11–14)

Macbeth is just such a gentleman: this is one of the richest moments of dramatic irony in all Shakespeare. Macbeth, who learns to put on a 'false face', becomes Cawdor point for point. Ross's 'rebellious arm 'gainst arm' – again, an image fleetingly suggestive of severed body-parts – is also replete with dramatic irony, for Macbeth the defender of the nation will soon become a traitor, worse than a rebel because he pulls down the temple of the monarchy from within.

After the murder of Duncan, Macbeth begins to realize that he is Cawdor: 'Glamis hath murdered sleep, and therefore Cawdor / Shall sleep no more, Macbeth shall sleep no more' (2.2.40–41). In the closing battle, Macduff will take the place that Macbeth took in the opening battle. Defeat will come from the arm of an other who is half the same: a brave warrior half of whose name is 'Mac'. The armed head of the traitor Macbeth, Thane of Cawdor, will be displayed on stage. This dead head is what Macbeth sees in Fuseli's painting: the weird sisters are 'Confronting him with self-comparisons'.

The face is constructed of wide-eyed fear. We cannot read from it the power of imagination that has been lodged inside the head. But then we stop to think: whose severed head, whose imagination, are we really witnessing? Certainly not that of the historical Macbeth; nor that of the actor whose body has worked through the performance. Where has the creation come from? From inside the head of the artist. Shakespeare and Fuseli outlive their bodies. Their art is like the oracular speech of the armed head. The head is Macbeth; it is also the artist. It follows that Macbeth is the artist. In accordance with the Romantic theory of art, we are to imagine Shakespeare throwing himself personally into his creation. Only by doing so, the theory goes, can he enable us as spectators to see ourselves in the artwork.

The strong imagination is complicit with transgression – this was the lesson that Shakespeare learned from Marlowe. Whether you are a writer, an actor, a painter, or a spectator, you will be more interested in Macbeth than in Duncan. You will be distinctly suspicious of Malcolm's calculated trial of Macduff in the dreary scene at the English court. If you are a young Romantic poet, thrilling to the blissful dawn of the French Revolution, you will identify with Macbeth – then when the Revolution turns to Terror your conscience will sound with a voice that cries 'Sleep no more'. So William Wordsworth records in the tenth book of *The Prelude*.

A personal joke on Fuseli's part supports a reading of his Macbeth as an image of the Romantic artist: the faces of the three weird sisters who point to the armed head are modelled on the face of Fuseli's own artistic mentor, Johann Jakob Bodmer. The *Sturm und Drang* aesthetician is re-imagined as the initiator of his pupil into the mystery of Romantic aesthetics: that art is the deepest 'Confronting with self-comparisons'.

The best analysis of Fuseli's great painting remains his own. Technically, it reveals that he followed the play in basing his structure on the mystical number three (three weird sisters, three prophecies, three acts of murder). Romantically, it voices the principle of self-confrontation, the doppelgänger effect:

> To say nothing of the general arrangement of my picture, which in composition is altogether triangular, (and the triangle is a mystical figure,) I have endeavoured to shew a colossal head rising out of the abyss, and that head Macbeth's likeness. What, I would ask you, would be a greater object of terror to you, if, some night on going home, you were to find yourself sitting at your own table, either writing, reading, or otherwise employed? would not this make a powerful impression on your mind?

Fuseli's description of his painting is also an intuition of the power of Shakespearean character to impress itself upon the mind. When the Romantic looks at Hamlet, he does not only see an embodiment of the idea of human 'character', an icon of consciousness: he sees himself. And when he looks at Macbeth, he does not only see an icon of humankind's capacity to make a contract with evil: he sees his own highest imaginings, in all their thrilling power, in all their darkness.

The two wings of the soul

Hamlet, Othello, Macbeth, Lear: think of these titles and one thinks first of a character, then of other characters and a story. *Romeo and Juliet*: think of this title and one thinks first of an idea. Millions of people who have never read a word of Shakespeare instantly associate Romeo and Juliet with the idea of being in love. Shakespeare's dramatization of their story has become Western culture's archetypal myth of youthful passion. Tourists flock to a courtyard in Verona and take photographs of 'Juliet's balcony'. A man who is a passionate admirer (and, in later usage, a frequent seducer) of women has been a 'Romeo' ever since the mid-eighteenth century, when the role was one of David Garrick's most celebrated stage creations. In Garrick's century, *Romeo and Juliet* was, indeed, the most frequently staged of all Shakespeare's plays.

Rumour had it that when Hector Berlioz saw Harriet Smithson as Juliet at the Odéon theatre in Paris in 1827, he instantly vowed that he would marry the actress and base his greatest work on the play. Berlioz himself said that this was an exaggeration, but there is no doubt that his *Roméo et Juliette* symphony was inspired by the performance.

The Charles Kemble production attended by Berlioz and his fellow French Romantics was based on a slightly cut text of Garrick's adaptation of the play. Garrick's major changes were as follows: he removed all reference to Romeo's being in love with Rosaline before meeting Juliet; he added a funeral procession for Juliet at the beginning of the fifth act, complete with sung dirge; and he altered the tomb-scene, so that Juliet awakes after Romeo has drunk the poison, but before he dies. More locally, Garrick reduced the original's use of rhyme, punning, and bawdy, in accordance with eighteenth-century decorum; he conflated and streamlined the scenes in the first half of the play involving Romeo, Mercutio, and Benvolio; and he raised Juliet's age from just under fourteen to just under eighteen.

Garrick regarded it as a blemish upon Romeo's character that he should be in love with Rosaline one moment and Juliet the next. Shakespeare did not start from such a conception of character. He began from conceptions of love. Romeo's love for Rosaline is conventionally courtly; it is shown to be artificial and hence superficial. His love for Juliet begins in similar fashion, but grows into something more profound. Shakespeare's principal interest was in discovering the linguistic means of representing this growth.

When Romeo and Juliet first speak to each other as they are dancing at the ball, they do so in the form of a sonnet, with the rhyme scheme *ababcbcbdedeff*. They weave a verbal dance to match their musical motion: Romeo speaks the first quatrain, Juliet the second (but picking up on Romeo's rhyme of 'this' and 'kiss'); the third quatrain is divided between them, then each delivers one line of the closing rhyming couplet (1.5.92–105). Their speaking in a sonnet, the conventional form of courtly love, establishes their relationship in the terms of traditional courtly artifice. Juliet's unobtainability, since she is betrothed to another while Romeo is a member of a rival household, is of a piece with this: the conventional courtly lover revels in the distance of his lady. It will, after all, give him the opportunity to write more pleading and despairing sonnets. But then Shakespeare sets about developing the love into something more real, in which the drive to consummation is a necessity and the act of severance a tragedy.

As the play progresses and the love is intensified, the poetic language is loosened. Shakespeare unshackles the lovers from the constraints of courtly verse and lets them speak with freshness and fluidity. The aubade, in which lovers part at dawn, was another conventional courtly form, but when Romeo looks out on the morning sky, he is no longer impeded by the sonneteer's rhymes and end-stops. High from his night's lovemaking, his sentences bound across the line-endings:

> It was the lark, the herald of the morn,
> No nightingale. Look, love, what envious streaks
> Do lace the severing clouds in yonder east.
> Night's candles are burnt out, and jocund day
> Stands tiptoe on the misty mountain tops.
>
> (3.5.6–10)

Romeo and Juliet was crucial to Shakespeare's artistic development, because its way of representing the intensification of Romeo and Juliet's love led the dramatist towards the fluid blank verse that he perfected in his mature tragedies. But at the same time, the play's frequent bouts of bawdy talk and violent male rivalry make it something more complicated than a hymn to love. By downplaying these variations of tone and adding a final love-duet in the tomb, Garrick reduced the play's complexity whilst simultaneously elevating Romeo and Juliet's love affair to iconic status.

Berlioz called his *Roméo et Juliette* (Opus 17) a 'Dramatic Symphony'. It is structured as follows:

1. Orchestral introduction – combat between the Montagues and the Capulets, tumult, intervention of the Prince.
   Prologue – choral recitative, concerning the ancient enmity of the two houses.
   Strophes – first transports of love which no one forgets. Sung text to the effect that first love is higher than all poetry, it is poetry itself, of which Shakespeare alone had the supreme secret and which he carried to the skies.
   Choral recitative – transition in which Mercutio tries to turn Romeo from reverie to gaiety.
   Scherzetto, with tenor solo concerning Queen Mab.
2. Romeo alone and melancholy; sounds of grand ball at the Capulets. Two orchestral themes (a larghetto and an allegro) in contrast, then united.
3. Serene night in the silent and deserted garden of the Capulets. Begins with chorus of guests saying goodnight after the ball, then Love-Scene represented orchestrally.
4. Queen Mab or the Fairy of Dreams (orchestral scherzo).
5. Funeral procession of Juliet (initially instrumental, then chorus of Capulets).
6. Romeo at the tomb of the Capulets – invocation, awakening of Juliet: 'outburst of delirious joy, broken by the first gripping of the poison; last anguish and death of the two lovers' (orchestral).
7. Finale (vocal) – choral reaction to the return of Romeo; maledictions on the lovers; sympathetic aria by Friar Laurence ('Poor children for whom I cry'); homily on reconciliation by Friar

Laurence; reunion between Montague and Capulet families sworn over the bodies of their dead children.

From a structural point of view, it is clear that Berlioz is following Garrick. He read Shakespeare in the French prose translation of Pierre Le Tourneur, whose version of *Romeo and Juliet* was based on Garrick and thus included such innovations as the funeral procession of Juliet (this was in fact cut from the 1827 Odéon performance, since the French censor did not allow priests on stage). The climax of the symphony is the passionate but brief reunion of the lovers when Juliet awakes before Romeo's death. The scene was Garrick's master stroke. It seared itself into Berlioz's memory of Harriet Smithson's performance. More than thirty years after the event, he remembered the moment (Fig. 18) as follows:

> [Romeo] dashes upon the funeral couch, snatches the beloved body from it, tearing the veils and the winding-sheet, and brings it to the front of the stage where he holds it upright in his arms. Juliet gazes languidly around her with her dim eyes, Romeo calls her by name, hugs her in a distraught embrace, smooths away the hair which is hiding her pale forehead, covers her face with mad kisses, is carried away with gusts of convulsive laughter; in his heart-rending joy he has forgotten that he is about to die. Juliet breathes. Juliet! Juliet!

The orchestral sixth movement of the symphony, entitled 'Romeo at the tomb of the Capulets', is intended to convey the emotions of this scene. Its close dependence on Garrick's adaptation was such that the printed score of the symphony, published in 1847, included a note to the effect that the movement 'should be omitted from every performance except those in which this symphony is presented before an elite audience extremely familiar with the fifth act of Shakespeare's tragedy with Garrick's ending'.

The opening movements of the symphony reflect Garrick's compression of the first half of the action, while the absence of any part for the Nurse takes to a logical extreme his diminution of the play's bawdy. But Berlioz also went back to the structure of the Shakespearean original: the reunion of the two families, which provided him with his finale, had been omitted from the Garrick and Kemble versions.

The *Roméo et Juliette* symphony is created out of a unique combination of choral and orchestral resources. Berlioz stressed that only the finale should be regarded as being in the domain of opera or oratorio. He explained his deployment of choruses in the preface to the libretto which was available to the audience at the first performance of the work in 1839:

> The genre of this work will surely not be misunderstood. Although voices are frequently used, it is neither a concert opera nor a cantata, but a choral symphony [*Symphonie avec chœurs*].
>
>   The voices are present almost from the start, but this is to prepare the mind of the audience for the dramatic scenes, whose feelings and passions are to be expressed *by the orchestra*. I also had it in mind to draw the choral forces gradually into the musical argument; if they appeared too abruptly they might damage the unity of the work. Thus the first prologue, where following the example of classical tragedy and Shakespeare's own drama, the chorus gives an outline of the action, is sung by only fourteen voices. Later on we hear (from off stage) the chorus of Capulets (men) alone; then in the funeral procession, Capulet men and women. At the beginning of the finale the *two full choruses* of Capulets and Montagues appear with Friar Laurence; and at the close the three choruses are united.

Because a chorus is a collectivity of voices, it serves to represent the community as opposed to the individual. The uniting of the different choral resources in the finale is a dramatic enactment of the knitting together of the community after the death of the lovers.

Only two characters from the play are given individual voices. A tenor solo sings an adapted version of Mercutio's speech about Queen Mab, while the closing choruses are punctuated by the expository and admonitory aria and recitative of Friar Laurence. Berlioz has finely intuited the importance of these two roles: Mercutio encapsulates the spirit of energy, youthfulness, and abandonment that pervades the first half of the play, while Laurence is an embodiment of the sober conclusion of the tragedy.

Queen Mab is associated with wild dreams. Berlioz introduces her twice. The scherzetto at the end of the first movement introduces the 'voice' of Mercutio in the same structural position as the Mab speech in the play, immediately before Romeo goes to the ball. But then the musical theme associated with Queen Mab is further developed in an orchestral scherzo after the central love-scene and before the funeral procession of Juliet. It thus becomes a musical representation of the fulfilment of Romeo and Juliet's love-dreams. At the same time, since many of Mab's effects are destructive, this interlude also brings forebodings of death. The music allows us simultaneously to imagine Romeo's dreams of the night he has just spent in the arms of his beloved and Juliet's nightmares whilst under the influence of the sleeping potion.

To anyone expecting a quasi-operatic version of the play, there is an extraordinary absence at the centre of *Roméo et Juliette*: the voices of the lovers themselves. In the strophes in the first movement, Berlioz steps outside the action and apostrophizes the idea of first love. A contralto voice asks what art could do justice to this feeling that is above all poetry. Perhaps, the voice continues, first love can become that very poetry of which Shakespeare alone knew the supreme secret. Berlioz's weak English meant that he only poorly understood the poetry of love spoken by Harriet Smithson and Charles Kemble on the stage of the Odéon, but their performance so moved him that he convinced himself that passionate love had found its quintessential expression. The experience of falling in love with Harriet Smithson was inextricable from the overwhelming power of Shakespeare. Berlioz saw that no words of his own or a librettist could equal Shakespeare. In accordance with his belief that music and love were the two wings of the soul, he took a different course and converted Romeo and Juliet into purely orchestral voices. As he wrote in his preface:

> In the celebrated scenes in the garden and the tomb, the dialogues of the two lovers, the asides of Juliet and the passionate declarations of Romeo, are not *sung* – the duets of love and despair are entrusted to the orchestra. . . . Such sentiments have often been sung – this is an attempt to find a different means of expressing them . . . instrumental language is richer, more varied, less punctuated, and thanks to its very indefinition, incomparably more powerful.

Love means two souls becoming as one. In spoken drama, it is difficult to hear two voices in unison. In a sung duet, it is possible, but the listener still hears the difference in registers between, say, the woman's soprano and the man's tenor. By rewriting the personae of Romeo and Juliet as orchestral 'voices', Berlioz can fully unite them.

Shakespeare's love-scenes begin with separation: in act two scene one, Juliet is aloft and Romeo below. They climax with union – the aubade of act three scene five – before the severance of exile and death. Berlioz creates a musical equivalent for Shakespeare's visual orchestration: at the beginning of the 'Scène d'amour', he scores high-pitched wood-wind to represent Juliet, deep cellos and horns for Romeo, but then as the movement unfolds there emerges a new melody which combines elements of each 'voice' and thus symbolizes the union of the lovers. 'The long final section', the musicologist Charles Rosen writes of the 'Scène d'amour', 'is subtle in a way that perhaps only Berlioz could have imagined and controlled: enough of the principal melody is retained to make it appear like a return, yet so much of it is transformed that it seems like a novel continuation'.

Classically, a sense of musical resolution is achieved by a movement from tonic to dominant and back. Rosen has observed how, in a bold breach of classical decorum, Berlioz withholds the dominant until extraordinarily late in the movement. The effect when it comes is of a climax in which profoundly pent-up feeling is given absolute release. Love affairs proceed from verbal dialogue to physical union. Berlioz finds a way of expressing this progression by means of the orchestra; he is thus able to 'stage' the consummation which no dramatist can show. At the same time, he can introduce motifs that are expressive of foreboding and hence anticipatory of the second half of the play.

Music allows the audience to imagine the mingling of bodies and souls. Its 'indefinition' means that it can appeal directly to the emotions without being filtered through the 'screen' of verbal or even visual representation. What is it like being in love and making love, or fearing that you will lose your love? Everyone knows that 'you cannot put the feeling into words'. You can, however, put it into music, even though there is no intrinsic connection between a particular musical cadence and the idea of consummation.

Traditionally, music has been made expressive of particular emotions by being linked to dramatic action, as in opera, to verbal articulation, as in oratorio, or to extrinsic information, as in 'programme' music or via a title. *Roméo et Juliette* provides a brilliantly original alternative. The vocal material in the first two movements signals to the audience that the symphony is not merely loosely connected to its source, as Berlioz's *King Lear* overture is broadly inspired by that play; the sung 'plot' actually sets in motion a kind of performance of the play. And since we know what is at the centre of the play, we realize that the central orchestral movements of the symphony are an expression of the passionate love that is iconically represented in the relationship between Romeo and Juliet. An icon is an archetypal *representation*; Berlioz goes beyond representation to the emotion itself. What is it like being in love and making love, or fearing that you will lose your love? I can't *tell* you about these feelings, but you can experience a *performance* of them if you listen to the third movement of the *Roméo et Juliette* symphony.

The kiss and the credo

'The truth is,' wrote George Bernard Shaw in 1901,

> that instead of *Otello* being an Italian opera written in the style of Shakespear, *Othello* is a play written by Shakespear in the style of Italian opera. It is quite peculiar among his works in this aspect. Its characters are monsters: Desdemona is a prima donna, with handkerchief, confidante, and vocal solo all complete; and Iagò, though certainly more anthropomorphic than the Count di Luna, is only so when he slips out of his stage villain's part. Othello's transports are conveyed by a magnificent but senseless music which rages from the Propontick to the Hellespont in an orgy of thundering sound and bounding rhythm; and the plot is a pure farce plot: that is to say, it is supported on an artificially manufactured and desperately precarious trick with a handkerchief which a chance word might upset at any moment. With such a libretto, Verdi was quite at home: his success with it proves, not that he could occupy Shakespear's plane, but that Shakespear could on occasion occupy his, which is a very different matter.

Genius can make time run in reverse. The hero of David Lodge's comic novel *Small World* comes to realize that there is a better book to be written on the subject of 'T. S. Eliot's influence on Shakespeare' than on that of 'Shakespeare's influence on T. S. Eliot'. Hamlet may not look the same after J. Alfred Prufrock's glum recognition that he is not Prince Hamlet, but he remains a living icon for the very reason that he is a character in whom reader after reader has recognized something of himself. Macbeth lives *because* he was reinvented as an icon of the Romantic imagination, Romeo and Juliet *because* they were immortalized anew in the music of Berlioz, Tchaikovsky, and Prokofiev. Shaw's paradox is deeply wise: one of the reasons why *Othello* continues to live is that, though written in the early seventeenth century, it gives the appearance of being influenced by the conventions of the Romantic opera of the nineteenth century.

Early in the second act of Shakespeare's tragedy, the first-act marriage still unconsummated, Othello lands in Cyprus and is reunited with Desdemona. He takes his wife in his arms and kisses her. To die at this moment, he says, would be to be most happy, for no greater contentment of soul is conceivable. How right he unwittingly is. At the beginning of the final scene of the play, convinced of Desdemona's infidelity, Othello comes to her chamber as she sleeps. He is about to 'Put out the light, and then put out the light.' He kisses his wife twice, perhaps three times. She wakes. But this is not the kiss that wakes the princess and brings a fairy tale ending: within minutes Desdemona has been smothered to death. Within a few more minutes, Othello has stabbed himself. His final words are 'I kissed thee ere I killed thee. No way but this: / Killing myself, to die upon a kiss.' He kisses the cold lips of Desdemona, and dies.

The repeated kiss is a dramatic motif which serves as iconic representation of Othello's love for Desdemona. At that first blissful moment on the Cyprus waterfront, Iago interjects with a characteristic aside:

> O, you are well tuned now,
> But I'll set down the pegs that make this music,
> As honest as I am.
>
> (*Othello*, 2.1.200–202)

The kiss is imagined as a kind of music, Iago as a destroyer of harmony. The operatic potential is immediately apprehensible. Add to it the musicality of Othello's soaring verse, the drinking song on the night of Cassio's fall from grace, the poignance of Desdemona's willow-song, and one sees Shaw's point: the play is tailor-made to become an opera. Gioacchino Rossini's 1816 version held the stage for much of the nineteenth century, until it was displaced by Giuseppe Verdi's, which was first performed at the Teatro alla Scala in Milan in February 1887.

Verdi and his librettist Arrigo Boito perceived the iconic force of the kiss. Boito restructured the plot of *Othello* in a number of economic ways. Shakespeare's first act is omitted altogether, so the opera begins with the storm which breaks up the Turkish fleet. Otello makes his first triumphant entrance as victor over the elements and saviour of Cyprus. The storm is then replicated in the stormy passions of Cassio's drunken fight with Montano and Otello's anger in response. Desdemona's entry, meanwhile, is held back until towards the end of the first act; she comes as a bringer of calm, her embrace quelling Otello's wrath. The climax of the act is a soaring love-duet during which Otello and Desdemona reminisce about their courtship. Incorporated here is Shakespeare's first-act narration of how Desdemona fell in love with Othello because of the dangers he had passed and he loved her that she did pity them.

For most of Verdi's first act there has been a large chorus on stage, representative of the public life to which Otello is committed in his capacity as a senior officer of the Venetian state. The stage is then cleared and his private life is given space in the closing moments. Otello and Desdemona are seen as iconic lovers, their mutual passion given voice in the form of the duet. They kiss to a beautifully resolved musical motif, which moves from the key of E to C major and back to E. Shakespeare's bare stage, thrust into the auditorium with no formal barrier between action and audience, no artificially dimmed lights, made for scenic fluidity. The nineteenth-century opera house, with its pictorial scenery, framing proscenium arch, and curtain drop, allowed instead for strong structural divisions. Each scene could be ended with a memorable visual tableau. The curtain comes down on the first act of *Otello* as the lovers are framed in their embrace, the love-star Venus shining over them.

Musical form and visual tableau enabled Verdi and Boito to 'iconize' the structural development of the drama. Towards the end of the second act of the opera, a quartet is sung by Otello and Desdemona, Jago and Emilia. The respective states of the two marriages are dramatized by the device of having different words sung to the same music. Desdemona tries to cheer Otello up; Otello, convinced of her infidelity, sings heartbroken 'asides'. Meanwhile, Jago is grabbing the handkerchief from Emilia. She is at first resisting, because she knows that he must have some evil scheme in mind; when forced to give in, she sings of her foreboding. The form of the quartet reminds the audience of the crucial fact that there are two married couples in this play.

Once Jago has the handkerchief, he uses it to confirm Otello's fears. The second act ends with the two men's vows: Otello's that he will have vengeance upon the unfaithful Desdemona, Jago's that he will devote himself to the service of his wronged master. Each sings his oath in a solo, but then they join in duet. Shakespeare's controlling idea at this point is a symbolic third marriage: 'I am bound to thee for ever', says Othello; 'I am your own for ever', says Iago (3.3.217, 482). In the opera, this bond is dramatized musically by the joining of the two characters' voices in the form of the duet. It is iconized visually by the tableau which ends the act: Otello and Jago are locked in an embrace, echoing that between Otello and Desdemona at the end of the previous act.

Jago gains complete ascendancy in the third act, by tricking Otello in the business of the dialogue with Cassio concerning the sexual charms of Bianca. The act ends with an off-stage chorus singing of Otello's glory, apostrophizing him as the lion of Venice, while on stage we see an utterly contrasting image. Otello lies on the ground in epileptic stupor, as Jago stands over him and proclaims 'See here the Lion!' In some productions, he places his foot on the Moor's face.

In the fourth act, the kiss motif re-emerges in the orchestra as Otello bends over the sleeping Desdemona and kisses her three times. But where the first act kiss was accompanied by the musical resolution E–C–E, here there is a dissonance. Fulfilment is forestalled as Desdemona awakes; instead of returning to E, the music goes into F minor. After Otello stabs himself, he makes to kiss the pale body of his beloved again: the opera ends with words which echo the end of the first act, 'Un bacio – un bacio ancora – un altro bacio' ('a kiss, another kiss, yet one more kiss'), and a tableau of the two dead lovers together on the bed. The elaborate visual resources of the nineteenth-century stage and the emotional force of the orchestra combine to transform Shakespeare's couplet, 'I kissed thee ere I killed thee. No way but this: / Killing myself, to die upon a kiss', into one of grand opera's most memorable representations of doomed romantic love.

Critics have often considered Othello's verse as a kind of music; Verdi does more than justice to the passion of his speech by transforming it into music itself. The emotional experience an audience undergoes in watching the play is not merely replicated but intensified in the opera. Similarly, Boito's rearrangements and simplifications of the plot strip the structural development of the play to its core; again, this has the effect of intensification, thanks especially to the iconic tableaux of the act-endings.

Boito made three major additions to the action of the original. In the second act, a chorus presents flowers to Desdemona: the scene serves to emphasize her beauty and to associate her with naturalness. Then in the final act she sings an Ave Maria as well as her willow-song: this serves to accentuate her spiritual purity.

Shortly before the flower scene, however, there is an addition for Jago. It is a self-revelatory solo in which he associates himself with a different kind of nature: the natural desire to destroy. He was born, he claims, from some vile germ of nature; he feels the primal slime flowing in his veins. It is as if he has learnt the harsh lesson of Darwinian natural selection: you must destroy your rivals in order to survive. The solo is structured as a parody of a Christian Credo; it is a negative anticipation of Desdemona's pious Ave Maria. For Boito's Jago, life is fashioned only to feed the worm of death. After death there is nothing; heaven is an old wives' tale.

Jago's Credo is often singled out as the one dramatic flaw in *Otello*. Does not the explicit statement of a creed of pure destructiveness diminish the mystery, and hence the power, of the character?

One of the things that makes Iago so compelling in the Shakespearean original is his apparent under-motivation. It is this which sets him apart from Richard III. When Richard tells us in soliloquy that he is determined to prove a villain in compensation for his physical deformity, we rather admire his honesty. We certainly like him for taking us into his confidence. 'Honest Iago', on the other hand, breaks all the rules of dramatic convention and does not even seem to be honest when he is soliloquizing to the audience. We can't take seriously his claims that what motivates him is the thought that both Othello and Cassio have been sleeping with Emilia. Besides the absurdity of the suggestion in itself, he doesn't love Emilia enough to care. We search instead for some deeper cause, or come to Samuel Taylor Coleridge's conclusion that we are witnessing the motive-hunting of motiveless malignity.

As Tolstoy took pleasure in observing, the Ensign in the Italian novella which *Othello* dramatizes is in love with the Moor's wife. He also believes that Desdemona is really in love with the Corporal: that is his motivation for destroying the Cassio figure. His animus is not directed towards the Moor. He hates Desdemona because she does not love him, so he decides that if he cannot have her himself, neither can the Moor. Shakespeare chose to remove this motivation of simple sexual jealousy. There is no precedent in the source for Iago's blunt statement that 'I hate the Moor' (1.3.378). Iago says 'I hate the Moor, / And it is thought abroad that 'twixt my sheets / He has done my office'. *And*, not *because*: sexual jealousy is tagged on as an after-thought, a spurious justification after the fact.

Iago's jealousy is a matter of permanent disposition, not specific cause. His wife knows this. When Desdemona says that she has never given Othello cause to be jealous, Emilia replies with words that are revelatory of her husband's nature:

> But jealous souls will not be answered so.
> They are not ever jealous for the cause,
> But jealous for they're jealous. It is a monster
> Begot upon itself, born on itself.
>
> (3.4.156–9)

Boito made the distinction well when he said in the prefatory notes for his libretto that Othello is Jealousy (i.e., specifically caused and directed sexual jealousy), whereas Iago is Envy. He is envious of everyone because they have qualities – of whatever kind – which he lacks. Francis Bacon wrote in his essay 'Of Envy':

> A man that hath no virtue in himself ever envieth virtue in others. For men's minds will either feed upon their own good or upon other's evil; and who wanteth the one will prey upon the other; and whoso is out of hope to attain to another's virtue will seek to come at even hand by depressing another's fortune.

There could be no better gloss on the character of Iago. The most revealing thing he says about himself is that Cassio must die because 'He hath a daily beauty in his life / That makes me ugly' (5.1.19–20).

This is his attitude not only to Cassio, but also to Othello, Desdemona, Emilia, and even Roderigo, who is at least capable, in however debased a way, of feeling the sensation of love.

By stripping Iago of the specific motivation which the character has in the source, Shakespeare made him into an iconic embodiment of pure malice. This is not to say that he is motiveless: his motivation is that he has a mind but no heart, he is capable of thought but not of love, and he therefore wants to destroy love wherever he sees it. No critic has put this more clearly than William Hazlitt: 'Iago in fact belongs to a class of character, common to Shakespear and at the same time peculiar to him; whose heads are as acute and active as their hearts are hard and callous'. Iago has to destroy the love, virtue, or beauty of others so that he is not the victim of comparison with them.

Iago's motivation, then, is the desire *to do away with comparison*. He is the negative equivalent of the Antony and Cleopatra who want their love to be immeasurable, unparalleled. He wants a world in which it is no longer true

> that man, how dearly ever parted,
> How much in having, or without or in,
> Cannot make boast to have that which he hath,
> Nor feels not what he owes, but by reflection –
> As when his virtues, shining upon others,
> Heat them, and they retort that heat again
> To the first givers.
>
> (*Troilus and Cressida*, 3.3.91–7)

Iago will always come off the worse from the principle of reflection 'upon others'. That is why he takes a peculiar pleasure in transforming Othello into a 'retort' of himself – in act three scene three, Othello thinks that Iago is 'echoing' him, but in fact he is echoing Iago.

At the end of the play, Othello and Lodovico try to make sense of Iago by calling him a devil. God and the Devil, heaven and hell are conceptions which function according to the principle of reflection. Iago, however, does not have the links with the supernatural that characterize those driving-forces of *Hamlet* and *Macbeth*, the ghost and the weird sisters. He is, wrote Verdi in a letter, 'humanity, that's to say a part of humanity, the ugly part'. This is why it seems to me that Boito's Darwinian Credo is true to the character: Iago is Shakespeare's pre-imagining of a world which is no longer anchored by the moral order made possible by the reflective principles of good and evil. Iago does not commit himself to a contract with the devil in the manner of Dr Faustus. He inhabits a world in which there is no moral principle, there is only the fact of life and death.

'Darwinian' is one word for such a world. Another is 'existential'. Rivers, the anti-hero of William Wordsworth's play, *The Borderers*, proclaims his allegiance to

> the only law that wisdom
> Can ever recognize: the immediate law
> Flashed from the light of circumstances
> Upon an independent intellect.
>
> (3.5.30–33)

Rivers does not only create his autonomy, his sense of self, from his deeds; he also creates his own structure of values. According to traditional moral values, his deeds are criminal. To him, that is an irrelevance. What matters is that he has invented himself through his actions. He is, in this sense, an existential hero, the ancestor of Meursault, protagonist of Albert Camus' *L'Étranger*.

In his preface to *The Borderers* Wordsworth acknowledged that Rivers is also a descendant of Iago. Hazlitt and Boito saw the corollary of Iago's rejection of preordained moral law. His only law is that of action. Iago therefore becomes a dramatist. Hazlitt writes:

> instead of employing his invention on imaginary characters, or long-forgotten incidents, he takes the bolder and more desperate course of getting up his plot at home, casts the principal parts among his nearest friends and connections, and rehearses it in downright earnest, with steady nerves and unabated resolution.

And he becomes an actor, the only versatile player in his cast of character-types (the cuckolded husband, the handsome youth, the gull, and so forth). Boito writes:

> One of his talents is the faculty he possesses of changing his personality according to the person to whom he happens to be speaking, so as to deceive them or to bend them to his will.
>
> Easy and genial with Cassio; ironic with Roderigo; apparently good-humoured, respectful and humbly devoted towards Otello;

brutal and threatening with Emilia; obsequious to Desdemona and
Lodovico.

'Existence precedes and rules essence' proclaimed Jean-Paul Sartre in
Being and Nothingness. Do you believe that there is some essence to
human being that can be known in itself – call it conscience, call it
consciousness? You do? Then your icon is Hamlet. Or do you believe
that we are nothing but the roles we play, that the only form of being
is *action*? Yours is Iago.

10

THE LAWS OF THE
SHAKESPEAREAN UNIVERSE

Professor Eddington with the same insolence
Called all physics one tautology;
If you describe things with the right tensors
All law becomes the fact that they can be described with them;
This is the Assumption of the description.
The duality of choice thus becomes the singularity of existence.

(William Empson, 'Doctrinal Point')

Dr Bowdler's problem play

Thomas Bowdler 'imbibed an hereditary desire to be doing good'. So said his nephew in a family memoir. In 1788 Dr Bowdler travelled in France, 'where he marked with a penetrating eye the state of the public mind, and foretold, on his return, the approach of some great crisis in that unhappy country.' Undeterred by this gloomy prognosis, Bowdler set out to turn the impending upheaval to the advantage of his own piety and desire to do good. He found a silver English lining in the French Revolutionary cloud:

> The terrible effects which followed served happily, first to awaken a deep and serious alarm, and then to rouse a spirit of vigilance and exertion, of loyalty and religion, among ourselves: the best and ablest men united together, and associations were formed for the preservation of all that is valuable to the Christian, and the member of society.

Bowdler joined one such association, the Proclamation Society, which had been formed with the purpose of carrying into effect a royal proclamation for the encouragement of piety and virtue, and the punishment of vice, profanity, and immorality. The Society worked for the tightening of regulations in houses of correction and the suppression of licentious prints and publications. In 1802 it was reconstituted as the Society for the Suppression of Vice.

Throughout the 1790s, while Paris was torn apart by Jacobin disregard for traditional order and morality, Dr Bowdler did all he could to assist in the improvement of the morals of the lower orders in London. He had, however, been frail in health since a near fatal accident at the age of nine, and in 1800 he was almost broken by his exertions on behalf of the undeserving poor. He retired to the seaside. He realized that for the rest of his life he would have to carry forward his work by indirect means. How could he continue to improve the morals of the lower orders without leaving his study?

His twin sister, Henrietta Maria Bowdler, gave him the answer. She was equally pious, but healthier and more energetic. In her early thirties she had published two volumes of highly successful poems and essays; she then produced an anonymous set of *Sermons on the Doctrines and Duties of Christianity*, which went through no fewer than fifty editions. The Bishop of London was so impressed by them that he announced that if the clergyman who had written them identified himself, he would be glad to grant him a living in his diocese.

Then in 1807, Henrietta Maria published another anonymous work: *The Family Shakespeare*. She explained her ambition in a preface:

> Twenty of the most unexceptionable of Shakespeare's Plays are here selected, in which *not a single line is added*, but from which I have endeavoured to remove every thing that could give just offence to the religious and virtuous mind. My object is to offer these Plays to the public in such a state, that they may be read with pleasure in all companies, and placed without danger in the hands of every person who is capable of understanding them.

The edition described itself as 'chiefly intended for family reading'. This was a Shakespeare made safe for girls and boys. Dr Bowdler saw his opportunity. In the course of the next decade he took over his sister's work and set himself the task of expurgating the remaining sixteen plays of the First Folio. In 1818 his name (and his alone) appeared on the title-page of the complete *Family Shakspeare, in Ten*

Volumes; in which nothing is added to the original text; but those words and expressions are omitted which cannot with propriety be read aloud in a family. Henrietta's anonymity remained a prime concern, for it was not regarded as ladylike to publish. Thus did brother Thomas gain the credit – if that be the word – for the entire undertaking.

Which one of Shakespeare's plays, we might ask, would especially interest a former member of the Proclamation Society who was concerned with the moral cleansing of the city? With, say, the elimination of prostitution and the strict punishment of extramarital sexual activity? At first glance, the obvious answer would be the play on this very theme: *Measure for Measure*. Does it not begin with the Duke of Vienna confronting the dilemma that for the previous fourteen years he has 'let slip' the state's tight laws against sexual indulgence? Bowdler must have thrilled to the first impression Shakespeare gives us of the ultra-puritanical deputy, Angelo, who is appointed to suppress prostitution and make an example of those fornicators unlucky enough to have been caught out by extramarital pregnancy.

But as he continued his work on the text of *Measure for Measure*, Dr Bowdler ran into two problems. For one thing, sexual licence was so central to the play that it was impossible to make sense of the plot without referring to it. If you are not going to allude to premarital sex, how can you explain the arrest of Claudio for getting Julietta pregnant before marriage? How can you bowdlerize something so inherently licentious as the chief business of the play, the trick of substituting Mariana for Isabella in the bed of Angelo? Bowdler's first problem, then, was textual. His second was interpretive. Angelo's own fall into sexual desire exposes a hypocrisy which, once contrasted with the engaging vitality of the inhabitants of the fleshly underworld (Lucio, Pompey, Froth, even the condemned Barnardine), made it very difficult to turn the play as a whole into an apology for sexual repression.

Contemporaneously with Bowdler's work, the politically radical theatre critic William Hazlitt attended a production of *Measure for Measure* at Covent Garden. His review for Leigh Hunt's liberal newspaper *The Examiner* combined relish for the play with a notable dig at Bowdler's kind:

Shakespear was the least moral of all writers; for morality (commonly so called) is made up of antipathies, and his talent consisted in sympathy with human nature, in all its shapes, degrees, elevations, and depressions. The object of the pedantic moralist is to make the worst of every thing; *his* was to make the best, according to his own principle, 'There is some soul of good in things evil.' Even Master Barnardine is not left to the mercy of what others think of him, but when he comes in, he speaks for himself. We would recommend it to the Society for the Suppression of Vice to read Shakespear.

For Hazlitt, Shakespeare's liberal lesson was the very opposite of what the anti-Vice brigade recommended. By giving a voice to every disposition, Shakespeare dissolves the ready distinction between virtue and vice; he offers an education in humanity, not a sermon in morality.

How, then, did Bowdler deal with his task? On turning to *The Family Shakspeare* we find that *Measure for Measure* is, exceptionally, furnished with an editorial preface. In it, Bowdler lays out what he sees as the problem of the play: the character of Angelo. His 'wickedness' is described as 'atrocious', as, indeed, unprecedented in history. For Bowdler it was appalling that although Angelo does not carry through his crimes – thanks to the bed-trick and the convenient death of Ragozine, whose head is substituted for Claudio's – he thinks that he has done so, which is just as bad: 'his guilt is as great as it would have been, if the person of Isabella had been violated, and the head of Ragozine had been Claudio's'. Angelo betrays the trust reposed in him by the Duke, he threatens not just execution but slow, torturous death for Claudio if Isabella does not yield her body to him, and even when she has (he thinks) gratified his carnal desire, he breaks his word and orders the prison authorities to go ahead with the brother's execution. To represent a character so evil as superficially pious and morally rigorous was offensive enough, but worst of all was the fact that Angelo gets away without a fitting punishment:

> This monster of iniquity appears before the Duke, defending his cause with unblushing boldness; and after the detection of his crimes, he can scarcely be said to receive any punishment. A hope is even expressed that he will prove a good husband, but for no good reason – namely, because he *has been a little bad*.

Samuel Taylor Coleridge had expressed the same indignation a few years earlier:

the pardon and marriage of Angelo not merely baffles the strong indignant claim of justice – for cruelty, with lust and damnable baseness, cannot be forgiven, because we cannot conceive of them as being morally repented of – but it is likewise degrading to the character of woman.

Bowdler also objected to the Duke's trifling with Isabella in the fifth act, the unnecessary length of time for which he allows her to suppose her brother dead. He found an inconsistency in Lucio, who is Claudio's friend in the first act, but assists Angelo, Claudio's apparent murderer, in the fifth. Lastly, he complained that 'the indecent expressions with which many of the scenes abound, are so interwoven with the story, that it is extremely difficult to separate the one from the other'.

For all these reasons, Bowdler abandoned his attempt to bowdlerize the play. Instead, he reprinted in *The Family Shakspeare* the acting edition of the day: the text of John Philip Kemble's long-running Covent Garden production with Sarah Siddons, the greatest actress of the age, as Isabella. This had the advantage from Bowdler's point of view of omitting the appearance of the unmarried pregnant Julietta and cutting the scene with Mariana at the moated grange in which explicit plans for the bed-trick are laid.

But even with these omissions, the subject, the tone, and the morally questionable ending combined to make *Measure for Measure* Shakespeare's most problematic play from the point of view of Family values. In the course of the nineteenth century the bounds of acceptable taste progressively narrowed and the play was less and less frequently performed on stage. At the end of the century, critics began calling it a 'problem play' – they meant that its main concern was to address a moral problem which could not be readily resolved within the conventions of either comedy or tragedy, but what the term really reveals is that the age's idealized conception of Shakespeare had great difficulty in accommodating the play. In particular, it seemed impossible to reconcile the title's biblical precept of equal justice ('with what measure ye mete, it shall be measured to you again') with the unequal treatment of Isabella (made to think that her brother is dead when he is not, made to kneel in public and plead for the life of the man who has almost raped her) and Angelo (made to marry a woman who loves him and allowed to retain his rank as Deputy).

Genius does not pull it through?

In 1922 Sir Arthur Quiller-Couch, King Edward VII Professor of English Literature in the University of Cambridge, wrote the introduction to *Measure for Measure* in the Cambridge University Press's new edition of the plays. This scholarly enterprise was perceived in its own time to be at the leading edge of modern Shakespeare studies, but Quiller-Couch's reading of the play remained squarely in the nineteenth-century tradition. It was by no means Bowdlerian or 'Victorian' in the sense of prudish: 'Q', as he always signed himself, told his readers with a certain relish that *Measure for Measure* is about 'the fun of sex' just as much as it is about the potential tragedy that can follow from sexual intrigue. But, modern as this admission may have been, Q shared the view of the great majority of nineteenth-century readers that there was 'something morally or artistically untrue' about this work, that 'in *Measure for Measure*, striking play though it be, genius does *not* manage to pull it through.' What is wrong with the play? Q asks – 'Evidently *something* is wrong, since the critics so tangle themselves in apologies and interpretations.'

Q devoted the longest section of his introduction to a particular example of the critical tangle. He examined the conflicting attitudes which had been taken towards Isabella. He declined to judge her for himself, but instead considered how previous critics, especially female ones, had judged her. What he found was that 'the critics can make nothing of her or – which is worse – they make two opposite women of her, and praise or blame her accordingly.'

Anna Jameson in her book on Shakespeare's female characters, *Characteristics of Women*, published in 1832, had argued that 'Isabella is distinguished from Portia [in *The Merchant of Venice*] and strongly individualized by a certain moral grandeur, a saintly grace, something of vestal dignity and purity'. These were the qualities which Sarah Siddons had drawn out in her much admired performance in the role. They are finely caught in William Hamilton's painting of the scene in which Isabella first confronts Angelo, with Lucio lurking behind her and the Provost standing at the right hand of the smitten Deputy (Fig. 19, executed in 1793 for the Dublin Shakespeare Gallery). Isabella's classical profile and costume suggest a Roman Vestal Virgin, while the sweeping arm gesture conveys the character's uncompromising moral force.

Yet for another female critic, Charlotte Lennox, writing in her *Shakespear Illustrated* of 1753, Isabella was anything but noble. Lennox pointed to the character's extraordinary outburst in response to Claudio when he says that for him to be put to death will be a far worse fate than for her to sleep with Angelo:

> O, you beast!
> O faithless coward, O dishonest wretch,
> Wilt thou be made a man out of my vice?
> Is't not a kind of incest to take life
> From thine own sister's shame? What should I think?
> Heaven shield my mother played my father fair,
> For such a warpèd slip of wilderness
> Ne'er issued from his blood. Take my defiance,
> Die, perish!
>
> (3.1.137–45)

As far as Lennox was concerned, the Christian duty of mercy and the close kinship between Isabella and Claudio ought to have led the character to have sympathized with her brother and at the very least comforted him in his fears. 'One might have expected mild expostulations, wise reasonings, and gentle rebukes' – his desire to live ought to have been understood, reprehensible as is his lack of concern for his sister's chastity. At the beginning of the scene, the Duke, disguised as a friar, has delivered to Claudio a homily on the ills of life, which has temporarily reconciled him to death. Lennox could not understand why Isabella does not say something similar in response to her brother's terrified lines about the body lying in cold obstruction and becoming a kneaded clod, the spirit imprisoned in the viewless winds. What Isabella unleashes instead is a 'torrent of abusive language' which goes so far as to imply that her own mother might have been an adulteress. Such abuse, wrote Lennox, bespeaks 'the manners of an affected prude, outrageous in her seeming virtue; not of a pious, innocent and tender mind'.

Quiller-Couch did not take sides in the debate. He admitted that it had crossed his mind that Isabella and Angelo might conceivably be 'two pendent portraits or studies in the ugliness of Puritan hypocrisy', but he dismissed the thought and granted that Isabella must be regarded as an 'honestly conceived' heroine. Yet if this is so, how is it that she can regard not sleeping with Angelo as a necessity to save her own soul, but have no qualms about acting as a procuress (a Mistress Overdone?) in arranging for Mariana to commit the very act of fornication from which she herself shrinks? She argues to Angelo that Claudio's fornication was only a venial sin, but regards the fornication that Angelo demands of her as mortal. She pleads to Angelo with eloquence that he should show mercy to Claudio, but she has no words of either mercy or eloquence for Claudio himself. The whole of her character is an inexplicable mix of eloquence and dumbness – with Angelo in the second act she is a brilliant rhetorician, yet in the fifth act she and Claudio do not speak on their reunion, nor does she reply to the Duke's proposal of marriage.

For Q, all this gave the impression that Shakespeare had failed to articulate his central idea clearly. T. S. Eliot made a similar criticism of *Hamlet* at around the same time. Common sense suggests that what is revealed by the diametrically opposed readings of Isabella offered by Mrs Lennox and Mrs Jameson is that 'the dispute itself – the mere fact that intelligent readers can hold such opposite views of a character which, on the face of it, should be simplicity itself – is proof that the play misses clearness in portraying its most important character'.

There is a similar problem with the Duke: is he a guardian angel watching over his subjects, or a meddling puppeteer who is more concerned with the thrill of secret manipulation than the happiness and well-being of his people? Whilst disguised as the Friar, he tells Claudio that Angelo was only testing Isabella and did not really intend to sleep with her; he says that he knows this because he is Angelo's confessor. This is clearly a lie: how could an unknown friar have got himself so quickly into the position of confessor to the acting governor of the state? It hardly reflects well on the character's integrity that he lies with swiftness and without compunction, and that the identity he adopts is that of a friar who has no qualms about breaking the secret of the confessional. In the very final speech of the play, the Duke commends Mariana to Angelo by saying that he has confessed her and knows her virtue. But he has only put on holy orders as a theatrical costume, never taken them before God: he has no entitlement to hear a confession.

With the help of his co-editor, John Dover Wilson, Q attempted to get round some of the problems of *Measure for Measure* by proposing that the text as printed in the First Folio was in some way inaccurate or incomplete. If we could recover Shakespeare's lost original, all would be made clear. But, although there are a number of local textual inconsistencies and difficulties, this is wishful thinking. The printed text is basically sound. The problem of *Measure for Measure* simply could not be solved within the analytical frame of reference of Quiller-Couch's nineteenth-century critical vocabulary, with its demand for consistency of characterization and 'either/or' conclusions – either Mrs Jameson is right about Isabella or Mrs Lennox is, either the Duke is a quasi-divine figure or he is a machiavellian manipulator.

I say 'critical' because the strongest creative writers in the nineteenth century, whether George Eliot and Flaubert in fiction or Ibsen and Strindberg in drama, did not themselves come to 'either/or' conclusions about their characters, their fictive worlds. Ibsen, by offering 'both/ and' portrayals of strong-minded women under the pressure of hard sexual circumstance, brings us closer to an understanding of Isabella than any nineteenth-century critic can. But *Measure for Measure* could only be appreciated in the vocabulary of formal criticism once it was viewed within a different frame of reference. That frame of reference was a specifically twentieth-century one. What I would describe as the first twentieth-century reading of the play emerged from Cambridge University in the late 1920s. Astonishingly, it took shape in the essay work of an undergraduate. I shall summarize the reading, then place it in its context, then ask what made it possible by considering what was available to the Cambridge undergraduate in the late twenties that had not been available to the Cambridge professor in the early twenties.

William Empson discovers the twentieth-century Shakespeare

The breakthrough was not a new interpretation; it was a new style of interpretation. For Q, the problem of *Measure for Measure* stemmed from the difficulty of choosing between readings. The way round the problem was to admit the simultaneous validity of contradictory readings.

Begin with a local example:

An ambiguity of the fifth type occurs when the author is discovering his idea in the act of writing, or not holding it all in his mind at once, so that, for instance, there is a simile which applies to nothing exactly, but lies half-way between two things when the author is moving from one to the other. Shakespeare continually does it: –

> Our Natures do pursue
> Like Rats that ravyn downe their proper Bane
> A thirsty evil, and when we drinke we die.

Evidently the first idea was that lust itself was the poison; but the word *proper*, introduced as meaning 'suitable for rats,' but also having an irrelevant suggestion of 'right and natural,' and more exact memory of those (nowadays phosphorus) poisons which are designed to prevent rats from dying in the wainscot, produced the grander and less usual image, in which the eating of the poison corresponded to the Fall of Man, and it is drinking water, a healthful and natural human function, which it is intolerable to avoid, and which brings death. By reflection, then, *proper bane* becomes ambiguous, since it is now water as well as poison.

The passage under discussion occurs early in *Measure for Measure* (1.2.120–22). Claudio is explaining to Lucio why he has been arrested: for his sexual 'liberty', for succumbing to his bodily desire for Julietta. The point of the image is that rat poison works by a delayed reaction, giving you a better chance of escaping the stench and infection of the vermin's decaying body: the rat dies not when it takes the poison, but when, made thirsty by the poison, it drinks. The thought begins with the simple moral idea that we have a natural inclination for lust which is our undoing. The turn in the thought effected by the completion of the simile gives us the complicated, disturbing idea that our undoing may be the result of a bodily function that is as necessary and unreprehensible as to drink water. *Ambiguity* makes it possible for us to regard sexual desire, the chief matter of *Measure for Measure*, as simultaneously our source of life and our poisonous well. My quotation is from William Empson's *Seven Types of Ambiguity*, published in 1930.

Now proceed from a local analysis to an implicit reading of the central encounter of the play, the relationship between Angelo and Isabella:

> In her youth
> There is a prone and speechlesse dialect
> Such as move men.

[1.2.170–72]

This is the stainless Isabel, being spoken of by her respectful brother. *Prone* means either 'inactive and lying flat' (in retirement or with a lover) or 'active,' whether as *moving men*, by her subtlety or by her purity, or as *moving* in herself, for pleasure or to do good. *Speechlesse* will not give away whether she is shy or sly, and *dialect* has abandoned the effort to distinguish between them. The last half-line makes its point calmly, with an air of knowing about such cases; and, indeed, I feel very indelicate in explaining Claudio's meaning. It is difficult to put the workings of the mind into a daylight which alters their proportions without an air either of accusation or of ribaldry; he is making no judgment of his sister's character, and only thinking that as a weapon against Angelo she is well worth being given a try.

Claudio's instinct is that his best chance of life will be for Isabella to plead on his behalf before Angelo. He thinks that the battle will be half won before she even opens her mouth. The physical appearance of her 'youth' will move Angelo. How could he not be affected by a pure young nun? But what kind of effect will she have? 'Youth' is traditionally associated with the heat of sexuality, while 'prone' introduces the fleeting idea of Isabella lying flat on a bed. The indelicacy may be risked: Isabella is sent to Angelo not merely because of her purity and her powers of persuasion, but also because Claudio and Lucio know full well that she has the power to move the vital spirits through a man's body and make his penis stiffen. Sure enough, when Isabella goes to Angelo, she inflames him with an image of herself prone on a bed:

> Th'impression of keen whips I'd wear as rubies,
> And strip myself to death as to a bed
> That longing have been sick for, ere I'd yield
> My body up to shame.

(2.4.101–4)

The ambiguity whereby Claudio simultaneously says 'Isabella will affect Angelo's good nature' and 'Isabella will affect Angelo's desire' prevents us from passing the kind of single 'either/or' judgement that had been characteristic of earlier readings of the play. Empson throws off Bowdlerian prudery by means of a throwaway tone ('I feel very indelicate . . .'), but his real innovation is the switch of gear whereby his analysis begins with 'either/or' (either inactive or active, either for pleasure or to do good, either shy or sly), then abandons 'the effort to distinguish between them' and implies that it has been 'both/and' all along.

To see Isabella's sexuality being used by Claudio and Lucio, and conceivably even herself, is to see that Angelo is not the main plot's only sexual user. The sub-plot is there, meanwhile, to spread the smell of sexual procurement throughout the city. To read the play thus is to see that in practice there can be no pure appeal to reason, justice, or mercy; emotions and bodily desires are always already complicit.

> It seems impossible even to praise the good qualities of Angelo without bringing into the hearer's mind those other good qualities that Angelo refuses to recognize. The most brilliant example of this trick in the play is the continual pun on *sense*, for sensuality, sensibleness (which implies the claim of Lucio) and sensibility (which implies a further claim of the poet).

An entire new reading of the play is spun from the thread of the word 'sense'. In the first act, Lucio tells Isabella that Angelo has no sexual appetite, that he is

> a man whose blood
> Is very snow-broth; one who never feels
> The wanton stings and motions of the sense,
> But doth rebate and blunt his natural edge
> With profits of the mind, study, and fast.
>   (1.4.56–60)

Here 'the sense' means 'sensuality'. From Lucio's point of view, Angelo's suppression of it is unnatural, but he knows that the image he is offering is one that will appeal to Isabella, since as a novitiate she is herself learning to blunt her bodily desires by means of prayer, study, and fast. When Isabella goes to Angelo, two senses of 'sense' clash with each other. He says: 'She speaks, and 'tis such sense' (such a good rational argument) 'That my sense' (my sensual desire) 'breeds with it' (2.2.145–6). For Angelo it is the very fact of an appeal to the mind that stimulates the body; hence the paradox, upon which his identity begins to collapse in self-tormenting soliloquy, that 'modesty may more betray our sense / Than woman's lightness' (2.2.174–5). And hence his descent into pure desire. Two scenes later he lets himself go: 'And now I give my sensual race the rein' (2.4.160). The bodily and the intellectual senses of 'sense' cannot be disentangled.

When Angelo says to Isabella, 'Your sense pursues not mine' (2.4.74), he means 'you are not following my argument', but he also means 'you are not desiring my body as I am desiring yours'. He qualifies the statement by saying 'Either you are ignorant, / Or seem so craftily, and that's not good.' Either she has no idea that he is making a play for her body or she has a perfectly clear idea and is cunningly not admitting it. Angelo has an 'either/or' mindset. 'What's this? What's this? Is this her fault or mine? / The tempter or the tempted, who sins most, ha?' (2.2.168–9). He can only regard himself as either the angel implied by his name or a devil masked as an angel. He would regard the rational sense of 'sense' as an angelic faculty, the bodily one as devilish. But if the different senses are collapsed, then so are the distinctions between tempter and tempted, angel and devil.

Isabella, too, has an 'either/or' mindset. Apply the same line of argument to her and one comes to a conclusion that is a more nuanced version of the thought which Quiller-Couch rejected, namely that Isabella and Angelo are in some paradoxical sense pendent portraits: 'It is [Angelo's] virtues and Isabella's between them that both trick him and nearly destroy Claudio.' In the final scene the Duke responds to Mariana's request to Isabella that she should kneel with her to beg for Angelo's life by saying 'Against all sense you do importune her' (5.1.430). If all senses of the word 'sense' may be read into 'all sense', then this 'final use of *sense* can carry a good deal of meaning':

> 'Against all reason' – 'all normal decent feeling' – 'all depth or delicacy of feeling'; whatever kind of *sense* is meant here, she lacks it. For a moment, in the elaborate and teasing balance of the play, Shakespeare turns even against mercy, or at least against the abstract rule of mercy from which [Isabella] acts. She is too otherworldly to feel the thing like a sane person; she is not sensual enough, the word might argue, to have tolerable human feelings.

'Sense' is by no means the only reiterated word in the play which refuses to be read in terms of 'either/or'. If 'move' as first used by Claudio suggests a sexual motion, then what are the Duke's motives for proposing to Isabella at the very end of the play with the words 'I have a motion much imports your good' (5.1.534)? Once we abandon 'either/or' as an interpretive principle it becomes possible to see the Duke as both disinterested and self-interested, both guardian angel and machiavellian plotter.

'Ambiguity' as the refusal of 'either/or' was an idea of William Empson's invention. *Seven Types of Ambiguity* proposes a gradual ascent from multiple meaning to radical paradox. A second-type ambiguity is more complicated than a first-type one, a third-type more complicated than a second, and so on up to the seventh type. The book's first example is a famous line from Shakespeare's seventy-third sonnet. Empson's analysis of it is rich and varied – it touches on biography and historical context as well as purely linguistic association – but not conceptually innovative. The principle of first-type ambiguity is that it is fundamental to poetry that 'a word, a syntax, or a grammatical structure, while making only one statement, is effective in several ways at once'. 'Bare ruined choirs where late the sweet birds sang' is a good line of poetry, Empson suggests, because it is multiply suggestive: the poet's comparison between his own ageing self and the silent 'choir' of a ruined monastery in late autumn holds for many reasons:

> because ruined monastery choirs are places in which to sing, because they involve sitting in a row, because they are made of wood, are carved into knots and so forth, because they used to be surrounded by a sheltering building crystallised out of the likeness of a forest, and coloured with stained glass and painting like flowers and leaves, because they are now abandoned by all but the grey walls coloured like the skies of winter, because the cold and Narcissistic charm suggested by choir-boys suits well with Shakespeare's feeling for the object of the Sonnets, and for various sociological and historical reasons ('for oh, the hobby-horse is forgot,' and the Puritans have cut down the Maypoles), which it would be hard now to trace out in their proportions; these reasons, and many more relating the simile to its place in the Sonnet, must all combine to give the line its beauty, and there is a sort of ambiguity in not knowing which of them to hold most clearly in mind. Clearly this is involved in all such

richness and heightening of effect, and the machinations of ambiguity are among the very roots of poetry.

Empson began writing analyses of this kind for his tutorials with I. A. Richards during his first two terms as an undergraduate student of English. This is how Richards remembered the origins of *Seven Types of Ambiguity*:

> [Empson] seemed to have read more English literature than I had, and to have read it more recently and better, and so our roles were soon in danger of becoming reversed. At about his third visit he brought up the games of interpretation which Laura Riding and Robert Graves had been playing with the unpunctuated form of [Shakespeare's sonnet] 'The expense of spirit in a waste of shame.' Taking the sonnet as a conjurer takes his hat, he produced an endless swarm of lively rabbits from it and ended 'You could do that with any poetry, couldn't you?' This was a Godsend to a Director of Studies, so I said, 'You'd better go off and do it, hadn't you?' A week later he said he was still slapping away at it on his typewriter. Would I mind if he just went on with that? Not a bit. The following week there he was with a thick wad of very illegible typescript under his arm – the central 30,000 words or so of the book.

In the preface to *Seven Types*, Empson himself acknowledged the debt to Robert Graves' treatment of Shakespeare's hundred and twenty-ninth sonnet in *A Survey of Modernist Poetry*. The debt is also demonstrable from the fact that the first section of *Seven Types* to find its way into print was an essay on 'Ambiguity in Shakespeare's Sonnet 16', which appeared in February 1929 in a student journal called *Experiment*, of which Empson was co-editor. The analysis went virtually unchanged into chapter two of the book.

The starting point for Empsonian ambiguity, then, was a reading of a Shakespearean sonnet. But why were Robert Graves and Laura Riding writing about Shakespeare in a book on Modernist poetry?

Their *Survey of Modernist Poetry*, published in 1927, was the book which gave popular currency to the term 'Modernist'. It was an attempt to explain and defend the new poetry of the 1920s and in particular to address its notorious difficulty. E. E. Cummings called himself 'e. e. cummings' and published poems that lacked punctuation; Modernism was therefore synonymous with obscurantism, self-indulgence, and

incomprehensibility. So the prejudice went. Graves and Riding introduced Shakespeare as a tactical weapon: by making him into a
Modernist, they could punch a hole in the case against the new poetry.

They therefore compared the heavily punctuated edited text of
Sonnet 129 which Quiller-Couch had included in his best-selling
Oxford Book of English Verse with the lightly punctuated text printed in
the original Quarto edition of 1609. In the original text, for example,
line three of the sonnet describes lust as 'periurd, murdrous, blouddy
full of blame', but in Quiller-Couch's text this becomes 'perjured,
murderous, bloody, full of blame', and so the meaning 'bloody full'
('full as with blood') is edited out. Graves and Riding were explicit
about their aim: 'By showing what great difference in the sense the
juggling of punctuation marks has made in Shakespeare's original
sonnet, we shall perhaps be able to sympathize somewhat with what
seems typographical perversity in a poet like Mr Cummings.' Prior to
the editorial intervention, the fluidity of punctuation meant that a
single Shakespearean line could stand for 'a number of interwoven
meanings'. Many different readings of individual lines in the sonnet are
expounded in support of the argument that

> The effect of [Quiller-Couch's] revised punctuation has been to
> restrict meanings to special interpretations of special words. Shake-
> speare's punctuation allows the variety of meanings he actually
> intends; if we must choose any one meaning, then we owe it to
> Shakespeare to choose at least one he intended and one embracing as
> many meanings as possible, that is, the most difficult meaning. It is
> always the most difficult meaning that is the most final. (There are
> degrees of finality because no prose interpretation of poetry can have
> complete finality, can be difficult enough.)

There are two principles here: the more interpretations the better, and
the most difficult meaning is the best meaning. From these principles it
becomes easy to move forward to a defence of T. S. Eliot's *The Waste
Land* and the lyrics of Cummings.

Shakespeare gave Empson more examples of ambiguity than any
other poet. *Macbeth*, a play exceptionally concerned with double
meaning or 'equivocation', was one of his two most frequent sources,
and the other was the *Sonnets*, which shows how deeply Graves' and
Riding's analysis left its mark. But by the time Empson reached the

seventh type of ambiguity he had extended the idea far beyond multiplication and difficulty. The identification of first-type ambiguities could legitimately be described as Gravesian; seventh-type ambiguity is uniquely Empsonian.

An ambiguity of the seventh type occurs when 'the two meanings of the word, the two values of the ambiguity, are the two opposite meanings defined by the context, so that the total effect is to show a fundamental division in the writer's mind.' Empson explained that 'the idea of "opposite" is a comparatively late human invention, admits of great variety of interpretation (having been introduced wherever there was an intellectual difficulty), and corresponds to nothing in the real world'; he added to this explanation a footnote which reads '$-a.b$ is contrary to a for all values of b'.

What is a seventh-type ambiguity like? It has a special intensity such as one finds in 'a gridiron pattern in architecture because it gives prominence neither to the horizontals nor to the verticals, and in a check pattern because neither colour is the ground on which the other is placed'. It may be heard as something 'like the stereoscopic contradictions that imply a dimension'. It resembles a dream as analysed by Sigmund Freud, in which 'the notion of what you want involves the notion that you must not take it'. We should approach the seventh type of ambiguity with awe, writes Empson. We are like Dante arriving at the centric circle of hell: 'We too must now stand upon our heads, and are approaching the secret places of the Muse.'

Claudio's lines about Isabella's 'prone and speechless dialect / Such as move men' are cited as an intensely compacted example of seventh-type ambiguity. Having worked in to the core of those lines, Empson moved concentrically out in his later books, *Some Versions of Pastoral* and *The Structure of Complex Words*, to a wider-ranging reading of *Measure for Measure* as a play that refuses 'either/or'.

There is nothing in Graves and Riding's analysis of sonnet 129 that approaches the radical paradox which Empson finds characteristic of a seventh-type ambiguity. What, then, made it possible for him to formulate the idea? Freud was one influence, as the comparison of ambiguity-work to dream-work suggests. But a source much closer to Empson's own world of 1920s Cambridge is hinted at in the dash of mathematical logic in the footnote added to the passage about how the 'idea of opposite' is neither an old nor a necessary conception. Freud himself might have said that what appears to be incidental or subliminal – the footnote – is in fact essential.

Quantum Shakespeare

The twentieth century began in 1905. That was the year of the first (unsuccessful) Russian Revolution, but far more importantly it was the year in which Albert Einstein advanced his first revolutionary scientific hypothesis.

In the seventeenth century Sir Isaac Newton had argued that light consisted of a stream of emitted particles. Newton's Dutch contemporary Christiaan Huygens had proposed to the contrary that light consisted of waves, not particles. By the early nineteenth century the wave theory seemed to have triumphed: light was regarded as a vibratory motion through the ether. Then in the 1860s James Clerk Maxwell demonstrated that light was in fact the visible portion of a broader spectrum of electromagnetic radiation. This was another triumph for the wave theory, albeit in modified form.

Experiments at the end of the nineteenth century showed that the energy of individual electrons emitted by a metallic surface when it was irradiated with ultraviolet light was dependent on the frequency, not the intensity, of the radiation, as should have been the case according to Maxwellian theory. This result led Max Planck, in the first years of the new century, to put forward his quantum theory of light: that radiation is non-continuous. Planck prepared the way for Einstein's formulation in 1905 of the revolutionary theory that light behaves as if it consists of bundles or 'quanta' of energy.

The equation in which Einstein laid out this hypothesis matched the results of the electron emission experiment, but was a complete paradox from the Maxwellian point of view, which regarded light as an electromagnetic wave and electrons as charged material particles. Einstein's hypothesis met with little favour until 1923, when Arthur Compton's measurements of X-ray scattering gave empirical confirmation that light quanta possess momentum as well as energy. Einstein's quanta were then given a name: 'photons'. The discovery of photons did not, however, mean a rejection of the wave theory and a return to Newton's view of light as particles. Certain features of photon emission were characteristic of wave motion. Einstein had done what had previously seemed impossible: fused two seemingly contradictory theories. Light behaves like both waves and particles.

This theory of the duality of light was part of the broader movement in twentieth-century physics to the hypothesis that all matter has both wave and particle aspects. During the mid-twenties, the new quantum physics supplanted the classical Newtonian model. In 1924 Louis de Broglie showed that under certain circumstances particles behave like waves; in the course of the next two years Erwin Schrödinger advanced an equation that seemed to fit the behaviour of both wave and particle motion, while Werner Heisenberg came to a similar conclusion by a different route.

In classical theory, exact measurements had been possible. The new theory proposed that quantities such as radiant energy are not constant, that they exist only in discrete amounts. Their behaviour is irregular and unpredictable. It follows that quantum physics can only calculate the *probability* of the results of an experiment. According to Heisenberg's 'uncertainty principle' or 'principle of indetermination', it is impossible to specify both the position and the momentum of a subatomic particle. Indetermination is not due to inadequate techniques of measurement: it is inescapable because the process of observing the position of a particle disturbs the particle's momentum, and vice versa. The corollary of Heisenberg's uncertainty principle was Niels Bohr's principle of complementarity: a full description of phenomena needs both wave and particle descriptions of radiation, despite their apparent mutual contradiction.

In England, the home of the new physics was Cambridge. In 1925 Paul Dirac, a twenty-three-year-old graduate student in the Department of Applied Mathematics and Theoretical Physics, read a proof copy of the seminal paper in which Heisenberg laid out the new quantum theory; the following year he produced his own mathematical deduction of 'The Fundamental Equations of Quantum Mechanics'. Then in 1930 he published the first full-length book in English on the subject: *The Principles of Quantum Mechanics*.

Also in 1930, another bright young Cambridge student, who had read for part one of the mathematics tripos, published a pair of book reviews. In the *Nation and Athenaeum* he wrote on Joseph Needham's *The Sceptical Biologist*. The review ends as follows: 'speaking of recent developments, I was sorry not to find Schrödinger in the index: his latest theory says that the more exactly you know the position of an atom the less exactly you know its velocity, and vice-versa.' And a few months later, in *The Criterion*, he made some sharp remarks about a book on *The Metaphysical Foundations of Modern Science*. This review refers knowingly to the Michelson–Morley experiment that had disproved the existence of the ether, an experiment which, by removing the idea that light always has to travel through something substantial, made it possible for Einstein to posit the equivalence of mass and energy. The review concludes with a discussion of relativity and how 'the view of space taken by modern physics will eventually alter our notion of reality'. The bright young student was William Empson.

Empson went to Cambridge University to read mathematics. Only after completing the first part of the Mathematical Tripos, ranking Senior Optime, did he change to the English Tripos in October 1928. Empson's biographer, John Haffenden, has persuasively demonstrated that the poetry which he was writing in the late twenties and early thirties was steeped in the new physics. 'The World's End' alludes to the curvature of space, 'Plenum and Vacuum' to the atomic theory of Rutherford, while 'Letter I' imagines the possibility of the sun becoming that kind of very dense star called a white dwarf. The penultimate line of that poem reads 'Flame far too hot not to seem utter cold'. This paradox is a poetic compacting of a passage in A. S. Eddington's 1927 Gifford Lectures on *The Nature of the Physical World*, concerning the way in which white dwarfs defy the laws of classical physics: 'the star could not stop losing heat, but it would have insufficient energy to be able to cool down'.

Empson's knowledge of the new physics was, I think, derived chiefly from what in a later review he called 'Eddington's monumental book'. The purpose of that book was not merely to describe 'the great changes of scientific thought which have recently come about', but to explore their philosophical consequences. Relativity and quantum theory, Eddington proposed, 'involve changes in our mode of thought about the world'. Might the new physics have been formative of Empson's criticism as well as his poetry? Let us consider the hypothesis that the innovations of Heisenberg and Schrödinger, so lucidly mediated by Eddington, led Empson to bring about changes in our mode of thought about literature.

It was during the first few months after he switched from Mathematics to English that Empson wrote the first draft of *Seven Types*. That draft seems to have become chapter two of the finished book. At the end of this chapter, the longest and the one which made most extensive use of Shakespeare, he explained his procedure and in so doing revealed the newness and contemporaneity of his method:

> Some readers of this chapter, I should like to believe, will have shared the excitement with which it was written, will have felt that it casts a new light on the very nature of language, and must either be all nonsense or very startling and new. A glance at an annotated edition ‚of Shakespeare, however, will be enough to dispel this generous illusion; most of what I find to say about Shakespeare has been copied out of the Arden text. I believe, indeed, that I am using in a different way the material that three centuries of scholars and critics have collected; without such a claim it is impertinent to add to the vast library about Shakespeare; but the difference here is merely one of interpretation.
>
> The conservative attitude to ambiguity is curious and no doubt wise; it allows a structure of associated meanings to be shown in a note, but not to be admitted; the reader is encouraged to swallow the thing by a decent reserve; it is thought best not to let him know that he is thinking in such a complicated material. So it is assumed, except when a double meaning is very conscious and almost a joke, that Shakespeare can only have meant one thing, but that the reader must hold in mind a variety of things he may have meant, and weight them, in appreciating the poetry, according to their probabilities. Here as in recent atomic physics there is a shift in progress, which tends to attach the notion of a probability to the natural object rather than to the fallibility of the human mind.

In the eighteenth and nineteenth centuries, editors regarded it as their business to *choose between* possible meanings. From Lewis Theobald to the first Arden editions of the early 1900s, the function of the footnote was to explicate the primary meaning of complex or obsolete words and phrases in order to clear up potential ambiguities. Empson does something different: he says 'both/and' instead of 'either/or'. In the case of a seventh-type ambiguity, he says 'both/and' of two things which according to eighteenth- and nineteenth-century modes of perception are by definition opposites. By doing so, he brought Shakespeare into the twentieth century, for what enabled him to do so was, I suggest, the 'recent atomic physics' in which uncertainty was attached 'to the natural object rather than to the fallibility of the human mind'. That last sentence is a clear allusion to the inexactitude of prediction in the quantum world.

Seventh-type Empsonian ambiguity is the literary-critical equivalent of quantum mechanics. In the Cambridge of 1922, Sir Arthur Quiller-Couch could only think in terms of either/or, so he could not make sense of *Measure for Measure*. In the Cambridge of 1930, Sir William Empson (as he eventually became) became the first man to see the literature of the past through quantum theory's altered notion of reality. He was able to think in terms of both/and, so he could make sense of *Measure for Measure*. Different measures which had hitherto been measured as opposites were seen afresh as resembling a check pattern in which 'neither colour is the ground on which the other is placed'. Erwin Schrödinger demonstrated mathematically that a hydrogen atom may have two energies at once, something impossible under previous atomic theory; William Empson demonstrated critically that a text may have two contradictory meanings at once, something impossible under previous literary theory.

An analysis of the literary-theoretical implications of this development would need a whole book in itself. Such a book might suggest that the swing from writer to reader that is described by the parabola of twentieth-century criticism is true to Heisenberg's uncertainty principle. 'The principle of indeterminacy', wrote Eddington, 'is epistemological. It reminds us once again that the world of physics is a world contemplated from within, surveyed by appliances which are part of it and subject to its laws.' So too with the world of literature; like a quantum-event, an ambiguity is only brought into being by an observer's perception of it.

But such a book ought also to suggest that the dissolution of absolutes which characterizes late-twentieth-century modes of criticism such as 'deconstruction' is a fallacious extension of seventh-type ambiguity. As Empson noted in one of those reviews written in 1930, relativity is an ill-named theory since it says not that everything is relative, 'but that a new thing (not space but the velocity of light) was found which could be treated as absolute'. The problem with deconstruction is that it has no equivalent for the velocity of light. It is not an illiterate theory but an innumerate one.

So what is the literary-theoretical equivalent of the velocity of light? I propose that it is the genius of Shakespeare. In chapter six, it was shown that our idea of 'genius' grows from the eighteenth-century conception of Shakespeare. Shakespeare is not an example of genius: he is the premiss for genius. Einstein is our century's prime exemplar of genius, but it would not have been possible to think of him as such without the Shakespeare effect of the previous two centuries.

Empson is Modernism's Einstein among literary critics. His 'both/ and' is the twentieth century's most powerful contribution to the understanding of Shakespeare because it is both a microscopic and a macroscopic way of seeing. It begins with ambiguous words and syntaxes – think of them as the wavicles which are the literary work's smallest unit of energy – but it can be extended to the work as a whole. It enabled Empson to apply an 'uncertainty principle' to every aspect of Shakespeare. To a word as small as *not*: 'Shakespeare's use of the negative is nearly always slight and casual; he is much too interested in a word to persuade himself that it is "not" there, and that one must think of the opposite of its main meaning'. And to a creation as large as Falstaff: 'to stretch one's mind round the whole character', Empson writes, 'one must take him, though as the supreme expression of the cult of mockery as strength and the comic idealization of freedom, yet as both villainous and tragically ill-used'. To see that something *is* there in a play even when a speaker says that it is not and to judge a character in different ways simultaneously are to view Shakespeare under the aspect of a quantum world. What made the difference between 1922 and 1930 was the new physics of 1923 to 1928.

Iconoclasts and vigilantes

Shakespeare has proved himself peculiarly adaptable to a world of ambiguity, uncertainty, and relativity. Like the fittest organisms in the natural world, he survives. He is a triumph of evolution, mutating in order to cope with a changed cultural environment. If Shakespeare the man was *mobile*, how much more so the body of his work has remained.

The evolutionary potential of the plays is proof of their genius. But we also need to ask what it is in the nature of the plays that gives them this potential. Has their survival been the result of qualities inherent within them or has it been a matter of historical contingency? When we start speaking of uncertainty and relativity, we may find ourselves asking whether Shakespeare's endurance might itself be an uncertainty, whether his generally assumed greatness might not be relative rather than absolute.

In an earlier chapter we met the New Iconoclasts who stormed the world of Shakespeare studies in the 1980s. Their argument was that those who have made claims for Shakespeare's greatness have always been claiming him in the name of their own ideology. The iconoclastic Terence Hawkes proposes that 'all we can ever do is use Shakespeare as a powerful element in specific ideological strategies'. According to Hawkes,

> no text offers values or meanings that exist as essential features of itself. Shakespeare's plays are not essentially this or essentially that, or essentially anything. They are, to take up Wittgenstein's metaphor, far more like natural phenomena, mountain ranges, pieces of scenery, out of which we *make* truth, value, 'greatness', this or that, in accordance with our various purposes. Like the words of which they are composed, the plays have no essential meanings. It is *we* who mean, *by* them.

If meaning and value come from the reader and the audience, not the text and the performance, there is in theory no reason why Shakespeare should be of any more use than, say, Bugs Bunny – we could make meaning by means of the cartoons just as well as the plays.

This alarming conclusion brought a new group of players onto the field: vociferous opponents of the New Iconoclasts, we may call them the Anti-PC Vigilantes. They patrolled the university course catalogues and the review pages of the more serious newspapers, perhaps even went incognito to the odd academic conference or symposium, then reported back to the general public in a jeremiad to the effect that the young were being indoctrinated in the creed of 'Political Correctness'. The Vigilante would call his book something like *Tenured Radicals: How Politics has Corrupted our Higher Education*. In it he would announce his appalled discovery that 'The very idea that the works of Shakespeare might be indisputably greater than the collected cartoons of Bugs

Bunny is often rejected as antidemocratic and an imposition on the freedom and political interests of various groups'.

Unfortunately, he – it was nearly always a 'he' – failed to advance any arguments as to why the works of Shakespeare should be regarded as indisputably greater than the collected cartoons of Bugs Bunny. All he did was to assert that Shakespeare and the other canonical works of Western literature constituted 'our' tradition and that this was reason enough to cherish them. As traditionalists, the Vigilantes needed to believe in the value of the Western canon, but as free marketeers they had difficulty in justifying as opposed to merely proclaiming it. Margaret Thatcher famously said, 'you can't buck the market': if the market is always right, doesn't it follow that if the market wants Bugs Bunny, then the rabbit must prevail over the Bard? But the Vigilantes preferred not to have this thought; they said instead that we must have Shakespeare because he is a source of 'timeless wisdom'. Since their examples of 'timeless wisdom' were things like Ulysses' speech on degree in *Troilus and Cressida*, the Vigilantes gave fuel to the Iconoclasts' argument that Shakespeare is nothing but an ideological tool.

So it was that New Iconoclasts and Anti-PC Vigilantes played into each others' hands: both groups accepted the premiss that the passing on of Shakespeare to new generations of students was a way of shoring up 'traditional' – that is to say white male European – value-structures. The Vigilantes thought of Shakespeare as a good way of maintaining the tradition; the Iconoclasts wanted to set him aside in order to give a chance to black, female, and socially 'low' traditions.

But we have seen that Shakespeare has also belonged to a variety of 'low' traditions, that he gave a voice to Jack Cade as well as the Lord Say, and that he has appealed to the artisan and the colonized as well as the gentleman and the government minister. And, more than any other figure in the 'Western canon', he has become a world genius. Shakespeare's cross-cultural appeal is the rock on which both Vigilantism and Iconoclasm founder.

The Iconoclasts remain an irritant because they do not allow us to take Shakespeare's iconic status for granted. They force us to scratch further at the matter of why he and not some other writer became the world genius of literature.

How do I show my approval of a suit?
Chiefly by wearing it often

Ludwig Wittgenstein, the greatest philosopher of the twentieth century, was puzzled by Shakespeare. He was of the view that 'Shakespeare's similes are, *in the ordinary sense*, bad'. But then, if Shakespeare was a bad poet, how is it that he has been so much admired? Since Wittgenstein could not accept the orthodox explanations for Shakespeare's greatness (the power of his language, the richness and variety of his characterization), he came to the conclusion that 'It may be that the essential thing with Shakespeare is his ease and authority and that you just have to accept him as he is if you are going to be able to admire him properly, in the way you accept nature, a piece of scenery for example, just as it is'.

It is to this statement that Terence Hawkes refers in the passage I quoted earlier when he 'takes up Wittgenstein's metaphor'. But I believe that he is misrepresenting Wittgenstein's position. The correct conclusion to draw from the incommensurability of traditional criteria of aesthetic judgement (such as 'are his similes good or bad?') with demonstrable emotional and cognitive effect (the admiration of many) is not that meaning and value inhere in the reader rather than the work. The correct conclusion is that the traditional criteria of aesthetic judgement must be abandoned. Wittgenstein's remark about Shakespeare must be seen in the context of the broader project of his later philosophy, which was in fact a kind of anti-philosophy.

One day Wittgenstein buttonholed Dr F. R. Leavis in a Cambridge street, said without any prelude, 'Give up literary criticism!' and walked away. Leavis perceived the encounter in terms of the old battle between philosophy and literature. He was (uncharacteristically) dumbstruck at the time, but afterwards wished that he had retorted 'Give up philosophy!' That he conceived of this retort shows that he didn't know Wittgenstein well or understand his work, for Wittgenstein was always telling his own students to 'Give up philosophy!' and was forever trying to do so himself – as when he became a hospital porter. Furthermore, his later work was a relentless attempt to do away with the questions that philosophy had traditionally tried to answer.

Giving up literary criticism (Leavis's 'common pursuit of true judgement') and giving up philosophy (the quest for truths in meta-physics and epistemology) are necessary because they rely on a search for foundations: what is the foundation of knowledge, what is the essence of great art? This kind of search, says Wittgenstein, may be appropriate in science, but it is not appropriate in areas such as religion and aesthetics. In those areas, to ask for a foundation or an essence is to ask the wrong question.

Traditional aesthetic theory – the attempt to define the true nature of the beautiful – makes it sound as if we respond to a work of art by thinking, 'This is beautiful.' The theorist then asks, 'What is the essence of this beauty?' But we don't usually think, 'This is beautiful,' when we read a book, look at a painting, or watch a play. As Empson put it in *Seven Types of Ambiguity*, 'What is needed for literary satisfaction is not, "This is beautiful because of such and such a theory," but "This is all right; I am feeling correctly about this; I know the kind of way in which it is meant to be affecting me."'

Our sense of aesthetic excellence is manifested not in theory but in practice: by our gestures as we take in the work of art, our degree of absorption in the book, the length of time we spend looking at the painting, the frequency with which we return to the play. Wittgenstein says: 'How do I show my approval of a suit? Chiefly by wearing it often, liking it when it is seen, etc.' This does not mean, as Hawkes would have it, that the suit has no inherent meaning or value: its meaning is to clothe us, its value is in fitting well and lasting for a long time. That is what a great work of art is like. It does not wear out; it will continue to look good even as fashions change.

Our posture and gesture as we read or watch and listen; our return to what we have read or seen or heard before; the conversations with our friends which are inspired by what we have read or seen, through which in our clumsy way we re-perform the work: these are the testing-grounds of aesthetic greatness. An audience of hundreds so absorbed in the play that you can *hear their silence* in the theatre. A reader concen-trating so hard on his book that he is oblivious to his surroundings: look at the posture of John Keats as he reads, a picture of Shakespeare looking down over his shoulder (Fig. 20). A composer knowing instinctively that music and love are the two wings of the soul, that *Romeo and Juliet* is the greatest of all love-stories and that he must accordingly remake it musically. Such effects *are* the Genius of Shakespeare in action.

We can describe the activity of aesthetic appreciation, but it is impossible to describe what it is a response to, for to do so 'we would have to describe the whole environment'. Literary critics in the line that ran from Coleridge to Leavis argued that aesthetic excellence depended on organic unity, the contribution of each part of the artwork to the whole. But to describe this kind of excellence adequately you would have to describe all the parts and demonstrate how each of them contributed to the whole – the only economic way of doing this would be to reproduce the whole, which would take you back to where you started. Unlike most literary theorists, William Empson was also a practising poet. He therefore knew that 'The analysis of a poem can only be a long way of saying what is said anyhow by the poem it analyses'. It is no good breaking a poem down into sense, feeling, tone, and intention, in the manner proposed by I. A. Richards in his *Practical Criticism*. The process of apprehending an artwork is not like that: 'one cannot give or state the feeling directly, any more than the feeling of being able to ride a bicycle'. Asked what a piece of his music *meant*, Robert Schumann played it again.

It is in the context of this argument that we must read Wittgenstein's remarks on Shakespeare. That Shakespeare's similes are bad is a suitably dramatic way of announcing that we shouldn't bother ourselves with the traditional aesthetic criteria. The proof of his greatness is in its effect, in the reactions and actions it brings about. 'You just have to accept him as he is if you are going to be able to admire him properly' doesn't mean that Shakespeare doesn't inherently mean anything in particular; it means that 'greatness' should be thought about in terms of effects, not causes.

This, it seems to me, is the only way we can satisfactorily answer the question of why the works of Shakespeare are indisputably greater than the collected cartoons of Bugs Bunny. Internal causes can always be disputed: 'You might think Aesthetics is a science telling us what's beautiful – almost too ridiculous for words', remarks Wittgenstein, 'I suppose it ought to include also what sort of coffee tastes well'. But specific effects can be observed: 'Perhaps the most important thing in connection with aesthetics is what may be called aesthetic *reactions*'. In the intensity and variety of the reactions and actions it provokes, the 'Shakespeare Effect' is greater than the 'Bugs Bunny Effect'.

That is an unfair comparison because Shakespeare has been around for longer than Bugs Bunny. A better comparison would be with the 'Ben Jonson Effect'. Jonson's works were available in a collected edition from around the same time as Shakespeare's; when the English theatres reopened after the Restoration, Jonson held a more prestigious position than Shakespeare in terms of both influence and revivals (his *Epicoene* fathered more of the best of Restoration drama than did any Shakespearean comedy); in aesthetic theory, his art was more admired than Shakespeare's. But, as the eighteenth century unfolded, the Jonson Effect waned while the Shakespeare Effect waxed. In particular, the Shakespeare Effect started working outside the author's own native country, something that happened barely at all with the Jonson Effect. If the argument of the New Iconoclasts were right, it would be as possible to 'mean by Jonson' as to 'mean by Shakespeare', but it has not been possible so to do.

In answer to the question 'Why has the Shakespeare Effect been greater than the Jonson Effect?', the New Iconoclast will reply: 'Because Shakespeare is a site of greater cultural authority than Ben Jonson – he is a talisman which people want to have on the side of their own ideology'. But this argument is strictly circular: why is Shakespeare a site of greater cultural authority than Ben Jonson? Because people have made a greater investment in making meaning out of him. Why have people made a greater investment in making meaning out of him? Because he is a site of greater cultural authority. Etc. Etc. We need another explanation.

Since the Shakespeare Effect has been and is so much greater than the Jonson Effect, I conclude that it is possible to make judgements about 'greatness'. But still we need to ask what it is about the plays themselves that exercises this great effect. Wittgenstein insists that we must attend to the whole effect. It is no use picking out some individual feature – elegance of plot, complexity of character, inventiveness of language. Some other writers have as good plots as Shakespeare, as complex characters and equally compelling poetry (often, indeed, written in a more accessible and less self-indulgent language). But the effect of those other writers is not so great as the Shakespeare Effect.

Wittgenstein was an ambitious and optimistic young philosopher. In his *Tractatus Logico-Philosophicus* (1922) he attempted to demonstrate that we can infer the logical structure of reality from the logical structure of language. But the attempt could not account for certain illogical things like religious and aesthetic experience. Since these were things whereof we cannot speak logically, the young Wittgenstein thought that we should remain silent about them.

The older Wittgenstein renounced the confidence of the *Tractatus* and reined in the ambitions of philosophy. He also found a way of talking of those things about which he had previously said we should keep silent. But he discovered that in order to talk about them usefully and to avoid lapsing into nonsense, he had strictly to circumscribe the terms in which he conducted the conversation. Indeed, what he did was to pay close attention *to* the terms of the conversation.

Imagine arguments about things like metaphysics and aesthetics as analogous to games. A game makes perfect sense according to its own rules; you only run into trouble if you start trying to play it by the rules of another game. The later Wittgenstein's favoured method of arguing was the 'language game'. He says: let us attend to the particular thing we are doing with words here, let us not attempt to make language instrumental in a passage to some higher realm of metaphysics. This is what he means by giving up philosophy. Giving up literary criticism would mean something similar: let us attend to the particular thing Shakespeare is doing or making happen with words and actions here, let us not attempt to pass to some higher realm of aesthetics.

Performative criticism

What is the best name for this kind of philosophy, this kind of literary criticism? In 1955 the Oxford philosopher J. L. Austin published a book called *How to Do Things with Words*. To make philosophers regard their profession as a matter of doing things with words was Wittgenstein's most enduring achievement. Austin was especially interested in utterances which effect an action by the act of being spoken (promises and apologies, for instance). He coined a new word for this kind of utterance: 'performative'. What his book demonstrated was that many kinds of utterance ordinarily classified as statements have an element of performativeness. Wittgenstein, who had died just a few years earlier, would not have been surprised by this conclusion; he would have recognized that *performative* is exactly the right name for his own later philosophical procedure. His method was to choose an example and work it through with close linguistic attention; the working through did not *lead to a conclusion*, it *performed the point*.

Two consequences followed from this method. The first was that Wittgenstein never again made a general theoretical statement like that of the *Tractatus*. The second was that he never published another book: his performative method meant that he had to perform his philosophy in notebooks, conversations, seminars, and lectures. To commit a position to print would have been to put an end to the performance, to stall the process of working through and thinking aloud which was the whole point of the enterprise.

What analogies are there for the performative way of thinking? The game is one, as we have seen. Another is the dream. An intellectual born in Vienna in 1889, as Wittgenstein was, could not but have been fascinated by Freud's attempt to decipher the grammar of dreams. A dream performs a psychological function for the dreamer. Like a game, a dream makes perfect sense according to its own rules.

A third performative kind of thinking is theatre. Indeed, theatre has the best claim to be the original performative mode. See this and you see another meaning of Wittgenstein's 'Give up philosophy!' Philosophy was born with Plato, who regarded his enterprise as a rival one to that of theatre. Though it grew from the profoundly dramatic method of the Socratic dialogue, the Platonic pursuit of wisdom and of essence could not abide theatre's implicit claim that everything is performance. By returning thinking to the performative mode, Wittgenstein was bringing to an end the centuries-long battle between philosophy and theatre. Giving up philosophy means acknowledging the superiority of theatre's way of doing things.

In the English language since Shakespeare's time, the words *perform* and *play* have had a special association with acting. The creation of that association in conjunction with the creation of a public theatre may be regarded as the most enduring achievement of Shakespeare and his contemporaries. There is a beautiful propriety about the fact that *The Oxford English Dictionary*'s earliest citation for the special sense of 'perform' as 'to act a part in a play' is Prospero to Ariel: 'Bravely the figure of this harpy hast thou / Performed, my Ariel' (*The Tempest*, 3.3.83–4).

Like a dream-world, a play-world has its own rules. Wittgenstein says:

Shakespeare and dreams. A dream is all wrong, absurd, composite, and yet at the same time it is completely right: put together in *this* strange way it makes an impression. Why? I don't know. And if Shakespeare is great, as he is said to be, then it must be possible to say of him: things *aren't like that* – and yet at the same time it's quite right according to a law of its own.

Like a language-game and a dream, a Shakespeare play has what we may call a *performative truth*. Its truth, Wittgenstein suggests, is achieved not in spite of but because of the wrongs of decorum, the absurdities of fable and the composite mingle-mangle of styles that is Shakespeare's distinctive strangeness. In front of Shakespeare, Wittgenstein says both 'It's all wrong, this is not how things are' and 'It's quite right, this is how things are'. As with the question of the nature of light, it is only in the twentieth century that it has become possible to say two such apparently contradictory things simultaneously.

A performative literary criticism will be a manifestation of how Shakespearean drama, in Wittgenstein's phrase, 'makes an impression'. It is not only theatre companies who perform Shakespeare, not only actors who interpret Shakespearean roles. To undertake a 'reading' of Shakespeare, whether re-creative (e.g. Berlioz) or critical (e.g. Empson), is also to perform him. People have gone on performing Shakespeare in all sorts of different ways for four hundred years: such is his genius. Wittgenstein might have said that the Genius of Shakespeare is not a factual hypothesis, but a truth-function of the difference it makes to the lives of those who maintain it.

One of the things that makes Shakespeare so performable is his memorability. A good performance depends on an actor becoming word-perfect in a script. Shakespeare's are the best scripts in the business not least because they stick in the mind. William Hazlitt said something simple, important, and empirically true about the old play of *Gorboduc*, which is sometimes described as the first English tragedy: 'As a work of genius, it may be set down as nothing, for it contains hardly a memorable line or passage'. There is no other writer like Shakespeare for condensing ideas and feelings into memorable words and phrases. Furthermore, his memorability is not restricted to language. There is that peculiarity of emotive gesture singled out by Tolstoy. And, as I suggested in the previous chapter, his plays also achieve memorability through iconic 'visible representation'. That is why even if you dispense with the dialogue of *Romeo and Juliet*, you still have an unforgettable idea of what 'Romeo and Juliet' stand for. And that is why with Hamlet you get a dramatic creation so memorable that he can be lifted from his play and put down in a novel by Goethe or a psychological treatise by Freud, where he manages both to remain himself and to become the epitome of struggling, searching, dreaming humankind.

I have tried to adopt the performative approach in this book. Like Wittgenstein with his language-games, I have tried to offer a performative description of the Genius of Shakespeare. My assumption has been that it is impossible to 'describe the whole environment' and I have accordingly preferred to imagine the Genius of Shakespeare as a field of forces in space-time. In part one, I examined the origins of the field in William Shakespeare's education, his social mobility, his generic variety, his actor's art of perpetual impersonation, his contest with Marlowe, his capacity to absorb source materials while resisting single-mindedness in explanation, tone, or judgement. I also 'performed' a reading of the sonnets in which I began from a determination not to tie them to biography, but was forced by their power of suggestion to tell my story of Southampton, Will Shakespeare, and Mrs Florio. In part two, I have traced some of the effects of the force-field by attempting to restage the performances of the history plays in different traditions of nationhood and of the major tragedies in various kinds of Romantic art. A performance always takes place in both space and time, which is why I have traced the shapes of some of the plays, such as *Macbeth* and *Romeo and Juliet*, while also attending to their continuing life in cultural time.

This approach seems to me the only possible way of avoiding the two pitfalls into which Virginia Woolf thought that all Shakespearean critics fell. Every critic finds him or herself in Shakespeare. Woolf thought that all Shakespearean criticism was autobiographical and therefore inadequate, and that this inadequacy was one reason why Shakespeare continues to be read. Of course my readings of Shakespeare are autobiographical, but since they are sometimes other people's readings — George Lamming's, Verdi and Boito's, William Empson's — their inadequacy is not that of what might be called 'single aspect' criticism.

Virginia Woolf also thought that, even with a single reader, one reading always superseded another. She concluded that 'the truest account of reading Shakespeare would be not to write a book with a beginning, middle, and end; but to collect notes without trying to make them consistent'. Since I think something different about Shakespeare each time I read him, I have not tried to offer a sequential 'reading' of his career or a scene-by-scene analysis of any of his works. The moves within each individual game are infinitely variable; they are not our best way to the general laws of the Shakespeare-world.

It must, however, be stressed that to play Shakespeare-games, and to acknowledge the autobiographical in the critical, is not to '*make* truth, value, "greatness", this or that' out of Shakespeare in the manner supposed by the New Iconoclasm. For what we discover when we play our Shakespeare-games thoughtfully is that they have rules. These rules are not the invention of the reader. By discovering what Wittgenstein calls the 'family resemblances' between the many Shakespeare-games, it becomes possible to articulate the laws of the Shakespearean universe. The Shakespeare-world, Wittgenstein said, is 'quite right according to a law of its own'. What then is that law?

A law of its own

'Shakespeare' may be thought of as a vast collection of games. Games in which the oldest and most enduring stories – children coming to terms with their parents; men and women falling in love, fearing infidelity, seeking power, renouncing power, growing old, dying well – are made new. Games in which public is pitched against private, young against old, female against male, inheritance against environment; games of yearning and loss, of will and revenge, of sobriety and wit. And, in a bewildering spiral, games which are resolved by games within the game – by cross-dressing and dressing up, disguising and play-acting. Each play-world has its own particular rules – you can make moves in Arden that you can't make in Rome – but I think that we can discern two laws which all the plays obey.

The first law is that truth is not singular. Formal recognition of what may be called 'the aspectuality of truth' is a key feature of many different twentieth-century cultural fields. Albert Einstein perceived it in atomic physics, William Empson in literary criticism. Wittgenstein perceived it in his later philosophy when he used the idea of 'aspects'. He meditated upon a famous drawing in a work of *Gestalt* psychology:

This is a drawing of a duck. This is a drawing of a rabbit. Now you see a duck; now you see a rabbit. Both the duck aspect and the rabbit aspect are 'true', but try as you might you cannot see them both at one and the same time.

Long before the twentieth century, Shakespeare's genius was attuned to aspectuality. Both the Hal aspect (call it the rule of providence) and the Falstaff aspect (call it the rule of the body) are truths of the *Henry* plays, but you cannot see them both at one and the same time. Both the Prospero aspect and the Caliban aspect are truths of *The Tempest*, but you cannot see them both at one and the same time. Again, inherent in the conception of desire performed by many of the plays and sonnets is the truth that, as Empson put it, 'the notion of what you want involves the notion that you must not take it, and this again involves the "opposite defined by your context," that you want something different in another part of your mind.' Shakespeare's aspectual representation of truth led to, among other things, his self-contradictory political afterlife, my subject in chapters seven and eight.

The formal origin of Shakespeare's ambidextrousness was the rhetorical training he received in school. The main purpose of an Elizabethan grammar school education in the arts of rhetoric was the preparation of future public and private servants. By developing a persuasive way with words, one was readying young men to argue a case in secretarial correspondence, council, diplomatic exchange, or law-court. Essential to the training was the ability to argue either side of a case with equal force. This is still a staple in the education of lawyers. Good oratory is thus like good acting: by deploying a full range of suasive linguistic effects, orator and actor make their audience believe – make them feel – the truth of the 'voice' they are animating. It is essential to the effect that the voice is *performed*. Intonation, pitch, pause, and gesture contribute to the emotive effect as much as argument, figurative device, and image. That is the key link between rhetoric and Renaissance drama.

Sixteenth-century educational theory also proposed that active virtue could be learnt through the study of the classic texts of ancient Greece and Rome: read about the noble Aeneas and you will become a little noble yourself. In this respect, the theatre was an advance on the schoolroom. Educational practice was confined to the formal analysis and imitation of vocabulary, syntax, and grammar. The theatre allowed for full rhetorical performance of a kind which could have a far greater effect than any mere philological exercise. In his *Apology for Actors*, Thomas Heywood defended the theatre from its Puritan antagonists by just such an argument.

But the Puritans had a case – a case, indeed, as old as Plato. Granted, the theatre presents to the public virtuous personae who are voiced so powerfully that one is moved to wish to be like them. But the well-trained dramatist and actor will, with equal force, give voice to vicious personae. In the theatre, we will see alluring Cleopatras and scheming Iagos as well as sturdy Caesars and noble Othellos. What is to stop us being moved to wish to be like the sirens and machiavels? In practice, audiences do tend to be more stirred by the voices of Richard III and Edmund the Bastard than those of the virtuous Richmond and Edgar. When we go to the theatre, we are more interested in characters who appeal to theatricality than those who appeal to morality.

As far as Renaissance humanist theory was concerned, this was a place where ideals and pragmatics fell apart. Ideally, a humanist education should have been a stirring to virtue. Pragmatically, it was technical, not moral – what the state needed were men of linguistic skill, never mind to what end those skills were deployed. The art of arguing both sides with equal conviction was a two-edged sword.

In the long term, it was Shakespeare's mastery of the art of making so many different voices persuasive that led to his renewability. Good rhetoric means having an effect on your audience; what I have called the Shakespeare Effect has been so strong, so varied, and so persuasive because Shakespeare was such a good rhetorician. By rhetoric I mean the full art of animating a voice, not the narrower technical sense of mastering tropes and schemes – the latter were but a part of the art of voicing. Since the eighteenth century, Shakespeare has been admired above all for two things: the range of his characters and the inventiveness of his language. The two go closely together, for it was by investing so many of his dramatic persons with memorable language that Shakespeare animated more voices than did any of his contemporaries. And because he animated so many opposing voices, he has been able to speak to many later dispositions.

Prior to the new way of thinking which became possible with such twentieth-century developments as *Gestalt* psychology and quantum physics, the person who came nearest to an understanding of Shakespeare's aspectuality was John Keats, writing under the influence of William Hazlitt. For Hazlitt, the key to Shakespeare's genius was his open-mindedness, his lack of egotism, and freedom from bias, his capacity to see both sides of a question and to empathize equally with all:

> The striking peculiarity of Shakspeare's mind was its generic quality, its power of communication with all other minds – so that it contained a universe of thought and feeling within itself, and had no one peculiar bias, or exclusive excellence more than another. He was just like any other man, but that he was like all other men. He was the least of an egotist that it was possible to be. He was nothing in himself; but he was all that others were, or that they could become. He not only had in himself the germs of every faculty and feeling, but he could follow them by anticipation, intuitively, into all their conceivable ramifications, through every change of fortune or conflict of passion, or turn of thought. He had 'a mind reflecting ages past,' and present: – all the people that ever lived are there. There was no respect of persons with him. His genius shone equally on the evil and on the good, on the wise and the foolish, the monarch and the beggar.

Keats heard Hazlitt lecture to this effect and concluded that the true poet must be a chameleon, must take 'as much delight in conceiving an Iago as an Imogen'. Shakespeare refuses to swear allegiance either to the principle of reflection (call it Hamlet-in-soliloquy) or to that of improvisation (call it Iago). He was the supreme exemplar of what Keats called *negative capability*: a willingness to be content with 'half knowledge', to remain in uncertainty and doubt 'without any irritable reaching after fact and reason'. Keats regarded this quality as the necessary condition of all great art.

Negative capability is a brilliant formulation because it holds together a negative and a positive term in the exact manner of Heisenberg's 'uncertainty principle'. How can negativity be a capability, how can uncertainty be a principle? Since Keats lived in a Newtonian universe of 'fact and reason', he could only articulate negative capability as a form of scepticism which he opposed to scientific truth; he had to leave Shakespeare undecided between two possibilities. In the quantum universe, we have discovered that undecidability is the condition of scientific truth and that contraries are equally true. Light has both wave and particle aspects, though wave and particle equations are incompatible with one another; an electron has both momentum and coordinates, but both cannot be specified at the same time. Undecidability, as Empson perceived in that crucial passage of *Seven Types*, is a condition of nature, not a fallibility or predilection of the interpreting mind. In an aspectual world, *Negative capability* becomes comprehensible as a law rather than a mystery. The sonnets can be understood as both autobiographical and fictive, Hamlet can be seen as both iconic and elusive.

To simplify, we may say that 'negative' corresponds to the rabbit/Falstaff/Caliban, 'capability' to the duck/Hal/Prospero. But if we do so, we must recognize that this is indeed a simplification. The duck-rabbit is a neat icon of aspectuality, but it only has two aspects. Each of Shakespeare's plays has many more than two. Every character has a point of view, while more and more aspects are revealed through the unfolding of the action. The duck-rabbit is experienced in a moment on the page, whereas the Shakespearean drama is experienced through time in the theatre.

The law of aspectuality governs many dramatic and poetic worlds; in itself, it does not make Shakespeare unique. What is it, then, that sets Shakespeare apart from even his most talented contemporaries, that gives him his unique capacity to be reperformed again and again through history?

In chapter four, I proposed that the key gift which belonged to Shakespeare, but not to Christopher Marlowe, was experience as an actor. Faustus and Hamlet endure because each of them seems to be both himself and Everyman, both intensely individualized and an embodiment of the restless intellectual activity that is the unique mark of our species. But Faustus cuts an awkward figure when horsing around on stage; Hamlet's extra dimension is the adept role-playing which goes with his love of theatre. Marlowe's heroes never quite recognize that Everyman is a player; that is their pathos and their limitation. Shakespeare's most memorable characters are irresistibly drawn to game-playing – Richard of Gloucester's wooing of Lady Anne, Rosalind's dressing-up, Falstaff's play extempore, Hamlet's 'Mousetrap', Cleopatra's celerity in dying, and so the list goes on. That is their glory and their mobility.

In chapter five, I argued that the peculiar power of Shakespearean characterization stems from the way in which the motivations that drive his source-narratives are removed. Instead of being predetermined, identity is performed through action. At the same time, a vacuum is created in the space which belongs to motive; spectators and readers rush in to fill that vacuum, thus performing their own versions of the play. A greater variety of greatly different performances is thus possible than is the case with, say, the plays of Ben Jonson, which tend to be pre-scripted by character 'type'. Volpone is by nature cunning, whereas Falstaff is no single thing by nature but potentially everything by performance.

This suggests that the second law of the Shakespeare world is the idea of performativity itself. The performative truth of human 'being', recognized by both Shakespeare and Wittgenstein, is that being and acting are indivisible. For the later Wittgenstein, the truth of a proposition is indivisible from the language in which it is performed. For Shakespeare, 'All the world's a stage / And all the men and women merely players'. This idea had often been stated before Shakespeare, but Shakespeare did not state it, he performed it. Because the idea is performed, the force of 'merely players' is not qualifying ('only players') but absolute ('wholly players').

Wittgenstein wrote, in English, in one of his unpublished notebooks:

Suppose we ask the question: 'Are people murdered in tragedies or aren't they?' One answer is: 'In some tragedies some people are murdered and not others.' Another answer is, 'People aren't *really* murdered on the stage and they only pretend to murder and to die.' But the use of the word pretend here is again ambiguous for it may be used in the sense in which Edgar pretends to have led Gloucester to the cliff. // But you may say: oh no! Some people really die in Tragedies, e.g. Juliet at the end of the play whereas before she pretended to have died. // 'Oh no they don't pretend at all: Edgar pretends to be a peasant to lead Gloucester to the edge of the cliff [but] he is *really* Gl.'s son // Gloucester is *really* blind.' // We shall say the words 'really' 'pretend' 'die' etc. are used in a peculiar way when we talk of a play and differently in *ordinary life*. Or: the criteria for a man dying in a play aren't the same as those of his dying *in reality*. But are we *justified* to say that Lear dies at the end of the play? Why not.

'But the use of the word pretend here is again ambiguous for it may be used in the sense in which Edgar pretends to have led Gloucester to the cliff.' In the world of the play, Edgar pretends to be Poor Tom but then pretends to be a peasant who pretends to lead Gloucester up a hill to the edge of a cliff. Gloucester is really blind. In the theatre, the actor pretending to be Edgar is dressed in a different costume and uses a different voice from the ones with which he began the play; he leads another actor across the flat stage. The other actor is pretending to be blind. For the purposes of 'ordinary life', we make a choice: it is really thus (life) or it is only a pretence (theatre). But Edgar's playing transfers the choice: the pretence is that he is a peasant and that they are approaching the edge of Dover Cliff; the reality is that he is Gloucester's son and that Gloucester is blind. If Gloucester is really blind and Edgar is really Edgar, not the peasant he is pretending to be, then there is no reason why we should not say that Lear really dies at the end of the play.

Wittgenstein's remarkable meditation comes to the core of the Shakespeare-world. He has seen that 'the striking peculiarity of Shakespeare's mind' (Hazlitt's phrase) was both to make us say and to prevent us from saying, 'The words "really" "pretend" "die", etc., are used in a peculiar way when we talk of a play and differently in ordinary life.'

Another word for 'striking peculiarity of mind' would be genius. As I pointed out in my first chapter, 'genius' in Shakespeare's time meant 'particular disposition'. Many of the boldest of Shakespeare's departures from his sources were injections of *performance* or self-conscious allusions to theatre. Edgar's leading of Gloucester to the edge of Dover Cliff is based on an incident described in Sir Philip Sidney's *Arcadia*, a non-dramatic work: there is an enormous difference between the narration of a pratfall and the enactment of one. Similarly, the most telling effect of dramatizing Lodge's *Rosalynd* is that a character's cross-dressing is doubled by the cross-dressing of the actor playing that character. There is no precedent in Plutarch for the pivotal moment in *Julius Caesar* when, immediately after the stabbing, the assassins perform the dramatic ritual of smearing their hands with Caesar's blood and Cassius alludes to the future theatrical performance which the audience is witnessing – 'How many ages hence / Shall this our lofty scene be acted over, / In states unborn and accents yet unknown'. Also without a source in Plutarch is Cleopatra's 'The quick comedians / Extemporally will stage us . . . and I shall see / Some squeaking Cleopatra boy my greatness / I'th' posture of a whore' – lines spoken on the Jacobean stage by a 'boy' of the kind regarded by Puritan antagonists of the theatre as worse than whores. *The Winter's Tale*'s most striking variation of Robert Greene's *Pandosto* is Paulina and Hermione's performance of bringing a statue to life.

Among Shakespeare's most original and distinctive plays are *A Midsummer Night's Dream* and *The Tempest*, both of which contain plays within plays and dissolutions of the distinction between reality, performance, and dream:

> Methinks I see these things with parted eye,
> When everything seems double.

I have had a dream past the wit of man to say what dream it was. Man is but an ass if he go about t'expound this dream.

> These our actors,
> As I foretold you, were all spirits . . .
> . . . We are such stuff
> As dreams are made on, and our little life
> Is rounded with a sleep.

What is the peculiar disposition, the genius, which makes Shakespeare unlike any of his contemporaries? There are other dramatists among his contemporaries who wrote extraordinary poetry and brought an astonishing range of human experience to the stage. There are precedents in early Tudor dramatic 'interludes' for the idea of the play within the play; there are precedents in Lyly for the cross-dressing of the boy actor. But no other successful poet of the period was an actor through almost all his working life. No other dramatist among his English contemporaries combined so many manifestations of the figure of 'the theatre of the world'. No other writer returned so obsessively to what Borges in his fable 'Everything and Nothing' called 'the fundamental identity of existing, dreaming and acting'.

Shakespeare or . . .?

Aspectuality and performativity are ways of thinking about Shakespeare which enable us to see beyond both the traditional paradigm which locates meaning in the text and the New Iconoclasm which transfers it to the reader.

When we are children, our parents take us to a farm or a petting zoo, and we learn that a certain animal is a duck, another is a rabbit, and another is a cow. If we are then shown a drawing of a duck, we say 'duck', of a rabbit, 'rabbit', and of a cow, 'cow'. Shown a duck-rabbit, we will say either 'duck', 'rabbit', or 'now it's a duck, now it's a rabbit'. But we will not say 'cow'. The image of the duck and the image of the rabbit are both in the drawing; they have been put there by the 'author' of the drawing. Yet at the same time the drawing only becomes a 'duck' or a 'rabbit' when someone looks at it and thinks 'duck' or 'rabbit'. If someone looks at the drawing and thinks 'cow', they have not learnt the rules of the perception-game. *Henry V* is a celebration of patriotism; *Henry V* is a critique of patriotism. These aspects of the play are drawn by Shakespeare but also *drawn out* by readers, performers, and spectators of Shakespeare. A reader who says '*Henry V* is a celebration (or critique) of whatever I want it to be a celebration (or critique) of – vegetarianism, for instance' is like someone who looks at the duck-rabbit and says, 'This is a drawing of whatever I want it to be a drawing of – a cow, for instance.'

The New Iconoclasm is in error when it says, 'Like the words of which they are composed, the plays have no essential meanings.' Words have semantic range, but they also have semantic limits. The error is the result of a leap from ambiguity to radical indeterminacy. Einstein's theory of light was an explanation of the aspectuality of things, not a

recipe for unbridled scepticism; Heisenberg's principle of indetermination showed that the presence of an observer alters the observed, but it
did not call into question the very existence of the observed. 'Both/
and' does not license a free for all; that Shakespeare is changed by being
performed does not mean there is no Shakespeare. The plays do not
mean anything and everything just because they mean many things.

The meaning of a performance is to be found in the process of
performance, which requires both writer and reader, actor and spectator. The genius of Shakespeare is neither the style nor the matter of
Shakespeare; it is certainly not the wisdom that can be extracted from
Shakespeare. It is the process of Shakespeare, that which is performed
by the performance. As with the later Wittgenstein, the working
through does not *lead to a conclusion*, it *performs the point*.

The performance has two laws: aspectuality and performativity. It is
these laws which give so many of Shakespeare's games the capacity to
be played successfully in an almost infinite number of different cultural
circumstances. At the same time, there have been – and will be –
cultural circumstances in which it has been and will be impossible to
play Shakespeare's games successfully. The law of tragicomic aspectuality was not accepted in the French court theatre of the late seventeenth
century, so Shakespeare was not played there; a law against performativity was enacted in England in 1642, so Shakespeare was only rarely
performed publicly until that law was repealed eighteen years later.

Could any writer except Shakespeare have become the world-genius
of literature? If aspectuality and performativity are the prerequisites,
then the drama is the only possible form in which a world-genius can
work, since the drama is the only literary form that is fully performative
and aspectual. All good literary works are aspectual, but the drama is
fully so because it disperses the authorial voice. It allows each character
to embody a different 'aspect', each character is essential to the whole,
but only one character speaks at once and the author does not single
out any individual character/aspect as the embodiment of 'the truth'.
All literary works have to be 'performed' by their readers, but only the
drama is fully performative because it is premissed on the act of
impersonation.

The aspectual, negatively capable dramatist will be equally at home
in many different kinds: tragedy of honour, comedy of love-intrigue,
historical play. The favoured form will be one which recognizes, on

the duck-rabbit principle, the different faces of the same thing – it will therefore be a mingling of tragedy and comedy. This will also allow for a mingling of high and low: the dramatist will be equally able in the representation of all ranks of men and women; the plays will appeal equally to all ranks. The dramatist's knowledge of the performativeness of things will require some kind of Fool-figure who is simultaneously inside and outside the action, who will frequently parody the language and habits of the serious characters. Devices such as disguises and plays-within-plays will also perform performativeness. Only a writer such as this, I suggest, could have become the world-genius.

Does this prescription answer to the disposition of any writer save William Shakespeare? He has, I think, just one rival.

During the reign of King Charles II of England in the late seventeenth century, the ground was laid for the triumph of Shakespeare in world literature and Great Britain in world power. By the end of the nineteenth century, Shakespeare's world-domination was secure. The work of translation which began with August Schlegel and Ludwig and Dorothea Tieck in Germany had made this possible. Shakespeare ceased to be English and became world-historical. He was translated not only into many languages and many different national theatrical traditions, but also into many different forms: the novel, beginning with Goethe, Scott, Stendhal, and Hugo; music, pre-eminently in Berlioz and Verdi; painting, as with Fuseli; psychoanalysis, beginning from Freud. He could therefore endure, as Thomas Carlyle predicted he would, even as Britain declined: 'Indian Empire will go, at any rate, some day; but this Shakspeare does not go'.

During the reign of King Charles II of Spain in the late seventeenth century, the ground caved in beneath his nation's world power. Soon all that was left of that world power was the Spanish language, which has penetrated throughout the Americas and beyond, as English has become a world language. But because England rose and Spain declined, English has taken Shakespeare around the world whereas Spanish has not taken an author around the world, beloved as Cervantes' Don Quixote remains in high culture. Suppose that the Counter-Reformation had stamped out Protestantism or that the Spanish Armada had succeeded in 1588 or that the pattern in the time of the two Charles IIs had been reversed. Who then would have become the world-genius of literature?

When Leonard Digges went to Spain in 1611, he discovered the answer: 'our Will Shakespeare' (born 1564) would have met his match in 'their Lope de Vega' (born 1562). Lope de Vega, not Shakespeare, was the Mozart of literature. 'This monster of nature', as Cervantes called him, reportedly began writing poetry at the age of five, plays at the age of ten. Often it is asked how Shakespeare could have written so many and such varied plays. The number of them is somewhere between thirty and forty. The number of Lope de Vega's was somewhere between five hundred and eighteen hundred, of which well over three hundred survive.

Like Shakespeare, Lope was born of humble origins; his father was an embroiderer, whereas Shakespeare's was a glover. Unlike Shakespeare, he lived a life as dramatic as his plays: a string of love affairs (usually with married women), service with the Armada, ordination as a priest (which did nothing to stop the love affairs). Like Shakespeare, he wrote poetry as well as plays – but far more of it. In the sonnet form alone, he penned nearly two thousand miniature anatomies of erotic desire. Shakespeare only managed one hundred and fifty-four.

Like Shakespeare, Lope wrote for a public courtyard theatre, where performances were attended by all social classes. His characteristic form was a mingle of tragedy and comedy, high and low, the poetic voice accordingly shifting from elegance to coarseness. His sources were as varied as Shakespeare's: classical history and mythology, vernacular chronicles, ballads, folklore, Italian dramas, and novellas. He dramatized the conflicts of rulers and subjects, husbands and wives, fathers and children, rivals in love. He wrote comedies of intrigue, where identities are mistaken, entrances and exits unexpected, and women quite likely to disguise themselves in men's clothing. He wrote tragedies in which comic interludes provide both light relief and ironic comment. He wrote histories which shaped his nation's sense of its own past.

His plays embrace a vast array of characters: convicts, pimps, whores, parasites, conmen, vagrants, astrologers, gangsters, friars, hired assassins, farmers, merchants, cooks, travellers, wet-nurses, counts, dukes, princes, queens, kings, God, and the devil. His women are frequently rebellious, energetic, and courageous, whilst his men are more often on the make both sexually and socially. In all this, he has a Shakespearean myriad-mindedness.

Like Shakespeare, he was wily in his aspectuality. In *Fuenteovejuna* (written between 1612 and 1614), an entire community joins together to kill a tyrannical local lord and everyone sticks together, refusing to name the murderer. Under one aspect, this is a revolutionary play. But eventually the people are pardoned by the king: under another aspect, the drama is respectful of the mercy and judgement of the established monarchy.

Equally two-handed are the comedies of intrigue. In *El perro del hortelano* ('The dog in a manger', 1613), the countess Diana is in love with her secretary, Teodoro. She feels she cannot marry him because of their difference in status, but she is determined to prevent him from marrying anyone else. The plot is resolved by Diana's ingenious servant, Tristán (the witty 'gracioso' figure who is an equivalent to the Shakespearean clown): he persuades a nobleman that Teodoro is his long-lost son. Dramatically, this leads to a brilliant parody of a 'recognition' scene; thematically, it satisfies honour but simultaneously ridicules the demand for honour to be satisfied.

Aspectual vision is also typical of Lope's tragedies. In *El castigo sin venganza* ('Punishment without vengeance', 1631), the Duke of Ferrara's young second wife is having an affair with his illegitimate son, Federico. The Duke traps his son into unwittingly killing the stepmother he loves and thus condemning himself to death. This is punishment without revenge: Federico is put to death by due process of law, not by a carnal bloody act of private vengeance. But it is also revenge without punishment: Federico is punished for a crime which he did not intend to commit, in revenge for a crime which he did.

One respect in which Lope was unlike Shakespeare is that he actually wrote a formal manifesto for his art, *The New Art of Making Plays in this Age*. It is a wittily self-deprecatory piece of work, which recommends locking away all classical precepts and concentrating instead on pure entertainment for the masses. I've written four hundred and eighty-four plays, says Lope, and only six of them obeyed the rules (this was in 1609 – he went on churning out plays until his death in 1635). His only rule was to imitate the actions of men and paint the customs of their age. This was a traditional classical idea, but Lope saw that its consequence was the rejection of classical purity of genre:

> Tragedy mixed with comedy and Terence with Seneca, though it be
> like another minotaur of Pasiphae, will render one part grave, the

other ridiculous; for this variety causes much delight. Nature gives us good example, for through such variety it is beautiful.

With mingled action comes linguistic doubleness: 'Equivocation and the uncertainty arising from ambiguity have always held a large place among the crowd, for it thinks that it alone understands what the other one is saying.'

Above all, Lope was fascinated by the power of playing: 'Deceive the audience with the truth', he advises in *The New Art*. His *Lo fingido verdadero* ('Pretence turned truth') is among the most astonishing of all plays ever written about the performativeness of things. The Roman actor Genesius plays before the Emperor a story of his character's conversion to Christianity upon hearing the voice of an angel. In the course of the play-within-the-play, he is himself converted – at the cost of his life. He comes to see that from the perspective of eternity all of life is a play:

> God has written my cues for me,
> all my entrances and exits,
> all my acts are written in him.
> For all the world is an actor,
> and without these cues all is lost.

As performative as he is aspectual, Lope de Vega wrote plays of every kind which appealed to every rank. He answered to every element of my prescription for a world-genius in literature. But Spain went into decline and Lope was not translated. The whole of Shakespeare has been translated into scores of languages; less than ten per cent of Lope's surviving plays has ever been translated into English.

Twentieth-century physics has made the idea of the co-existence of 'alternative universes' easier to comprehend. Picture an alternative world in which Spain triumphed over England. Lope would then have triumphed over Shakespeare and I would be writing a book called *The Genius of Vega*. What do we learn from our picture? That the apotheosis of Shakespeare was and was not a matter of historical contingency. It was a contingency insofar as it happened to be Shakespeare, not Lope. But it was a necessity because the chosen one had to be a particular kind of genius and could therefore only have been Lope or Shakespeare.

. Notes

Place of publication of all works cited is London, unless otherwise stated. All Shakespearean quotations are followed by line reference to *The Complete Works*, ed. Stanley Wells and Gary Taylor (Oxford, 1986), though the text has sometimes been silently emended. All Marlowe quotations are from *Complete Plays and Poems*, ed. E. D. Pendry and J. C. Maxwell (London, 1976). Spelling is modernized in all my quotations, and all dates are given according to the year end of the New Style calendar.

1. A Life of Anecdote

page 3 'As all that is known': Quoted, Samuel Schoenbaum, *Shakespeare's Lives* (Oxford, 1970), p. 174.

page 4 PRO documents: See David Thomas, *Shakespeare in the Public Records* (1985).

page 4 Stratford documents: For a full account of all the documentary evidence, see Samuel Schoenbaum, *William Shakespeare: A Documentary Life* (Oxford, 1975). The marriage documents are held in Worcester.

page 5 'A Man's life of any worth': Journal-letter to George and Georgiana Keats, written in spring 1819. *The Letters of John Keats*, ed. H. E. Rollins, 2 vols (Cambridge, Mass., 1958), 2.67.

page 6 representative truth of anecdote: The 'anecdotal' method in literary criticism has become associated with the 'New Historicism' which seeks to read texts as manifestations of 'the circulation of social energy'. Typically, a New Historicist reading will begin with some strange nugget of information – for instance, that the Elizabethan explorer Martin Frobisher brought home a Baffin Island Eskimo to display in London – and then proceed to a politicized reading of a literary work (the Baffin Island Eskimo is transformed into Caliban). The method produces dubious history but good narrative. Ironically, given that New Historicism is premissed on the idea that texts are written less by individual authors than by the social energies of the age, the method works much better as a biographical device than a socio-historical one. The most elegant practitioner of it is Stephen Greenblatt, a biographer at heart – he first developed the method in his book on Sir Walter Ralegh (1973), which was as interested in the life as the works. The meaning of 'anecdote' as 'an amusing or striking incident' emerged specifically in the context of *gossip* in the early-eighteenth-century world of coffee house essayists and Grub Street hacks. Historians should be sceptical about gossip, but it is the spice of biography.

page 6 'I was killed i'th'Capitol': *Hamlet*, 3.2.99–102.

page 8 'I will [that the boys be] taught': Quoted, E. I. Fripp, *Shakespeare Studies* (1930), pp. 34–5; see, more generally, T. W. Baldwin, *William Shakspere's Small Latine and Lesse Greeke*, 2 vols (Urbana, Illinois, 1944).

page 10 Shakespeare's classical learning and the school syllabus: See Baldwin, *Shakspere's Small Latine*; Jonathan Bate, *Shakespeare and Ovid* (Oxford, 1993); Charles and Michelle Martindale, *Shakespeare and the Uses of Antiquity* (1990); J. A. K. Thomson, *Shakespeare and the Classics* (1952).

page 10 'the poop whereof was of gold': *Narrative and Dramatic Sources of Shakespeare*, ed. G. Bullough, 8 vols (1957–75), 5.274, spelling modernized.

page 14 'Doll, I charge thee': Gabriel Harvey, *Four Letters and certain Sonnets, especially touching Robert Greene and other parties by him abused* (1592), ed. G. B. Harrison (1922), 'The Second Letter', pp. 13, 22.

page 15 'Yes, trust them not': *Greene's Groatsworth of Wit* (1592), ed. D. A. Carroll (Binghamton, New York, 1994), pp. 84–5.

page 15 'O tiger's heart': *True Tragedy*, 1.4.138.

page 16 'in disguised array': Preface to *Menaphon* (1589), *The Works of Thomas Nashe*, ed. R. B. McKerrow, 5 vols (1910, repr. Oxford, 1958), 3.312, 323–4. Greene's usage of 'bombast' for over-swollen verse is also derived from Nashe's preface: 'swelling bombast of bragging blank verse' (p. 311). Nashe's particular object of attack seems to have been the tragedy of Thomas Kyd and the old *Hamlet* play which was in the repertoire at this time. We do not know who wrote the original lost *Hamlet*: Kyd has often been proposed, but Eric Sams has suggested that it was an early work of Shakespeare himself, which he then revised around 1600. This is pure speculation, but if it is correct, then Nashe's attack must be regarded as the first allusion to Shakespeare's work – see Sams, *The Real Shakespeare* (New Haven and London, 1995), pp. 68–72.

page 17   Henry VI Part One: Confusingly, it was probably written *after* the plays which the Folio calls *Henry VI Parts Two & Three* – the latter were originally a two-part play, *The First Part of the Contention betwixt the Two Famous Houses of York and Lancaster* and *The True Tragedy of Richard Duke of York*. They are about civil war, whereas *Henry VI Part One*, which may be regarded as a 'prequel', gains its dramatic energy from war against France.

page 17   'my self have seen': Quoted, E. K. Chambers, *William Shakespeare: A Study of Facts and Problems*, 2 vols (Oxford, 1930), 2.189.

page 21   'younger sort' and '*Friendly Shakespeare's Tragedies*': Chambers, 2.214–15.

page 22   Return from Parnassus: Quotations from *The Three Parnassus Plays*, ed. J. B. Leishman (1949). There are no explicit allusions to Shakespeare in the first of the three plays, *The Pilgrimage to Parnassus*. This vitiates Eric Sams' argument in his *The Real Shakespeare* that the character of Studioso, introduced in that play, is a portrait of Shakespeare. *The Pilgrimage* is a purely 'Cambridge' play; sustained reference to the London literary scene is an innovation in the two parts of *The Return*.

page 22   'Thrice fairer than my self': *The First Part of the Return from Parnassus*, lines 986–1001, slightly misquoting *Venus and Adonis*, 7–12.

page 22   'Now is the winter': *The Second Part of the Return from Parnassus*, lines 1838–9.

page 23   'they smell too much': *The Second Part of the Return from Parnassus*, lines 1766–72.

page 23   Titus characterized: For a full account, see the introduction to my Arden edition (1995).

page 23   'Who loves not': *The Second Part of the Return from Parnassus*, lines 301–4.

page 24   'One evening when *Richard III*': Wilkes, *General View of the Stage* (1759), pp. 220–21. Manningham in Chambers, 2.212.

page 25   'Not without mustard': *Every Man in his Humour*, act three scene one.

page 25   'sharp mustard rhyme': *The Scourge of Villainy*, book 1, poem 2.

page 26 Jonson's allusions to Shakespeare: Collected in Chambers, 2.205–10.

page 26 'A good and wise man': Jonson, *Horace, his Art of Poetry made English* (1640), lines 633–5.

page 27 'I remember the Players': *Timber: or, Discoveries*, passage repr. in Chambers, 2.210.

page 29 'Poets are born, not made': Digges, 'Upon Master William Shakespeare', repr. in Chambers, 2.232–4.

page 30 'much like the *Comedy of Errors*': Chambers, 2.327–8.

page 31 'solid but slow': Chambers, 2.245.

page 31 'Shakespeare was Godfather': Sir Nicholas L'Estrange, in Chambers, 2.243.

page 32 Borges' allegory: Borges, fable translated by James Irby in *Labyrinths: Selected Stories and other Writings* (New York, 1964), pp. 248–9.

2. SHAKESPEARE'S AUTOBIOGRAPHICAL POEMS?

page 34 Aubrey's anecdotes: Relevant extracts from Aubrey's *Brief Lives* are reprinted in E. K. Chambers, *William Shakespeare: A Study of Facts and Problems*, 2 vols (Oxford, 1930), 2.252–4.

page 35 'little Personal Story': 'Some Account of the Life, etc. of Mr William Shakespear', in *The Works of Mr William Shakespear . . . Revis'd and Corrected . . . by N. Rowe, Esq.*, 6 vols (1709), 1.i.

page 35 'He had the Honour'; 'Queen *Elizabeth*': 'Life', pp.viii–x.

page 37 'The Elizabethans wrote': John Buxton, *Sir Philip Sidney and the English Renaissance* (3rd edn, 1987), p. 22.

page 37 'It betrays more': A. W. von Schlegel, *A Course of Lectures on Dramatic Art and Literature*, trans. John Black (rev. edn, 1846), p. 352.

page 38 order of the sonnets: See in particular Katherine Duncan-Jones, 'Was the 1609 *Shake-speares Sonnets* really Unauthorized?', *Review of English Studies*, NS, 34 (1983), 151–71.

page 39 Brown's division: Charles Armitage Brown, *Shakespeare's Autobiographical Poems* (1838), pp. 46–7.

page 40 Steevens' notes: Quoted in H. E. Rollins' invaluable Variorum edition of *The Sonnets*, 2 vols (Philadelphia, 1944), 2.336–7, 1.55.

page 41   Lee on Pembroke: *DNB* entries of 1889–91 on Mary Fitton, Lady Pembroke, and William Herbert, cited in Rollins, 2.199.

page 41   'Of course Lee had': Rollins, 2.200.

page 42   'Attempts have been made': *Dictionary of National Biography*, vol. 51 (London, 1897), p. 363.

page 42   'to a large extent undertaken': *Dictionary of National Biography*, vol. 51 (New York, 1897), p. 363.

page 42   Lee's 1898 *Life*: Sidney Lee, *A Life of William Shakespeare* (1898), chaps. 8 and 10.

page 43   'William Shakespeare was almost certainly': *Shakespeare's Sonnets*, ed. Stephen Booth (New Haven, 1977), p. 548.

page 43   parody of sonneteering: Katharine Wilson, *Shakespeare's Sugared Sonnets* (New York, 1974).

page 44   'It is agreed that': Empson, *Some Versions of Pastoral* (1935), p. 89.

page 54   'complete rubbish': Rowse, introduction to 2nd edn. of *Shakespeare's Sonnets: The Problems Solved* (1973).

page 55   Florio as agent: See Frances Yates, *John Florio* (Cambridge, 1934), p. 126. That Florio actively spied on behalf of Burghley is a strong inference, not a proven fact. It is certainly the case that some years earlier Burghley's right-hand man Walsingham had placed Florio in the French Embassy, incurring the suspicion of the ambassador. The spy 'Henry Fagot' (Giordano Bruno?) reported to Walsingham a conversation in which the ambassador, Châteauneuf, said, 'What about Maître Geoffroy, the doctor? In France they say he's a double agent, works both for the Huguenots and the Pope. They don't trust Laurent or Florio much either' – John Bossy, *Giordano Bruno and the Embassy Affair* (New Haven, 1991, repr. London, 1992), p. 59.

page 56   'We need not speak so much': *Florio his Firste Fruites* (1578), p. 71, end of discourse 31. Florio's Dialogue 32 is 'upon Lust': it consists of a multiplication of epithets ('O cruel monster, O beastly rage, O infernal Fury, thou inchastest the wise, thou deceivest the wise, thou overcomest the strong, thou subduest all men unto thy yoke' etc.) which anticipates the technique of Sonnet 129 – this would be ironic indeed if the dark lady really was Florio's wife.

page 56   Daniel and patronage: In 1594, Daniel.seems to have lost the patronage of the Countess of Pembroke and to have looked for support to the Essex circle, with which Southampton had strong links. Daniel's new patrofi in 1595 was Lord Mountjoy who, like Southampton, became one of the supporters of Essex's attempted *coup d'état*.

page 56 'accounted most fair': *Florio's Second Fruites* (1591), p. 131. We must be wary of attributing the opinions of the characters in Florio's bilingual dialogue to the author himself, but it is striking that the most impassioned voice in *Second Fruits* is that of a figure in the final dialogue (pp. 157–205) who says that love of women leads to nothing but the cuckold's horns, that 'Wretched is he and most accursed that in a woman puts his trust', for 'there is nothing in the world worse than a woman' – 'O abject, filthy, and accursed sex / like purgatory made men to vex'. Woman is compared to 'whitest Lilies' that grow 'from a stinking weed' (compare the final line of Shakespeare's bitter 94th sonnet: 'Lilies that fester smell far worse than weeds') and her changeability is displayed in a rhetoric similar to that of Rosalind's witty condemnation of her sex in *As You Like It*: 'Women are in churches, Saints; abroad, Angels; at home, devils; at windows, Sirens; at doors, pies; and in gardens, goats' (p. 175).

page 57 Florio children: See Yates, *John Florio*, pp. 54, 67–8. Florio and Samuel Daniel were both in Oxford from 1579–82. The marriage with Daniel's sister took place before 1585, when Joan was christened at the church of St Peter's in the Baylie, Oxford. Unfortunately, the parish register for the years prior to 1584 is missing. Aurelia was presumably born some time between 1580 and 1585, since by 1605 she was old enough to have married one James Molins and borne Florio a grandson; it was from the Molins family that John Aubrey learned of the relationship between Florio and Daniel.

page 58 belief in Mrs Florio: These speculations are indebted to the conversation of John Harding, who believes that Florio himself wrote the works of Shakespeare. It would be ironic if the true identity of the dark lady were in fact to have been uncovered as part of an anti-Stratfordian argument.

page 60 'a partiality for the picture': Quoted in Rollins, 2.221.

page 63 Sidney or Spenser: The proposal that 'our ever-living poet' might be a dead poet was made by J. M. Nosworthy in 'Shakespeare and Mr WH', *The Library*, 5th series, 18 (1963), 294–8. Nosworthy's extremely cogent case for the possibility of WH being a misprint has barely been noticed, save by Donald W. Foster in 'Master W. H., R.I.P.', *PMLA*, 102 (1987), 42–54, who adds additional support, but makes the improbable suggestion that 'our ever-living poet' refers to God. Like most theories concerning the *Sonnets*, the misprint one was first brought forward in Victorian times, but it was too unromantic to catch on.

3. THE AUTHORSHIP CONTROVERSY

page 66 'Shake-speare': Anti-Stratfordians like to hyphenate Shakespeare's name because it appeared thus on some of his title-pages, notably that of the *Sonnets*, and they think this strengthens the case for the name being a pseudonym. But in fact this form of hyphenation was a frequent printer's vagary of the period.

page 66 plays from beyond the grave: On *Macbeth* and the Gunpowder Plot, see Garry Wills, *Witches and Jesuits: Shakespeare's 'Macbeth'* (Oxford, 1994). Lewis Theobald recognized as long ago as 1733 that *Macbeth* is a thoroughgoingly Jacobean play written after the Union of the thrones of England and Scotland and after 'King James I had begun to touch for the *Evil*' – Preface to *The Works of Shakespeare* (1733), vol.1, p.ix. The touch of King Edward the Confessor supposedly had the power to cure scrofula, alluded to at *Macbeth*, 4.3.143–59; it was not until some time after August 1605, well past Oxford's death, that James began touching sufferers and hanging a gold coin round their neck in the manner described in the play. About 750 of the words which Shakespeare used in his post-1603 plays, but not his pre-1603 works, occur in Florio's Montaigne, published that year: the obvious inference is that Shakespeare read the translation closely – see G. C. Taylor, *Shakspere's Debt to Montaigne* (Cambridge, Mass., 1925), pp. 58–66.

page 68 carefully planned five-act structure: In modern texts the distinction is less easy to see than it should be because, ever since the First Folio of 1623, editors have imposed the five-act division on *all* Shakespeare's plays.

page 70 'by the dim light of Nature': The letter was first printed in full in E. K. Chambers, *William Shakespeare: A Study of Facts and Problems*, 2 vols (Oxford, 1930), 2.224–5.

page 70 Camden and Dethick: See Chambers, *William Shakespeare*, 2.22.

page 70 'the most pregnant wits': *Remains* (published 1605, but preface dated 1603), section on 'Poems', p. 8.

page 71 '*Players*, I love ye': *Microcosmos* (1603), p. 215.

page 71 'Teste W. Shakespea': See Charles Pennel, 'The Authenticity of the *George a Greene* Title-page Inscriptions', *Journal of English and Germanic Philology*, 64 (1965), 668–76. The play was printed in 1599; Buc was associated with the Revels Office from 1603. See further, an article on Buc's manuscript notes by Alan Nelson, forthcoming in *Shakespeare Quarterly*. I am grateful to Professor Nelson for sharing with me his research on Buc, whose manuscript notes on several play quartos provide hard evidence that Shakespeare was both player and dramatist.

page 72 'our Will Shakespeare': Digges' note is reproduced in Paul Morgan, '"Our Will Shakespeare" and Lope de Vega: An Unrecorded Contemporary Document', *Shakespeare Survey*, 16 (1963), pp. 118–20.

page 75 'degraded to the bottom of the page': Pope, Preface to *The Works of Shakespear*, 6 vols (1725), 1.xxii.

page 76 'unanimous Applause . . . too sincere': *The Weekly Journal: or the British Gazetteer*, 10 February 1728.

page 76 'See! T—': *Gentleman's Magazine*, November 1731; also published in the *Grub Street Journal*, 18 November 1731.

page 77 'GEORGE THE SECOND': *Double Falsehood*, ed. Walter Graham (Cleveland, Ohio, 1920), p. 26.

page 78 'fewer Flaws': Preface of the Editor, *Double Falsehood*, p. 29.

page 78 good imitation: For this argument, see Harriet C. Frazier, *A Babble of Ancestral Voices: Shakespeare, Cervantes, and Theobald* (The Hague, 1974), chap. 6.

page 78 features resembling Fletcher: See Gamaliel Bradford Jr., 'The History of Cardenio by Mr Fletcher and Shakespeare', *Modern Language Notes*, 25 (1910), 51–6.

page 80 plays included in Theobald's reading edition: These were restricted to those of the First Folio: *Double Falsehood* was thus excluded for the same reason as *Pericles*.

page 80 '*The History of Cardenio*': In 1995 Charles Hamilton published an edition of a Jacobean tragedy purporting to be Shakespeare and Fletcher's *Cardenio*, but that play is in fact by Thomas Middleton and is generally known to scholars as *The Second Maiden's Tragedy*.

page 82 'Every thing, Sir': George Hardinge, *Chalmeriana: or a Collection of Papers literary and political* (1800), p. 20.

page 83 Malone's 1790 edition: For Malone's importance in the shift from anecdote towards historical 'authenticity' in the scholarship of the later eighteenth century, and its ideological motivation, see Margreta de Grazia, *Shakespeare Verbatim: The Reproduction of Authenticity and the 1790 Apparatus* (Oxford, 1991).

page 85 'And with rude laughter': *Vortigern, An Historical Tragedy, in Five Acts; represented at the Theatre Royal, Drury Lane, on Saturday, April 2, 1796* (1799), p. 64.

page 85 'Thys Letterre': Quoted, Malone, *An Inquiry into the Authenticity of Certain Miscellaneous Papers and Legal Instruments* (1796), p. 26.

page 86 'urged, partly by the world': W. H. Ireland, *An Authentic Account of the Shaksperian Manuscripts, &c.* (1796), p. 9.

page 87 'has been dependent': Grafton, *Forgers and Critics: Creativity and Duplicity in Western Scholarship* (Princeton, 1990), p. 123.

page 87 Malone's idealizing, royalist view: On this, and its relation to the politics of the 1790s, see the more detailed discussion of the Ireland affair in my essay 'Faking it: Shakespeare and the 1790s', *Essays and Studies 1993: Literature and Censorship*, ed. Nigel Smith, pp. 63–80 (of which I have made some use here).

page 88 'The abundance of the contemporary': Sidney Lee, *A Life of William Shakespeare* (1898), p. 373.

page 88 painstaking work of refutation: The best such refutation is that of Irvin Leigh Matus, *Shakespeare, in Fact* (New York, 1994). Matus came from outside the academic Shakespeare establishment and began from a position of agnosticism, but ended up demolishing every pro-Oxford argument.

page 89 'Seas ill said': Connelly, *The Great Cryptogram* (Chicago, New York, and London, 1888), pp. 718–19.

page 91 'Hence it is': Samuel Ireland, *An Investigation of Mr Malone's Claim to the Character of Scholar, or Critic* (1797 or 1798), p. 87.

page 91 'The privy-council': Alexander Chalmers, *An Apology for the Believers in the Shakspeare-Papers* (1797), pp. 186n., 410.

page 93 'It is offensive': Amphlett, *Who was Shakespeare? A New Enquiry* (1955), p.xiii.

page 93 'to preserve them pure': Malone, *Inquiry into the Authenticity*, p. 2.

page 94 logical extreme of Anti-Stratfordianism: *The Autobiography of*

Malcolm X (New York, 1966), p. 185. On Sweet, see Schoenbaum, *Shakespeare's Lives*, pp. 626–7, to which my account of Anti-Stratfordian heresies is much indebted.

page 95 'The solution': *'Shakespeare' Identified* (1920), p. 5.

page 96 'removed to an excellent': Theodore Bacon, *Delia Bacon: A Biographical Sketch* (1888), p. 312.

page 97 haunted by the thought: On the authorship question and the uncanny, see chapter one of Marjorie Garber's *Shakespeare's Ghost Writers* (1987).

page 97 Freud's submission to the Looney hypothesis: See the chapter on Freud in Bloom's *The Western Canon: The Books and School of the Ages* (New York, 1994), which offers a Shakespearean reading of Freud that is superior to all Freudian readings of Shakespeare. The greatest literary fantasia on Hamlet and the ghost of his father in relation to Shakespeare's life and the name of his son is the debate between Stephen Dedalus and Buck Mulligan in the National Library scene of James Joyce's *Ulysses*, on which Bloom also has a dancing chapter.

page 98 handwriting in scene of *More*: The characteristics shared by 'Hand D' in *Sir Thomas More* and Shakespeare's known signatures were brilliantly argued for by Sir Edward Maunde Thompson in his contribution to *Shakespeare's Hand in the Play of 'Sir Thomas More'*, papers by A. W. Pollard, W. W. Greg, et al. (Cambridge, 1923), a book dedicated to the proposition 'that the writing of the three pages [of the 'ill May Day scene'] is compatible with a development into the hand seen in Shakespeare's considerably later extant signatures and explains misprints in his text; that the spelling of the three pages can all be paralleled from the text of the best editions of single plays printed in Shakespeare's life; and that the temper and even the phrasing of the three pages in the two crucial points involved, the attitude to authority and the attitude to the crowd, agree with and render more intelligible passages in much later plays' (p.v). For supporting evidence and discussion, see *Shakespeare and 'Sir Thomas More': Essays on the Play and its Shakespearian Interest*, ed. T. H. Howard-Hill (Cambridge, 1989).

page 98 'Peace, hear me! . . . For to the King': Addition II.D, 1–4, 110–18. For an annotated text of the whole play, see *Sir Thomas More*, ed. Vittorio Gabrieli and Giorgio Melchiori (Manchester, 1990).

4. Marlowe's Ghost

page 102   Zeigler, *It Was Marlowe*: Chicago, 1895.

page 102   Hoffman, *The Murder*: New York, 1955. More recent scholarship has shown that the widow Bull's dwelling, where Marlowe was killed, was not in fact a public house, but in the public perception his death was linked to a tavern because it occurred as a result of a quarrel over a bill or 'reckoning'. See William Urry, *Christopher Marlowe and Canterbury* (1988), pp. 83–6.

page 104   'strong misreading . . . prime precursor': Bloom, *The Anxiety of Influence: A Theory of Poetry* (New York, 1973), pp. 93, 94, 11.

page 106   'Imagine for a moment': Garber, 'Marlovian Vision/Shakespearean Revision', *Research Opportunities in Renaissance Drama*, 22 (1979), 3–9 (p. 3). Despite this wonderfully promising opening, the essay turns out to be no more than an outline sketch of one particular relationship, that between *Tamburlaine* and *Henry V*.

page 107   precise chronology of the early plays does not matter: This said, one needs a working chronology. What follows is an approximate one, though this cannot be the place to argue the case for it. For Marlowe: *Dido Queen of Carthage* (1586, probably in collaboration with Nashe), *1 & 2 Tamburlaine* (1587, based on the assumption that a shooting accident at the Rose Theatre that year was in a performance of part two), *Dr Faustus* (1588–9), *The Jew of Malta* (1590), *The Massacre at Paris* (1591), *Edward II* (1592). It is often assumed that Marlowe's major poem, *Hero and Leander*, was written in early 1593, when the theatres were closed, but I strongly suspect that Marlowe started it before then, and that it would have been known in manuscript (or at least known about) by Shakespeare. Thomas Lodge initiated the vogue for erotic Ovidian narrative poetry in 1589, and I don't think Marlowe would have waited four years to have a go himself, especially if he had already undertaken his translation of Ovid's *Amores* whilst still at Cambridge. For Shakespeare (those works treated in this chapter): *The First Part of the Contention* and *The True Tragedy* (1589–91), *1 Henry VI* (1592), *Venus and Adonis* (1593), *Sonnets* begun (1593), *The Rape of Lucrece* (late 1593), *Titus Andronicus* (late 1593 to early 1594), *Richard III* (1594), *Richard II* (1595), *Romeo and Juliet* (1596), *The Merchant of Venice* (1596), *1 & 2 Henry IV* (1597–8), *The Merry Wives of Windsor* (1598), *Henry V* (1599), *Julius Caesar* (1599), *As You Like It* (1599), *Hamlet* (1600),

Macbeth (1606), *Antony and Cleopatra* (1607), *The Tempest* (1611). I have no idea of the date of *The Two Gentlemen of Verona*, but it is usually assumed to be one of Shakespeare's earliest plays. The surviving text of *Titus Andronicus* belongs to early 1594, but it *may* be a revision of an earlier version of the play by Shakespeare and/or another dramatist.

page 108 opens where *Tamburlaine* closes: In an excellent study, *Rival Playwrights: Marlowe, Jonson, Shakespeare* (New York, 1991), James Shapiro argues (pp. 86–7) that this is where *Henry VI Part One* begins: he sees the funeral of Henry V and the language of hanging the heavens with black as deliberate echoes of *Tamburlaine*.

page 109 'fond and frivolous gestures': Printer's epistle to 1590 edition of the two parts of *Tamburlaine the Great*.

page 109 'Thou hast most traitorously': *First Part of the Contention*, 4.7.30–35.

page 111 *splitting* in *Henry VI Part One*: There is no evidence that there was any such thing as a *three*-part history play in the early 1590s. The three-parter was, I suggest, invented by Shakespeare in *Henry IV/Henry V*; it established a model which gave the compilers of the First Folio the idea of calling the three *Henry VI* plays parts one to three – they do not have that appellation prior to the Folio. I take *The First Part of the Contention* and *The True Tragedy* to be one of the many two-part plays that followed in the wake of *Tamburlaine, Part 1* to be an independent play, probably written later, possibly collaborative, almost certainly the *Harey the sixth* marked in Henslowe's diary as 'ne' (new?) on 3 March 1592, unquestion-ably the hit play of brave Talbot alluded to by Thomas Nashe in his *Pierce Penniless his Supplication to the Devil* (August 1592). Whilst I do not wish to apply a psychoanalytic straitjacket to the Marlowe/Shakespeare relation-ship, I have taken the term *splitting* from Melanie Klein's idea of splitting in infantile psychological development.

page 111 ten thousand spectators: Nashe, *Pierce Penniless*, sig.f3.

page 113 'Was this the face': *Dr Faustus*, 5.1.99–105. The first critic to discuss the significance of this link was Nicholas Brooke in 'Marlowe as provocative agent in Shakespeare's early plays', *Shakespeare Survey*, 14 (1970), 34–44.

page 115 catalogues of villainy: *Titus*, 5.1.124–44; *Jew*, 2.3.176–214.

page 115 'Olympus' top': *Titus*, 2.1.1–24; *Tamburlaine Part 1*, 1.2.100; *Dr Faustus*, 1st Chorus.

page 117 'The thirst of reign': *Tamburlaine Part 1*, 2.7.12–29. This passage sows a seed not only for Shakespeare but also for Marlowe himself: it is surely the first intimation of *Faustus*. The link with Richard of Gloucester is well discussed by Shapiro, *Rival Playwrights*, p. 95.

page 119 'Hamlet has no sooner': Trilling, *Sincerity and Authenticity* (1972), p. 13.

page 120 links between *Henry V* and *Tamburlaine*: See further, Shapiro, p. 100.

page 123 'Who ever loved': *As You Like It*, 3.5.82–3; *Hero and Leander*, 1.176.

page 123 'a little room': *As You Like It*, 3.3.11–12; *Jew of Malta*, 1.1.37. The term *The Reckoning* gave Charles Nicholl the title for his wonderful book on Marlowe's death (1992), which includes a discussion of the possible allusions in *As You Like It* (pp. 72–5).

page 123 cluster of Marlovian allusions: In addition, Touchstone compares his dilemma as a sophisticated courtier among simple country folk to that of Ovid among the Goths. The Elizabethans believed that the sophisticated Roman poet Ovid was exiled to the land of the barbaric Getes because of the scandal caused by his books of love, the *Amores* and *Ars Amatoria*. As Shakespeare was writing *As You Like It* came the news that Marlowe's own translation of Ovid's *Amores* was to be banned and burned by Bishops' order. The association between Ovid and Marlowe gains corroboration from Ben Jonson's play, *Poetaster*, performed soon after, in which the character of Ovid actually delivers on stage a very slightly adapted version of one of Marlowe's translations from the *Amores*.

page 123 *The Massacre at Paris*: I assume here that *The Massacre* is a late Marlowe play. If it is not, then Marlowe must be credited for first staging the 'murder of the writer' trope which so haunts Shakespeare.

page 127 parody of Barabas: Though this is complicated by the way in which *The Jew* is a tragedy which parodies the 'high' tone of tragedy (that parody is one of its chief idioms is clear from the fact that the character of Ithamore parodies Marlowe's own most famous poem, 'The Passionate Shepherd' – 4.2.102): the play is actually more complex and sophisticated than Shakespeare allows it to be, but then the suppression of the precursor-text's complexity is implicit in the art of 'strong misreading' by means of which the inheritor overcomes it.

page 128 Pyrrhus passages: Compare the whole of *Dido*, 2.1.210–88, and *Hamlet*, 2.2.452–99.

page 129 'I'll drown'; 'I'll burn': *Tempest*, 5.1.57; *Faustus*, 5.2.191.

5. SHAKESPEARE'S PECULIARITY

page 133 'Great men': 'Shakspeare, or the Poet' in *Representative Men* (lecture of 1846), *The Collected Works of Ralph Waldo Emerson*, vol. 4, ed. W. E. Williams and D. E. Wilson (Cambridge, Mass., 1987), p. 109.

page 135 *Diana Enamorada*: Montemayor's *Diana* was not published in English translation until 1598, several years after the probable date of composition of *Two Gentlemen*. Scholars who assume that Shakespeare read it have to suppose that he had enough Spanish to read the original, or that he got hold of a French translation which was available, or that he saw Bartholomew Yonge's English version in manuscript some years before it was published. Neither the second nor the third possibility is utterly implausible, but it seems to me much more likely that his inspiration was the earlier dramatization of the Felismena story performed by the Queen's Men. The parallels are of plot, not of verbal detail.

page 136 Shakespearean comedy grew from Lyly: Valuable accounts of Lyly's influence on Shakespeare are provided by G. K. Hunter, *John Lyly: The Humanist as Courtier* (Cambridge, Mass., 1962), Marco Mincoff, 'Shakespeare and Lyly', *Shakespeare Survey*, 14 (1961), 15–24, and Leah Scragg, *The Metamorphoses of Gallathea: A Study in Creative Adaptation* (Washington, DC, 1982).

page 138 falling into the love-trap: Lyly, *Gallathea* (performed about 1584, published 1592), act three scene one.

page 139 'tradition supplies': Emerson, 'Shakspeare, or the Poet', p. 113.

page 140 'A natural perspective': *Twelfth Night*, 5.1.214.

page 141 'Rosalynd and Alinda watch themselves': Brian Nellist, introduction to Thomas Lodge, *Rosalynd* (Keele, Staffs., 1995), p. 16.

page 143 '"You may see," quoth Ganymede': Lodge, *Rosalynd*, ed. Nellist, p. 49.

page 144 'that willing suspension': Coleridge, *Biographia Literaria* (1817), chap. 14.

page 145 'There were six of us': trans. Richard Freeborn, in Turgenev, *First Love and other Stories* (Oxford, 1989), p. 203.

page 145 a woman travelling alone: See the story of Apolonius and Silla in Barnabe Riche, *Riche his Farewell to the Military Profession*, repr. in

Geoffrey Bullough, *Narrative and Dramatic Sources of Shakespeare* (8 vols, 1957–75), 2.349–50.

page 145 'where they two in private': Greene, *Pandosto*, in Bullough, *Narrative and Dramatic Sources*, 8.158.

page 146 Lennox, *Shakespear Illustrated*: 2 vols, 1753; a third vol. added, 1754.

page 146 'much less absurd': Lennox, *Shakespear Illustrated* (1753), 2.75.

page 147 'a firm, indubitable conviction': L. N. Tolstoy, 'Shakespeare and the Drama', trans. V. Tchertkoff, repr. in *Shakespeare in Europe*, ed. Oswald LeWinter (Cleveland, Ohio, 1963), p. 225. Quotations in next paragraphs from pp. 256, 246–7, 250.

page 149 Albany: *King Lear* (Folio text), 5.3.231, 274–6.

page 149 'Human life'; 'strange': 'Shakespeare and the Drama', pp. 282, 237.

page 149 foreshadowed his own tragic ending: The resemblance between late Tolstoy and the Lear he despised have been discussed in a marvellous essay by George Orwell, 'Lear, Tolstoy and the Fool', in his collection, *Shooting an Elephant* (1950), and some fine pages in Harold Bloom's *The Western Canon* (pp. 57–9).

page 150 'Sincerity': 'Shakespeare and the Drama', p. 269.

page 151 Samurai remaking: Kurosawa, *Ran* (Greenwich Film Productions, Paris, and Nipon Herald Films, Tokyo, 1985).

page 151 'However unnatural': 'Shakespeare and the Drama', p. 260. Subsequent quotation from pp. 260–61.

page 152 Lear; Macduff: *Lear*, 5.3.285, *Macbeth*, 4.3.212–18.

page 152 'Great genial power': Emerson, 'Shakspeare', pp. 109–10.

6. THE ORIGINAL GENIUS

page 157 Shakespeare's vocabulary: The *Harvard Concordance to Shakespeare* lists thirty thousand words, but this includes singulars and plurals, inflected verb forms, etc.

page 165 *Plays*, 1647: I use the name 'Beaumont and Fletcher' as convenient shorthand for the plays in the 1647 Folio of works attributed to that pair of dramatists; in fact, many of them were either by Fletcher alone or Fletcher and another collaborator, most frequently Philip Massinger.

page 166 'Shakespear was one ... If Shakespear': Dennis, *An Essay on the Genius and Writings of Shakespear* (1712), pp. 1, 3–4.

page 167 'who by the mere Strength': *The Spectator*, no.160, quoted from the edition of D. F. Bond, 5 vols (Oxford, 1965).

page 168 'Shakespeare is a wonderful Genius': Quoted from *Shakespeare: The Critical Heritage 1623–1801*, ed. Brian Vickers, 6 vols (1974–81), 2.215.

page 168 'the Genius of our Isle': 'An Epistle to Mr. Southerne', *Critical Heritage*, 2.265.

page 169 nationalism and Francophobia: On this, see Gerald Newman, *The Rise of English Nationalism* (1987) and Linda Colley, *Britons: Forging the Nation, 1707–1837* (New Haven, 1992).

page 169 'It may be true': Berlin, 'Nationalism: Past Neglect and Present Power', in his *Against the Current: Essays in the History of Ideas* (New York, 1980), p. 346.

page 170 'True Poesy is magic': Maurice Morgann, *An Essay on the Dramatic Character of Sir John Falstaff* (1777), p. 71.

page 172 'Great Wits': Pope, *An Essay on Criticism* (1711), lines 152–5.

page 173 'refined the language'; 'imagination gave way': Johnson, 'Dryden', *Lives of the English Poets* (1779–81, repr. 1906), 1.305; T. Warton, *Observations on the Faerie Queene* (1754), quoted from 2nd edn (1762), 2.111.

page 173 'we know, in spite of Mr. R—': Dryden, 'Letter to John Dennis', *Of Dramatic Poesy and other Critical Essays*, ed. George Watson, 2 vols (1962), 2.178.

page 174 'Those scatter'd Sparks': Gildon, *The Complete Art of Poetry* (1718), *Critical Heritage*, 2.322–3.

page 174 'In my style I have professed': Dryden, *Of Dramatic Poesy*, 1.231. The word 'force', with its suggestions of superhuman strength and perhaps of a divine force that takes over the poet, frequently recurs in discussions of Shakespeare's original genius.

page 175 Charmian's death: T. S. Eliot, 'Dryden the Dramatist', *The Listener*, 22 April 1931, p. 681.

page 175 'Few things in Shakespear': *The Complete Works of William Hazlitt*, ed. P. P. Howe, 21 vols (1930–34), 4.229.

page 176 'Shakespeare is above all writers': Johnson's Preface of 1765, *Critical Heritage*, 5.57, 60–61.

page 176 Cavendish: Margaret Cavendish, Duchess of Newcastle, *CCXI Sociable Letters* (1664), letter CXXIII.

page 177 'What are the lays': Joseph Warton, *The Enthusiast*, lines 168–75, in *Critical Heritage*, 3.121.

page 178 'By degrees, the mind': Akenside, *The Pleasures of Imagination* (1744), bk.3, lines 380–85, quoted from *The Poetical Works of Mark Akenside* (1845).

page 179 'he was surprized': James Boswell, *The Journal of a Tour to the Hebrides with Samuel Johnson* (1785), entry for Thursday, 30th September.

page 179 'Learning we thank': Edward Young, *Conjectures on Original Composition* (1759), pp. 36–7. Subsequent quotations from pp. 34, 29, 81, 78, 26–7.

page 181 the grand, the terrible, the melancholy: 'das Artige, das Zärtliche, das Verliebte'; 'das Grosze, das Schreckliche, das Melancholische' – Gotthold Ephraim Lessing, *Werke*, 8 vols (München, 1973), 5.71.

page 182 'the darling genius': *Briefe über Merkwürdigkeiten der Literatur*, ed. Alexander von Weilen (Heilbronn, 1890), p. 121.

page 182 'to explain him, feel him': *The Romantics on Shakespeare*, ed. Jonathan Bate (1992), p. 39. Subsequent quotations from pp. 40, 48.

page 183 Goethe's own innate genius: See further, Michael Beddow, 'Goethe on Genius', in *Genius: The History of an Idea*, ed. Penelope Murray (Oxford, 1989), pp. 98–9. My first attempt at an analysis of 'Shakespeare and Original Genius', from which I have drawn some material here, is published in the same book.

page 184 'an analogue of the unduplicatibility': McFarland, 'The Originality Paradox', in his *Originality and Imagination* (Baltimore, 1985), p. 5.

page 184 'the commonwealth of letters': Hazlitt, 'On the Aristocracy of Letters', *Works*, 8.208. For Hazlitt the domain of letters is like a democratic republic in that positions in it are not predetermined by birth or rank, but like an aristocracy in the Greek sense that it values *aristos*, the best.

page 184 'the creative, and self-sufficing power'; 'a man speaking to men': Coleridge, *Biographia Literaria*, ed. James Engell and W. Jackson

Bate, *The Collected Works of Samuel Taylor Coleridge* vol. 7 (in 2 vols),
(Princeton, 1983), 1.31; Wordsworth, 1802 addition to Preface to *Lyrical
Ballads*, as paraphrased by David Bromwich, 'Reflections on the Word
Genius', in his *A Choice of Inheritance: Self and Community from Edmund
Burke to Robert Frost* (Cambridge, Mass., 1989), p. 27.

page 185   nationalism in the eighteenth century: On this, see Benedict
Anderson, *Imagined Communities: Reflections on the Origin and Spread of
Nationalism* (1983).

page 185   'A foreign greatness': Ralph Waldo Emerson, *Representative
Men* (1850, repr. in *Essays and Representative Men*, 1904), p. 370.

7. THE NATIONAL POET

page 187   'The relations which hold society': Speech printed under the
heading 'Poison of a new British Disease', *The Independent on Sunday*, 16
January 1994, p. 2, quoting *Troilus and Cressida*, 1.3.101–18.

page 188   'justice resides': 'recides' in the early texts: most editors emend
to 'resides', but the Latinate 'recides' meaning 'falls back, falls down' is
possible – and equally suggestive that 'justice' is an unstable, problematic
idea.

page 190   Alice Walker and Shakespeare: 'Eng Lit Students learn to get
by without Shakespeare', *The Sunday Telegraph*, 2 February 1992, p. 1.

page 190   The New Iconoclast argument: This story is told in books like
Gary Taylor's *Reinventing Shakespeare* (1989), Michael Dobson's *The
Making of the National Poet* (Oxford, 1992), Margreta de Grazia's *Shakespeare
Verbatim: The Reproduction of Authenticity and the 1790 Apparatus* (Oxford,
1991), Hugh Grady's *The Modernist Shakespeare* (Oxford, 1991), Terence
Hawkes' *That Shakespeherian Rag* (1986) and *Meaning by Shakespeare* (1992),
and, with a supporting American inflection, Michael Bristol's *Shakespeare's
America, America's Shakespeare* (1990). Although I disagree with its main
line of argument, Gary Taylor's book has been an especially valuable
stimulus to me.

page 192   Hawkes on Bradley and Raleigh: 'A Sea-Shell' and 'Swisser-
Swatter', both repr. in *That Shakespeherian Rag*.

page 192   'Is Literature gossip'; 'Life in the process': *The Letters of Sir
Walter Raleigh (1879–1922)*, ed. Lady Raleigh, 2 vols (1926), 1.142, 147.

page 193   'I have just been asked to examine': *Letters*, 1.179.

page 194   'A small British expeditionary force': Raleigh, quoted in *That Shakespeherian Rag*, pp. 63–4.

page 195   'The Age of Elizabeth': *Shakespeare's England*, 2 vols (Oxford, 1916), vol. 1, p. 1.

page 195   'Thee, SHAKESPEARE, to-day': *Shakespeare's England*, vol. 1, p. xxii.

page 196   Shakespeare in German propaganda: See Balz Engler, 'Shakespeare in the Trenches', *Shakespeare Survey*, 44 (1992), pp. 105–11.

page 197   Gollancz: *Shakespeare Tercentenary Observance in the Schools and other Institutions* (1916), pp. 11, 15.

page 198   'is put into the mouth': *Shakespeare's England*, vol.1, pp. 9–10.

page 198   *Faber Book of English History in Verse*: Quotations from pp. 70, 75, 163, 171.

page 201   'Henry, because he did not know': *Characters of Shakespear's Plays* (1817), repr. in *The Romantics on Shakespeare*, ed. Jonathan Bate (1992), p. 364.

page 202   'This is an anthology': Preface to *This England* (Oxford, 1915).

page 202   'a system of vast circumferences': Thomas, from the essay 'England' in his *The Last Sheaf*, repr. in *A Language not to be Betrayed: Selected Prose of Edward Thomas*, ed. Edna Longley (Manchester, 1981), p. 231.

page 204   'a clear stage was needed': Raleigh, *William Shakespeare*, English Men of Letters (1907), pp. 189–90.

page 204   'we never could forgive': *Romantics on Shakespeare*, p. 360.

page 205   'Well, fare thee well': *2 Henry IV*, 2.4.386–8.

page 205   Falstaff's Arthurian quotations: *2 Henry IV*, 2.4.32–4; *Henry V*, 2.3.9–10. See further, A. D. Nuttall, in his wonderful reading of Hal and Falstaff in *A New Mimesis: Shakespeare and the Representation of Reality* (1983), p. 152: 'Falstaff, who cannot get on with live King Henry, is on the best of terms with dead King Arthur. If a sense of England as a ruined Arcadia or Eden survives at all in *Henry IV* it is because of Falstaff. This comes partly from the language of the Falstaff scenes with its preference for immemorial, rustic ways of measuring time'.

page 207   Protestant Harry: In an excellent essay called 'Why is Falstaff Fat?' (*Review of English Studies*, 47 [1996], 1–22), David Womersley argues that Shakespeare made his version of Sir John Oldcastle a fat and indulgent vice-figure instead of a lean and sober martyr in order to hold up King Harry instead of the historical Oldcastle as the true exemplar of Protestant virtue. I am, however, less convinced than Womersley that the plays unequivocally endorse Harry and the Protestant way.

page 208 'We wish Henry a glorious': Bradley, 'The Rejection of Falstaff', in his *Oxford Lectures on Poetry* (1909, repr. 1965), pp. 260, 262.

page 208 'Would I were in an alehouse': *Henry V*, 3.2.12–13.

page 209 'he dies where he lived': Morgann, *An Essay on the Dramatic Character of Sir John Falstaff* (1777), p. 21.

page 209 'The goodness is in Lob': *Selected Letters of Robert Frost*, ed. Lawrance Thompson (1965), p. 164.

page 209 'Lob': Thomas's poems are quoted from *Collected Poems*, ed. R. George Thomas (Oxford, 1978, repr. 1981).

page 210 'When icicles hang': *Love's Labour's Lost*, 5.2.898–900.

page 210 'idol Ceremony': *Henry V*, 4.1.235–7.

page 211 'One man said to me': *A Language not to be Betrayed*, p. 229.

page 212 Feeble and Bates: *2 Henry IV*, 3.2.232–6; *Henry V*, 4.1.113–16; quoted, *The Middle Parts of Fortune* (1929; repr., 1977), pp. 1, 198.

page 212 'the fundamental necessities': *Middle Parts of Fortune*, p. 50. Subsequent quotations from pp. 156, 193–4.

page 214 'I say *self*-educated': *The Life of Thomas Cooper written by himself* (edn of 1875), p. 43. Subsequent quotations from pp. 34, 43, 134, 163, 228.

page 215 'The young spring morn': *Cooper's Journal*, no. 21, week ending 25 May 1850, p. 328.

8. ALL THE WORLD HIS STAGE

page 218 'fair vestal': *A Midsummer Night's Dream*, 2.1.158. See the extraordinary range of allegorical interpretations in the relevant note to H. H. Furness's New Variorum edition of the play (Philadelphia, 1895), pp. 75–91.

page 222 'a play that deals with crises': Müller, translated by Manfred Pfister in *Shakespeare in the New Europe*, ed. Michael Hattaway, Boika

Sokolova, and Derek Roper (Sheffield, 1994), p. 76. My examples here are taken from the essays in this collection which are devoted to twentieth-century Eastern European readings of the plays. An earlier version of some of this chapter appeared under the title 'Shakespearean Nationhoods' in both this collection and *Shakespeare e la sua eredità . . .*, ed. G. Caliumi (Parma, 1993).

page 223 'When to dark doubts': *A Book of Homage to Shakespeare* (Oxford, 1916), p. 237. Subsequent quotations from pp. 552, 339, 228.

page 225 'There is no European nation': *Waverley*, ed. Claire Lamont (Oxford, 1981), p. 340. All quotations from this edition.

page 227 'Scott's greatness': Lukács, *The Historical Novel* (1937), trans. Hannah and Stanley Mitchell (1962), p. 35.

page 228 'Through some odd process': 'Sir Walter Scott', in *The Spirit of the Age*, in Hazlitt's *Complete Works*, 11.64. Hazlitt also wrote an essay differentiating between Scott and Shakespeare on the grounds that the novelist is bound to historical accidentals ('the levers of custom', 'quaint, old-fashioned dresses', 'grotesque backgrounds or rusty armour'), whereas Shakespeare proceeds from historical particulars to human essentials (*Complete Works*, 12.340–1). This relates to my argument that Shakespeare realized the accidentals – and Scott learnt from this – but in proceeding to the essentials, to larger patterns, he provided a model which could be applied to the accidentals of later ages.

page 228 'confident against the world'; 'all air and fire': *Waverley*, p. 264; *1 Henry IV*, 5.1.116–17; *Henry V*, 3.7.21 (actually *'pure* air and fire').

page 230 'the modern sense of honor': Welsh, *The Hero of the Waverley Novels* (New Haven, 1963), pp. 208–9.

page 230 Scott's Burkean Shakespeare: For another account of Scott's Shakespeare in relation to conservative nationalism, with a particular emphasis on *Woodstock*, see Nicola J. Watson, 'Kemble, Scott, and the Mantle of the Bard', in *The Appropriation of Shakespeare*, ed. Jean Marsden (Hemel Hempstead, 1991), pp. 73–92.

page 230 'English drama': Peter Raby, *'Fair Ophelia': A Life of Harriet Smithson Berlioz* (Cambridge, 1982), pp. 46–7. For 'lieutenant de Welling-ton', some accounts have 'aide de camp de Wellington' – see Roger Fayolle's introduction to Stendhal's *Racine et Shakespeare* (Paris, 1970), p. 23.

page 230 'To write tragedies': Heading to chap. 1 in Stendhal, *Racine et*

Shakespeare (1823), my trans. Stendhal's 'errements' suggests 'vagaries' as well as 'ways'.

page 231 'Shakespeare *is* drama': Preface to *Cromwell*, in Hugo, *Théâtre Complet I*, Bibliothèque de la Pléiade (Paris, 1963), p. 422. My trans.

page 232 'I come now to the supreme': *The Memoirs of Hector Berlioz*, trans. David Cairns (1969), p. 95. Berlioz always called Harriet Smithson 'Henriette'. The evening after *Hamlet*, she played Juliet. See my next chapter for Berlioz' response to that role.

page 233 'The first page of his': 'Oration on Shakspeare', trans. in G. H. Lewes, *The Life and Works of Goethe* (2 vols, 1855; Everyman repr., n.d.), p. 94.

page 233 'I was finishing': *Memoirs*, p. 131. The quotation is from Auguste Barbier.

page 234 'The scaffold, the judges': Berlioz, *Lélio or the Return to Life: Lyric Monodrama Opus 14b* (printed for 1855 Weimar performance, repr. New York, 1975), p. 2. My trans.

page 235 'I want to go away': *Lélio*, p. 23.

page 235 'Why reflect? . . . may SHAKESPEARE': *Lélio*, pp. 62–3.

page 235 'For the first time': André Maurois, *Olympio: La Vie de Victor Hugo*, trans. Gerard Hopkins (1956), p. 474.

page 236 'I shall translate Shakespeare': Hugo, *William Shakespeare*, trans. Melville B. Anderson (1886, repr. Freeport, New York, 1970), p. 7.

page 236 'The poet of England': My trans., from editorial commentary in *Oeuvres Complètes de Victor Hugo: Philosophie – II: William Shakespeare*, édition de l'Imprimerie nationale (Paris, 1937), p. 425.

page 236 'In contemplating Shakespeare': *William Shakespeare*, p.vii.

page 237 'The great Greek': Amédée Rolland, review cited in *Oeuvres Complètes de Victor Hugo: Philosophie – II: William Shakespeare*, p. 439, my trans.

page 237 'He strides' . . . 'The school hates Shakespeare': *William Shakespeare*, pp. 214–15, 209, 210, 250, 288, 289.

page 238 'Shakespeare without a muzzle' . . . 'Teach! learn!': *William Shakespeare*, pp. 211, 296–8, 307.

page 238 'The soul of the people': *William Shakespeare*, pp. 307–9. Subsequent quotations from pp. 289, 397, 355.

page 241 'new historicist' readings: Typical is the introduction to Stephen Orgel's 1987 Oxford edition of *The Tempest*, which has become as influential for its generation as Frank Kermode's 1954 Arden edition of the play was for the previous one. Orgel twice mentions Octave Mannoni's pioneering interpretation of *The Tempest* in relation to colonialism, but on each occasion passes straight from it to a liberal white interpreter. First: 'The most important treatments of the relevance of colonialism to the play are Octave Mannoni's *Psychologie de la colonisation* (1950), published in England as *Prospero and Caliban*; Stephen J. Greenblatt's brilliant 'Learning to Curse'...' (p. 24n.). And secondly: '[Jonathan] Miller, in a 1970 production at the Mermaid, based his view of the relation of Prospero to Caliban and Ariel on Octave Mannoni's metaphorical use of these figures in his analysis of the revolt in Madagascar in 1947, *La Psychologie de la colonisation*' (p. 83). For a good liberal who is manifestly troubled by the white tradition's silencing and marginalization of blacks, Orgel is here remarkably adept in his own silencing of the major – 'brilliant' indeed – black interpretations of the two decades between the publication of Mannoni's book and the readings of Miller and Greenblatt. Typical, too, is Eric Cheyfitz's *The Poetics of Imperialism: Translation and Colonization from 'The Tempest' to 'Tarzan'* (New York and Oxford, 1991): the author claims that Frantz Fanon is his 'immediate inspiration for reading *The Tempest*', then remarks that 'his name should remind us that Shakespeare's play is the possible prologue not only for the literature of the United States, but for a significant body of Caribbean literature' (p. 23) – yet the rest of the book has nothing to say about that body of literature. Given the silence of most critics, it is imperative to salute Rob Nixon's pioneering article, 'Caribbean and African Appropriations of *The Tempest*', *Critical Inquiry*, 13 (1986–7), pp. 557–78, to which I am much indebted. The material is also surveyed briefly in Alden and Virginia Vaughan's *Shakespeare's Caliban: A Cultural History* (Cambridge, 1991). There is a substantial body of French exegetical criticism devoted to Césaire's play. On Edward Brathwaite's 'Caliban' poem, see my essay 'Caliban and Ariel Write Back', *Shakespeare Survey*, 48 (1995), pp. 155–62.

page 242 'You tried to violate'; 'The "Prospero complex"': O. Mannoni, *Psychologie de la colonisation* (Paris, 1950), trans. Pamela Powesland as *Prospero and Caliban: The Psychology of Colonization* (1956), pp. 106, 110.

page 242 'what is interesting'; 'toward Caliban': Fanon, *Black Skin, White Masks*, trans. Charles Lam Markmann (1968), pp. 93, 107.

page 243 'a way of presenting' . . . 'The tone suggests an intimacy': *The Pleasures of Exile* (1960), pp. 9, 13, 15, 116.

page 246 'the berries whereof': Quoted, Orgel's Oxford edn., p. 214.

page 248 'a tiny house stinking': Lamming's *Pleasures of Exile*, p. 49, translating a passage from Césaire's autobiographical poem, *Cahier d'un retour au pays natal.*

page 249 'Rape! rape!': 'Violer! violer! Dis-donc, vieux bouc, tu me prêtes tes idées libidineuses' – Césaire, *Une tempête* (Paris, 1969), p. 27.

page 249 'To me': Quoted in S. Belhassen, 'Aimé Césaire's *A Tempest*', in *Radical Perspectives in the Arts*, ed. Lee Baxandall (Harmondsworth, 1972), p. 176.

page 249 'For Ariel, like Caliban': *Pleasures of Exile*, p. 99.

page 250 exchange about naming: *Une tempête*, pp. 27–8, my trans.

page 250 Renan to Jacobinism: Renan's *Caliban: suite de 'La tempête'* (1878), written in reaction against the Paris Commune of 1871, imagines that Caliban's rebellion was successful, but that due to his ineptitude and corruption he becomes a bad ruler, the embodiment of Renan's hatred of the *demos*. See further, Ruby Cohn, *Modern Shakespeare Offshoots* (Princeton, 1976), pp. 272–5. On Caliban and Jacobinism, see my *Shakespearean Constitutions: Politics, Theatre, Criticism 1730–1830* (Oxford, 1989), pp. 95–6, 178–80.

9. FROM CHARACTER TO ICON

page 251 '*Resemblance* by Portrait': Puttenham, *The Arte of English Poesie*, ed. G. D. Willcock and A. Walker (Cambridge, 1936), p. 243.

page 252 *Shakespeare's Remarkable Characters*: This example was published in 1774 by a Scottish academic, William Richardson.

page 258 'Hamlet is, through the whole play': General Observation on *Hamlet* in Johnson's edition.

page 258 'It was not until the nineteenth century': *The Collected Works of Ralph Waldo Emerson*, ed. W. E. Williams and D. E. Wilson (Cambridge, Mass., 1987), vol. 4, p. 117.

page 258 Bradley: *Shakespearean Tragedy* (1904), p. 98n.

page 260 Serlo: The figure is based on Friedrich Ludwig Schröder, author of the version of *Hamlet* which was performed in eighteenth-century Germany.

page 260 'It is clear to me': *Wilhelm Meister's Apprenticeship*, trans. Eric Blackall, vol. 9 of *Goethe's Collected Works* (New York, 1989), p. 146 (bk. 4, chap. 13).

page 261 'the prevalence of the abstracting': Coleridge, *Table Talk* (1835), entry for 24 June 1827.

page 261 'He persists in the inactivity': Hegel, *Aesthetics: Lectures on Fine Art*, trans. T. M. Knox (Oxford, 1975), p. 584. Subsequent quotations from pp. 1213, 1230, 1231–2.

page 263 'The play is built': *The Standard Edition of the Complete Psychological Works of Sigmund Freud*, trans. James Strachey et al., vol. 4 (1953), pp. 264–5. The idea was first developed in a letter from Freud to Wilhelm Fliess, 15 October 1897. Though a footnote in the first edition of *The Interpretation of Dreams* (1900), the analysis was incorporated into the main text in the 1914 edition; in the 1919 edition, Freud added a footnote drawing attention to the fuller development of a psychoanalytic explanation of Hamlet in the work of his disciple, Ernest Jones, which was eventually expanded and published as *Hamlet and Oedipus* (1949).

page 266 'There is living in Rome': Quoted, Eudo Mason, *The Mind of Henry Fuseli: Selections from his Writings* (1951), p. 69.

page 267 'Consider it as the unalterable': Aphorism 200, *Mind of Fuseli*, p. 344.

page 267 'the supreme master of passions': Lecture 3 of 1801, *Mind of Fuseli*, p. 343.

page 268 Kean as Romantic actor: See further, *Shakespeare: An Illustrated Stage History*, edited by Jonathan Bate and Russell Jackson (Oxford, 1996), chap. 5.

page 269 'the actor moving across the stage': Giulio Carlo Argan, 'Fuseli, Shakespeare's Painter', in an Italian edition of Shakespeare's plays, ed. C. V. Lodovici (Einaudi, 1960), trans. in Gert Schiff's introduction to *Henry Fuseli*, catalogue of Tate Gallery exhibition (1975), p. 11.

page 272 lighting of first production: Though on a winter's afternoon, dusk would presumably have been falling by the fifth act, in which the speech occurs.

page 273 'All apparatus': Lecture 4 of 1805, *Mind of Fuseli*, p. 218.

page 273 'It is not by the accumulation': Aphorism 58, *Mind of Fuseli*, p. 218.

page 275 painting of *Macbeth, Banquo and the Witches*: Similar to, but not identical with, the version of the same subject that is my Fig. 16. See William L. Pressly, *A Catalogue of Paintings in the Folger Shakespeare Library* (New Haven, 1993), p. 56.

page 277 Bodmer's face: See Gert Schiff, *Johann Heinrich Füssli 1741–1825: Text und Oeuvrekatalog*, 2 vols (Zürich and München, 1973), 1.514 (no.881).

page 277 'To say nothing of': *The Life and Writings of Henry Fuseli*, ed. John Knowles, 3 vols (1831), 1.189–90.

page 281 '[Romeo] dashes upon': Berlioz, *A travers chant*, trans. in Ian Kemp, '*Romeo and Juliet* and *Roméo et Juliette*', *Berlioz Studies*, ed. Peter Bloom (Cambridge, 1992), p. 74. This essay is the best brief introduction to Berlioz's symphony, from the point of view of both its music and its relation to Garrick and Shakespeare.

page 281 'should be omitted': Berlioz's note, trans. in Julian Rushton, *Berlioz: Roméo et Juliette* (Cambridge, 1994), p. 88.

page 282 'The genre of this work': Berlioz's 1839 preface, trans. in Rushton, p. 87.

page 283 'In the celebrated scenes': Berlioz's 1839 preface, my trans.

page 284 'The long final section': Rosen, *The Romantic Generation* (Cambridge, Mass., 1995), p. 559. Following point from p. 563.

page 285 'instead of *Otello* being': G. B. Shaw, 'A Word More about Verdi', in *London Music in 1888–89 as heard by Corno di Bassetto (later known as Bernard Shaw) with some further Autobiographical Particulars* (1937, repr. 1950), p. 394.

page 287 Jago: Though pronounced 'Iago', the character's name was spelt 'Jago' in the original score and programme; I use this spelling to distinguish between the play and the opera.

page 290 'A man that hath no virtue': Bacon, *The Essays*, ed. John Pitcher (1985), p. 83.

page 291 'Iago in fact belongs': *Characters of Shakespear's Plays*, in *The Complete Works of William Hazlitt*, ed. P. P. Howe, 21 vols (1930–34), 4.206.

page 291 'humanity, that's to say': Letter of Verdi to Domenico Morelli, 7 February 1880.

page 292 'instead of employing his invention': Hazlitt's *Works*, 4.207.

page 292 'One of his talents': Boito, Preface to 'Disposizione scenica' for *Otello*, trans. in Julian Budden, *The Operas of Verdi*, vol. 3 (rev. edn., Oxford, 1992), p. 328.

10. THE LAWS OF THE SHAKESPEAREAN UNIVERSE

page 294 'Doctrinal Point': Empson, *Poems* (1935), p. 34. 'Tensor' is an abstract mathematical entity used in describing the transformation of coordinates; it was through the calculus of tensors that Einstein satisfied the postulate of general relativity.

page 294 'imbibed an hereditary'; 'The terrible effects': *Memoir of the late John Bowdler Esq., to which is added some account of the late Thomas Bowdler, Esq. Editor of the Family Shakspeare* (1825), pp. 303, 305.

page 295 'Twenty of the most': *The Family Shakespeare* (1807), p. vii.

page 296 'Shakespear was the least moral': Review published 11 February 1816, in *The Complete Works of William Hazlitt*, ed. P. P. Howe, 21 vols (1930–34), 5.283. The quotation is from *Henry V*, 4.1.4.

page 297 'his guilt is as great': *The Family Shakspeare* (1818), 2.1–2.

page 298 'the pardon and marriage': Coleridge, in *The Romantics on Shakespeare*, ed. Jonathan Bate (1992), p. 453.

page 298 'the indecent expressions': *The Family Shakspeare* (1818), 2.1–2.

page 299 Q on something wrong: *Measure for Measure* (Cambridge, 1922), p.xiii.

page 299 the dispute over Isabella: Quiller-Couch's 1922 introduction, pp. xxvii–xxx.

page 303 'An ambiguity of the fifth type': William Empson, *Seven Types of Ambiguity* (1930), p. 195. Following quotation from pp. 257–8.

page 305 'It seems impossible even': William Empson, *Some Versions of Pastoral* (1935), p. 111. Empson developed this *aperçu* in 'Sense in *Measure for Measure*', chapter 13 of his *The Structure of Complex Words* (1952).

page 306 'It is [Angelo's] virtues': *Some Versions of Pastoral*, p. 113.

page 306 '"Against all reason"': *Structure of Complex Words*, pp. 279–80.

page 307 'because ruined monastery choirs': *Seven Types of Ambiguity*, p. 3. In the second edition (1947), the parenthesis was altered to the more sober 'the protestant destruction of monasteries; fear of puritanism'.

page 308 '[Empson] seemed to have read': Richards, 'William Empson', in '*Furioso*: A Special Note', *Furioso*, 1, No.3 (Spring 1940), supplement following p. 44.

page 309 'By showing what great difference': *A Survey of Modernist Poetry* (1927), p. 64. Subsequent quotations from pp. 68, 74.

page 310 definitions of seventh type: *Seven Types of Ambiguity*, pp. 244–9.

page 313 Empson's scientific reviews of 1930: repr. in William Empson, *Argufying* (1987), pp. 528–33.

page 313 Haffenden: 'The Importance of Empson (I): The Poems', *Essays in Criticism*, 35 (1985), 1–24.

page 313 'the star could not stop': Eddington, *The Nature of the Physical World* (Cambridge, 1928), p. 204.

page 313 'Eddington's monumental book': Review written in 1941, repr. in Empson, *Argufying*, p. 584.

page 313 'changes': *The Nature of the Physical World*, pp.v, 4. For the more general influence on literary modernism of Eddington's popularizations of the new physics, see Gillian Beer, 'Eddington and the Idiom of Modernism', in *Science, Reason, and Rhetoric*, ed. H. Krips et al. (Pittsburgh, 1995), 295–315.

page 314 first draft of *Seven Types*: I am grateful to John Haffenden for this information and for letting me see relevant unpublished work of his and of Empson's.

page 314 'Some readers of this chapter': *Seven Types of Ambiguity*, pp. 102–3.

page 315 'The principle of indeterminacy': *The Nature of the Physical World*, p. 225.

page 315 'but that a new thing': *Argufying*, p. 531.

page 316 'Shakespeare's use of the negative'; 'to stretch one's mind': *Seven Types of Ambiguity*, p. 262; *Some Versions of Pastoral*, p. 109.

page 317 'all we can ever do'; 'no text offers values': *Meaning by Shakespeare* (1992), pp. 3, 76.

page 317 'the very idea that the works': Roger Kimball, *Tenured Radicals* (New York, 1990), p.xii.

page 319 'It may be that the essential thing': Wittgenstein, *Culture and Value (Vermischte Bemerkungen)*, ed. G. H. von Wright and Heikki Nyman, trans. Peter Winch (Oxford, 1980), p. 49e.

page 319 'Give up literary criticism!': F. R. Leavis, 'Memories of Wittgenstein', in his *The Critic as Anti-Philosopher*, ed. G. Singh (1982), pp. 129–45, discussed by Hawkes in *Meaning by Shakespeare*, pp. 75–6.

page 320 'What is needed for literary satisfaction': *Seven Types of Ambiguity*, pp. 322–3.

page 320 'How do I show my approval': Wittgenstein, *Lectures and Conversations on Aesthetics, Psychology and Religious Belief compiled from notes taken by Yorick Smythies, Rush Rhees and James Taylor*, ed. Cyril Barrett (Oxford, 1970), p. 5.

page 321 'we would have to describe': *Lectures on Aesthetics*, p. 7.

page 321 'The analysis of a poem;' 'one cannot give or state': *Seven Types of Ambiguity*, pp. 322, 301.

page 321 'You might think Aesthetics': *Lectures on Aesthetics*, p. 11.

page 321 'Perhaps the most important thing': *Lectures on Aesthetics*, p. 13, my italics (the reactions cited at this point are negative ones).

page 324 the superiority of theatre's way: In an attempt to keep philosophy pure, Austin (puritanically?) excluded 'things said on stage' from his theory of performativeness, claiming that they were not 'serious' – see Christopher Ricks, 'Austin's Swink', in his *Essays in Appreciation* (Oxford, 1996). Austin did not have the benefit of the later notebooks in which Wittgenstein refuses to set aside such questions as 'Is a ballet dancer sincere?' and 'Are people murdered in tragedies or aren't they?'

page 325 'Shakespeare and dreams': Wittgenstein, *Culture and Value*, p. 83e.

page 325 'As a work of genius': *Lectures on the Dramatic Literature of the Age of Elizabeth*, in Hazlitt's *Complete Works*, 6.194.

page 327 'the truest account of reading Shakespeare': Brenda R. Silver, ed., '"Anon" and "The Reader": Virginia Woolf's Last Essays', *20th Century Literature*, 25 (1979), p. 432.

page 328 duck-rabbit: In *Shakespeare and the Problem of Meaning* (Chicago, 1981), Norman Rabkin offers a duck-rabbit reading of *Henry V*, but without reference to Wittgenstein.

page 328 'the notion of what you want': *Seven Types*, p. 246.

page 330 'The striking peculiarity': Hazlitt, 'On Shakspeare and Milton', in *The Romantics on Shakespeare*, p. 181.

page 330 Keats: letters to Richard Woodhouse, 27 October 1818 ('What shocks the virtuous Philosopher delights the cameleon Poet'), and to George and Tom Keats, 21–7 December 1817 ('at once it struck me, what quality went to form a Man of Achievement especially in Literature & which Shakespeare possessed so enormously – I mean *Negative Capability*').

page 332 'Suppose we ask the question': Wittgenstein, *Nachlass*, manuscript notebook, reel 13, pp. 42–3, cited in Peter Hughes' seminal article, 'Performing theory: Wittgenstein and the trouble with Shakespeare', *Comparative Criticism*, 14 (1992), 71–86. Hughes argues that, as with Tolstoy, Wittgenstein dispraised Shakespeare out of the anxiety of influence – he saw that Shakespeare had arrived at his own destination long before he got there himself. My attention was first drawn to Wittgenstein's musings on Shakespeare by George Steiner's W. P. Ker Lecture, 'A Reading against Shakespeare', now reprinted in his essay collection, *No Passion Spent* (1996).

page 334 'How many ages'; 'The quick comedians': *Julius Caesar*, 3.1.112–14; *Antony and Cleopatra*, 5.2.212–17.

page 334 'Methinks I see'; 'I have had a dream'; 'These our actors': *A Midsummer Night's Dream*, 4.1.188–9, 202–4; *The Tempest*, 4.1.148–58.

page 335 'theatre of the world': See the classic study by Anne Righter (Barton), *Shakespeare and the Idea of the Play* (1962).

page 337 'Indian empire will go': Carlyle, 'The Hero as Poet', lecture of 12 May 1840, in *The Romantics on Shakespeare*, pp. 255–6.

page 338 between five hundred and eighteen hundred: the lower figure is the most conservative scholars' estimate, the higher is Lope's own (exaggerated?) claim.

page 339 manifesto for his art: *Arte nuevo de hacer comedias en este tiempo* (1609, in verse), all quotations from prose trans. by William T. Brewster, *The New Art of Writing Plays* (New York, 1914).

page 340 'God has written my cues': act three of *The Great Pretenders* (Bath, 1992), David Johnston's free translation of *Lo fingido verdadero* for the Gate Theatre's stunning 1991 production.

ACKNOWLEDGEMENTS

The writing of this book was made possible by the award of a British Academy Research Readership, a visiting fellowship at the Folger Shakespeare Library in Washington, DC, and an Andrew Mellon Fellowship at the Huntington Library in San Marino, California, for all of which I am deeply grateful. The hospitality of Barbara Mowat and Georgianna Ziegler at the Folger and Roy Ritchie at the Huntington was especially appreciated.

For permission to reproduce illustrations, the publishers and author would like to thank the following: Folger Shakespeare Library (1, 2, 4, 8–10, 17, 19), Henry E. Huntington Library and Art Collection (3), Kunsthaus, Zürich (12), Yale Center for British Art: Paul Mellon Collection (6), National Portrait Gallery, London (20), Tate Gallery, London (11, 13, 15), Victoria and Albert Museum: The Theatre Museum (18).

An earlier version of part of chapter seven was delivered as my inaugural lecture in the University of Liverpool, and published in *English*, Spring 1993. Earlier versions of sections of some other chapters were tried out in the form of conference papers and lectures: I am grateful for the invitations which gave me these opportunities (special thanks to Yasunari Takahashi, Akiko Kusunoki, and Yuji Kaneko of the Shakespeare Society of Japan, Alessandro Serpieri of the Associazione Italiana di Anglistica, and, for an invitation to speak in Sofia, Michael Hattaway, Derek Roper, and Boika Sokolova).

For comments on draft material, I am most grateful to Paul Baines, Kent Cartwright, Katherine Duncan-Jones, Julian Ferraro, Robert Knapp, Christopher Ricks, Bruce Smith, and Stanley Wells. I am deeply indebted to Christopher Ridgway and Paula Byrne for their reading of the entire typescript. My thinking about the sonnets has been stimulated by conversations with John Harding and Edward Burns, though neither of them will agree with my conclusions. Lidia Garbin helped to make the index.

I am extremely grateful to my astute copy editor, Nicholas Blake. I would like to thank my agent, David Godwin, for placing the book, and Jon Riley and Peter Straus at Picador, and Susie Chang at Oxford University Press (New York), for their faith in it.

INDEX